STUDIEN ZU LITERATUR
UND ERKENNTNIS

Herausgegeben von
STEFAN BÜTTNER
ARBOGAST SCHMITT
GREGOR VOGT-SPIRA

Band 20

BINGHAO HU

A Systematic Research of the Platonic Perception-Theory

Plato's Analysis
of Human Beings' Perception Ability
Derived from the Conditions
of the World's Perceptibility

Universitätsverlag
WINTER
Heidelberg

Bibliografische Information der Deutschen Nationalbibliothek
Die Deutsche Nationalbibliothek verzeichnet diese Publikation
in der Deutschen Nationalbibliografie;
detaillierte bibliografische Daten sind im Internet
über *http://dnb.d-nb.de* abrufbar.

Zugl.: Marburg; Univ., Diss., 2021

ISBN 978-3-8253-4850-2

Dieses Werk einschließlich aller seiner Teile ist urheberrechtlich geschützt.
Jede Verwertung außerhalb der engen Grenzen des Urheberrechtsgesetzes
ist ohne Zustimmung des Verlages unzulässig und strafbar. Das gilt insbesondere
für Vervielfältigungen, Übersetzungen, Mikroverfilmungen und die Einspeicherung
und Verarbeitung in elektronischen Systemen.
© 2022 Universitätsverlag Winter GmbH Heidelberg
Imprimé en Allemagne · Printed in Germany
Druck: Memminger MedienCentrum, 87700 Memmingen
Gedruckt auf umweltfreundlichem, chlorfrei gebleichtem
und alterungsbeständigem Papier.

Den Verlag erreichen Sie im Internet unter:
www.winter-verlag.de

Herrn Prof. Arbogast Schmitt gewidmet

Contents

Preface 9

Introduction 11
   1 The theme and method of this work 11
   2 The current research situation of Plato's perception-theory 16
   3 Introduction of the main contents of this research 24

1 The generation of the perceptible world and perception subject 33
   1.1 The generation of the perceptible object: the sensible world 33
      1.1.1 Primary research 33
         1.1.1.1 The generation of the world soul 34
         1.1.1.2 The generation of the world body 36
         1.1.1.3 The combination of the world body and world soul 39
         1.1.1.4 Conclusion 40
      1.1.2 Further inquiry 41
         1.1.2.1 The Identity of the Demiurge: Intellect, Maker and Father, and Zeus 42
         1.1.2.2 The Platonic elemental theory 47
         1.1.2.3 How to understand the (world) soul? 55
         1.1.2.4 Rethinking the Platonic way of explaining the generation of the universe 59
         1.1.2.5 Conclusion 65
   1.2 Human being as perception subject and his generation 67
      1.2.1 The four kinds of perceiver 67
      1.2.2 The generation of the human being as perception subject 69
         1.2.2.1 The generation of the immortal and mortal human soul 69
         1.2.2.2 The generation of the human body 81
         1.2.2.3 The combination of the human body and soul 82
      1.2.3 Conclusion 89

2 The generation of the affected and unaffected perception 91
   2.1 The generation of the affected perception 92
      2.1.1 The preconditions of the generation of the affected sense perception 92
      2.1.2 Detailed analysis of the preconditions of the affected perception's generation 95
         2.1.2.1 The motion of acting and being affected and the generation of sense-affection 96
         2.1.2.2 The motion of the affection from body to soul 108

      2.1.2.3 The perfection of the soul's perception-ability:
           discrimination and comprehension 113
  2.2 The generation of the unaffected sensation 117
  2.3 Conclusion 121

3 The kinds of perception and their cognitive abilities 125
  3.1 The kinds of sense perception in Plato 125
    3.1.1 The Proclean and Aristotelian models and their origins in Plato 126
    3.1.2 Comprehensive research of the different kinds of perception
        in Plato 137
  3.2 The cognitive power of the affected and unaffected perception 144
    3.2.1 The cognitive ability of the affected sensation 144
        3.2.1.1 The categories of the affected sensation *per se* 145
        3.2.1.2 The truth of the affected sensation 150
    3.2.2 The cognitive dynamis of the unaffected sensation 162
        3.2.2.1 The first category 'Substance' and the unaffected
            sensation *per se* 162
        3.2.2.2 The truth of the unaffected sensation and its reason 167
    3.2.3 Conclusion: different kinds of sensation and their determinate
        cognitive dynameis 175

Bibliography 183

Preface

This book is based on my dissertation submitted to the Institute of Classical Philology, Philipps University of Marburg in November 2020. After the viva in March 2021, I began to revise it, which, however, took more time than was expected. Now at the conjuncture of its publication, I would like to write a short preface about my studies and lives in Marburg to commemorate it.

The day I arrived in Marburg was October 3, 2014, when I was still struggling with the language: although I had learned German in China, it was another thing to apply it in the 'real' life. Hence, I enrolled in a language class for international doctoral students. Six months later, i.e., in summer semester 2015, I started to learn Ancient Greek in the Institute of Theology. Miss Rosin, our teacher for this class, was very enthusiastic about teaching; being deeply influenced by her, I usually got up at 6 o'clock, reading Greek on the bus and later in the classroom of the eldest building of the University of Marburg. My hard work was not bootless, two semesters later (summer 2017), I passed the Greek exam 'Graecum'. During this period, I also took the class about the Aristotelian *De anima* of Prof. Schmitt, which was held in the Institute of Philosophy. In the next year, i.e., 2018, I finally started to learn in the Institute of Classical Philology, the classes I took are: ancient Greek style and syntax, Plato's *Republic*, Aristotle's *Politics*, etc. From the teaching of Prof. Sabine Föllinger, Dr. Brigitte Kappl, and Mr. Thomas Busch I benefited a lot. Meanwhile, the Research Colloquium was held together with other teachers and doctoral students, i.e., Dr. Diego De Brasi, Dr. Bernadette Banaszkiewicz, Dr. Sven Meier, Sebastian Klinkmüller, Christoph Hammann, Daniel Fuchs, Hans Noack, Hinrik Vollbracht, and David Schindler. Beside the classes in our institute, I also studied Plato's *Theaetetus* with Prof. Alexander Becker, where I met Dr. Bernhard Longinus, who was in charge of an ancient philosophical reading group. Together with others (mainly Julia Gebhard, Dieter Budde, and Robert Whitley) we read Aristotle's *Metaphysics* and *Nicomachean Ethics* in Café Vetter or Café Q; with Bernhard we also read the *Categories* and *De anima*, sometimes in Café Pause.

The daily lives were also wonderful. I had made many friends in the classes, especially Eike Quast, with whom I always went to the university canteen. During the holidays I travelled to many cities visiting friends, went to churches, and read the *Bible* with neighbours like Miss Reuter as well as many other Chinese students. This was a great consolation during the coronavirus pandemic.

Now back to the dissertation and its publication. Originally, I preferred to write a dissertation about the relationship between the Platonic epistemological and ethical theory. Yet due to the wide range of this theme, I finally decided to write a dissertation about only a small part of it, namely the sense-perception theory. This work could not have been finished without Prof. Schmitt's supervision, who offered help in almost every step: determination of a possible theme, selection of the valuable literature, revision of the arguments, etc. Usually, at 17:00 o'clock I went talk with him about the written parts. In his workroom teemed with huge amounts of books, he expressed his opinion in a cordial voice – which is an image now deeply imprinted in my memory. On his 65th teaching anniversary, I met Prof. Stefan Büttner (University of Vienna), Prof. Wolfgang Bernard (University of Rostock), and Prof. Rainer Thiel (University of Jena), who had also written their dissertation with Prof. Schmitt. In August 2018, I, Sebastian Klinkmüller, and Dr. Sven Meier held an academic conference and invited them to give a lecture. After that I asked Prof. Büttner whether he could supervise my dissertation, and luckily, he promised to be my second supervisor. In the next two years I emailed him a lot, asking for help and advice, and every time he answered quickly and kindly.

As scheduled, the disputation was held on March 25, 2021. Besides the two supervisors Prof. Schmitt and Prof. Büttner, Prof. Föllinger, Prof. Gregor Vogt-Spira, and Prof. Elisabeth Rieken were also on the Doctoral Committee. Due to the pandemic, it was held virtually. Thanks to Sebastian, I had practiced several times, and the disputation turned out to be a happy ending. Miss Bettina Herrmann in the Dean's Office had done a lot for the submission of the dissertation, the organization of the disputation, and other related things. Therefore, here I would like to express my cordial appreciation.

After the disputation I talked with Prof. Schmitt about its publication, who suggested containing it in the series 'Studien zu Literatur und Erkenntnis', edited by him together with Prof. Stefan Büttner, and Prof. Gregor Vogt-Spira. So I wrote an email to the other two co-editors. After having received their permission I emailed Dr. Andreas Barth, head of the university publishing house Winter in Heidelberg, who also agreed to publish my work.

I would like to thank Dr. Christina Hünsche, Kathrin Sternberger, Dirk Hoffmann, Ralf Stemper, Selina Sannemann, and Sarah Bohn for their work in publishing this book, without whose help the publication would have been impossible.

I am appreciated that the CSC (Chinese Scholarship Council) had offered me a four-year scholarship to accomplish my studies in Marburg. Many thanks also go to GNU (Guizhou Normal University) for their funding its publication.

If the readers have any question or problem when reading this book, please feel free to email me: hubinghao0507@foxmail.com.

Binghao Hu
Guizhou Normal University

Introduction

Today a research of Plato's perception-theory appears to be an unnecessary work, if not a waste of time, since the modern psychophysics and physiology, in the eyes of many people, enable us to know enough about this subject.[1] Such an opinion, however, reveals firstly the very fact that we know too little about the meaning of "perception" in Plato: for him this term concerns not only the physiological process of sensation like seeing and hearing, but also encompasses many other aspects, for instance the generation of the sensible world including all perceptible things like the fixed stars, all animals, and planets, and the becoming of the all kinds of perception subject like the human being, both his body and soul – today we prefer to call the latter 'mind', or more physically, 'brain'. Moreover, Plato divides the perception into different kinds, which possess distinct cognitive abilities. Performing these abilities, the perception results occasionally in the generation of various feelings and emotions, of which the most significant are pleasure and pain. The determinate feelings and emotions pertaining to sensation lead to certain kinds of desires and wills, which function as the motivation of our practical activities. These aspects construct together a system of perception, which embraces the generation of the sensible object and subject, the becoming of different kinds of human sensation, the discrimination and comprehension of the sensibles, and the feelings and wills originating from such a cognitive activity. Such a systematic perspective, I believe, automatically reveals the reason and value of a systematic investigation into the Platonic perception-doctrine: it is more complex and in certain sense even more reasonable as the modern sense perception theory; it enables more cognition of the natural and social world; and last, but not least, it shows us how to be a good person.

In the following I will introduce this systematic exploration in three steps: firstly, a clarification of the theme and methods of this study, which includes a demonstration of the harmony of the Platonic and Aristotelian philosophy; then a summary of the current studies about the perception-theory in Plato, Aristotle and the Neoplatonists, especially Proclus; at last, there will be an introduction of the main contents of each chapter.

1 The theme and method of this work

With this investigation I prefer to display the Platonic view of the most important aspects of sense perception. Systematically and logically these aspects can be arranged in the following order: (1) the generation of the whole sensible world, which can be considered as the perception object, and the coming to be of the perception subject, especially the human being. Given that for Plato both the universe and human being are

---

[1] For the modern studies about perception, see for example May (2007); Mather (2011); Jones (2017); Schellenberg (2018); Shottenkirk, Curado and Gouveia (2019); Sathian & Ramachandran (2020).

living creatures, the description of their generation embraces two parts, i.e., that of the body and soul. (2) The whole process of the generation of a single perception. There are four main conditions to be fulfilled for such a generation: (a) the existence of the sensible object and sensation subject; (b) the becoming of the affected sense-affections; (c) the progress of these affections to the soul; (d) the soul's activity to discriminate these affections. Considering that the Platonic perception includes two fundamental types, i.e., the affected and unaffected sensation, the generation of the unaffected sensation requires two more conditions: the desire to discriminate the substance of the sensibles after having perceived the sensible qualities, and the combination of the memory-image with the fresh perception in the soul. (3) Following the clarification of the generation of perception I will continue to determine the kinds of perception and their corresponding cognitive abilities. In exploring the different kinds of perception, I shall offer a classification in a comprehensive view, for hitherto there is still no complete research of the sensation-types grounded on Plato's own dialogues. The truth of perception varies in accordance with the distinguished kinds, hence the analysis of the sensory truth should be performed in according to the division of the affected and unaffected sensation.

The aim and frame of this work requires it to be systematic and historical. Systematic because it concerns the most important aspects of perception that are systematically organised: the generation of perception objects and subjects, the becoming of the affected and unaffected sensation, their classification and cognitive dynameis of discrimination and comprehension. Historical due to the immanent development of the Platonic doctrine of sense perception: proceeding from Plato the following Platonists including Aristotle have significantly developed and completed this theory, for example Aristotle has conceived the category-theory, and some Neoplatonists have developed the soul-vehicle doctrine.

Yet the argument that the Platonic perception-theory is more thinkable than the modern science requires a proof, at least a comparison between the Platonic and modern perception-theories. In this study this job is done at many points, for instance after the introduction of the generation of the sensible world there will be a reflection of this Platonic generation-theory in comparison with the modern theories like the Big Bang and Darwinism, from which we can derive that on the one side the Platonic notion 'Demiurge' is not simply a religious role, rather it can be discriminated and comprehended with knowledge,[2] on the other side the modern world-generation theories lay too much emphasis on chance and materials, which result in their less persuasiveness (section 1.1.2.4); in describing the generation of the human soul I shall show that the notion of 'soul' in Plato signifies primarily the faculty of cognition and motion, and it results in no body-soul dualism, which is a core issue for the modern philosophers like Descartes (section 1.2.2.1); in the description of the incarnation of the mortal human

---

[2] For an epistemological interpretation of the notion 'god' in Plato (and Aristotle), see Schmitt (2019). Because of this cognitive possibility the human being can 'become like god'. For the notion of 'becoming like god' in Plato, see Merki (1952); Passmore (1970); Roloff (1970); Annas (1999) 52–71; (2019) 541–542; Sedley (1997) 327–339; (1999) 309–328; (2017) 319–337; Van den Berg (2003) 189–202; Armstrong (2004) 171–183; Van Riel (2013) 19–24. Cf. Sedley (1999) 309n1; (2019) 628n2; Annas (2019) 542n14.

soul-form I will try to point out that for Plato the generation of our organs are clarified not in the physiological sense, rather it is established in accordance with position, structure and dynamis (section 1.2.2.3); and the interpretation of the generation-process of perception will refute the Cartesian and Kantian doctrine for their taking this process as purely passive (section 2.1.2.3).

Now let us turn back and throw light on one crucial problem: the harmony of Plato and Aristotle. As said above, a historical research of the Platonic perception-theory naturally involves the Platonic tradition, of which the most important are Aristotle and the Neoplatonists.[3] The agreement between Plato and the Neoplatonism is clear and evident, but their relationship with Aristotle is a troublesome issue, especially the harmony between Plato and Aristotle. To solve this problem I should firstly clarify the necessity of an explanation of their harmony: expect for the reason that a historical research of Plato's perception-theory can hardly be entitled 'historical' without the necessary references of Aristotle's related doctrines, the subject matter itself requires also a determination of their harmony: Plato does not write any treatise on perception, his doctrines can be found in the *Timaeus*, *Theaetetus*, *Philebus*, *Republic*, *Laws*, and many other dialogues, while Aristotle's *De anima* concentrates on the theme of the faculties of soul, of which the research of perception occupies almost one third of the whole treatise, which makes it an indispensable work of an investigation into Plato's perception-doctrine. However, considering the seemingly contradiction between these two philosophers one may hesitate to quote Aristotle as direct warranty of Plato's theory: for example, in the first book of *De anima* alone there exists already a considerable amount of accusations against Plato.[4] Although the seemingly criticism is already corrected or answered by the commentators in late antiquity, one wonders whether they are in harmony in general sense: after all, Aristotle's 'criticism' covers a huge range of Plato's thought, and the research of his perception-theory concerns not only the sense perception, but also the theory of soul, god, matter, and so on. Thus, an apology of the harmony of Plato and Aristotle is the precondition of both the validity of Aristotle's testimony and the reasonableness and continuity of Plato's perception-theory.

Primarily we should determine the meaning of 'harmony' (συμφωνία), which appears to be a perennial problem, albeit for the most Neoplatonists it is less problematic. Certainly 'harmony' denotes not 'identity',[5] for we all know that Aristotle 'contradicts' Plato, frequently verbally though.[6] Yet the fact is, sometimes Aristotle and

---

[3] Indeed the term 'Neoplatonism' originates from the early nineteenth century scholarship, and it is not suitable to describe the Platonism in the late antiquity, since substantially those Platonists tend not to be 'neo'. Cf. Coulter (1976) 1; Gerson (2005) 2; (2010) 3. Gerson (2010) 3 argues in this sense that we should abandon this term. However, considering that my research is immanent and historical, the Neoplatonists will naturally be in harmony with Plato (and Aristotle), hence, this term could be remained. Adamson (2015) 206 also asserts that there is no necessity to change this term, for geographically there is no misunderstanding of this term, at least in Europe.

[4] For example, 404b16f.; 405b14, 26–27; 407b2f.; 411b5–6.

[5] For example, Gerson (2005) 5, 8. Yet according to Hadot (2015) 42 there are still scholars holding this idea, for instance Helmig (2009) esp. 371.

[6] For the argument that their distinction is verbally, see Simplicius, *In Phy.* 1249, 12–13, where he attributes this difference to the approaches of their examination. Cf. Gerson (2005) 7. A

Plato tackle the same issue with different approaches: for example, the Neoplatonist Simplicius declares at the beginning of his *Categories*-commentary that Aristotle tends to examine things in accord with nature, thus he always begins with the views based on sense perception. Plato, however, observes natural things in the view of their relation to things 'above nature' (ὑπὲρ φύσιν).[7] Hence Aristotle's criticism of Plato's doctrines, e.g., the Form-theory, reveals not their contradiction, rather their different view of this subject-matter.

Given that the term 'harmony' indicates in no way 'identity', and Aristotle's criticisms should be viewed at face value, we can emphasise that these two philosophers are harmony 'in most matters' (ἐν τοῖς πλείστοις), as argued by Simplicius and Olympiodorus.[8] With other words, the term 'harmony' signifies their coincidence in the most fundamental issues, for example the One, Substance, Soul, Motion, etc.[9]

The next question is whether such a kind of harmony is reasonable. This question could be answered in two aspects. Literally let us consider the testimonies from both Ammonius and Olympiodorus about the origin of the term 'Peripatetics':[10] Plato walks as he teaches, his pupils and successors Xenocrates and Aristotle are named the Peripatetics. They teach later respectively in Lyceum and Academy, but the places are neglected, and the followers of Aristotle are entitled 'Peripatetics', while the philosophers following Xenocrates are called 'Academics' – this fact reminds us that the term 'Peripatetics' relates originally to Plato's way of teaching,[11] and Aristotle is indeed a Platonist. Historically, their harmony is grounded on the necessary development of their philosophy. Generally the harmony of Plato and Aristotle results essentially from three factors:[12] (a) the tendency of Pythagoreanizing Platonism which can be found not only

---

seemingly exception is, speaking of the Aristotelian attack on Plato's theory of Forms, the Neoplatonist Philoponus prefers to contradict the assertation held by others (like Iamblichus, Ammonius, and Simplicius, who argue that indeed Aristotle does not intend to criticise Plato, rather those people who have wrongly understood Plato). He insists that at this point Aristotle really disagrees with Plato. The assertation of Philoponus can be found in his *De aeternitate mundi contra proclum* 29, 2–13 and *In Anal. post.* 243, 9–13. For the declaration of Simplicius, see his *In Phys.* 1155, 8–1156, 3. Cf. *In de caelo* 557, 1–21. For that of Ammonius, see Asclepius, *In Met.* 233, 25–40; Philoponus, *In de an.* 116, 26–28. Cf. Golitsis (2018) 73–75, 77–78.

[7] See Simplicius, *In Cat.* 6, 19–32; Elias (or David) *In Cat.* 120, 31–121, 3. Cf. Chase (2003) 103n89; Gerson (2005) 6–7. This claim minimizes Syrianus' accusation (*In Met.* 81, 26–30; 195, 2–9) against Aristotle for his problematic reading of Plato and other earlier philosophers. Cf. Golitsis (2018) 70.

[8] Simplicius, *In Cat.* 7, 31–33; Olympiodorus, *In Gorg.* 41, 9, 1–4. Cf. Gerson (2005) 6.

[9] See the testimonies from Photius *Bibliotheca* 214. 2, 172a2–9; Porphyry *De. Reg. An.* (frag. 302F, 6 Smith); *Suda* P 2098, 8–9 (= frag. 239T Smith); Elias, *In Porph. Isag.* 39, 6–8; etc. Cf. Gerson (2005) 9; Hadot (2015) 41.

[10] Ammonius, *In Cat.* 3, 9–16; Olympiodorus, *Prolegomena to Platonic Philosophy* 5, 18–30. Cf. Gerson (2005) 8n24.

[11] In fact, many Platonic dialogues are also exercised in this form: the *Symposium* is told on the way to city (173b7–8); the *Laws* are discussed during walking (625a7–c5); so does the *Phaedrus* (227b7f.).

[12] See Hadot (2015) 50.

in the Platonists like Speusippus and Xenocrates in the Old Academy,[13] but also in Aristotle and his first successor Theophrastus.[14] In this movement Eudorus of Alexandria, whose doctrine about the first principles is derived from both Plato's late dialogues and the Pythagoreanism, is recognised to be the first Pythagoreanizing Platonist, and followed by Moderatus of Gades, Nicomachus of Gerasa, Theon of Smyrna, and the others.[15] In this tendency the Neoplatonist Iamblichus itemises seven heads of the Pythagorean school, while according to the anonymous *Life of Pythagoras* in Photius' *Bibliotheca* Plato and Aristotle are the ninth and tenth successor of Pythagoras,[16] which indicates that in this view their thoughts are coincident. (b) The movement in the Academy that proceeds from Antiochus of Ascalon who claims the harmony of the philosophy of Aristotle and Plato. Antiochus does not resort to the Pythagoreanism, rather turning from the Sceptical Academy back to the Old Academy, he claims the close relationship between the Old Academy and the philosophy of the Peripatetics. Knowing as the first Platonist to harmonise Plato and Aristotle, his work is carried on by many Middle-Platonists and almost all Neoplatonists.[17] (c) Lastly the systematisation of the Platonic Philosophy as well as that of the Aristotelian thought lead inherently to their harmonisation.[18] For example, with reference to the state of the soul in the perception-process both Aristotle and Plato agree that the soul is not passive (see section 2.1.2.3); and the three kinds of perception in Aristotle's *De anima* have their origin in Plato, because speaking of the soul-parts both Plato and Aristotle agree that the soul is both bipartite and tripartite, and in accordance with different logoi (λόγοι) and dynameis the soul can be divided into many parts (see section 3.1.1).

With this brief account we can proclaim that the harmony of Plato and Aristotle designates their concordance in many aspects including the fundamental principles and many specific issues. Beginning at least from the Middle-Platonist Eudorus of Alexandria, this harmonisation-tendency is the logical and natural result of the development of the Platonic and Aristotelian philosophy. To harmonise them, the Platonists in late antiquity do not hesitate to use the Aristotelian terms and conceptions to explain Plato's theories, for example, Aristotle's dynamis-activity model in clarifying the Platonic sense-generation doctrine (section 2.1.2.1); and Proclus applies the seemingly Aristotelian term 'substance' (οὐσία) to annotate the three differentiated parts of soul (see section 3.1.1). Therefore, we are endorsed to quote Aristotle in clarifying Plato's perception-theory.

---

[13] Speusippus writes *On Pythagorean Numbers*, Xenocrates is author of the book *Pythagoreia*, Cf. Burkert (1972) 64–65; Tarán (1981) 89n415; Dillon (²1996) 21–22, 37–38; (2003) 39, 89ff.; Zhmud (2013) 328–330.
[14] Cf. Zhmud (2013) 331–342; Hadot (2015) 43.
[15] See Hadot (2015) 43. For the theory of the first principles in Eudorus of Alexandria, see Dillon (²1996) 126–129, for an introduction of the doctrines of Moderatus of Gades, Nicomachus of Gerasa, and Theon of Smyrna, see Dillon (²1996) 346–361, 397–399.
[16] Hadot (2015) 45.
[17] Dillon (²1996) 55–61; (2016) 183–201; Gerson (2005) 1–2; (2006) 185; Karamanolis (2006) 45, 51–65; Hadot (2015) 44, 49. Antiochus stresses that the Stoic school also proceeds from Plato, this point is also revealed in the given literature.
[18] See Karamanolis (2006) 11ff. Cf. Gerson (2005) 6; Hadot (2015) 50; Michalewski (2016) 219.

2 The current research situation of Plato's perception-theory

After the clarification of the theme and method of this study as well as the determination of the harmony between Plato and Aristotle we should turn to the contemporary studies about Plato's perception-theory, which falls into three parts: the research about the sense perception in Plato, Aristotle, and the Neoplatonism. (1) Regarding Plato's own views about perception, chronologically, two systematic studies should be mentioned at first, namely Büttner (2000) *Die Literaturtheorie bei Platon und ihre anthropologische Begründung*, and Grönroos (2001) *Plato on Perceptual Cognition*. Alone from the titles we can derive that they are two different works, and perhaps also with distinguished methods: in Büttner's study the interpretation of Plato's perception-theory occupies the first part which is entitled 'Plato's anthropology'. In the view of the different psychology between Plato and the modern philosophy, Büttner persuasively argues that in Plato there are three different soul-parts, each of them has the abilities of cognition, feeling and will, while in modern philosophy these three soul-abilities are separated from each other. In this framework the author explores the tripartition of the Platonic soul in the *Republic, Timaeus* and *Laws* (pp. 18–37; 111–122), and the cognition-feeling-will model (pp. 64–100),[19] of which the exposition of the perception-theory begins with the description of four different kinds of perception that are grounded on Aristotle's classification in *De anima*, continues with the examination of the generation of phantasia, memory, pleasure and pain, and desire, and ends with a summary of the whole process from the perceptive cognition, feeling, will, and finally to act. Such an elaborate explanation functions as a model of a further research of Plato's perception-theory, for firstly it is a work grounded on the detailed and insightful analysis of Plato's own texts, secondly it is not immanent, rather to justify the Platonic and Aristotelian doctrines this study goes out to compare with and criticise the related modern philosophical thought.

Grönroos' work takes another starting-point and goes in another direction: in *Theaetetus* Plato contradicts Protagoras' declaration that man is the measure of everything by asserting that this statement is based on a determinate view of perceptual cognition, and the misunderstanding of this cognitive ability leads to the inner conflation of Protagoras' doctrine in discerning perception, opinion and phantasia (chapter 1). Proceeding from this point Grönroos investigates these three abilities respectively: in chapter 2 there is primarily an examination of the sensory mechanism, especially that of sight and hearing, following with the exploration whether the sensible qualities are the things that are perceived by sense perception, and whether those qualities belong to the external sensible things and hence whether the perception recognises the external objects – the answers are positive (p. 47). For the theme of perception and cognition the author cautiously argues that the content of sense perception is rich enough to bring about cognition (p. 60), albeit the content of sense perception is not propositional (pp. 61–62). At the end of this chapter the author asserts that the soul is passive during the

---

[19] This model is utilised by the author to clarify the city-soul analogy in the *Republic*, see pp. 75–93.

process of perception (pp. 60–61; p. 64). The third chapter continues with a research of opinion in *Theaetetus*. Going further with the suggestion that perception is not propositional Grönroos believes that opinion is the first capacity to differentiate the colours from sounds and to assert "what X is" (pp. 79–85). In chapter 4 what he turns to phantasia, however, for him this term means 'appearance', and his examination of this notion still belongs to the specific theme, i.e., how Plato tackles the Protagorean assertion that man is the measure, but not to the perception-theory *per se*. Grönroos' investigation has many problems, yet the crucial one, I suppose, is his misunderstanding of the cognitive ability of perception, which leads to his wrong attribution of the difference between perception and opinion. For indeed through perception we can already discriminate determinate objects, i.e., the sensible qualities which are enmattered in the sensible things, e.g. the colours are discriminated by sight and the sounds by hearing, which reveals that the (peculiar) sensation alone can distinguish colours from sounds. Moreover, through the dynamis of perception we can declare "X is black" (cf. p. 82), although for X the perception discerns only 'a thing as such and such', not a certain thing, a thing determined by its substance. To discern the substance we must resort to the opinion, precisely, the 'opinion with perception' (δόξα μετ' αἰσθήσεως). So "what X is" is discriminated by this kind of opinion, while what the sensible qualities are, is discerned through the (affected) sensation. Moreover, the perception is conceptual and propositional, for it can discriminate "what X is", and according to the cognition-feeling-will framework it enables the corresponding feelings and thereby the determinate desires to act. Last, but not least, the state of soul is indeed not passive in the process of perceiving. These mistakes manifest that we should clearly determine the cognitive dynameis of perception and the state of soul during the perception process, and the exploration of the kinds of perception should also not be omitted.

After these two studies, in the year 2003, Prof. Schmitt publishes his book *Die Moderne und Platon: zwei Grundformen europäischer Rationalität*, and in 2012 its second edition is translated in English. In this work he illustrates the ground-breaking idea that in Europe there are two paradigms of rationality, one is the Platonic-Aristotelian tradition, which also includes the Medieval philosophy, the other is the Stoic way of thought, which also dominates the philosophy from Renaissance on.[20] With this fundamental division he goes into their difference in epistemology, of which the perception has a role to play. His examination of sense perception is grounded on the principle that to think something is to discriminate and comprehend its proper object, and to be the object of thought the object requires to be something determinate, for what is thinkable is something determinate,[21] so the perception has its determinate objects, i.e., the sensible qualities like colours and sounds, not the external sensible things. After re-stressing that in Plato and Aristotle there exists the cognition-feeling-will model in comparison with the modern philosophy (see chapter 6) – which is already raised by Büttner (2000) – Schmitt begins with a study of the cognitive dynamis and the related feeling and emotion of perception and opinion. In his elaborate analysis of the peculiar function of perception (section 7.3.1, pp. 303–309) there are two especially valuable

---

[20] See (2012) 519–548.
[21] See Schmitt (2012) 46–48. In this sense Schmitt declares (pp. 217–225) that 'einai' (εἶναι) is the principle of cognition.

points: firstly he stresses that the sensible object is not external, rather it is something internal, something subjective, thus in the perception-activity there is an identity of internal and external, subjective and objective,[22] according to this assertation the claim that sense perception is nothing but a passive-receptive act is criticised (p. 307); secondly he introduces the Aristotelian dynamis-activity model to clarify that before the activity of seeing and hearing, the colours and sounds are merely potentially as they are, only in the activity of the soul's discrimination they are real colours and sounds for us (pp. 306–307). Moreover, Schmitt emphasises that according to Plato and Aristotle the first time we recognise the (external) object as object, is in the discrimination-activity of opinion, or with the Aristotelian terms, 'incidental perception', which refutes Grönroos' announcement that the sense perception recognises the external objects through the contents of sensible objects. Following this analysis of perception in the sense of itself Schmitt turns to the character of the sensibles, which in the view of Aristotle appears clear and evident for us though, confusing and abstract for the thing itself, i.e., the perception supplies still no knowledge of the individual objects (section 7.3.2, pp. 309–317). Regarding the 'opinion with perception' he stresses that it synthesises the sensible characteristics and grasps the substance of the individual object by logically discriminating its function which relates inherently to the substance.[23] Yet the opinion's dynamis is still broader, i.e., it always seeks to derive a universal aspect from the individual case, which can be exemplified by the fact that the children tend to call all men 'father', all women 'mother' (section 7.3.3, pp. 317–322). In this sense the distinction between perception and opinion is evident: the former discriminates merely the sensible qualities, not the sensible things like table or statue, for the discrimination and comprehension of their function – through which their substances can be recognised – is ascribed to the cognitive ability of opinion (p. 322f.).

Indeed Schmitt's study of the Platonic perception-doctrine proceeds already from his dissertation *Die Bedeutung der sophistischen Logik für die mittlere Dialektik Platons*, in which he tackles Plato's criticism of the Pre-Socratic philosophers and Sophists in respect of their doctrines about the perception-cognition and object-cognition.[24] Following this work he writes a thesis entitled "Zur Erkenntnistheorie bei Platon und Descartes" in 1989, which develops later into a systematic research named *Denken und Sein bei Platon und Descartes*, of which the principle that 'einai' (εἶναι) is the criterion of thought is re-asserted and applied in his interpretation of Plato's perception and

---

[22] Schmitt (2012) 303. Cf. p. 306 about the identity of subject and object in discriminating the sounds. For a similar analysis of this point, see section 2.1.2.3.
[23] To illustrate this point Schmitt (p. 318) quotes Philoponus' statement (*In de an.* 4, 21) that what involves here is 'the deduction of the universals from the sensibles' (τὸ ἐν τοῖς αἰσθητοῖς καθόλου συλλογίσασθαι). Later (p. 321), he argues for the requirement of a three-fold discrimination in discriminating a given sensible object as a scissors: Discriminating the sensibles: silver, long, sharp, hard, etc.; discriminating the function that is realised in this gathering of sensibles; and distinguishing this function purely for itself. For his clarification of the notion 'function', see pp. 326–331.
[24] Schmitt (1974) esp. 26–72; 132–240.

opinion.[25] In an essay written in 2002 Schmitt researches into the Aristotelian notion of 'synaesthesia' (συναίσθησις) in accordance with the latter's framework of sense-perception theory.[26] Then he goes back to Plato in 2006 and finishes the article 'Platonism and Empiricism',[27] of which his argument is: in Plato and Aristotle despite the fact that the sense perception is confusing, abstract and universal, it constitutes the beginning of the empirical cognition. Now, I suppose, the crucial points of his comprehension of the Platonic perception-theory are all proved, so in the following works like *Wie aufgeklärt ist die Vernunft der Aufklärung: Eine Kritik aus aristotelischer Sicht* he systematises Aristotle's perception-theory in comparison to the Stoics and the modern philosophy (esp. pp. 109–137), and in his newest treatise about the knowledge of the god he summarises the Platonic and Aristotelian way from sense perception to intellect.[28]

Now I turn to the other unsystematic studies about the sense perception in Plato. Considering the fact that (a) there are a multitude of essays and monographs involving one or some aspects of this subject matter, and (b) a detailed summary of all studies goes beyond the concern of this work, and some of them are already mentioned by Büttner (2000) and Grönroos (2001), I will introduce some of the most valuable studies after 2000, and several important interpretations that are not included in these two systematic studies, and my personal review will be given only when it is necessary. According to the organisation order of my own research I shall begin with the literature about the cosmology, cosmogony, and philosophy of science in the *Timaeus*. Chronologically they are: Brisson and Meyerstein's work[29] that compares Plato's world generation model with the Big Bang theory; Gregory's research into Plato's philosophy of science (2000) and the ancient Greek cosmogony (2007) which also concern the comparison of Plato and modern cosmology and cosmogony;[30] Johansen's work (2004) that prefers to exhibit the 'goodness in the cosmos as Plato sees' (p. 2);[31] the revised book of Mohr (2005) concerns the space, time, the mechanism Flux and world soul;[32] the treatise of Carone (2005)[33] involves the Platonic cosmology and ethics, which begins with a research of the *Timaeus*-Demiurge (pp. 24–52) and continues with an

---

[25] Schmitt (2011) 93–109. Strikingly the author does not cease at this point, he points out the way from perception and opinion to Plato's form-theory, see pp. 109–116.

[26] Schmitt (2002) Synästhesie im Urteil aristotelischer Philosophie.

[27] A similar essay entitled 'Platon und das empirische Denken der Neuzeit' is published in the same year, see (2006b) 77–109.

[28] Schmitt (2019) Gibt es ein Wissen von Gott? Plädoyer für einen rationalen Gottsbegriff, pp. 59–127. For a summary of his general scientific research until the year 2018, see Bernard (2018) 9–19.

[29] Brisson and Meyerstein (1995) Inventing the Universe: Plato's *Timaeus*, the Big Bang, and the Problem of Scientific Knowledge.

[30] Gregory (2000) Plato's Philosophy of Science; (2007) Ancient Greek Cosmogony, of which pp. 140–162 are about Plato's doctrine.

[31] Johansen (2004) Plato's Natural Philosophy: A Study of the *Timaeus-Critias*. Also see his article (2008) The *Timaeus* on the Principles of Cosmology.

[32] Mohr (2005) God and Form in Plato: The Platonic Cosmology. This book is revised from an earlier edition (1985) The Platonic Cosmology.

[33] Carone (2005) Plato's Cosmology and Its Ethical Dimensions.

exploration entitled 'cosmic god and human reason in the *Timaeus*' (pp. 53–78); Sedley (2007) summarises the notion of Demiurge in Plato's *Gorgias* and *Timaeus* as divine craftmanship;[34] Broadie (2012) examines several important aspects of the *Timaeus* like the Demiurge, the Paradigm, the construction of world body and soul, the establishment of the immortal souls, the notion of Chora (χώρα), etc;[35] Van Riel (2013) checks the Platonic notion of gods in a metaphysical perspective;[36] O'Brien (2015) offers then a chronological study of the notion of Demiurge from Plato to Plotinus.[37] Except for these monographs and essays there are also some important compilations like Calvo and Brisson (1997), Wright (2000), Sharples and Sheppard (2003), Mohr and Sattler (2010), and Chiaradonna and Galluzzo (2013).[38] Here two decisive issues of the modern interpretations should be pointed out: (a) most of the scholars intend not to compare the Platonic cosmos model with the modern theories like the Big Bang, yet such a comparison, I will argue in section 1.1.2.4, benefits us in recognising the rationality of Plato's thought – at this point the studies of Bernard, Schmitt, and Gregory must be praised.[39] The research of Brisson and Meyerstein does concentrate on both the Platonic world-generation doctrine and the Big Bang theory, yet their conclusion is false, for they insist that both theories are grounded on "a set of irreducible and indemonstrable formulas, pure inventions of the human mind, retained solely through recourse to his simple operative argument: 'it works'."[40] In this view the 'scientific' knowledge insisted by them is factually the Platonic discursive thinking that corresponds to mathematics and the mathematic physics in the Big Bang theory, while Plato's notions of Demiurge, gods and intellect (νοῦς) and the role of chance in the Big Bang theory are ruled out of this study, in this view the Platonic Demiurge is understood as a 'mystical illumination' (p. 2), which is a misunderstanding of Plato's doctrine. (b) The most studies neglect the research of the ancient Platonists, especially that of the Neoplatonists, for example, Proclus' commentary on *Timaeus*. One of the consequences of this omission rests on the misunderstanding of the notion of Demiurge: many scholars do not think that he is the divine Intellect, rather something others like the world soul, the form of the Good, and

---

[34] Sedley (2007) esp. 109ff.
[35] Broadie (2012) Nature and Divinity in Plato's *Timaeus*.
[36] Van Riel (2013) Plato's Gods.
[37] O'Brien (2015) The Demiurge in Ancient Thought. For Plato's doctrine of Demiurge, see pp. 18–35.
[38] Calvo and Brisson (1997) Interpreting the *Timaeus-Critias*: Proceedings of the IV Symposium Platonicum; Wright (2000) Reason and Necessity: Essays on Plato's *Timaeus*; Sharples and Sheppard (2003) Ancient Approaches to Plato's *Timaeus*; Mohr and Sattler (2010) One Book, the Whole Universe: Plato's *Timaeus* Today; Chiaradonna and Galluzzo (2013) Universals in Ancient Philosophy.
[39] Bernard (1998) 'Teleologie' und Naturphilosophie bei Platon; (2002) Die Entvölkerung des Himmels. Der moderne Naturbegriff und die platonische Daimonogie. For the research of Schmitt, see above n22 and n30, for that of Gregory, see n32. See also Campbell (2000) Zoogony and Evolution in Plato's *Timaeus*; Gloy (2000) Platons *Timaios* und die Gegenwart; Röd (2000) Platonische und neuzeitliche Kosmologie; Leggett (2010) Plato's *Timaeus*: Some Resonances in Modern Physics and Cosmology; Paparazzo (2015) Does Present-Day Symmetry Underlie the Cosmology of Plato's *Timaeus*? A Response to D. R. Lloyd.
[40] Brisson and Meyerstein (1995) 1–2.

so on. This can be exemplified by the work of Carone (2005), who rightly argues that the Demiurge is a kind of intellect (pp. 35–42), yet falsely attributes this intellect to the cosmic soul (pp. 42–51).

With reference to the sense perception theory in the *Timaeus* we can also resort to the articles of Brisson (1997), Hirsch (1997), Reydams-Schils (1997), Ierodiakonou (2005), Lautner (2005), Lorenz (2012), Wolfsdorf (2014), Remes (2014), Fletcher (2016), McCready-Flora (2018), and Calvo & Maria (2018).[41] Speaking of the Platonic perception doctrine in the *Theaetetus* I prefer to mention the monographs of Polansky (1992), Dorter (1994), Hardy (2001), Becker (2007), Tschemplik (2008), Giannopoulou (2013), and Kahn (2013)[42] – it is worthy to point out that (a) Kahn rightly emphasises the qualitative identity of the subjectively perceived object with the external object (pp. 92–93), (b) he rightly views the nature of perception as a system of movements (p. 91), but this argument is wrongly grounded on the attribution of the Act-Being affected upon model to Plato – and the essays written by Day (1997), Lee (1999), Osborne (2003), Thaler (2016), and Keeling (2019).[43] For the perception theory in other dialogues we have the papers of Bedu-Addo (1991), Baltzly (1996), Sansone (1996), Perl (1997), Rosen (1999), Craig (2001), Darchia (2003), Ganson (2005); Modrak (2006), Eisenstadt (2011), Pitteloud (2014), King (2016), Larsen (2017), (2018), and Tuozzo (2018).[44]

---

[41] Brisson (1997) Plato's Theory of Sense Perception in the *Timaeus*; Hirsch (1997) Sinnesqualitäten und ihre Namen (zu *Tim.* 61–69); Reydams-Schils (1997) Plato's World Soul: Grasping Sensible without Sense perception; Ierodiakonou (2005) Plato's Theory of Colours in the *Timaeus*; Lautner (2005) The *Timaeus* on Sounds and Hearing with Some Implications for Plato's General Account of Sense Perception; Lorenz (2012) The Cognition of Appetite in Plato's *Timaeus*; Wolfsdorf (2014) Timaeus' Explanation of Sense-Perceptual Pleasure; Remes (2014) Plato: Interaction Between the External Body and the Perceiver in the *Timaeus*; Fletcher (2016) Aisthēsis, Reason and Appetite in the *Timaeus*; McCready-Flora (2018) Affect and Sensation: Plato's Embodied Cognition; Calvo & Maria (2018) The Crafting of Mortal Soul in Plato's *Timaeus*.

[42] Polansky (1992) Philosophy and Knowledge: A Commentary on Plato's *Theaetetus*; Dorter (1994) Form and Good in Plato's Eleatic Dialogues: The *Parmenides*, *Theaetetus*, *Sophist*, and *Statesman*; Hardy (2001) Platons Theorie des Wissens im "*Theaitet*"; Becker (2007) Platon: *Theätet*; Tschemplik (2008) Knowledge and Self-Knowledge in Plato's *Theaetetus*; Giannopoulou (2013) Plato's *Theaetetus* as a Second *Apology*; Kahn (2013) Plato and the Post-Socratic Dialogue: The Return to the Philosophy of Nature.

[43] Day (1997) The Theory of Perception in Plato's *Theaetetus* 152–183; Lee (1999) Thinking and Perception in Plato's *Theaetetus*; Osborne (2003) Knowledge is Perception: A Defence of *Theaetetus*; Thaler (2016) Judgement, Logos, and Knowledge in Plato's *Theaetetus*; Keeling (2019) Pathos in the *Theaetetus*.

[44] Bedu-Addo (1991) Sense-Experience and the Argument for Recollection in Plato's *Phaedo*; Baltzly (1996) Socratic Anti-Empiricism in the *Phaedo*; Sansone (1996) Socrates' "Tragic" Definition of Color (Pla. *Men*. 76d–e); Perl (1997) Sense perception and Intellect in Plato; Rosen (1999) The Problem of Sense Perception in Plato's *Philebus*; Craig (2001) The Strange Misperception of Plato's *Meno*; Darchia (2003) Colour Perception in Plato's *Phaedo* and Democritus' Treatise *About Colours*; Ganson (2005) The Platonic Approach to Sense Perception; Modrak (2006) Plato: A Theory of Perception or a Nod of Sensation; Eisenstadt (2011) The Affects and Senses in Plato's *Charmides*; Pitteloud (2014) Is the Sensible an Illusion? The Revisited Ontology of the *Sophist*; King (2016) Sensation in the *Philebus*:

(2) The research of Aristotle's perception-theory. For the Aristotelian doctrine of sense perception there are more literature, part of the reason lies in the fact that he has written the treatise *De anima*, in which he tackles the sense perception by ascribing it to the abilities of the soul, so the scholars can find most of his sensation doctrines in this work. Let us begin with the interpretations of this work: Bernard's dissertation (1988)[45] about the Aristotelian perception theory in comparison with the Cartesian and Kantian doctrine is still one of the best studies in this field. In analysing the contexts of the *De anima* he resorts not only to the modern literature, but also to the commentaries of the ancient Platonists like Themistius, Philoponus, Simplicius, etc. His interpretation explicitly manifests that being distinguished from the modern philosophy, in the eyes of Aristotle the soul is not passive and receptive in the perception process, rather its activity of discrimination is spontaneous (pp. 221–233). Everson's treatise (1997) supplies a relative comprehensive collection of the contexts involving the sense perception, i.e., not only the *De anima*, but also the *Metaphysics*, *Physics*, *On sense*, GC (*De generatione et corruptione*), PA (*De partibus animalium*), *Posterior Analytics*, and so on.[46] In the same year Johansen's PhD thesis is published, the main concern of this study, however, is focused on the sense-organs and their role in the course of sensation, especially the peculiar sensation sight, hearing, touch and smell. Additionally the author also argues that for Aristotle there is no material changes in the perceiver.[47] Gregoric (2007)[48] investigates the appearance of the notion 'common sense' in Aristotle's philosophical framework (chapter 1), examines the terminological use of this phrase the *De anima*, *De partibus animalium* and *De memoria et reminiscentia* (chapter 2), and explores its role in perceptual discrimination, and other higher cognitive capacities which bear the title 'common sense' though, goes factually beyond it (chapter 3). The work of Herzberg (2010)[49] concerns the determinate cognitive abilities of sense perception and its relationship with knowledge. Interestingly, in chapter 5 Herzberg examines the function of sense perception in acquiring the knowledge by resorting to the argument about experience (ἐμπειρία) and the distinct cognitive way of 'prior by nature' and 'prior for us' in the *Posterior Analytics* II 19. Despite the elaborate analysis, there are also mistakes in this study, for instance, he wrongly argues that the notion 'common sensation' exists not in Plato, rather it is an innovation of Aristotle (p. 137). At last Johansen (2012) supplies a complete investigation into the four dynameis of the Aristotelian soul in the *De anima*, i.e., nutrition, perception, locomotion, and intellect.[50]

Common to Body and Soul; Larsen (2017) The Place of Perception in Plato's Tripartite Soul; (2018) Are there Forms of Sensible Qualities in Plato? Tuozzo (2018) Sense Perception and Explanation in the *Phaedo*.

[45] Bernard (1988) Rezeptivität und Spontaneität der Wahrnehmung bei Aristotle. Versuch einer Bestimmung der spontanen Erkenntnisleistung der Wahrnehmung bei Aristoteles in Abgrenzung gegen die rezeptive Auslegung der Sinnlichkeit bei Descartes und Kant.
[46] Everson (1997) Aristotle on Perception.
[47] Johansen (1997) Aristotle on the Sense-Organs.
[48] Gregoric (2007) Aristotle on the Common Sense.
[49] Herzberg (2010) Wahrnehmung und Wissen bei Aristoteles: Zur epistemologischen Funktion der Wahrnehmung.
[50] Johansen (2012) The Powers of Aristotle's Soul.

Given the fact that there are many ancient commentaries on the *De anima*, we should not eschew the studies in this field: Blumenthal (1996)[51] introduces primarily some important aspects involving the commentaries and the commentators like the background of these commentaries, their identity, the Neoplatonic psychology, and offers an overview of all Neoplatonic commentaries (chapter 1). In the second part he summaries the commentaries according to the following order: firstly, the nature and divisions of the soul, then its abilities of perception, memory, imagination, reason, and intellect. The book of Perkams (2008) encompasses the commentaries of Philoponus, Priscian (Ps.-Simplicius) and Stephanus of Alexandria. The brief analysis of their interpretations of sense perception theory enables us to grasp the commentators' thought about this issue, although the subject-matter of perception is not the main concern of this work.[52] At last, Tuominen's outstanding research helps us to get a comprehensive view of the perception theory under the ancient commentators from Alexander of Aphrodisias to Simplicius. The discussion about sense perception is included in two sections, i.e., firstly the part of epistemology (pp. 52–66), then a specific chapter entitled 'psychology: perception and intellect' (pp. 158–184).[53]

(3) Finally, I will introduce some literature about the Neoplatonism,[54] especially Proclus, whose *Timaeus*-commentary will be one of the main resources in my interpretation of the generation of the sensible universe and the human being. For the perception-doctrine of Proclus the first study I prefer to recommend is Blumenthal's article written in 1982,[55] then Siorvanes' systematic introduction of Proclus' philosophy, in which he summarises some of the most important contributions made by Proclus in clarifying the Platonic perception theory, for example the theory of soul-vehicles (pp. 131–133), the interpretation of the world soul, human soul and supra-cosmic soul (pp. 140–148), and the element-theory (pp. 209–247).[56] The collection edited by Perkams and Piccione (2004)[57] embraces three essays about the perception doctrine in Proclus: Lautner on Proclus' fourfold division of sense perception (pp. 117–135); Opsomer researches into the unregulated souls in Proclus (pp. 136–166); and Perkams explores the theme of the substantial diversity of the human soul (pp. 167–185). The study of Martijn (2010)[58] concentrates on the aspect of Proclus' natural philosophy as theology and its application in his *Timaeus*-commentary. Kutash (2011) researches into the *Timaeus*-commentary in the view of the 'ten gifts' sent by the Demiurge, which is originally a theme supposed by Proclus. However, the first gift, i.e., the perceptibility of

---

[51] Blumenthal (1996) Aristotle and Neoplatonism in Late Antiquity: Interpretations of the *De anima*.
[52] Perkams (2008) Selbstbewusstsein in der Spätantike: Die neuplatonischen Kommentare zu Aristoteles' *De anima*. For Philoponus' analysis of sense perception, see pp. 110–122; for that of Priscian, see pp. 196–209; for that of Stephanus of Alexandria, see pp. 239–251.
[53] Tuominen (2009) The Ancient Commentators on Plato and Aristotle.
[54] For a summary of the general research of Neoplatonism from the year 2005 to 2015, see Adamson (2015) Neoplatonism: The Last Ten Years.
[55] Blumenthal (1982) Proclus on Perception.
[56] Siorvanes (1996) Proclus: Neo-Platonic Philosophy and Science.
[57] Perkams & Piccione (2006) Proklos: Methode, Seelenlehre, Metaphysik.
[58] Martijn (2010) Proclus on Nature: Philosophy of Nature and its Methods in Proclus' Commentary on Plato's *Timaeus*.

the universe, is barely touched.[59] In another collection published in 2017 Finamore and Kutash examine the world soul and human soul according to Proclus.[60] At last Van Riel (2017) expounds the causes of the perceptibility of the world in the Proclean perspective.[61]

3 Introduction of the main contents of this research

After the summary of the current research of the perception theory in Plato, Aristotle, and Proclus, I should turn to the introduction of the main contents of this study, which will fall into three chapters: the first one deals with the generation of the sensible world and the perceiver, namely human beings, the second chapter describes the becoming of the affected and unaffected perception, and the last chapter explores the kinds of perception and their corresponding cognitive abilities, i.e., their dynameis to discriminate and comprehend their own objects.

The clarification of the genesis of the whole universe is composed of two sections, i.e., a primary research (1.1.1) and a further investigation (1.1.2). The primary study aims at a brief description of the generation of the world soul (1.1.1.1), world body (1.1.1.2), and their combination into a living creature which is deemed to be a sensible god (1.1.1.3). The world soul and world body are fashioned by the Demiurge after receiving the forms from the Paradigm. The features of the world soul and body shall be explained with the Proclean five-aspects framework, namely their (essential) existence (ὕπαρξις), harmony (ἁρμονία), form (εἶδος or σχῆμα), dynamis (δύναμις), and activity (ἐνέργεια). The world soul (*Tim.* 35a1–37c5) will be clarified as follows: (1) its essential existence is an entity including three intermediate ingredients, viz. the mingled Substance (οὐσία), Sameness (τὸ ταὐτόν) and Difference (τὸ ἕτερον or τὸ θάτερον). (2) The harmony of the world soul means that as a mingled unification it can be divided into many harmonious parts through the harmonic (musical) and arithmetic proportions, so that each of its parts possesses a determinate harmony. (3) This whole separated world soul is now set in the form of one single line, which is divided again into two sections, they are put together at the centre in a X-form, and the Demiurge fashions these two parts into two circles and joins them up at one point, in which way the form of the world soul is fashioned. (4) The dynamis of the world soul is twofold, i.e., to move and to discriminate. (5) The activity of the world soul rests on the actuality of its dynameis of motion and cognition (section 1.1.1.1). With reference to the world body: (1) the world is sensible, so it must be visible and tangible, namely it encompasses fire and earth, and further air and water. (2) The four kinds of elements must be bound together, so there must be a certain bond (δεσμόν, 31c1) that can hold them in a unity in the sense of numbers, volumes and dynameis, which designates a continuous proportion Fire: Air = Air: Water = Water: Earth. (3) With this proportion the Demiurge fashions

---

[59] Kutash (2011) The Ten Gifts of the Demiurge: Proclus on Plato's *Timaeus*. Her mention of the perceptibility or sense perception can be found in pp. 50; 62–63; 92–93; 105; 124; etc.
[60] Finamore & Kutash (2017) Proclus on the *Psychê*: World Soul and the Individual Soul.
[61] Van Riel (2017) How Can the Perceptible World be Perceptible? Proclus on the Causes of Perceptibility.

the world into a sphere which will move in the circular manner at the same place after it is ensouled, this is the form of the world body. (4) The world body is self-sufficient, and is established to act and to be affected upon completely by itself and in itself. (5) The activity of the world body, namely its self-nutrition and circular motion, is initiated by the implantation of the world soul (section 1.1.1.2). As for the embodiment of the world soul in the world body, the Demiurge, according to the 'possible myth' or 'possible logos' (εἰκὼς μῦθος/ εἰκὼς λόγος), sets the soul in the middle of the world body, so the world soul extends to the surface of the world body and encompasses it, initiating the motion of the whole universe and its beginning as a living god, in which way the 'one, single, solitary' (ἕνα μόνον ἔρημον, *Tim.* 34b5) universe comes eventually to be (section 1.1.1.3). This is the primary research of the world-generation.

The further research embraces four parts, i.e., the substance of the Demiurge (1.1.2.1), the generation and reconstruction of χώρα (1.1.2.2), the nature of the world soul (1.1. 2.3), and a comparison of the Platonic world-generation theory with the modern theories like Darwinism and the Big Bang (1.1.2.4).

The definition of the Demiurge is a controversial topic, to clarify his real identity I will mainly resort to the interpretation of Proclus: Summarising the previous interpretations from the Middle Platonist Numenius to his own teacher Syrianus, Proclus points persuasively out that the Demiurge is (1) a divine intellect as the cause of the entire universe (Proclus, *In Tim.* I 311, 1–14); (2) Maker and Father of the universe (*In Tim.* I 311, 14–25); and (3) Zeus, which is affirmed both by Orpheus and Plato (*In Tim.* I 312, 26–317, 20).

Regarding the χώρα I shall primarily elucidate that it originates not from the Demiurge, rather from the One, the Unlimited, and the One Being. Thus, under the influence of the Paradigm it possesses the traces of elemental forms and moves disorderly, which signifies that the Demiurge can merely reconstructs it after having persuaded it and received the forms from the Paradigm. So, with numbers and logoi the Demiurge establishes the five polyhedrons for the five elements ether, fire, air, water, and earth, which are further used to constitute the elemental bodies and the matter for the whole universe, the fixed stars, the planets, the human beings, and all others. Considering the proportion of the volumes (τοὺς ὄγκους, 56c3) of these four polyhedrons – tetrahedron for fire, octahedron for air, icosahedron for water, and cube for earth – the Platonic Timaeus stresses that their multitudes, movements and the other dynameis (τὰ πλήθη καὶ τὰς κινήσεις καὶ τὰς ἄλλας δύναμεις) are also proportional, and these proportional features partially determine that the sensible things as well as the sensible qualities proceeding from the quantitative characters of the polyhedrons and elemental bodies are also proportional, which implies that there is no role for the chance to play in the genesis of the whole universe as well as the natural things (section 1.1.2.2).

In the further investigation of the soul, I shall focus on one of its most important features, i.e., its being both generated and not generated, and clarify this character with the soul's own logos and dynamis, namely self-motion. This determinate nature of self-motion, however, originates substantially from the soul's intermediate essence: it is an entity of three mingled ingredients Substance, Sameness and Difference. This implies that we can clarify the soul's coming to be and coming not to be by resorting to its very substance. For example, in the view of the soul's divisibility and indivisibility: the soul is mixed from both indivisible and divisible Substances, thus being indivisible the soul can be called 'intelligible' and 'eternal', and in terms of its divisibility it can be entitled 'temporal' and 'the first among the things that are generated' – as described at *Laws* 895a5–b7 and 896a5–b2. So substantially with reference to its divisible parts the soul is generated, while given its indivisible parts it is not generated (section 1.1.2.3).

In section 1.1.2.4 there will be a reflexion of the whole description of the Platonic world-generation theory. This theory, given that it is based on the epistemology, is more reasonable than the modern generation-doctrines like Darwinism and the Big Bang: firstly the latter two theories are essentially similar to some of the ancient theories like that of Democritus and Epicureanism, for they all lay too much emphasis on the materials, while in Plato the Chora is attributed to the subsidiary cause (συναίτια), and it is persuaded by the Demiurge to participate in the world-generation, so that the becoming of the universe results not merely from the change of the materials, rather from both the activity of the intellectual Demiurge and the necessary reconstruction of the materials (Chora), which is apparently more reasonable than the Big Bang. Secondly, both Darwinism and the Big Bang cannot be entitled 'scientific' due to their dependence on the chance (τύχη). Despite the complexity of their clarifications, the function of chance is substantially decisive for both doctrines, yet this decisive role of chance in explaining the generation and change of the whole universe leads logically and inherently to an unreasonable result: as chance is now the precondition of all kinds of natural science, and the Evolution and the generation of the cosmos cannot be repeated and proved, our natural knowledge turns out to be quite doubtful. Whereas the Platonic doctrine supplies primarily a mathematic clarification of the generation of the world soul and world body, moreover, the principle and reason of this generation, i.e., the divine intellect, is also thinkable for us.

The second part of the first chapter involves the generation of the perception subject, viz. the human being. To elucidate the becoming of human beings, however, I will primarily explore the kinds of perception subjects in Plato (section 1.2.1), for knowing the other types of perception subject enables us to discriminate the human being from the other sorts of perception subject which possess different kinds of perceptual abilities. According to Proclus' summary there are totally three classes, four kinds of perception subject: the first class includes the whole universe and the fixed stars due to their unaffected and common perception; the second class denotes the human being who is credited with the 'common and affected' perception; the last class holds the 'divided and affected' perception, which belongs to plants.

Like the exposition of the world-generation, the description of the coming to be of the human being falls into three parts: the generation of the human soul (1.2.2.1), the human body (1.2.2.2), and the embodiment of the human soul (1.2.2.3). This kind of soul embraces two forms and three kinds of vehicles: the immortal soul resides in the divine vehicle, while the mortal soul has two vehicles, i.e., the pneumatic and the earthly. The immortal and divine soul form is fashioned by the Demiurge and in the same way as the establishment of the world soul, the unique difference rests on their purity (*Tim.* 41d4–e2), hence the divine human soul part is akin (συγγενεῖς, 47c1, d1) to the world soul, which means that it also possesses two circles and moves by itself. In the same context we are also informed of this soul form's being immediately mounted in a chariot-vehicle after it is established (ἐμβιβάσας ὡς ἐς ὄχημα, 41e1–2). This vehicle is also moulded by the Demiurge, and the ingredients used to mould it are ether, which are also used to form the astral bodies, so that the immortal souls can firstly be distributed to the astral stars and living there as encosmic citizens – at this point I will prove that the Neoplatonic soul-vehicle theory proceeds directly from Plato, for in Plato the ether is already deemed to be the fifth element used to create the heaven, and in the following part about the second vehicle I will argue that the term 'pneuma' (πνεῦμα) in Plato's dialogues hints already at a possible meaning of a material vehicle. The mortal souls and their vehicles are fashioned by the young gods in the manner of imitating their father, hence the mortal souls share the immortality of the divine souls, and survive the (bodily) death: this point can be literally illustrated by the Myth of Er in the *Republic*. The mortal vehicles are twofold, both are composed of the four elements, yet the pneumatic vehicle, in which the mortal soul perceives, is simpler than the shell-like one, which partially enables the earthly individual life. Here we see three kinds of soul lives: the heavenly life in the ether-vehicle, the middle one in the pneumatic vehicle, and the earthly in the shell-like vehicle.

The human body, or the earthly vehicle of the mortal soul form, is also established by the young gods. The materials utilised to fashion them are the elements borrowed from the universe. They are unified into a unity by the young gods who weld them together with a multitude of small 'rivets', which reveals that the harmony of the human body is so tiny that it cannot be held on for a long period. This shell-like body, seen from outside, has a head, a body, and four limbs, of which the head is moulded for the immortal soul part, and the body and limbs are sent to it so that the body can move in all directions. For the sake of perception, the gods set the sense-organs in the face, and the eyes and ears are bestowed to the human being for their beneficial function in the study of the natural things. Unlike the world body, the human body requires nutrition from outside to maintain its existence and growth, which indicates its ability to produce affections that can influence the soul, although it is created to be the soul's servant (section 1.2.2.2).

The implantation of the human soul into the earthly body is stated in three passages, i.e., *Tim.* 42a3–b2, 43a5–44d2, and 69c5–72e1, of which the first one belongs originally to the 'the fated laws' (νόμους τε τοὺς εἱμαρμένους, *Tim.* 41e2–3) that is declared by the Demiurge, the second context depicts the incarnation of the immortal soul form, and the last one concerns the embodiment of the mortal part. In the first passage the Demiurge ascribes the reason of the embodiment or descent of the immortal souls to necessity, and the incarnation results in both the beginning of the living human life on the earth and the generation of all kinds of sensation, feelings, emotions, and desires due to the forcible bodies affections. Moreover, the circular movements of the divine soul will also be impeded by the bodily movements and affections including the sensation. The second context affirms the possible influence of the bodily movements on soul, for in the initial period of the incarnation, or for every infant, neither the body nor the soul can control the other, rather 'with force' (βίᾳ, *Tim.* 43a7) they are moved and move mutually, thus the whole life moves in all six directions without any measure (43a7–b4). When the influence of the body, especially that of growth and nutrition, becomes weaker and the rotations in the soul recover their path and govern the whole life, this situation will be altered. And depending on whether a human being receives the right education or not he can either escape from the disease of soul or go back to Hades after the death of the shell-like body. In the third passage Plato describes the specific embodiment of the mortal soul which includes two further parts, i.e., the thymos-formed (θυμοειδές) and the appetitive (ἐπιθυμητικόν). The former is incarnated in the breast, while the latter is embodied in the belly. Strikingly, instead of a view of modern physiology the Platonic Timaeus describes the implantation with an interpretation-model of the position, form (structure), and dynamis of the related organs. The reason of this model is located at the young gods' purpose to make the generation of the mortal human life a perfect generation which can participate in the intellect (*Tim.* 42e2–4, 71d5–7).

After the description of the generation of the sensible universe and the human being who undergoes the sensible affections, I will examine the becoming of the sense perception in chapter 2. Given that in Plato there are two basic kinds of perception corresponding to the mortal and immortal soul, i.e., the affected sensation (παθητικὴ αἴσθησις) and unaffected sensation (ἀπαθὴς αἴσθησις), I will firstly determine the becoming of the affected sensation (2.1), then the generation of the other kind (2.2).

From the passages at *Theaetetus* 156a5–b2, *Philebus* 34a3–5, *Timaeus* 42a3–6, 43b6–c7, and 69c5–d6 we can conclude that in order to engender an affected sensation four preconditions must be fulfilled: the existence of the sensibles and the perception subject, namely the human body and soul; the generation of an affected sense-affection; the progress of this affection to the soul; and the activity of the soul's dynamis to discriminate this affection (section 2.1.1). Considering that the generation of the sensible cosmos and that of the human being is already described in the preceding parts, I will concentrate here on the last three conditions (section 2.1.2): A sense-affection comes to be, normally when two elemental movements, one from the sensibles, the other from the sense-organs, encounter with each other in the neighbouring area, and join together in giving birth to a unified elemental movement which can move back to the sense-organ. The meeting of both elemental movements, according to the principle 'like to like' (ὅμοιον πρὸς ὅμοιον, *Tim.* 45c4), should be homogeneous (ὁμοῖος) and commensurate (σύμμετρος), and there must exist medium through (with) which they can move: water and air are the media for the affections of colour, sound and odour, while flesh is the medium for taste and touch. The daylight plays a decisive role in the generation of sense-affection, for it initiates the existence and growth of all sublunary natural sensible things including all media, thus it would not be deemed to be a medium, rather a determinate entelechy (ἐντελέχεια) and perfection (τελειότης) of what is transparent. At this point one can already refute the application of the modern philosophical terms like 'active' and 'passive' in describing the process of the affection-generation, for both the sensibles and the perceiver are not opposite, rather the elemental movements from them are homogeneous and commensurate. Moreover, this homogeneity is not decided by the sensibles, rather the elemental movements proceeding from the sense-organs (section 2.1.2.1).

The motion of the affected sense-affection from the meeting-place to the sense-organ is not a simple physical motion or physiological process, rather a qualitative movement from dynamis to activity, or a kind of generation, for this affection exists previously not in the sense-organ. The state of the sense-organ is altered as the affection-motion moves in it, for its dynamis to discriminate the external homogeneous and commensurate elemental movements is now realised. The movement from the sense-organ to the soul also needs the existence of a proper media. And this sense-affection movement to the human soul, taking the elemental motion as its substrate, is necessary, for the sense-organ is unable to recognise the affection, only the soul, as the principle and reason of all kinds of motion including the generation of all sensibles, possesses the dynamis to discriminate the affected sense-affection, in which sense the progress of affection to soul is a kind of reversion (2.1.2.2).

The dynamis-activity model can also be used to explain the change of the (mortal) soul's state, as it discriminates the affection that exists rightly in itself. In perceiving the affections the soul, not as the modern Cartesian and Kantian philosophy argues, (1) is not passive, which is exemplified in *Symposium* 220c–d: Socrates is said to stand outside thinking for a whole summer day without any food or drink, in which situation the bodily affections must be quite forcible, yet concentrating on his thought those affections are neglected by Socrates, which means that only when the soul is ready to perceive, the affection can be perceived; (2) discriminates not the external sensible things, but the internal affection, for apparently after approaching to the soul the affection assails the soul and the latter perceives this affection spontaneously, which indicates that in strict sense the perception is 'subjective' and 'internal', not 'objective' and 'external'. The discrimination and comprehension of the affections enable us to grasp the sensible qualities like sounds and colours though, not the substance of the sensible things, for what the soul discriminates is not the external objects like 'a man' or 'a statue', rather 'a white as such', 'a motion as such', and so on (section 2.1.2.3).

The second part of chapter 2 will describe the generation of the unaffected sensation, namely the opinion with sensation (δόξα μετ' αἰσθήσεως): as the affected sensation corresponds both to the Aristotelian 'peculiar and common sensation', and Proclus' 'perception of the mortal soul', the unaffected perception is equal to the Aristotelian 'incidental sensation' and the 'perception of the immortal soul' in Proclean sense. The generation of such a kind of perception is clarified in *Philebus* 38b6–d10, where the Platonic Socrates declares that when the present (affected) sensation is combined with a memory-image in the soul, the soul will announce the substance of the sensibles like 'this object that locates beside the rock under the tree is a man'.

The following task is to determine the kinds of perception and their cognitive abilities, which constitutes the chapter 3. In the first section of the examination of the sensation-types I will demonstrate that both the Aristotelian threefold sensation model and the Proclean perception theory originate from Plato's doctrine, whereas Plato's classification of the perception-sorts is more complex as what is exhibited in both models (section 3.1.1). Summarily for Plato the sensation includes two fundamental kinds, i.e., the affected and unaffected sensation, which correspond respectively to the mortal and immortal soul form. Both kinds can be further divided into two types: the affected sensation *per se* and the affected sensation mixed with other cognitive faculties such as phantasia and memory, and the unaffected sensation *per se* and the unaffected sensation mingled with further cognitive dynameis like the discursive thinking. For the affected sensation *per se* there exist the perception in strict sense, i.e., in the sense of its cognitive ability, and the perception in broad sense, namely feelings like pleasure and pain, emotions, and desires. With reference to the affected sensation in strict sense there are two further types: one is generated because of the inner desire to perceive, the other comes to be by chance. For all kinds of affected sensation in the strict sense there are occasions on which they can precisely discriminate, yet sometimes their discrimination results to contradictions – on this occasion the immortal soul will be summoned up to participate in the discrimination of the objects. Whether there is contradiction or not, all mortal sensation-types are generated from the affections involving either the whole body (touch) or merely a peculiar part of body (sight, hearing, smelling and taste). At last, in the perspective of the function in the study of the natural science, sight and hearing can be separated from the other senses, for the motion in the heaven and the harmony of the music is akin to the rotations of our immortal soul. To elucidate these classifications, I will draw a diagram at the end of section 3.1.2.

According to the framework of the 'affected-unaffected sensation' the research of the cognitive dynamis of perception will fall into two steps, i.e., that of the affected sensation (3.2.1) and the unaffected sensation (3.2.2). Each of them will begin with a determination of the correspondence between the Platonic perception-kinds and the Aristotelian (enmattered) categories. Then there will be an examination of their truth and a clarification of this truth.

The cognitive range of the affected sensation *per se* is covered by the Aristotelian categories expect for the first one, i.e., Substance. For those enmattered and sensible categories can be discriminated by the sensible objects of the peculiar and common sensation: quality, motion, rest, shape, size, number, and oneness. This correspondence exists not only in Aristotle, but also in Plato, for all categories and the sensible objects can be equally found in Plato's dialogues (section 3.2.1.1). For the truth of the affected sensation *per se* one should say that the peculiar sensation perceives always with precision, for its cognitive dynamis relates essentially to its objects, for example the sight has substantially colours, which is declared in *Charmides* 167b5–169a1; as for the truth of the common perception, however, holding no peculiar sense-organs it can merely perceive through the five peculiar organs, which leads to its possible fallibility. What we discriminate through the peculiar and common perception, however, is confusing, abstract, and universal, for on the one side the sensible things are always moving, on the other side the mortal soul is unable to grasp the forms. Under the affected sensation there is another kind of sensation, namely the affected sensation with help of memory and phantasia, which can also be right and wrong, yet when the memory is combined with the affected sensation to discern the substance of the sensibles, it turns out to be the unaffected sensation *per se*, viz. the opinion with sensation (section 3.2.1.2).

The unaffected sensation *per se* corresponds to the first Aristotelian category, i.e., the Substance that comes to be in the bodies. The cognitive range of this kind of perception covers factually all generated things, not only the natural ones, but also social affairs like justice and courage, and it concerns not only the individual, but also general things. For example, discerning the deep voice as father the children tend to call all men father. Moreover, the unaffected sensation *per se* can also partially recognise the Platonic 'common things' such as What-is (τὸ ἔστιν, *Theaet.* 185c4–5), What-is-not (τὸ οὐκ ἔστιν, 185c5), Substance and Non-substance (οὐσίαν [...] καὶ τὸ μὴ εἶναι, 185c8), etc., for the opinable things are the images of these things, as manifested in the Line-Analogy of *Republic* (section 3.2.2.1). This opinion with affected perception can precisely discriminate its objects, for there is 'true opinion' (τὸ δοξάζειν ἀληθῆ, *Theaet.* 200e5) without knowledge, yet there also exists possibility to give birth to the 'mis-opinion' or 'other-opinion (ἀλλοδοξίαν, 189b12; τὸ [...] ἀλλοδοξεῖν, 189d5; τὸ ἑτεροδοξεῖν, 190e2), which results on the one side from the mis-combination of the fresh affected sensation with the proper memory-image, on the other side from the features of the opinable things which are changeable. As for the unaffected sensation with support of the discursive thinking, it discriminates not only the substance, but also the cause of such a substance, and due to the help of the discursive thinking, this cognitive dynamis is always right (section 3.2.2.2). Lastly, I will exemplify the whole description of the cognitive dynamis of perception with the finger-passage in *Republic* 523a10–525a8.

1 The generation of the perceptible world and perception subject

Given that for Plato it is a general method to research into the generation of certain subject matter, for example in the *Republic* the exploration of the definition of the concept 'justice' begins with the description of the generation of a just city (369a6–b9), and in fact the *Timaeus* also begins with the generation of the cosmos (27a5–7), in this chapter, I will concentrate on the generation of the perceptible object, i.e., the physical world, and the perception-subjects – primarily the human being. The research of the generation of the sensible world (1.1) consists of two steps: at first a primary research which is devoted to offer an outline of the world-generation, i.e., the generation of the world soul, world body and their combination (1.1.1). For the general readers who have interest in Plato's theory of the world-generation such an overview shall be sufficient, but for the Platonists and professional researchers it is still not persuasive, hence following this primary research there will be a further inquiry (1.1.2) that deals with the more fundamental issues such as the definition of the Demiurge (1.1.2.1), the meaning of 'Chora' (χώρα) and its reconstruction (1.1.2.2), the essence and nature of the world soul, (1.1.2.3), and whether the Platonic generation-doctrine continues to be convincing when we compares it with the modern theories such as the Big Bang and Darwinism (1.1.2.4). In the second section of this chapter, after having clarified that how many kinds of perception subjects there are (1.2.1), I will continue with an exposition of the generation of the human being (1.2.2). The account of this subject matter, following the description of the generation of the universe in section 1.1.1, shall also encompass three parts: the establishment of the human soul (1.2.2.1), that of the human body (1.2.2.2), and their unification into a living human being (1.2.2.3).

1.1 The generation of the perceptible object: the sensible world

1.1.1 Primary research

Speaking of the primary research of the generation of the world one should bear in mind that for Plato the phrase 'sensible world' indicates the complete natural world that embraces both body and soul. The world soul is evidently not sensible, nonetheless, the whole sensible world, including all celestial and sublunary natural things, cannot exist without the soul: Plato declares at *Timaeus* 28b8–c2 that the whole world is generated, for it has a body, it is sensible and tangible, and it can be recognised by the opinion with perception (δόξῃ μετ'αἰσθήσεως). Although this statement is originally the answer to the question 'whether the world has come to be', it endorses the assertion that, according to Plato, what is sensible is the whole natural world that consists of all celestial and sublunary things. Moreover, as the universe moves in a certain way, there must be a reason to initiate and maintain such a motion, which implies that the universe must have a soul, because for Plato it is the soul that causes all physical movements;[62] and it is necessary for the soul to be in the world body, for there exists nothing in the outside (*Tim.* 33c1–2). In this respect the primary research should include three aspects: the generation of the world soul (1.1.1.1), that of the world body (1.1.1.2), and at last their combination into the whole moving and perceptible universe (1.1.1.3).

1.1.1.1 The generation of the world soul

It is the Demiurge who has established the whole sensible world according to the Paradigm[63] generated from the Good, or the One. The work of the demiurgic creation begins with the establishment of the world soul, goes further with the fashion of the world body, and ends with their unification. Regarding the relation of the world soul and world body, the Platonic Timaeus asserts explicitly that the former is earlier than the latter: "the god made soul prior to body and more venerable (πρεσβυτέραν) in birth and excellence, to be the body's mistress and governor" (*Tim.* 34c4–5).[64]

In the sight of the Neoplatonist Proclus,[65] who has written a marvellous commentary on Plato's *Timaeus*, the account of the generation of the world soul should be explained with three aspects: its essence (οὐσία), its dynamis (δύναμις) and its activity (ἐνέργεια),[66] for they exist by nature in everything. The essence of the soul, however, is both single and triple, since it is three-fold: (essential) existence (ὕπαρξις), harmony (ἁρμονία) and form (εἶδος or σχῆμα), and all of them are in one another. According to this account, the description of the soul-generation encompasses five parts: (1) existence, (2) harmony, (3) form, (4) dynamis, and (5) activity.

(1) The (essential) existence of the world soul (*Tim.* 35a1–a8). The soul is an entity including three ingredients, namely the mingled Substance (οὐσία), Sameness (τὸ ταὐτόν), and Difference (τὸ ἕτερον or τὸ θάτερον). The Platonic Timaeus introduces two kinds of Substance: one is the indivisible Substance that is 'ever in the same state' (ἀεὶ κατὰ ταὐτὰ ἐχούσης, 35a1–2), and indicates the eternal hypostasis which is intellectual, the other is the divisible Substance which 'becomes in bodies' (περὶ τὰ σώματα γιγνομένης, 35a2), and exists entirely temporally. The Demiurge compounds a third form (εἶδος) from the analogical things of both kinds of Substance, in the same way he blends things that are analogical to the indivisible and divisible Sameness, and the

---

[62] *Tim.* 36e2–5. Cf. *Laws* 896b1–2, 896d8.
[63] *Tim.* 28a6–b1. Cf. 29b3–4. Analogically Plato proclaims at *Rep.* 592b3 that the discussed city is a paradigm in the heaven.
[64] In this study the translation of the *Timaeus* is taken from Cornford (1937). According to Proclus (In *Tim.* II 115, 2–10), the term 'πρεσβυτέραν' can be understood in two ways: (1) in the sense of their essence (οὐσία). The soul is closer to the Demiurge, while the body is far away from him. (2) In the temporal sense. The time in the soul is senior and more divine as the time in the body.
[65] Proclus, *In Tim.* II 125, 10–127, 11.
[66] This is originally the research-order of Iamblichus' *De anima*, which is possibly taken from Aristotle's *De anima*. See Baltzly (2009a) 21–22.

indivisible and divisible Difference, which brings forth the mixed Sameness and Difference (35a1–6). With force he combines this intermediate Difference with this mixed Sameness, then joins them with the intermediate Substance into a unity.

(2) The harmony of the world soul (*Tim.* 35b1–36b5). After the unification of these three ingredients, the Demiurge ceases not, rather he divides the united whole – as it was a long strip – into many parts, so that each part is a blending of all three elements. This division is quite remarkable because it is arithmetic and harmonic.[67] First he takes one portion from the unified whole, then double of this, the third portion is one and a half as the second, the fourth is double of the second, the fifth is three times as the third, the sixth is eight times as the first, and the seventh is 27 times as the first. These portions form a series 1–2–3–4–8–9–27 that can be separated into two tetractys: 1–2–4–8 and 1–3–9–27. The former numbers are even and square, whereas the latter are odd and cube, and we can also find that 1+2+3+4+8+9=27.[68] The Demiurge continues by placing two means (i.e., the harmonic and arithmetic) in each interval, which "give rise to intervals of 2/3, 4/3 and 9/8 within the original intervals" (36a7–9). Through this division we obtain 1, 9/8, 81/64, 4/3, 3/2, 27/16, 243/128, 2 [...] 27.[69] In this division process what dominate are the harmonic (musical) and arithmetic proportions bestowed by the Demiurge. By virtue of these proportions all intervals are proportional divided and compound of all three reconstructed ingredients. In this sense these proportional intervals, together with the harmonic and arithmetic means, indicate the harmony of the world soul.

(3) The form of the world soul (*Tim.* 36b5–c6). All divided parts are now formed in one line, which is divided again into two parts. These two parts are fashioned into two circles that are responsible for the motion of the whole world: The Demiurge splits the whole composition lengthways into two same parts, puts them together at their centres in the form of letter 'X', bends them round into two circles, and joins them up at one point. Now there are two circles sharing the same centre. Setting both circles in circular movements at the same place, the Demiurge makes one circle outer, the other inner. The outer movement belongs to the nature of the 'Same', while the inner the 'Difference'.[70]

(4) The dynameis of the world soul (*Tim.* 36c6–d7). The circle of the Same is announced to revolve horizontally to the right, while the movement of the Difference diagonally to the left. The Demiurge assigns the supremacy to the rotation of the Same and Uniform (ταὐτοῦ καὶ ὁμοίου, 36d1) by making it "single and undivided" (μίαν γὰρ αὐτὴν ἄσχιστον, 36d1), and be responsible for the motion of the fixed stars, while the

---

[67] However, this implies not that the world soul itself is number, as Xenocrates tends to believe. See Heinze (1892) fr. 68. Cf. Baltes (1972) 74.
[68] Cornford (1937) 66–70. That the number 1 is both even and odd, see Aristotle, *Metaphy.* 986a17.
[69] Cf. Brisson and Meyerstein (1995) 35.
[70] Here the circles of 'Same' and 'Difference' are different from the 'Sameness' and the 'Difference', two of the three ingredients of the world soul: According to Timaeus the long band of soul-stuff is the blending of all three ingredients, for he says "τὴν σύστασιν πᾶσαν" (36b7), so that both circles consist of the blended Substance, Sameness and Difference. Indeed, the circle 'Same' and 'Difference' signify the form and dynameis of the world soul in governing the whole world. See Proclus, *In Tim.* II 258, 1–25.

circle of Difference is inferior and corresponds to the movements of the seven planets.[71] Hence the (self-)motion of the world soul can initiate the proportional motion of the whole universe. This is the world soul's dynamis of motion, its cognitive dynamis will be introduced together with its cognitive activity.

(5) The two-fold activities of the world soul (*Tim.* 36d8–37c5). The world soul's activities of cognition and motion are based on its dynameis, this can be revealed by the following account. After the establishment of the world body the Demiurge joins the body and soul together, centre to centre. The soul extends immediately from the centre to the circumference of the world body, revolving within its own and initiating a divine beginning of an unceasing and rational life for the whole time (36d8–e5).[72] This dynamis of movement must proceed from the circle of the Same, since it is an ability which covers the whole world.[73] The cognitive activity and the corresponding dynamis are grounded on the principle 'like knows like'.[74] As the world soul is established from the intermediate Substance, Sameness and Difference which are both divisible and indivisible, it knows the Substance, Sameness and Difference themselves. So as a logos arises in the soul, when it is related to the circle of Difference and carries message throughout the whole soul, there becomes firm and right opinion and belief; when it is concerned with the rational things and the circle of Same, necessarily there will be intelligent and knowledge.[75] Proclus comments elaborately on this point by emphasising that: "through the logoi which the Demiurge has bestowed upon it [the world soul], it cognises both the things prior to it and those posterior to it […] Going into itself, it learns that it is itself the logos of all things, since all knowledge is brought about through the similarity of the one who knows to what is known".[76]

1.1.1.2 The generation of the world body

With five aspects (existence, harmony, form, dynamis, and activity) the generation of the world soul is descripted. In the same manner the generation of the world body will be introduced:

(1) The substantial existence of the world body (*Tim.* 31b5–9). The universe is generated, and it is perceptible. As sensible object it must be visible and tangible, because for us the corresponding sensation sight and touch are prior to the others.[77]

---

[71] Proclus, *In Tim.* II 259, 1–3, 25–29. Cf. Aristotle, *GC* 336a31–b10. See Baltzly (2009a) 246–247.

[72] For a summary of this body-soul-relation in respect of motion, see Aristotle, *De an.* 406b26–407a2. For a refutation of the Aristotelian criticism of the Platonic doctrine in *De an.* 407a2f., see Priscian (Pseudo-Simplicius), *In de an.* 40, 1–41, 6.

[73] Cf. Cornford (1937) 93.

[74] Aristotle, *De an.* 404b17: γινώσκεσθαι γὰρ τῷ ὁμοίῳ τὸ ὅμοιον. This principle appears also in Crantor (see Plutarch *de an. procr.* 1912F) and Proclus (*In Tim.* II 135, 30–136, 1; II 298, 1–299, 33; etc.). Cf. Cornford (1937) 64–65, 94.

[75] *Tim.* 37b3–c3. Cf. Proclus, *In Tim.* I 251.

[76] Proclus, *In Tim.* II 298, 22–28. Tr. Baltzly. In this sense there is no wonder for Plato to assert at *Laws.* 896d–e that the soul governs the whole universe.

[77] Cf. Proclus, *In Tim.* II 6, 1–7, 18.

Visibility is inaccessible without fire, for (a) the visible things (like colours) are products of the lights, (b) sight is akin to the light of the day (45c3–7), (c) the connection of the visible object and sight cannot be realised without light.[78] Tangibility can be possible through (first of all) earth, for the earth is primarily solid (55d8–56a1).[79] In this sense the Demiurge establishes the world body from fire and earth.

(2) The harmony of the world body (*Tim.* 31b9–32c4). Because fire and earth, as sensible things that undergo change by virtue of their determinate properties, are opposite elements, there must be intermediate elements to connect them, for only in this way the world body can be generated as a unity. As fire and earth are three-dimensional elements, there must be at least two intermediates to join them: in the *Timaeus* they are air and water.[80] These four elements, as Timaeus teaches us later, are taken from the Chora (χώρα), which due to the lack of logos[81] and measure (53a8–9) keeps moving disorderly in the pre-cosmic conditions and processes in this state only some 'vestiges' (ἴχνη, 53b2) of the elemental nature (53a9–b2).[82] The Demiurge re-constitutes these elemental vestiges with forms and numbers (53b4–5), so that the four proportional elements can be generated (see section 1.1.2.2). Now they are formed into the world body by the Demiurge with proportion, which is a persuasive proof that the world is created as possibly perfect as it can be: he gives the elements a configuration by using a certain bond (δεσμόν, 31c1) that can hold them in a unity in the sense of numbers, volumes and dynameis (ἀριθμῶν τριῶν εἴτε ὄγκων εἴτε δυνάμεων, 31c5).[83] This reveals that the generation of the sensible world, even in respect of the world body, is not by chance.

Such a kind of proportion, instead of a discrete analogy like 8:4 = 6:3, is indeed a continuous one (ἀναλογία συνεχής) like 8:4 = 4:2. In this sense the proportion under discussion is Fire: Air = Air: Water = Water: Earth.[84] The reason of such an analogy rests on the fact that (a) Plato demands a perfect symmetry;[85] (b) only with such a proportion the four elements can be joined together in an incessant unity from which the universe can be fashioned.

---

[78] Proclus, *In Tim.* II 7, 33–8, 6. For the generation of the sight-affection, see section 2.1.2.1.
[79] For a more detailed explanation of the tangibility of the earth, see *Ibid.* II 10, 16–12, 15.
[80] That all creatures are composed of the four elements, see *Philebus* 29a10–b1.
[81] For the meaning of the term λόγος in Plato, see Theon of Smyrna, *Philosophi Platonici exposition rerum mathematicarum ad Platonem utilium*, 73, 11–15 and Proclus, *In Tim.* I 246,10–248, 6.
[82] At *Laws* 898b6–9 Plato describes a motion that is akin to the complete lack of intelligence (ἀνοίας ἂν ἁπάσης εἴη συγγενής), such a motion resembles the very pre-cosmic movement of these element-vestiges.
[83] This is a translation according to Calcidius (*In Tim.* § 21) and Proclus, *In Tim.* II 20, 10–28, 7, both annotate the phrase in the same way. For a detailed analysis of this translation, see Baltzly (2007) 11–16. One important point is that, according to Proclus, what Plato indicates with this phrase is not only a mathematical proportion, but also physical, which is neglected by many scholars such as Cornford (1937) 44n3 (who translated 'numbers, solids and squares') and Pritchard (1990) 182–193. For the research of the theory of numbers in the Platonic tradition, see Radke-Ulmann (2003) Die Theorie der Zahl im Platonismus.
[84] See Calcidius, *In Tim.* § 16.
[85] Taylor (1928) 96.

(3) The form of the world body (*Tim.* 32c5–33c1). With this perfect proportion the Demiurge fashions the world body into a (sensible) sphere that moves circularly. As a perfect creation the world has three properties: (a) it is a whole and complete living being; (b) it is the single one, nothing is left out; (c) it is free form oldness and sickness (32d1–33a3). The Demiurge bestows the cosmos the sphere-shape which is 'fitting and akin to its nature' (31b1–2), for (a) the cosmos is to embrace all living creatures in itself (33b2–4), analogically sphere is the very form that can comprehend all figures; (b) sphere is the most perfect and uniform figure at all, and the Demiurge wants the world to be a uniformity (33b4–c1). In addition, because the universe is visible and tangible, the sphere is also sensible.

(4) The dynameis of the world body (*Tim.* 33c1–34a1). Due to its determinate shape the universe is smooth and has no sensible organs, and there exists nothing in the outside. Thus, the world body is self-sufficient and is designed "to act and be acted upon entirely by itself and within itself" (33c7–d2). However, when it is ensouled, it becomes a living creature (30c2–31a1). As a living creature it must possess a certain kind of sensation.[86] But what sort of a perception the cosmos has? Proclus declares that its perception is the kind that imitates intellect and encompasses the sensible object in itself. He comments at *In Tim.* II 84, 5–20:

> Therefore the whole cosmos is both vision and what is visible, and it really is 'grasped by perception and opinion' (28a2) by virtue of its sensing itself and holding opinions concerning itself, for it is grasped by these [sc. perception and opinion] in the primary manner. So the knowledge in it is utterly complete and the sense perception is undivided, and the universe is all things: sense object, sense organ and sense [...] Just as the particular bodies have been brought together by the universal body, so too in the universal sense the many [individual] senses are encompassed. [This kind of perception] does not know [only] the colours or the sounds of sensible things, but rather the whole essence of them in as much as it is end mattered and individual, because it possesses the sensible essence and is sensible in itself rather than merely possessing them accidentally. (Tr. Baltzly).

So, the dynameis of the world body rests on its being self-sufficient, and after being ensouled it has a determinate perception which includes all sensibles. Such a sensation is an imitation of the intellect, for the world is created by the Demiurge who is indeed the divine intellect.[87]

(5) The activity of the world body (*Tim.* 34a1–8).[88] Given the essence and shape of the world body it nourishes by itself, being initiated by the soul it moves in an appropriate way, i.e., in circular motion, a movement which is regulated by the Demiurge. This motion is similar to the movement of intellect and reason (νοῦν καὶ φρόνησιν, 34a2–3), because it always moves "in the same place and within its own limits" (34a3–4).[89] Fur-

---

[86] Proclus, *In Tim.* II 82, 20–25; III 296, 3–4.
[87] For the clarification that the Demiurge is the divine intellect, see section 1.1.2.1.
[88] At 34a9–b3 there is a description of the world body that is originally irrelevant to the current issue, but still it is included in Proclus' commentary, so I also take it as a part of the account of the world body.
[89] Cf. *Laws* 898a3–b4.

thermore, as a simple motion the circular movement has no opposite motion, and it also needs no feet to realise this motion, in this reason the world body has no legs or feet.

This is the description of the world body's generation: As a sensible existence it is visible and tangible, which implies that it is formed from fire and earth. Being opposite elements there bound to be at least two intermediate elements to join them into a single body, which turn out to be air and water. The Demiurge fashions the four elements by unifying them with proportion and shaping them into a sphere, which is smooth and self-sufficient. As a work of the Demiurge the world body is perfect and uniform, its cognitive dynamis, after being ensouled, is an imitation of the intellect, while the manner of its movement is like that of the intellect and reason.

1.1.1.3 The combination of the world body and world soul

Having discussed the essence, harmony, shape, dynamis and motion of the world body and the world soul, Timaeus turns now to their combination (34b3–9): the soul is set by the Demiurge 'in the middle' (εἰς τὸ μέσον, 34b2) of the world body and thus caused to extend from the centre to the circumference of the body, initiating the circular movement of the whole universe. In this manner the 'one, single, solitary' (ἕνα μόνον ἔρημον, 34b5) cosmos is generated. Through its excellence (δι' ἀρετὴν, 34b6) the universe is autarchic, needing no acquaintance or friend. In respect of all these factors it is regarded as a blessed god (εὐδαίμονα θεὸν, 34b8).

For a better understanding of this unification, one must explain the term 'in the middle', the extension of the soul, and the universe's being 'one', 'single' and 'solitary': the first two points explain the way of the world's ensoulment, while the last one determines the essence of the universe. (1) Proclus reminds us that in the sentence "in the middle he set a soul" (34b3: ψυχὴν δὲ εἰς τὸ μέσον αὐτοῦ θείς), Plato does not write 'the soul', but 'a soul', which results in a substantial distinction:[90] 'the soul' denotes that the whole soul is set in the middle, while 'a soul' implies merely one of its dynameis. For in the world soul there is a hypercosmic, transcendent soul that transcends the universe and exercises authority over everything. This kind of soul, or this certain aspect of the world soul, through which the world has a connection with the intellect, is a monad, which implies that this hypercosmic soul is designed to be above all kinds of cosmic souls. Proceeding from the hypercosmic and transcendent soul, the cosmic souls "apportion themselves around about the cosmos and are present in all parts of the universe in a manner appropriate to each".[91] In this sense 'the middle' – or 'the centre', considering the concrete shapes of the whole universe and the planets in it – can be that of the whole world, the Earth, the Sun, and any other sphere. Beginning with the dynamis of the soul which is placed 'in the middle' Timaeus shows the process of ensouling:[92] from the dynamis of the world soul in the middle to that in the whole

---

[90] Proclus, *In Tim.* II 105, 15–106, 9. Tr. Baltzly.
[91] *Ibid.* II 106, 2–4. Tr. Baltzly.
[92] Here we meet the typical Neoplatonic three-fold mode of procession (πρόοδος), remaining (μονή), and reversion (ἐπιστροφή). See Proclus, *In Tim.* I 414.29–415, 3. Cf. Siorvanes (1996) 105–109.

universe and the hypercosmic aspect, through which the intellect is connected. Proclus summarises this explanation by claiming that: "in the middle of it he placed Soul which is the same thing as saying 'giving even the centre participation in soul and stretching it throughout the universe, he sent forth its dynameis to make a whole, while leaving outside the universe an even more divine [power] which has been established from itself and sustains the whole cosmos in a transcendent manner'" (Proclus, *In Tim.* II 107, 24–28. Tr. Baltzly). This interpretation corresponds to the claim at *Laws* 898e8–899a4, where Plato shows us the three ways through which the soul guides the world: governing in the round bodies like the Sun and human being; forming a body from the elements from outside; and being without body but still possessing certain wonderful dynameis. The hypercosmic soul in the *Timaeus* is the third kind of souls of the *Laws*, and the other two kinds are the souls in the cosmos.

(2) Following the aforesaid paragraph, it is evident that one dynamis of the world soul is placed in the middle, and it starts to extend from the centre to the outside of the world body. This extension is later than the activity of the world soul (36e2–5). Given that it is the Demiurge who puts the soul 'in the middle', the ensoulment is twofold: on the one hand the process of the combination is initiated by the Demiurge, for it is he who moulds and unifies the world body and world soul; on the other side the process is finished by the self-moving activity of the world soul, as it expands three-dimensionally from the centre to the outmost heaven.[93]

(3) 'one', 'single' and 'solitary'.[94] These three termini indicate three corresponding reasons of the world: the final, the paradigmatic and the demiurgic (τὴν τελικήν, τὴν παραδειγματικήν, τὴν δημιουργικήν, Proclus, *In Tim.* II 109, 18–19). The final cause denotes the One, or the Good, the paradigmatic reason is the intelligible, and the demiurgic cause is certainly the Demiurge. Because the universe is generated as one single existence which reverts upon the One, it is 'one'. The universe is 'single', because it shares the intelligible: the cosmos is fulfilled with all sensible things and thus being complete. Being 'solitary' in terms of the world's ability of preserving itself. Proceeding from these three aspects, i.e., being 'one' with reference to its substantial existence (κατὰ τὴν ὕπαρξιν), being complete, and self-sufficient, the sensible universe can be denominated as 'a blessed god'.

1.1.1.4 Conclusion

In the primary answer to the question 'how is the sensible world generated' I have clarified that (1) the world soul is a mixture of three blended ingredients Substance, Sameness and Difference: they are firstly unified together and then divided into intervals through arithmetical and harmonic proportions. Setting all those divided portions in the form of one single line, the Demiurge cuts it into two halves and puts them together at the centre in a 'X' form, then he bends them in two circles, the outer one, which is called the 'Same', is responsible for the motion of the fixed stars, while the inner one, possessing the name 'Difference', is designated to be in charge of the motion of the

---

[93] Proclus, *In Tim.* II 108, 20–22.
[94] *Ibid.* II 109, 16–110, 4.

seven planets. Since the world soul is composed of the blended Substance, Sameness and Difference, according to the principle 'like knows like', it is endorsed to participate in opinion, reason, and intelligence; moreover, moving the whole universe it can recognise every logos in the created universe. (2) The world body is composed of four elements that are proportional rearranged from their disordered pre-cosmic vestiges. With the proportion in sense of numbers, volumes and dynameis the Demiurge fashions the world body into a sphere whose circular movement resembles the intelligible motion. Since the universe does not have any organ in the outside, it is self-sufficient and has a peculiar sort of perception which imitates the intellect. (3) The universe is generated as a living thing, a blessed god. As the Demiurge joins the world body to the world soul, the soul stretches immediately from the centre to the surface of the body and envelops it, initiating the unceasing circular motion of the complete sensible universe.

Such a description of the generation of the whole perceptible world manifests that: (1) the sensible world is ordered and proportionally generated, and as a living being it possesses a certain kind of sensation. A chaotic and discordant perceptible world is refused by Plato (29a5–8). Furthermore, all sensible objects exist in the cosmos, for nothing is left in the outside of it. And the universe itself, being visible and tangible, is naturally perceptible. (2) The world soul, as a mixed entity of the indivisible and divisible Substance, Sameness and Difference, is entitled to discriminate and comprehend all corporal and incorporable existences in the sensible universe, which implies that the human soul – substantially it is created in the same way as the world soul – also has an ability to recognise the whole sensible world. (3) The Platonic world-generation doctrine, unlike the corresponding theories like the Big Bang, rules the chance out: for in the eyes of Plato the world generates from the activity of the demiurgic intellect, which is essentially different from the function of chance.

1.1.2 Further inquiry

A further, more essential investigation into the issue of the world's generation is necessary, because, despite the primary answer, there are still many problems to be solved. For instance, (1) who is the Demiurge? (2) Why he has the dynamis to create the universe? (3) What is the so-called Chora? (4) How can the discordant elemental vestiges be reconstructed? (5) Whether the soul is generated or not? (6) How to understand the soul's essence of being an intermediate entity? And finally, (7) why should we take this Platonic interpretation-system to expound the generation of our universe? In the further research the first two questions will be answered in 1.1.2.1; the following two inquires will be solved in section 1.1.2.2; the part 1.1.2.3 deals with the fifth and sixth questions; and the last one will be treated in 1.1.2.4.

1.1.2.1 The Identity of the Demiurge: Intellect, Maker and Father, and Zeus

Plato acknowledges at *Timaeus* 28a3–5 that it is difficult to find the Demiurge, i.e., Maker and Father of the universe, and having found him it will also be impossible to tell everyone. This claim indicates the difficulty of an exegesis of the Demiurge, which is revealed by the related academic debate lasting from the first Platonists, i.e., Aristotle and Xenocrates, to the modern scholars like Taylor, Cornford, Cherniss, Baltes, Brisson, etc.[95] Usually the opinions about this issue are divided into three categories: (1) the Demiurge is the intellect (νοῦς) without being a soul;[96] (2) he is the soul, either the world soul or the reason in the soul;[97] (3) the other interpretations, for example, the intelligible Paradigm.[98] The first explanation is close to the right answer, yet it is still too simple to grasp the real nature of the Demiurge. The best elucidation of the notion 'Demiurge' should be ascribed to Proclus, however, considering that his clarification is based on a quite complex theological system, it is better to look at a summary of his marvellous theological system at first:[99]

---

[95] Some of the previous studies are summarised by Gerson (1990) 76; Karfik (2004) 130–133; Carone (2005) 29–52; Erler (2007) 458–459; Pietsch (2008) 580–581.

[96] See for example Hackforth (1936) 4f.; Solmsen (1942) 113; Brisson (1974) 81–84; Guthrie (1978) 512, 275n1; Mohr (1985) 183; (2005) 189–195; Menn (1992) 556, 558; (1995) 10–13, 19–24; Hoffmann (1996) 286; Strange (2000) 409n21; Schäfer (2005) 82–83; Pietsch (2008) 580; Kahn (2010) 73–74; Wolfe (2010) 54; Hoenig (2018) 30.

[97] For instance, Taylor (1928) 71, 82; (⁶1949) 442; Cornford (1937) 38–39; Cherniss (1944) 425f., 607 n359; Vlastos (1964) 407; Theiler (²1965) 69–74; Tarán (1971) 372–407, n34; Lee (1976) 89; Robinson (²1995) 102; Carone (2005) 43–46; Long (2010) 43n15; Silverman (2010) 55; O'Brien (2015) 23.

[98] See Baltes (1996) 89f.; Dörrie & Baltes (1998) 265n24. Arthur (1936) 49 suggests that he is 'Self-Transcending Fecundity'; Ostenfeld (1997) 170 supposes that the Demiurge is "an all-embracing Form including many sub-Forms"; Lisi (2007) 109 and Rheins (2010) 215ff. attribute the Demiurge to be the Form of the Good discussed in the *Republic*.

[99] This diagram is taken from Opsomer (2006a) 281–282. See also his clarification in (2000) 113–143.

I. The One
  1. The One, i.e., the first God
II. The transcendent Gods
  2. The intelligible Gods (Being)
      2.1. *limit*, unlimited, intelligible being
      2.2. limit, *unlimited*, intelligible life
      2.3. limit, unlimited, intelligible intellect (*mixture*)
  3. The intelligible-intellective Gods (Life)
      3.1. *being*, life, intellect
      3.2. being, *life*, intellect
      3.3. being, life, *intellect*
  4. The intellective Gods (Intellect)
      4.1. triad of the "parents"
          4.1.1. pure intellect (Kronos)
          4.1.2. intellective life (Rhea)
          4.1.3. demiurgic intellect (Zeus)
      4.2. triad of the "immaculate"
          4.2.1. Athena
          4.2.2. Korè
          4.2.3. Kourètes
      4.3. the 'seventh divinity'
III. The Gods of the World
  5. The hypercosmic Gods (assimilative)
      5.1. demiurgic triad (= Zeus): Zeus$_2$, Poseidon, Hades
      5.2. life-giving triad (= Kore): Artemis, Persephone, Athena
      5.3. converting triad (= Apollo)
      5.4. immaculate triad (= Corybantes)
  6. The hypercosmic-encosmic Gods (*apolutoi*)
      6.1. demiurgic Gods: Zeus$_3$, Poseidon$_2$, Hephaestus
      6.2. guardian Gods: Hestia, Athena$_2$, Ares
      6.3. life-giving Gods: Demeter$_2$, Hera$_2$, Artemis$_2$
      6.4. educating Gods: Hermes, Aphrodite$_2$, Apollo$_2$
  7. The encosmic Gods
      [analogous to the preceding]
      celestial gods   not errant: stars;
                                  errant: planets
      sublunary gods
  8. The universal Souls
  9. The Superior Kinds (intelligible souls)
      Angels
      Demons
      Heroes

In this diagram we can see that the Demiurge is the 'demiurgic intellect (Zeus)' in 4.1.3, and there are still other Gods above and under him. To clarify this location and definition of the Demiurge in Proclus' system, man should read his commentary prudentially. Before expounding his own ideas Proclus firstly summarises the previous studies of this subject matter.[100] According to him there are three gods by Numenius:[101] the first god is entitled 'Father', the second 'Maker', and the third 'Product' (ποίημα), which is the cosmos (I 303, 27–304, 5). For Numenius the Demiurge is the first and second god. Proclus criticises him for counting the Good (One) together with the gods, confusing the order of the paternal principle and the One, and separating the 'Father' from the 'Maker' in speaking of the Demiurge (I 304, 5–22).

Following Numenius, Harpocration denominates the first god 'Ouranos and Kronos', the second 'Zeus and Zên' (Δία καὶ Ζῆνα, I 304, 27), and the third 'Heaven and Cosmos'. He combines the first and second god by defining the first god as 'Zeus and King of the intelligible thing' (Δία [...] καὶ βασιλέα τοῦ νοητοῦ, I 304, 39). As in the case of Numenius Proclus reproaches him for treating the first principle (Good) as Father (I 304, 22–305, 6). On the same ground the doctrine of Harpocration's father, Atticus, is also censured by Proclus (I 305, 6–16).

After these three Middle Platonists Proclus turns to Plotinus, who conceives the Demiurge as twofold: one is in the intelligible world (ἐν τῷ νοητῷ), the other is the leader of the universe (τὸ ἡγεμονοῦν τοῦ παντός),[102] and asserts that in the intelligible realm, between the One and the Cosmos, there are the true heaven, the kingdom of Kronos, and the Intellect of Zeus.[103] These opinions are praised by Proclus.[104]

Following Plotinus comes Amelius, who propounds a notion of threefold Demiurges who are Intellects and Kings: one 'who is', one 'who has', and the last one 'who sees' (τὸν ὄντα, τὸν ἔχοντα, τὸν ὁρῶντα, I 306, 2–3).[105] The first Intellect (Demiurge) is really what it is, the second is the Intelligible (I 306, 4–5) in him, having the Intelligible which is prior to himself and plainly participating in him, the third too is the Intelligible in him, but having the Intelligible in the second and seeing the first Intellect (Demiurge). Applying these three Demiurges and Intellects to the three Kings in Plato (*Ep. II*, 312e1–4), i.e., Phanes, Ouranos and Kronos, Amelius assumes that Phanes is the very *Timaeus*-Demiurge. Proclus embraces the idea that the set of gods is triad, however, he

---

[100] Proclus, *In Tim.* I 303, 24–310, 2. In the following of this section (1.1.2.1) the location of the quotations will be directly given in the text. For the notion of Demiurge in the first Platonists, see O'Brien (2015) 24–27, where we are told that Aristotle ignores this notion in his *DC*; Philip of Opus attributes the Demiurge to a rational world-soul in *Epinomis*; while Speusippus and Xenocrates tend to deconstruct this concept.

[101] Places (1973) *Numénius Fragments*, fr. 21. Cf. Dillon (²1996) 366–367; Frede (1987a) 1055.

[102] This thought is indeed a summary of *Enn.* 3. 9.1, 23–27. Cf. Runia and Share (2008) 160 n625.

[103] Runia and Schare (2008) 160n628 assert that Proclus derives these explanations from *Enn* 5.1.3, 24ff. and 5.8.13.

[104] In addition to Proclus' exegesis, Opsomer (2006a) 273 claims that Plotinus "equated the demiurge with intellect but transferred as many of his activities as he could to the soul".

[105] This triad 'to be, to have, to see' is applied to Proclus' theory of Intellect at *In Tim.* I 242, 27–30, 244, 25–30. Cf. Opsomer (2006a) 274n61. Further discussions about this passage are located at 361, 26–362,9 and 398, 16–26. Cf. Runia & Share (2008) 160n631.

stresses that there should be a monad prior to the triad (I 306, 14–21), because on one side Plato has the habit to develop the multiplicity to unity, on the other side, considering that both the Paradigm and the universe are single, there is no reason to deny that the Demiurge is also single (I 306, 21–31).

Deviating from Plotinus, Porphyry calls the Demiurge the hypercosmic soul, and regards its Intellect as the Paradigm, the Living-thing-itself (τὸ αὐτοζῷον).[106] Proclus contradicts the concept that the Demiurge is a soul by stressing that (1) Plato constantly calls the Demiurge Intellect, but never soul; (2) there are things which participate not in the soul, yet the whole universe takes part in the demiurgic Providence (πρόνοια); (3) the divine creative activity creates intellect and gods, but the soul cannot engender things beyond the psychic rank (I 306, 31–307, 14).

Iamblichus, following Plotinus, attributes the entire intelligible cosmos between the cosmos and the One (in Plotinus' view) to the Demiurge, and declares that in the Demiurge all things, such as the Being itself and the intelligible cosmos, exist 'demiurgically', in which sense the Demiurge is in accordance with the Orphic Zeus. Proclus refuses the suggestion that the Demiurge is on behalf of the complete level between the cosmos and the One, for there would be no place for the Kings prior to Zeus. Those Kings, according to Proclus' another work *On the Speech of Zeus in the Timaeus*, are firstly (three) intelligible triads, then three intelligible-intellective triads, following with the intellective hebdomad, in which the Demiurge is assigned to the third rank among the Fathers – the first triad in the hebdomad (I 307, 14–309, 13).[107]

Theodorus, a pupil of Porphyry and Iamblichus, asserts like Amelius that there are totally three Demiurges. However, instead of being set directly after the One they are assigned to be on the side of the intelligible-intellective gods: the first is entitled 'Essential Intellect' (οὐσιώδη νοῦν, I 309, 17), the second 'Intellective Essence' (νοερὰν οὐσίαν, I 309, 17), and the third 'Source of Souls' (πηγὴν ψυχῶν, I 309, 18). Furthermore, he argues that "the first is indivisible, the second has been divided into wholes, the third has effectuated the division as far as the individual beings".[108] The main problem of this explanation, like in the case Amelius, is that the so-called three Demiurges do not exist, rather one is actually the intelligible Paradigm of the Demiurge, one is the demiurgic generative Dynamis, and the last one is the real demiurgic Intellect (I 309, 23–25).

Syrianus proclaims that the Demiurge, single as he is, is the god who defines 'the limit of the intelligible gods' (τὸ πέρας τῶν νοερῶν θεῶν). Being filled by the 'intelligible monads' and 'the sources of life' (τῶν νοητῶν μονάδων καὶ τῶν τῆς ζωῆς πηγῶν, I 309, 9–10), the Demiurge conceives the whole creation and governs two worlds: the hypercelestial world and the celestial world.[109] In the whole demiurgic order there exist four causes: Wholes holistically, Parts holistically, Wholes partially, and Parts partially. The Demiurge, who is a monad, has the universal care of the whole world, thus

---

[106] Sodano (1964), fr. 41. Cf. fr. 53 and Proclus, *In Tim*. I 431, 20–23.
[107] See above pp 38–39.
[108] Proclus, *In Tim*. I 309, 17–20: τὸν μὲν ἀδιαίρετον, τὸν δὲ εἰς ὅλα διῃρημένον, τὸν δὲ καὶ τὴν εἰς τὰ καθ' ἕκαστα διαίρεσιν πεποιηνένον. Tr. Runia & Share.
[109] Proclus supposes that there are three kinds of gods: the hypercosmic gods, the hypercosmic-encosmic gods and the encosmic gods. See *Ibid*. I 269, 26–30.

corresponds to the first cause. The demiurgic fathers, i.e., the hypercosmic gods, the hypercosmic-encosmic gods, and the encosmic gods constituting a triad which depends on the demiurgic monad and partly processes his dynamis, are accordingly in response to the other three causes. Proclus accepts Syrianus' interpretation without hesitation and further develops it. For him, the Demiurge is: (1) A divine Intellect who is the cause of the entire universe (I 311, 1–14). Being established in the intelligible field he is full of dynamis, through which he creates all things. Thus, Timaeus calls him 'Intellect' (29a6–b1)[110] and 'the best of the causes' (29a6), who looks at the eternal, intelligible Paradigm (29a3). Proclus argues that the Demiurge's looking towards the Paradigm proves that he is different from the primary intelligible gods, for the Paradigm belongs to the intelligible Gods.[111] As Intellect the Demiurge is separated from the 'intelligible-intellective Gods (Life)',[112] and 'the best of the causes' signifies that he is above all other demiurges, both hypercosmic and encosmic. Considering the Platonic doctrine in *Phaedo*, man can affirm this Proclean interpretation, for Plato does agree that the Intellect, ordering all things and placing each of them in the best place, is the order and cause of everything (*Phaedo* 97b9–c5).

(2) Maker and Father of the whole universe (I 311, 14–25). According to Proclus there are three kinds of intellective gods: the pure intellect (Kronos), who continues to abide by his own nature, the intellective life (Rhea), who is defined as cause of life, and the demiurgic intellect who establishes and activates souls with the mixing bowl (*Tim.* 41d4), yet generates the intellect by himself (30b4). The Demiurge, who creates intellect, must be the third intellective father, because Plato calls him 'Maker and Father' (ποιητὴν καὶ πατέρα, 28c3–4). Proclus interprets that:

> [1] 'Father' and 'Maker' are the extremes. The former holds the peak position in the intelligibles and is prior to the royal series, the latter occupies the limit of this rank (i.e., of the royals). The one is the monad of the Paternal divinity; the other has inherited the creative dynamis in the universe. In between both is the one who is 'Father as well as Maker' and the one who is 'Maker as well as Father' (I 311, 28–312, 2. Tr. Runia & Share).[113]

> [2] Each of the divine beings is named after his own particularity, even if he contains all attributes. The one who is 'Maker' only is cause of the encosmic creatures, the 'Maker and Father' is cause of hypercosmic and encosmic creatures, the 'Father and Maker' is cause of intellective, hypercosmic and encosmic creatures, and the one who is Father only is cause of intelligible, intellective, hypercosmic and encosmic creatures (I 312, 21–26. Tr. Runia & Share).[114]

---

[110] The text-location of this term 'Intellect', given by the editor Diehl (1903) 311, is 29a; the translators Runia & Share (2008) 166 attribute it to 39a7, which, I think, is an erratum: it should be 29a7. Yet the fact is, in 29a Timaeus does not mention this term, so I suppose that either it is located at another place (for instance *Phaed.* 97b9–c5, see below), or what Proclus means is that from 29a6–b1 we can derive that the Demiurge is the Intellect.
[111] Proclus, *In Tim.* I 229, 19–27; 269, 9ff.
[112] For this notion and its relationship with Demiurge, see *Ibid.* I 411, 3ff., 420, 2ff., 431, 12ff.
[113] Cf. *Ibid.* III 168, 15–169, 9. See Runia & Share (2008) 166n661.
[114] Cf. Proclus, *In Tim.* III 209, 2–12. See Runia & Share (2008) 167n664.

(3) Zeus, as affirmed both by Orpheus and Plato (I 312, 26–317, 20). Although Plato leaves the *Timaeus*-Demiurge unnamed, in the other dialogues he does certify that he is Zeus: for example, *Craty.* (395b1–3), *Gorg.* (523a–524a), *Laws* (716c2–3), *Phileb.* (30d1–2), *Polit.* (272b2, 273b1–2), *Min.* (319c3), *Protag.* (321c–322d). In the Orphic poems the Demiurge is also affirmed to be Zeus.[115]

To summarise, according to the Proclean ontological and theological interpretation the Demiurge is the divine Intellect who fabricates the entire universe, who is the Maker and Father of the whole world, and who is regarded as Zeus in Plato's dialogues and Orphic poems.

1.1.2.2 The Platonic elemental theory

In this section I will continue to solve the problems about the notion Chora (χώρα): (1) what it means, and (2) how can it be formed, i.e., how can the elemental vestiges – in terms of a lack of proportion and measure – be fashioned with the regular geometrical figures and thus become the substratum (ὑποκείμενον) of the whole sensible world. To answer the first question, we should explain the origin of Chora and its role in the generation of the world, whereas the research of the second issue will begin with a description of the proportional generation of the elements with geometrical figures, continue with an interpretation of the proportion in respect of number, motion and dynamis of the elements, and end with a brief clarification of the interchange under the elements.

(1) The meaning of Chora. To establish the cosmos the Demiurge needs to persuade the Necessity (*Tim.* 48a2–3), so that with form and measure he can fashion the pure material possessing merely vestiges of the regular elements (53a8–b7). For he does not mould the world from nothing, rather with the reconstructed elements in the Chora.[116]

At *Timaeus* 48e4f. the concept of Chora is firstly introduced as a third genus (substance) expect for the intelligible entities and the sensible things. Plato asserts that it is "a difficult and obscure form which can be brought to light with logoi (χαλεπὸν καὶ ἀμυδρὸν εἶδος ἐπιχειρεῖν λόγοις ἐμφανίσαι, 49a4)". However, the logos used to describe the (original) Chora is indeed not determinate, for the Chora itself is without certain form: as 'mother' (μητρί, 50d3, μητέρα, 51a5), 'nurse' (τιθήνην, 49a7, 52d5) and 'recipient' (ὑποδοχὴν, 49a6) of all becoming things, it is able to receive everything without taking any character from them (*Tim.* 50b7–c4), i.e., it is unlimited, full of potencies and extended. In this respect Chora is always 'what is of such and such a quality' (τὸ τοιοῦτον, 49d7), and the kind of reasoning which is suitable to delineate it is a determine kind of bastard (λογισμῷ τινι νόθῳ, 52b3).[117]

That the Chora is not generated by the Demiurge, can be obviously demonstrated by Timaeus' assertion that Being, Chora and Becoming exist even before the cosmos is

---

[115] Kern (1922) *Orphicorum fragmenta*, esp. fr. 165–168.
[116] The causes of the world-generation are thus twofold: The Demiurge or Intellect is the main cause, the Chora and the elements in it is the subsidiary cause (συναίτια).
[117] Many scholars argue that the Chora resembles the Aristotelian notion 'matter' (ὕλη). For an analysis of this issue, see Claghorn (1954) 8–19.

created (50d2–4). This statement implies that the cause of the Chora is prior to the Demiurge, for it has the same priority as Being, which is above the Demiurge in the Proclean theological order: indeed, quoting the contexts at *Philebus* 23c9–10 and 27b7–9,[118] where the God has revealed the Limit and the Unlimited in the Beings, Proclus argues that the One and the Unlimited are the causes of the Chora, because only the One can generate the Limit and Unlimited, and the Limit is related to form and measure.[119] Proclus goes further by declaring that the Chora, or with the Aristotelian term, the Matter, generates from both the One and the Unlimited that is "prior to One Being" (τῆς πρὸ τοῦ ἑνὸς ὄντος, I 385, 13), and in the sense that it can be formed, it is potential being, which means that it can also be said to proceed from One Being. Originating from the One it is 'a good of a kind' (ἀγεθόν πῄ, I 385, 15), proceeding from the Unlimited it is 'a thing without limit' (ἄπειρον), as potential being it is 'the most indistinct being' (ἀμυδρότατον ὄν, I 385, 15).

Although the Chora proceeds from these mentioned principles, i.e., the One, the Unlimited, and the One Being, what brings it forward are the causes of the second and third level in the Proclean theological system, i.e., the transcendent gods and the gods of the world. For the Chora contains the traces of forms and a disordered motion under the influence of the Paradigm, which is the cause of the production of form and the order among these forms.[120] Receiving the forms from the Paradigm, the Demiurge reconstructs the elements vestiges in the Chora with numbers and logoi, fashioning them firstly into bodies without qualities, then with primary qualities. To create the rest lives, the hypercosmic and encosmic gods take the bodies from the Demiurge and regulate them further.

Now it is evident that the Chora originates from the One, the Unlimited, and the One Being. After it is regulated by the Demiurge and the elements in it are formed by number and measure, the elemental bodies are produced for all living creatures,[121] i.e., the universe itself, the fixed stars, the planets, human beings, and all rest lives in the universe. In this sense it is entitled 'subsidiary cause' (συναίτια) by Plato's Timaeus.

(2) The proportional reconstruction of the elements. The next question is, how can the elements be formed with certain figures and how the physical qualities are generated from their quantitative properties. A brief answer is that the elements are reconstructed by the Demiurge with the perfect geometrical figures, i.e., right-angled triangles, and in virtue of the certain physical dynameis of these material figures the sensible qualities are eventually produced.

That the four elements are the first bodies encompassing certain geometrical shapes and pure materials, is the precondition of a possible generation of the physical world. These shapes (tetrahedron, octahedron, icosahedron, and cube) are bestowed by the Demiurge, who prefers to create perfect bodies. As said above, the materials are already

---

[118] Proclus does not mention the text at 27b7–9, yet what he means can be proved with this passage.
[119] Proclus, *In Tim.* I 384, 22–385, 3. That the Limit concerns form and measure, see *Phileb.* 25a7–b3.
[120] *Ibid.* I 387, 28–29. For the relation of the visible things' generation and the traces of forms, see *Ibid.* I 270, 14–21; 383, 17–22; 387, 12–19.
[121] *Tim.* 31b5ff., 53c5ff. Cf. *Phileb.* 29a9ff.

there, before the universe is established. The argument that these bodies can be formed with the four polyhedrons consisting of the right-angled triangles is as follows (53c5–e1): the four elements fire, air, water, and earth are obviously bodies, as a body it must have depth, which is bounded by surface. Every rectilinear surface is established by triangles, under which the right-angled triangles have two kinds, i.e., the right-angled isosceles and the right-angled scalene, this is the principle (ἀρχή) of the elements. To construct four possibly perfect (κάλλιστα) bodies (53e1–54a1) corresponding to fire, air, water, and earth Plato, according to the 'possible account' (κατὰ ἐικότα λόγον),[122] chooses the right-angled triangle (a half equilateral) – of which one hypotenuse is double as long as the other – as the 'element and seed' (στοιχεῖον καὶ σπέρμα, 56 b3–5) of the tetrahedron (fire), octahedron (air), and icosahedron (water), while the right-angled isosceles as that of the cube (earth). These figures can be better explained with the following diagram:[123]

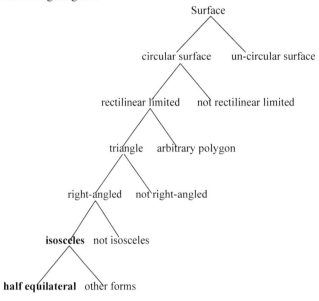

We see that the two triangles chosen by the Demiurge are the perfect and beautiful figures: the right-angled isosceles and the right-angled half equilateral.[124] The two triangles and the polyhedrons composed of them, however, are not pure geometric shapes

---

[122] Considering that for Plato the cosmos is image of something determinate (29b1–2: τόνδε τὸν κόσμον εἰκόνα τινὸς εἶναι), the account of the generation of the universe is certainly a possible account. For the cosmos as image, see Proclus, *In Tim.* I 334, 30–337, 7.
[123] This diagram is taken from Gaiser ([2]1968) 156, Fig. 46.
[124] *Tim.* 54a1–3. One can ask why the Demiurge selects the right-angled triangle, but not the circle, as the elementary figure, for the circle is evidently perfecter as the right-angled triangle. The reason, however, is that Plato has bestowed the circle to the world soul and the world body. Gaiser ([2]1968) 514n38 points out that Plutarch has handled this question at *Platon. quaest.* 5, 1003B–1004C.

without motion, life or physical dynameis, rather they hint at the active and demiurgic dynameis of the nature.[125] When Plato declares that bodies are established from surfaces, he means that the physical surfaces do have depth.[126] If one insists to ask about the relation of the *Timaeus*-polyhedrons and the abstract geometrical forms, the answer is that the polyhedrons are enmattered forms (τὰ εἴδη τὰ ἔνυλα),[127] or the elemental forms are imitations of the immaterial principles.[128]

These triangles are now constructed in two ways: (1) for the second right-angled triangle:

> if a pair of such triangles are put together by the diagonal, and this is done three times, the diagonals and the shorter sides resting on the same point as a centre, in this way a single equilateral triangle is formed of triangles six in number. If four equilateral triangles are put together, their plane angles meeting in groups of three make a single solid angle, namely the one (180°) that comes next after the most obtuse of plane angles. When four such angles are produced, the simplest solid figure is formed, whose property is to divide the whole circumference into equal and similar parts. A second body (the octahedron) is formed of the same (elementary) triangles when they are combined in a set of eight equilateral triangles, and yield a solid angle formed by four plane angles. With the production of six such solid angles the second body is complete. The third body (the icosahedron) is composed of one hundred and twenty of the elementary triangles fitted together, and of twelve solid angles, each contained by five equilateral triangular planes; and it has twenty faces which are equilateral triangles (*Tim.* 54d9–55b3).[129]

(2) For the first right-angled isosceles:

> But the isosceles triangle went on to generate the fourth body, being put together in sets of four, with their right angles meeting at the centre, thus forming a single equilateral quadrangle. Six such quadrangles, joined together, produced eight solid angles, each composed by a set of three plane right angles. The shape of the resulting body was cubical, having six quadrangular equilateral planes as its faces (*Tim.* 55b5–c2).

Apart from these four figures Plato also mentions another shape, i.e., the dodecahedron, which is used by the Demiurge for the creation of the whole world.[130] This figure cannot be constructed from the mentioned two kinds of right-triangles, rather from the isosceles triangle whose base angle is two times as its vertical angle (i.e., an acute triangle, 72°, 72° and 36°).[131] As the image of the world the dodecahedron is most akin to the most

---

[125] Syrianus, *In Meta.* 86, 2: δραστικὰς δὲ καὶ δημιουργικὰς δυνάμεις τῆς φύσεως αἰνίττεται.
[126] Simplicius, *In de caelo* 648, 11–23.
[127] Proclus, *In Tim.* III 357, 10. Cf. Timaeus of Locros, *De nat.* 215, 13–15.
[128] Cf. Siorvanes (1996) 223; Opsomer (2012) 168–169.
[129] The reason, why the Demiurge takes six elementary triangles to form one single equilateral triangle, is symmetry and proportion according to Simplicius, *In de caelo* 576, 16–19.
[130] *Tim.* 55c4–6. Cf. Brisson (2003) 193; Simplicius, *In de caelo* 12, 16–27. Remarkably, to prove that for Plato there are five simple bodies, Simplicius cites a fragment of Xenocrates.
[131] Cf. Cornford (1937) 218.

perfect figure, i.e., sphere[132] – this manifests that the Demiurge, recognising the pure spere and dodecahedron in the Paradigm and knowing that dodecahedron is the shape that is most akin to sphere, takes this fifth element, fills it with the proportional connected four elements. As these reconstructed elements keep moving and expand the dodecahedron into a sphere, the Demiurge establishes the world body with the shape of sphere – a proof of this calculation can be found in *Phaedo* 110b5f., where the Platonic Socrates describes the real earth as a ball that includes 12 leather pentagons. For in the ancient times, one can produce a leather ball out of 12 regular leather pentagons, logically with dodecahedron the Demiurge can also mould the spherical world.[133]

In this manner the 'elements and seeds' of the four elements are reconstructed. There are several levels in the process of the establishment of the polyhedrons: At first the two basic triangles, i.e., right-angled isosceles and scalene, then the two kinds of surfaces respectively composed of these two triangles, at last the four polyhedrons originating from them. The dodecahedron is an exception of this rule because it is established from another 'seed' and is utilised to create the whole universe.

With these polyhedron-forms the element vestiges are reconstructed. These polyhedrons, however, cannot decide the final shapes of the elements, for each element is composed of a massive number of corresponding material figures with different bigness, consequently the shape of the element depends not on the shape of a single ingredient.[134] Besides, a single polyhedron is still too small to be seen, i.e., only a large (proportional) bulk of them is perceptible for us (56b7–c3). Considering the proportion of the volumes (τοὺς ὄγκους, 56c3) of these four polyhedrons Timaeus stresses that their multitudes, movements and the other dynameis (τὰ πλήθη καὶ τὰς κινήσεις καὶ τὰς ἄλλας δυνάμεις) are also proportional, once the Necessity is persuaded by the Demiurge and the Chora is reconstructed (56c3–7).

This statement about the proportional relation of the numbers, movements and the other dynameis of the polyhedrons recalls the passage of the generation of the world body (section 1.1.1.2), where the four elements are alleged to be joined together with a continuous proportion Fire: Air = Air: Water = Water: Earth in the sense of numbers, volumes and dynameis. One could ask whether two proportions are the same, and what can we derive from the frequent application of the term 'proportion'. For the first question a positive answer should be refused, because, despite that both proportions are utilised by the Demiurge to establish the sensible cosmos, they are obviously applied in difference levels: (1) the construction of proportional polyhedrons is the beginning of the generation of all perceptible elements, while the proportion between the elements is the guaranty of the world body's perfection. (2) The proportion between the elements in forming the world body is a proportion that connects all four elements, whereas the proportion of the polyhedrons are used to ensure the perfection and reconstruction of the elements themselves – this indicates that such a proportion is physically more fundamental than the former one. As for the second question we should proclaim that,

---

[132] See Timaeus of Locros, *De nat.* 216, 20–21: τὸ δὲ δωδεκάεδρον εἰκόνα τῷ παντὸς ἐστάσατο, ἔγγιστα σφαίρᾳ ἐόν.
[133] See Plutarch, *Qu. Plat.* 1003c; Proclus, *In Tim.* III 141, 13–24; Damascius, *In Phaed.* II 132, 2–11. Cf. Cornford (1937) 219n1; Baltes (1972) 123–124.
[134] Cf. Simplicius, *In de caelo* 648, 24–650, 15 and 657, 10–659, 10.

obviously, the application of the proportions in distinct levels reveals that the construction of the perceptible cosmos is thoroughly rational and logical, or with Plato's own words, it is fashioned as perfect as possible. In this sense we can assert that the Demiurge, i.e., the divine Intellect, ensures the possibly perfect generation and proportional reconstruction of all elements, while the role of the chance is excluded.

Now let us take a closer look at the proportional volumes, movements and dynameis of the polyhedrons and elements: (1) the proportion of volumes and numbers – considering the faces of tetrahedron (fire), octahedron (air) and icosahedron (water) are 4, 8 and 20 – can be explained both by the amount of the faces of every single polyhedron,[135] and by their specific bigness, if a certain multitude of polyhedrons are joined together. (2) A research of the motion of the polyhedrons and elements is particularly important for the investigation of the sensible physical world.[136] This issue, however, is not handled in the *Timaeus*. Rather the movements of the five polyhedrons are described at *Laws* 893c5–e1,[137] where the fifth element dodecahedron is declared to move at one place and in a circle (περιφορά, 893c9), the other four polyhedrons move forward in many locations, and when they move on one surface, they gliding, when many, rolling (τῷ περικυλινδεῖσθαι, *Laws* 893e1). In *De caelo* Aristotle also discusses the rolling of the four polyhedrons,[138] albeit his aim is to argue that these movements are contrary to that of the elements like fire, which consists of pyramids though, moves linearly. Are the five elements moving in the same way as their components? Obviously not, for indeed this happens only in case of the fifth element: The other four polyhedrons used to reconstruct the four elements are either gliding or rolling, while the four elements consisting of them move naturally in straight line, for instance fire goes naturally up, and the earth down,[139] and the other two elements also in straight line.[140] While the aether, being composed of dodecahedrons, also moves in circular way.[141]

---

[135] Cf. *Tim.* 56d6–e8.

[136] For Aristotle the study of nature is in the perspective of motion (*DC* 308a1–2. Cf. *Phys.* 8.1, 250b14–15, where the motion is treated as a kind of life of all naturally constituted things). Simplicius (*In de caelo* 677, 8–10) comments that nature "is a starting point of motion and the kind of starting point that is seen in motion".

[137] For the polyhedral movements, see my paper "Selbstbewegung und die physischen Bewegungen. Eine neue Interpretation der Bewegungsarten in Platons *Nomoi* X", in *Hermes* (forthcoming). To supplement I should stress that the world soul and Demiurge are not the reason of motion, rather that of the proportional movements.

[138] Aristotle, *DC* 307 a6–8. Although he uses another term 'κύλισις', what he means here is similar to Plato. Simplicius also uses the word 'κυκλική' to describe the movements of the polyhedrons, and he also stresses that their movements 'imitate' (μιμεῖται) the circular movement. See Simplicius, *In de caelo* 663, 10–12.

[139] Aristotle, *DC* 269a34–b1, 311a19–21, etc.

[140] *Ibid.* 312 a25–27. The gliding of the polyhedrons appears to be similar to the motion of straight line, but indeed this is not true, for the gliding is always on one surface of a polyhedron, a natural elemental body like fire does not have such a surface.

[141] Logically we can calculate that because the dodecahedron is used to fashion the world body, and the world body moves in circle, the aether, analogically, must also move in this way.

A further related problem is, in which way a mixed continuous body moves. Given such a continuous compound, like flesh or bone, is interwoven with a multitude of elements,[142] the answer is, its motion is decided by the part which predominates the whole body.[143] For example, the motion of the world body is in accordance with that of the aether and dodecahedron, i.e., it moves in its own place and in the circular manner.

(3) The proportional dynameis of the elements are listed by Calcidius and Proclus:[144]

Fire:	fineness (subtilitas)	mobility (mobilitas)	sharpness (acumen)
Air:	fineness (subltilitas)	mobility (mobilitas)	bluntness (obtunsitas)
Water:	corporeality (corpulentia)	mobility (mobilitas)	bluntness (obtunsitas)
Earth:	corporeality (corpulentia)	immobility (immobilitas)	bluntness (obtunsitas)

But how can these dynameis come to be? Both Proclus and Simplicius argue that they result from synthesised reasons such as shape, size, and motion. For example, the sharpness of the fire should be ascribed to the properties of the angles and sides of its figures (57a1–2), or more precisely, to the "fineness of the edges, the sharpness of the angles, the smallness of the particles, and the swiftness of the movement".[145] The reason of the mobility is that it is more difficulty for a square to move than a triangle, and the same for cubes than the other three polyhedrons: for the cube its apexes encounter the bases which have the same shape, while the apexes of the other three are dissimilar to their bases, moreover, their triangles are few and small, which implies that they are easier to move. Because of the principle that similar things – in the sense of shape, dynamis, and size – do not affect each other, the cube remains fixed, while the other three polyhedrons incline to move.[146]

That the elemental dynameis proceed from the quantitative properties (and the movements based on their quantities) of the four physical elemental bodies, is the principle to clarify the generation of the sensible affections (τὰ παθήματα, 61d1) and thus sensible qualities such as 'hotness', 'coldness', 'hardness', 'softness', 'heaviness', 'lightness', etc. (*Tim.* 61c3–64e8). Regarding the elements their qualities are posterior to the quantities. This is originally a hypothesis of Plato and the Pythagoreans, who hypothesise the triangles in the way that the astronomers use certain hypotheses: speaking of the principle of the elemental bodies they conceive that quantity and figure are 'higher' than quality, thus the triangles, which are established according to similarity and symmetry, can be regarded as the principle of bodies and further generated things.

---

[142] Simplicius, *In de caelo* 660, 19–24.
[143] Aristotle, *DC* 269a4–5, a28–30. Cf. Simplicius, *In de caelo* 38, 6–42, 16.
[144] Calcidius, *In Tim.* § 21; Proclus, *In Tim.* II 39, 21–24. Cf. Siorvanes (1996) 227; Opsomer (2012) 169. This diagram can also be used to explain the proportion of the four elements in establishing the world body.
[145] *Tim.* 61e1–4. Cf. Simplicius, *In de caelo* 664, 5–8: "the stabbing sharpness of the angle, the slicing fineness of the side, and the speed of the motion. One should also take into account size" (Tr. Mueller).
[146] *Tim.* 55e4–56a1, 56a7–b3. Cf. Simplicius, *In de caelo* 663, 6–13; 671, 17–20. For the principle that what is homogenous and identical cannot affect any thing that is similar to itself, see *Tim.* 57a3–5. Cf. Simplicius, *In de caelo* 663, 13–15.

The reason for such a hypothesis rests on the fact that (a) comparing with the qualities like hotness, coldness, dryness, and moistness, the differences in their figures are more akin to these bodies.[147] (b) More fundamentally, what exist originally in the Chora are the elemental vestiges that are pure materials without any proportion, yet as materials they are three-dimensional, which implies that for them a quantitative proportion is more inclined to be established as the qualitative proportion. Hence the geometrical figures are applied to reconstruct these vestiges, co-produce the proportional polyhedrons, elemental bodies, and their proportional movements. And their gathering leads to their sensibility as well as the generation of all sensible qualities. Therefore, the quantitative properties are decisive for the elemental and sensible qualities. From this account we can derive that: (a) given the proportion in number, motion and dynameis in the level of polyhedrons, it is justified to suppose that the sensible qualities originating from the quantities are also proportional. (b) Furthermore, as the material quantities and qualities are proportional, one can announce that the sensible things from these materials are also proportional, and correspondingly our perception must also be proportional, so that we can discriminate and comprehend these sensible objects.

After having discussed the proportion of the elements and their 'seeds and elements' in respect of number, motion and dynamis, it is time to observe their interchanges, or transformations. Plato asserts at *Tim.* 49b7–c7 that these four elements can change into each other in a cycle Fire–Air–Water–Earth–Water–Air–Fire, for when one element is dissolved and re-combined into another, it becomes the element which is naturally close to itself:[148]

> In the first place, take the thing we now call water. This, when it is compacted, we see (as we imagine) becoming earth and stones, and this same thing, when it is dissolved and dispersed, becoming wind and air; air becoming fire by being flamed; and, by a reverse process, fire, when condensed and extinguished, returning once more to the form of air, and air coming together again and condensing as mist and cloud; and from these, as they are yet more closely compacted, flowing water; and from water once more earth and stones: and thus, as it appears, they transmit in a cycle the process of passing into one another.

At *Timaeus* 56d6–e8 he confirms the transformation between fire, air, and water by resorting to the number of their composed triangles. However, considering the difference of these triangles and the triangles of the earth, Plato seems to deny the transformation between earth and the other three elements,[149] for he claims at 56d1–6 that:

> Earth, when it meets with fire and is dissolved by its sharpness, would drift about – whether, when dissolved, it be enveloped in fire itself or in a mass of air or of water – until its own parts somewhere encounter one another, are fitted together, and again become earth; for they can never pass into any other kind.

---

[147] Simplicius, *In de caelo* 565, 28–566, 4; 640, 33–641, 9; 941, 21–24.
[148] For a discussion of this problem, see *Ibid.* 665, 25–667, 9.
[149] This is also an Aristotelian refutation against some Platonists. See Aristotle, *DC* 306a1–17.

Yet Plato means not that earth cannot change into the other elements at all. What he stresses here is merely that the right-angled isosceles of the earth cannot form the other elements, which means no refutation of the transformation between earth and other elements, for they are all formed of triangles, when the right-angled scalene triangles are dissolved and are re-combined into the right-angled isosceles, the earth is able to transform into the other elements.[150] Considering this interpretation there is also no error in the assertion at 49b7–c7 – otherwise one must concede that Plato holds a contrary view on the same issue within ten Stephan numbers, which would be very ridiculous.

Because of the transformations of the elements and their variants all uncompounded and primary bodies are generated (57c6–d6, 58c5–64c3). For each kind of these elements there exist several variants (ἕτερα [...] γένη, 57 c8–9; ἕτερά [...] εἴδη, 58d3): since the sizes of the two basic triangles (right-angled isosceles and right-angled scalene) are different, the polyhedrons established from them are also distinct in size. Therefore, how many different sizes of the triangles there are, so many varieties there are in the four kinds (57d3). Given these differences the elements and their variants, and the sensible bodies generated from the composition and interweaving of these elements and their variants, are also different. These different sensible bodies, together with their sensible qualities, however, are not disordered, as said above, rather proportionally generated in the sense of number, motion, and dynamis due to the proportional features of the reconstructed polyhedrons and elements. These proportional numbers, movements and dynameis, proceeding from the demiurgic intellect, manifest the substance of the sensible individuals and their specific being, i.e., they enable each sensible quality to be 'something determinate' and thus be recognisable for the human being, who shares the divine intellect. Therefore, seeing the fire we can discriminate and comprehend that it is a fire (number), it moves up (motion), and it warms and dries the neighbouring air (dynamis).

1.1.2.3 How to understand the (world) soul?

In the primary research the (world) soul is deemed to be generated, however, in many other Platonic dialogues the soul is also declared to be not generated. This feature of being both generated and not generated is a point through the soul's very nature and logos, i.e., self-motion, will be introduced in this part. After pointing out that it is still insufficient to explain the soul's being both generated and not generated by resorting to its logos, I will turn to the soul's very essence which embraces three ingredients Substance, Sameness and Difference. Arguing that the intermediate Substance is not composed of the divisible and indivisible Substance themselves, rather of some analogous things, I will assert that the soul encompasses both kinds of Substance, in which sense it is not generated in respect of the indivisible Substance, while generated as a divisible Substance.

---

[150] Cf. Simplicius, *In de caelo* 644, 9–17. Gregory (2000) 201 and Opsomer (2012) 152 declare that the triangles can be dissolved, albeit they did not provide any textual evidence.

Plato declares at *Phaedrus* 246a1 that the soul is 'not generated and immortal' (ἀγένητόν τε καὶ ἀθάνατον), at *Phaedo* 95c1 that it is 'indestructible and immortal',[151] at *Republic* 611b9 'immortal',[152] whereas in the *Timaeus* the soul is claimed to be generated (γενέσει, 34c4), in the *Laws* it is viewed as an entity that is generated (895b4) and deemed to be self-motion (896a1–2). How can we understand the seemingly contrary assertion that the soul is both generated and not generated? Indeed, for Plato they are not opposite, rather they indicate the determinate feature of the soul: it is the first generated thing under all becoming things, yet simultaneously, it is also the last member of the eternal beings that are not generated. In other words, the soul functions on the one side as the principle of all generated and moving things, on the other side as an entity that generates itself and gives itself life:[153] At *Republic* 611c–d Plato's Socrates compares the real nature (τὴν ἀρχαίαν φύσιν, 611d1) of the soul to the shell-encrusted sea god Glaucon, through which he prefers to clarify that the soul's nature is originally more beautiful as it seems to be. The soul, Socrates declares, has a kinship with the divine and immortal things and things that always being.[154] This statement implies that the soul is a member of the eternal beings. That it is the very last, is emphasised at *Philebus* 66b8–c2, where Socrates attributes the abilities 'knowledges, arts, and the so-called right opinions' (ἐπιστήμας τε καὶ τέχνας καὶ δόξας ὀρθὰς λεχθείσας) to the soul itself,[155] and arranges it in the fourth place of all good things. Because in the *Republic* the soul is deemed to be akin to the eternal beings and in the *Philebus* it is arranged in the last place of the beings – the fifth place is pleasure, which is evidently not a kind of eternal being – it must be the last member of the everlasting beings.

In the *Phaedrus* and *Laws* the soul is deemed to be an entity that is indestructible and immortal because of its very logos of the essence:[156] self-motion. This 'nature' (ψυχῆς φύσεως, 245c2–3) is discussed at *Phaedrus* 245c1–246a2 and *Laws* 894d5–896a4. In the former passage the Platonic Socrates argues that what is moved by the others and moves others after being moved will cease to live as it stops moving. However, what moves both itself and the others will not stop living, since it never leaves off itself. Such a motion is thus the 'source and principle' (πηγὴ καὶ ἀρχὴ, 245c10) of all kinds of movements.[157] Considering this account the soul is: (1) not generated, for all generated things must generate from a principle that originates from nothing else, otherwise it needs another principle for its becoming. (2) immortal, since when it is mortal, how could it be the beginning of everything, especially after its death? Now as self-motion is the principle of all generated things, the soul is neither generated

---

[151] ἀνώλεθρόν τε καὶ ἀθάνατον. Cf. 106b1–2: ἀθάνατον καὶ ἀνώλεθρόν.

[152] This is the beginning of the demonstration of soul's immortality at *Rep.* 611a–612a.

[153] For these two explanations, see Proclus, *In Tim.* I 235, 7–16. Both Plato and Aristotle agree that the soul is the principle of changes and movements in the ensouled bodies, see Simplicius, *In Phys.* 286, 20–21. A modern study of this theme can be found in Menn (2012) 44–67.

[154] *Rep.* 611e1–3: ὡς συγγενὴς οὖσα τῷ τε θείῳ καὶ ἀθανάτῳ καὶ τῷ ἀεὶ ὄντι.

[155] This corresponds to the announcement at *Tim.* 37b6–c3: with the circle of Same the world soul recognises intellect and knowledge (νοῦς ἐπιστήμη), with the circle of Difference the right opinions and beliefs (δόξαι καὶ πίστεις).

[156] *Laws* 896a3: λόγον ἔχειν τὴν αὐτὴν οὐσίαν. Cf. *Phaedr.* 245e4, οὐσίαν τε καὶ λόγον.

[157] See above 1.1.1.1 the motion-activity of the soul.

nor mortal. In the *Laws* Plato takes another strategy to illuminate the logos of soul's substance: firstly, he divides two kinds of motion, i.e., self-motion and the movement which is moved by something else. Self-motion, according to logos (κατὰ λόγον, 894d10), is the first motion in the view of generation and strength (ῥώμη); the other-moved motion following it is the second motion, because obviously it is impossible for the other-moved movement to be the first motion. Rather, it is the self-motion that changes itself at first by causing itself to move, then alters another movement, and this other further another, until all things are moved. In another view (*Laws* 895c5f.), if somehow everything that has come into being should stand still, the self-motion would be the first that comes to be among them. For being unmoved by others there is no change prior to the self-motion and stands between itself and the Still, which means the self-motion is the nearest to the latter, whereas the other-moved motion is posterior to the dynamis that moves it, which indicates that there exist things between such a motion and the Still. In this sense the self-motion, being the first generation and the first that comes to be among things standing still, is the eldest and most powerful change of all (*Laws* 895b5–6).

Strikingly, (1) the soul is not generated in the *Phaedrus*, but generated in the *Laws*, and in both dialogues the ground is the self-motion, the soul's nature, logos, and dynamis.[158] It is the nature of the self-motion, on the one hand, to generate through itself and give itself a life:[159] The self-motion ensures the psychic constitution by itself, because it is an eternal being that can revert upon and constitute itself,[160] so the soul is generated. On the other hand, this generation is not in temporal sense, because (a) in the *Timaeus* the generation of the world soul is prior to that of the world body (34c4–5), thus this generation is also prior to the emergence of the time. (b) The soul is the last member of the eternal beings that participate not in time, in which sense it is not generated.[161] (2) The (world) soul is described in the *Timaeus* as an intermediate entity of the divisible and indivisible Substance, Sameness and Difference, and is established by the Demiurge. Given this origin it appears that there are two distinct kinds of the psychic nature: self-motion and the intermediate substance. However, strictly speaking the account of the soul's intermediate essence is a description of its 'composition' (σύστασις, *Tim.* 36d9) that clarifies its substantial existence, harmony, form, dynamis, and activity (to move and to recognise), whereas the self-motion indicates mainly its motion-dynamis (and activity). Hence, when Plato speaks of the psychic generation in the *Phaedo*, *Phaedrus* and *Laws* he speaks primarily of its dynamis (and activity) of movement, leaving its intermediate substance literally untouched.

Now we must observe this intermediate essence of the soul, because evidently it involves a more fundamental view of the soul and can better clarify the soul's being both generated and not generated. At *Laws* 895d1–5 Plato declares that each thing is to be thought in threefold, i.e., substance, the logos of substance, and name. In this

---

[158] 'Dynamis' because the ability to move itself and other things is one of the soul's dynameis.
[159] Proclus, *In Tim.* I 235, 15–16.
[160] Proclus, *The Elements of Theology*, prop. 42 and 189. For an English translation, see Dodds (²1963).
[161] Cf. Proclus, *In Tim.* II 117, 11. A bit later Proclus asserts that there are two kinds of generation, one in the case of soul, one in respect of body, see II 117, 20–21.

perspective the intermediate essence is the substance of soul, while the self-motion is the logos and dynamis of this essence:[162] In the description of the world soul's generation we have determined that the two circles of the world soul – relating inherently to the latter's self-motion and cognitive abilities – are composed of those three mingled ingredients. Considering the difficulty of this issue and the main concern of this work – the perception-theory of Plato – instead of an investigation into all three ingredients of the soul, I will concentrate on its being an intermediate Substance.

(1) The world soul appears to be a mixture of the indivisible Substance and divisible Substance (*Tim.* 35a1–4). Being established as a third form (εἶδος, 35a4) from both Substances, the soul is simultaneously indivisible and divisible. This signifies that it is an intermediate entity, occupying the middle position between the intelligible Substances which are always there and the sensible Substances which are generated in bodies.[163] According to this account the soul can be called 'intelligible' and 'eternal' in terms of its indivisibility, and 'temporal' and 'the first among the things that have come to be' – as described at *Laws* 895a5–b7 and 896a5–b2 – in respect of its divisibility.[164] Given this substance of the soul it is both generated (with regard to its divisible parts) and not generated (in terms of its indivisible parts).

(2) That the soul is an intermediate entity between the indivisible and divisible Substances, is evident. However, it is neither composed of these two Substances themselves nor a third Substance except for them, rather of things that are analogous to them,[165] and it is said to be a form which can present in both Substances: (a) Proclus has enumerate four reasons to vindicate the claim that the soul is not composed of the indivisible Substance and the divisible Substance themselves:[166] firstly it is unreasonable to mix two essentially contrary Substances; secondly the soul would be secondary to the divisible Substance, when it is composed of this kind of Substance itself; thirdly if the soul is a third beyond these two Substances, it must exist with the two Substances which are always preserved, however, these two Substances are destroyed in the blending of soul; as last, the Demiurge divides the three mixtures by 'took a portion' (μίαν ἀφεῖλεν […] μοῖραν, 35b4–5), if the soul is constituted from the indivisible Substance itself, it would be impossible to take a portion from it. (b) The other ingredients, i.e., the intermediate Sameness and Difference, make the soul distinct from an entity originating merely from the intermediate species of the two Substances,[167] because the mingled

---

[162] For self-motion as the logos of soul, see above n156. Strikingly, 'logos and dynamis' are the Aristotelian criterion of the division of soul-parts, see *De anima* 432b3–4 and section 3.1.1.

[163] Proclus, *In Tim.* II 129, 31–130, 1.

[164] *Ibid.* II 147, 28–29; 148, 1–2. For the intelligibility of the world soul see section (4) in 1.1.1.1. Aristotle also asserts at *De an.* 415b21–2 that the soul is the first motion.

[165] Proclus, *In Tim.* II 149, 5.

[166] *Ibid.* II 149, 14–150, 11.

[167] For this issue, see *Ibid.* II 132, 2–135, 20 and 155, 3–156, 24. To summarise: in the former passage Proclus cites the *Sophist* to argue that all things are composed of the five genera Substance, Sameness, Difference, Motion, and Rest. And without Sameness, "the whole would be dissipated"; without Difference, "the thing would be solely one without multiplicity" (II 133, 21–22). Because he says in the second text that, "in the soul, the Sameness unities each of the many Differences among the many parts with Being, while the Difference distinguishes the many Sameness" (II 155, 18–20). Tr. Baltzly.

origin of the world soul enables it to participate both in the indivisible and divisible Substance, Sameness and Difference. Based on this synthetic essence the soul can be divided with harmony means, be formed into circles, and possess certain dynameis and activities. If the soul is solely composed of the intermediate Substance, it would be difficult for all souls to have the same nature that is attributed to the world soul. Therefore it is evident that the soul is not established from the indivisible divisible Substance themselves, instead it is composed of the analogous things.[168] And we should not entitle the world soul 'the third Substance' in addition to the indivisible and divisible Substance, for (1) it is generated from them and thus depends on and subordinate to them, owning not the same position in the pre-cosmic order as both of them, (2) we know that in Plato's *Timaeus* this very third species is called Chora (*Tim.* 48e4; cf. 50c7, 52a8, d4), not the soul.

The term 'intermediate' is derived from the phrase 'in the middle', which is used both in the world soul-text and the passage about the world body.[169] Considering the different subject matter in both contexts and their essentially distinguished constitution – in the case of world body air and water function as bonds that can unify the contrary fire and earth into one body, in the former text the world soul, however, is generated as an intermediate entity, and it is not stipulated to unify the two Substances into one – the soul's intermediate essence is able to connect the two Substances, however, it joins them not by fashioning them into a physical body – for they are two kinds of Substances that cannot be connected in a physical way – rather by way of presenting in both of them. In this sense although the soul is not established from these two kinds of Substance themselves, considering that it is generated to be intermediate, it can present in both, and differentiating and comprehending them. Proclus offers a concise summary of this issue at *In Tim.* II 1, 13–19:

> Soul, however, has an essence of an intermediate nature. So just as it is arranged as intermediate between divisible and indivisible things, in this manner it is also the boundary between generated and ungenerated things, having a beginning that is generated in relation to intellect but being ungenerated in relation to corporeal nature. It also has this status by being the limit of eternal beings but the very first among the things that have been generated. (Tr. Baltzly).

1.1.2.4 Rethinking the Platonic way of explaining the generation of the universe

In the primary research and the further investigation we have seen many factors regarding the Platonic world-generation theory – the One (the Good), the three transcendent Gods including the intelligible Gods (Being), the intelligible-intellective Gods (Life), and the intellective Gods (Intellect), the Gods of the World including the hypercosmic Gods, the hypercosmic-encosmic Gods, the encosmic Gods, the universal Souls, and the

---

[168] In explaining the substance of the immortal human souls Proclus also touches this theme, see 1.2.2.1.
[169] In the soul-passage 35a3, a5, in the body-text 31c1, 32a1, a3–4, b1, b4.

Superior Kinds (intelligible souls),[170] moreover, the Chora, geometrical figures, materials, elements, quality, quantity, and so on. Hence, we cannot define this doctrine with a single modern scientific discipline. Rather, these subjects, together with many other unmentioned elements, should be attributed to various scientific fields: not only the cosmogony, mathematics, physics, biology, but also theology, metaphysics, ontology, epistemology, psychology, politics, ethics,[171] etc.

The generated cosmos is perceptible and moves in a certain manner, to realise this perceptible nature it requires a material body that is composed of elements processing determinate quantitative and qualitative properties; to attain and maintain its motion there must be a dynamis, which belongs to the soul, the self-motion: (1) The generation of these elements, however, is the result of the combination of Matter and Form: the mathematical Forms on the one side, the Chora that is filled with pure materials on the other. Their unification is initiated by the Demiurge, who, after receiving the forms from the Paradigm, reconstructs the disordered elemental vestiges. Indeed, the generation of the elements is a 'preparation' or primary step to establish the world body, for after having reconstructed them the Demiurge continues to fashion all four elements into a sphere, which is the shape of the very world body. As the Maker and Father bestows certain dynameis and movements on it by implanting the world soul into it, the everlasting sensible world is generated. (2) The world soul, however, is a divine entity that originates from the intermediate Substances, Sameness and Difference. Being divided and blended in the 'X' form with perfect proportions, it has the cognitive capacity to grasp both the perceptible and intelligible things, and the motion-ability that initiates its own movement and causes the motion of the others, viz. all things in the universe, in which sense it is older and prior to the world body. Having fashioned the cosmos, the Demiurge goes on to create the young gods and the other immortal entities like the immortal human soul, and the young gods shall take over the generation-work and fabricate the human beings and all other mortal creatures.

In this system the existence of the Demiurge and the other kinds of gods is necessary and recognisable. Necessary because the Demiurge is the order and cause of the sensible universe, for he orders all things and places them in the best place (*Phaed.* 97b9–c5); recognisable because instead of a simple speculation, the Demiurge, in the sense of the divine Intellect, is something determinate, discernible, and comprehensible for us. (1) To prove the necessity and usefulness of his existence and his crucial role in the world-generation one needs only to reflect on the generation of the elements: all perceptible things are composed of elements that are established from certain geometrical forms and the pure materials, and both the forms and the pure materials exist originally before the cosmos really comes to be. These two factors are obviously isolated in the pre-cosmic state until an agent engages in the generation-work by combining them together. Given

---

[170] For an elaborate exposition of this system as well as the factors in it, see Siorvanes (1996) 114–206.

[171] The political and ethical application of the generation of the world and human beings is not discussed above, even not in the *Timaeus*, but it is apparently expressed at *Tim.* 27a7–b6 and is the subject matter of *Critias* and *Laws*. For the research of the coherence and organic unity in the Platonic cosmology and ethics, see for instance Carone (2005), in which the involved Dialogues are the *Timaeus*, *Philebus*, *Politicus* and *Laws*.

that the fashioned elements and the universe built from them are determinate things, it is unimaginable to attribute this agent to the chance. To determine this agent, logically and factually one must deal with two problems: who is this very agent, and how can he join the pure forms to the pure materials. For Plato such an agent is entitled the 'Demiurge', who is the divine intellect, the Maker and Father of the world, and the Zeus, as already proved in section 1.1.2.1. The Chora, being influenced by the forms in the Paradigm, possesses the vestiges of the elements, so receiving the forms from the Paradigm, the Demiurge can reconstruct it with forms and numbers, or logos and measure, which are exemplified by the perfectly good geometrical figures. In this view the existence of the Demiurge in explaining the generation of the universe is indispensable and useful.

(2) However, the trouble is, whether we can really discriminate and comprehend such a notion of god, or at least know something certain about him, for if the Demiurge is the very agent who establishes the whole world, yet is still unknown to us, this concept of god would be nothing but a device that is intentionally fabricated by Plato, to which he can always resort, especially when there is a puzzle in his description of the world-generation, and such a theology or cosmogony would be 'inaccessible' for us.

As mentioned above, the account of the generation of the sensible cosmos requires a restricted justification of the necessary existence of the Demiurge, which, however, can be illustrated only when he is recognisable in a certain way. So how can we recognise the god? In section 1.1.2.1 we have determined that the Demiurge is the Intellect, Maker and Father, and Zeus, but this theological, ontological explanation is perhaps too elaborate and difficult for us to understand. Now instead of this clarification we should find other ways to recognise the concept of the Demiurge. Here is an epistemological view: we are told by Plato that one can 'ascend' from sense perception to opinion and belief, then to discursive thinking (διάνοια) and reasoning (λογισμός), and eventually to the intellect that corresponds to the knowledge about the One and the god. This is primarily revealed in the Line Analogy of the *Republic*:[172] the ascension begins with the sense perception with which we can perceive different sensible qualities like colour, taste, smell, hardness, sound, figure, number, oneness, motion, and rest.[173] These perceptible objects, however, cannot ensure us to acquire the essence of the sensibles, rather they are abstract and confusing in the sense that they never cease to change. Thus, we must ascend to the next cognitive dimension, namely the opinion, which is based on perception and makes a determinate judgement about the essence of the sensible objects, for example, a place that offers protection against wind and rain and can be used to sleep is a house, a sphere that simultaneously moves around the sun and rotates itself is earth, and so on. This manifests that through the 'opinion with sensation' we can recognise the dynamis and activity of the sensible objects, which relate inherently to its substance. Yet with perception as its ground this kind of opinion is restricted, for on the one hand, although the dynamis and activity proceed from the essence, they can be multiple and different according to time, place, relations, and so on, which makes it difficult to determine the underlying essence by resorting to them alone, for example, we can sleep both in a house and a car, so with the function of 'sleeping' we cannot distinguish a

---

[172] See especially 511d6–e4. Cf. Cludius (1997).
[173] For the comprehensive research of the cognitive capacity of perception (and opinion), see section 3.2.

house from a car; on the other hand, when the sensible object at issue is mixed, this sort of opinion is unable to discriminate the substantial qualities of one object from those of the others, for instance, it is possible for Socrates to be smaller than one person, but taller than another one, so it seems that Socrates is both small and tall, which leads to a contradiction. Moreover, through this opinion one cannot grasp the cause of the essence, which leads to a puzzle to clarify such an essence of the objects. Therefore, one should turn to the higher epistemological ability which enables the discrimination of one substance from others and determines the cause of the essence – these are the dynameis of the discursive thinking devoting itself to the discrimination of the nature of the numbers, geometrical figures and similar things of this level, such as the likeness, unlikeness, sameness, and difference. For example, through this ability we can recognise the reason of the substance of earth, both its determinate form and matter. As a capacity which concentrates on the causes of the object, it would not be confused by recognising the sensible qualities. The defect of this capacity, however, is located at its very postulate (ὑπόθεσις) like point in the geometry and 1 in the arithmetic: if the truth of the hypothesis cannot be verified and maintained, all discrimination and comprehension obtained through it would be fallible. So logically and inherently it is requisite to examine its postulate to attain a guarantee of its rightness. The Platonic doctrine to this issue is not merely an amendment, rather a substantial transformation: instead of more supplements he turns to the final principle (ἀρχή) which needs no postulate anymore. Such a science is called dialectic, whose cognitive dynamis is the very intellect, the highest power to recognise all things. For instance, the postulate of all numbers and geometrical figures including the elemental triangles is the existence of the 'monad', which can be exclusively recognised through the intellect,[174] the very dynamis that is attributed to the philosopher-kings in the *Republic* and the Demiurge of the *Timaeus*.[175] So as the philosopher-kings are able to see the Form of Good and regard the city of justice as paradigm of the real city,[176] the agent who uses his divine intellect to establish the real sensible universe should also do this by looking at the forms in the divine Paradigm. Thus, the Demiurge is epistemologically recognisable for us.

In another view[177] we can say that 'something determinate' (τί ἐστιν) is the criterion of cognition, and 'einai' (εἶναι) is the inner measure, so the different dimension of 'einai' of the cognitive objects corresponds to different cognitive dynamis.

The discrimination of this determinate 'einai' begins already with the sense perception, which is an analysis-activity of the different achievements of discrimination, for example the sight of the peculiar sensation discriminates the colours from other sensible qualities like sounds, because colours and sounds are determinate objects that bear

---

[174] That from the geometrical forms we can derive their previous entities and principles like line and point, see *Rep.* 510c1–511c2; Aristotle, *Metaphy.* 992a10–24. For the correspondence of the numbers 1-2-3-4, the figures point-line-depth-body, and the cognitive abilities nous-reason-opinion-perception, see Plato, *Epin.* 990c–991e; Aristotle, *Metaphy.* 1090b21–5 and *De an.* 404b17f.

[175] Here we should point out that the human intellect originates from the divine intellect and is an imitation of the latter.

[176] See *Rep.* 540a8–2: καὶ ἰδόντας τὸ ἀγαθὸν αὐτό, παραδείγματι χρωμένους ἐκείνῳ.

[177] Schmitt (2019) 59–127.

different 'einai'. So, something sensible implies something determinate in respect of the enmattered categories like quantity, quality, motion, rest, shape, size, oneness, and number, in this sense Aristotle declares that the sense perception perceives the form (εἶδος) of the sensibles (*De anima* 424a18–25).

However, the discrimination of the enmattered 'einai', or the divisible substance, requires another cognitive dynamis, hence, there must be a transformation of the cognitive dimension, i.e., from the sense perception to the opinion which is a complex synthesis of many perception-activities and discriminates the dynameis and activities of the sensible things, which originate substantially from their determinate 'einai' (substance).[178] For example we can opine that a house is to sleep after perceiving someone sleeps in it.

A further transformation is to discriminate the 'einai' of a determinate thing itself, for instance what is the determinate 'einai' of triangle itself: not the enmattered triangle in the sand, rather the logos of triangle itself, i.e., the sum of whose interior angles is always equal to two right angles. This kind of 'einai' is distinct from all others like "the sum of whose outer angles is equal to four right angles", for the former explains what comes from the triangle itself, namely triangle *qua* triangle. This dimension of 'einai' is discriminated by the discursive thinking.

Finally, we should examine the 'einai' itself, which is the inherent measure of all cognition. The discrimination and comprehension of it has no specific object anymore, rather the purely recognisable 'einai', which should be deemed as the sum of the whole possibility of being something determinate. The cognition of such an 'einai' relates to the intellect, which enables the possibility of all kinds of human cognition. So, the way from the sensibly determinate 'einai' to the 'einai' itself denotes the transformation of the cognitive abilities from sense perception to the (divine) intellect. Considering that the Demiurge is the divine Intellect, we can also say the change from perception to god.

With this clarification one can assert that the notion of Demiurge is epistemologically recognisable and distinguishable. His existence is the precondition of the possibility of the proportionally sensible world's generation, for through his divine Intellect he recognises the forms in the Paradigm, which enables him to persuade the Necessity (*Tim.* 47e5–47a5), reconstruct the Chora, and mould the sensible universe.

However, stepping back form this Platonic system, one wonders whether it is the unique and perfect clarification of the generation of the cosmos as well as its epistemological certainty. The first point evoking such a kind of dissatisfaction is the necessity to maintain the role of the Demiurge (and the subordinate gods): for Plato the notion of god(s) is not a speculation, rather the accessibility and possibility of the whole epistemology and the reason of the world-generation, yet such a possible and thinkable explanation is not the single one, for both in the ancient and modern time,[179] regarding the generation and epistemological certainty of the sensible world, there are a multitude of doctrines ruling the concept of god(s) out. For example, the Big Bang theory based on many mathematical and physical postulates manifests that the god is not indispensable

---

[178] See Schmitt (2019) 72–74, where Schmitt cites the contexts from the *Cratylus*, *Sophist*, *Republic* and *Metaphysics* to prove this point.

[179] For a summary of the ancient Greek cosmology, see Gregory (2007) Ancient Greek Cosmogony.

in clarifying the cosmos-generation,[180] and with Darwinism one can clarify the generation of all creatures and their biological features, including that of the human being. In this sense it appears reasonable to doubt whether the Platonic doctrine is a better doctrine in explaining the genesis and determination of the perceptible cosmos.

However, these so-called modern theories are (1) not essentially 'modern' on the one hand, and (2) not so reasonable as the Platonic (and Aristotelian) model on the other hand. For (1) The Darwinism has determinate likeness with the natural theory of Democritus and Epicureanism (like Titus Lucretius Carus), and it shares the self-preservation-doctrine of the Stoicism.[181] Moreover, both Darwinism and the Big Bang theory are the same as the cosmogony-theory of Empedocles due to their substantial dependence on the chance (τύχη).[182] (2) In both Darwinism and the Big Bang theory the chance plays a decisive role, which is indeed not reasonable: in the Big Bang theory the explosion is caused by chance,[183] thus in the empirical sense it is very hard to build a model to explain and verify such an explosion, and in the theoretical respect such a fact can barely ensure the precision of the scientific knowledge based on the cosmogony: the science is developed to explain the genesis and essence of the world. As the universe's generation is initiated by chance, the truth of science turns out to be quite doubtful. In this sense the generation doctrine based on the chance is criticised by Proclus when he interrogates: "why are there always beings, and how do events in nature happen in accordance with general laws, when things that arise by accident occur only rarely?"[184] The Darwinism tries to equate the chance to the immanent impulse that enables the evolution, making the chance the actual necessity of nature.[185] However, this doctrine has the same problem: if the chance is the necessary and final cause of revolution and our contemporary natural world, it must be recognisable, so that we can determine under which conditions such a revolution can take place, and hope that when the same environment is created, the revolution should happen again. Yet the truth is, as I know, until now there is no experiment which leads to a successful biological revolution. Moreover, if such a revolution really happens, it should not take place a single creature,

---

[180] For a description of this theory, see Brisson & Meyerstein (1995) 67–147. In pp. 8–12 the authors have compared this theory with the Platonic cosmogony. Astonishingly they have regarded these two theories as the 'parallel' doctrines devoted to bridge the 'hiatus irrationalis' between the intelligible science and the perceptible reality (p. 4). Such a defect results from their wrongly established premise that the 'scientific' knowledge is the very knowledge acquired by the 'hypothesis-deduction-testing' procedure, according to which the knowledge generated through 'divine revelation or mystical illumination', or from perception or habit, would not be taken into account; more ridiculously, they have argued that this difference of knowledge and non-knowledge is established by Plato and Aristotle (p. 2), yet the Platonic and Aristotelian doctrine of knowledge, as showed above, is to discriminate the certain 'einai' of the object with the suitable cognitive abilities. For the rejection of the assertation of Brisson and Meyerstein, see also Gregory (2007) 158–160.

[181] Campbell (2000) 145; Bernard (2002) 12; Schmitt (2012) 455, 467; (2019) 182.

[182] Bernard (1998) 25; (2002) 10; Schmitt (2012) 455–459.

[183] Gregory (2000) 18–22; (2007) 7.

[184] Proclus, In Parm. 790, 7–10. Tr. Morrow and Dillon. Cf. 785, 4–799, 22 about cosmos-generation.

[185] Schmitt (2012) 456–457.

rather in a big group, for only in this way such a revolution can be biologically inherited. But how can we regard such an inheritance as something happens 'by chanced', if it simultaneously occurs in many individuals? Therefore, Proclus asserts that: "neither nature nor God does anything in vain, and in general all such production comes about for the most part, whereas the accidental occurs rarely".[186]

Because of these difficulties, the chance applied to explain the cause of such material changes in both theories, i.e., collapse, explosion, cooling, revolution, growth, etc., should be replaced by another cause that can be theoretically determined and empirically studied. Such a kind of cause can be found in the Platonic world generation theory, of which the Demiurge plays a decisive role: he recognises the forms in the Paradigm and reconstructs the Chora, fashioning and combining the world soul with the world body, through which bringing forth the sensible cosmos. All related factors in this description, including the Demiurge himself as well as the forms and materials, are determinate objects of the cognitive abilities.[187]

With this brief argument it is evident that the Platonic Demiurge is not a speculation, rather it ensures the accessibility and precision of the scientific knowledge, the exclusion of this factor in explaining the whole natural world leads to nothing but the collapse of a reasonable clarification of our world. In this sense, the Platonic exposition of the world-generation, being neither the unique theory nor the most precise one, for Plato entitles it 'the possible account' (κατὰ τὸν εἰκότα λόγον), is nevertheless more reasonable than the other theories.

1.1.2.5 Conclusion

In the further investigation I have offered a comprehensive research of the Demiurge, the Chora, and the (world) soul. The discussion about the Demiurge aims at an exposition of his essence and dynamis. Despite various modern explanations the Proclean interpretation continues to be closer to Plato's original doctrine. For he summarises the previous studies in the Platonic tradition and sets the Demiurge in an elaborately constructed theological system including the whole range of entities from the One down to the intelligible souls of angels, demons, and heroes. In this view he entitles the Demiurge the 'demiurgic Intellect'. Such an Intellect is the cause of the complete universe, the Maker and Father of the cosmos, and is named Zeus in the Platonic

---

[186] Proclus, *In Parm*. 791, 34–36. Tr. Morrow and Dillon.
[187] In fact, the distinction between the cause of material and form is one of the main concerns of Plato's Philosophy. At *Phaed*. 97b8–102a1 the Platonic Socrates approves the doctrine of Anaxagoras that intellect is the cause of everything, but criticises him for his resorting to the materials like fire, air, earth, water, and similar things, in explaining the natural phenomena. To maintain the Intellect as the last cause on the one hand and clarify the phenomena with a plausible cause which is in accordance with the intellect on the other hand, Socrates introduces the hypothesis of form. For a systematic description of the Platonic form-theory in the *Phaedo*, see Radke-Ulmann (2002). Cf. Bernard (1998) 3–9; (2002) 13–15. Aristotle (*De an*. 416a9–18) also criticises the idea (of Empedocles) that the elements enable growth, and following Plato he also credits the growth to the soul.

dialogues und Orphic poems. To determine that the Demiurge is Zeus Proclus provide a large multitude of quotations from the Platonic dialogues. These citations are evident proofs that the Proclean explanation is the one that agrees with Plato's own thought (1.1.2.1).

The Chora originates not from the Demiurge, rather from the One, the Unlimited, and the One Being, for Timaeus claims that Being, Becoming and Chora are three species that exist even before the universe is generated. To reconstruct the Chora, or the disorderly moving materials possessing merely the traces of the elements, the Demiurge bestows the possibly beautiful proportions on them, i.e., the geometrical figures like the right-angled isosceles and right-angled half equilateral, and the figures that are established from them, for example tetrahedron, cube, octahedron, icosahedron, and dodecahedron. Since these figures are proportionally formed and enmattered, they possess proportional volumes, movements and dynameis, and the elements composed of them are also proportional. Moreover, according to these proportional properties in terms of numbers, volumes, movements and dynameis, these elements can both transform into and interweave with each other, initiating all kinds of elemental and corporeal movements that result in the generation of all kinds of qualities. And the sensible qualities, as they must exist in a material body, are also proportional generated and altered. In this sense the objects of the sense perception, i.e., the whole universe, is proportionally perceptible (1.1.2.2).

That the world soul consists of three ingredients, i.e., the intermediate Substance, Sameness and Difference, is already clarified in the primary research (see section 1.1.1). In the further research I have concentrated on the soul's character and reason of being both generated and not generated: in the *Phaedo*, *Phaedrus*, *Republic* the soul is declared to be immortal, indestructible, and not generated, and according to the assertion in the *Republic* and *Philebus* it is the last member of the eternal beings. However, in the *Laws* the soul is deemed to be the first generation, because its logos and dynamis is self-motion. With self-motion man can clarify the soul's being not generated and generated, although a thorough interpretation is possible only when man resorts to its very essence involving the three intermediate ingredients, especially the Substance, which initiates its logos and dynamis, i.e., self-motion. For being an intermediate entity, the soul possesses the ability to unify the indivisible and divisible Substance in manner of presenting in both. Although the soul is not composed of the two kinds of Substance themselves, it consists of things that are analogous to them, thus it obtains the feature of being generated in terms of the divisible Substance, and not generated in respect of the indivisible Substance (1.1.2.3).

The whole system about the generation of the world is grounded on a strict cognitive theory, which can be understood in a scientific view: with distinguished cognitive dynamis we can determine different objects, for example, with sight one can see the colours in a determinate way. In this view our universe, as a leaving creature with body and soul, can be recognised through not only sensation and opinion, but also discursive thinking and intellect, for all cosmic things possess determinate 'einai', which corresponds to different cognitive abilities. In this Platonic world-generation doctrine the Demiurge plays the decisive role, and as the divine Intellect his cognitive dynamis and activity are explainable and demonstrable. In the modern time there do exist other theories appearing to be more scientific than the platonic system, like the Big Bang theory and Darwinism, however, both focus mainly on the material aspect of the universe, and to explain the generation of the natural world they resort essentially to the chance, which is barely recognisable. On this ground the Platonic interpretation of the world-generation continues to be a more reasonable doctrine which can be explained in a more thinkable manner (1.1.2.4).

1.2 Human being as perception subject and his generation

In this section I will expound the generation of a kind of perception subject, namely the human being. For after explaining the generation of the perceptible object, i.e., the entire universe, logically it is requisite to focus on the perception subject, primarily its coming to be. No doubt that for us the perception subject denotes the human being and his very soul, yet it is worthwhile to inquire firstly how many kinds of perception subjects there are, for in addition to the human being there are still many other kinds of creatures that can perceive. Moreover, an investigation of all these sorts can reveal the broad range of Plato's perception-theory, and with such an explanation we can confirm the heterogeneity and homogeneity between the human perception and the other kinds of perception, which enables us to attain a deeper understanding of the human perception. In this sense this chapter falls into three parts: firstly, a description of all kinds of perception and the corresponding subjects (1.2.1), then a clarification of the generation of the human soul, his body, and their combination into a living creature (1.2.2), finally a conclusion of this whole chapter (1.2.3). Considering that these issues are mainly handled in Plato's *Timaeus*, I will resort especially to the Proclean *Timaeus*-commentary to explain the related issues.

1.2.1 The four kinds of perceiver

Proclus announces at *In Tim.* II 83, 16–84, 5 that in Plato one can find four kinds of sense perception, which can be logically divided into three classes, as he does at *In Tim.* III 286, 2–287, 10.[188] The first class is the unaffected and common perception (ἡ ἀπαθὴς αἴσθησις καὶ κοινή, III 287, 7–8) corresponding to the first two kinds of sensation: the first and most authoritative (πρωτίστη καὶ κυριωτάτη, II 83, 17; 84, 6) perception is attributed to the whole universe,[189] which contains all sensation objects, sense-organs, and sensation in itself (II 83, 14–15; 84, 11–14). Such a sensation holds no separate organs like eyes and ears, i.e., it is the 'undivided' (ἀδιαίρετος, II 84, 12), 'single' (μία,

---

[188] Cf. Blumenthal (1982) 2–4; Lautner (2006) 117–136; Baltzly (2009b) esp. 266–279.
[189] See 1.1.1.2, part (4). For the perception of the whole universe (world soul), see Reydams-Schils (1997) 261–265; Baltzly (2009b) 261–281. Baltzly also compares the cosmic sense perception with the modern perception theory. Aristotle also attributes this kind of perception to the world soul, for it has 'an inborn perception about harmony' (*De an.* 406b30: αἴσθησίν τε σύμφυτον ἁρμονίας ἔχῃ).

II 85, 20) sensation, or the 'joint-perception' (συναίσθησις, II 83, 23).[190] Imitating the intellect (νοῦν), or the Demiurge,[191] the universe neither changes to another nor extends out of itself, for in that case it would be incomplete. And it discriminates not only the sensible qualities like colours and sounds, but also their whole essence (οὐσία), because instead of possessing them accidentally, the universal sensation owns the sensible essence by itself (II, 84, 16–20; cf. 84, 28). The second kind of perception goes outside, but is completely in activity, since it always apprehends the whole recognisable objects and is free from the affections that can be received by specific and enmattered organs. This perception belongs to the young, created gods who are in charge of the fixed stars.[192] As divine creatures (ζῷα θεῖα, *Tim.* 40b5) they are announced to be well-rounded (εὔκυκλον, 40a5), being visible as they will (ἂν ἐθέλωσιν, 41a5)[193] and circling around (περιπολοῦσιν φανεῶς, 41a4) in the cosmos, just like the world body. However, unlike the world body moving only in circular manner, the young gods (i.e., the astral gods) move simultaneously forward (40a5–b2). The second class of perception involves the so-called common and affected sensation (ἡ κοινὴ μέν, παθητικὴ δέ, *In Tim.* III 287, 8) of human beings. Such a kind of perception, necessarily being affected by the sensibles, is deemed to be a mixture of 'susceptibility and cognition' (πείσεως καὶ γνώσεως, II 83, 28), i.e., it begins with sense-affection and ends up in cognition and discrimination. The last class is the divided and affected perception (ἡ διῃρημένη καὶ ἐμπαθής, III 287, 8–9), which is unable to recognise the forms of the sensible objects such as hot and cold, rather it distinguishes whether the affection is pleasant or painful. According to *Timaeus* 76e8–77c4 this sort of perception subject belongs to the plants.[194]

Now it is evident that there are four kinds of perception in the *Timaeus*, and each has its certain features: (1) The first two kinds require no affections, since they have the highest perception-form, i.e., the joint-perception. With this form they can perceive the whole sensible objects that are generated and enmattered in a body.[195] (2) The human perception begins with the generation of sense-affection and ends with the discrimination of this affection. Obviously, there must be somatic organs to co-produce these affections with the external sensibles, for the human being cannot perceive these sensible qualities without his bodily sense-organs – this implies that an investigation into the generation of the perception subject in respect of human beings must begin with the generation of his body and soul. (3) The perception of the plants has the single ability to

---

[190] For a detailed explanation of this term συναίσθησις, see Lautner (2006) 118–122. For this notion in Aristotle, see Schmitt (2002) 109–148.

[191] Cf. Proclus, *In Tim.* II 85, 25, where he stresses that the universe is eyeless because it is an image of the intellective god (κατ'εἰκόνα τοῦ νοητοῦ θεοῦ). At III 100, 28–30 he re-asserts that the perception of the cosmos is an image (εἰκών) of the intellect.

[192] Proclus does not clearly assert that such a kind of perception belongs to the young gods, but according to his description they should be the possessors. Cf. Baltzly (2007) 145n279.

[193] For an analysis of the gods' visibility by virtue of their will, see Proclus, *In Tim.* III 194, 20–196, 10.

[194] Here the perception of animals is not mentioned, which, in this specific context, should be the same as the human perception.

[195] Cf. *Tim.* 28b8–9, 31b5–6.

discriminate the pain and pleasure brought by the affections, which reveals that its cognitive power is the simplest of all living creatures.

1.2.2 The generation of the human being as perception subject

Given that the present theme is the generation of the determinate kind of perception subject, i.e., the human being – first of all his soul and in a limited sense also his body – our research, as in the case of the world-generation, should fall into three parts: the generation of the human soul, both its immortal and mortal form, their vehicles, and the fated laws that all human souls should obey (1.2.2.1), the establishment of the human body, which is actually the third vehicle of the human soul, i.e., the shell-like vehicle (1.2.2.2), and their combination into a living creature, which is divided into two parts, i.e., the embodiment of the immortal soul-form, and that of the mortal part (1.2.2.3). In this interpretation I will resort further to the *Timaeus*-commentaries of Calcidius and Proclus, and in the last section I shall stress that for Plato the description of the incarnation of the mortal part is different from the modern biological theories.

1.2.2.1 The generation of the immortal and mortal human soul

Following the preceding Neoplatonists like Iamblichus and Syrianus, Proclus asserts that in Plato's *Timaeus* the individual human soul consists of two parts, or two forms,[196] i.e., the immortal part and the mortal part, and of three kinds of vehicles for the sake of their motion, cognition, and descent, viz. the divine, luminous vehicle moulded by the Demiurge, the mortal pneumatic vehicle and the shell-like earthly body established by the young gods.[197] This explanation, I suppose, should not be merely regarded as a Neoplatonic doctrine, for on the one side it is grounded on the very Platonic context, e.g. the generation of the immortal soul, its entrance into the divine vehicle in the *Timaeus* 41d4–e2; the creation of the mortal soul and the second, pneumatic vehicle which is adhered to it in 42c2–d2; the construction of the earthly body and the incarnation of the soul into this body at 42e5–43a6. On the other side what is not explicitly stated by Plato but explained by the Neoplatonists, for instance, the way of the becoming of the mortal soul and its pneumatic vehicle, can nevertheless be derived from Plato's own words.[198]

---

[196] Although the soul has two different parts, they form the single human soul together. Given that the mortal soul-form has two further parts, there exists a tripartite soul theory in Plato's oeuvre. For an interpretation of this theory, esp. its origin and its relation to music, see Taylor (1928) 496–499.

[197] For Proclus's doctrine of the origin, descent, and ascent of the human soul, see his *Elements of Theology*, §§ 184–211 and *In Tim.* III 236, 31–238, 26. For a summary of this topic, see Finamore and Kutash (2017) 131–134.

[198] Thus, in the Platonic tradition there is no problem about the body-soul relation, which, however, is one of the important issues in the modern philosophy like in Descartes. For the soul-body relation in the *Timaeus*, see Sorabji (2003) 152–162. For a brief study of this relation in the old Academy, see Dillon (2020) 349–356. Despite the vehicle-theory displayed

In this view the investigation into this theme should begin with the description of the divine soul-form's generation and the establishment of its divine, luminous vehicle, and continue with the clarification of the becoming of the mortal soul and its corresponding vehicle(s). Now, with reference to the divine soul-form Plato stipulates:

> Having said this, he turned once more to the same mixing bowl wherein he had mixed and blended the soul of the universe, and poured into it what was left of the former ingredients, blending them this time in somewhat the same way, only no longer so pure as before, but second or third in degree of purity. And when he had compounded the whole, he divided it into souls equal in number with the stars, and distributed them, each soul to its several star. There mounting each as into a vehicle, he showed them the nature of the universe and declared to them the fated laws (*Tim.* 41d4–e2. Tr. Cornford, with slight reversion).

In this quotation we are taught how the Demiurge fashions the divine human soul-form. There are three remarkable points in this statement: (1) The ingredients and the method applied to mould this human soul-form is declared to be similar to that of the world soul and the young gods' souls. For the immortal human soul-form is established from the rest of the ingredients that are mixed and blended to fashion the soul of the whole universe and the young gods, and they are fashioned in the same way, i.e., by using the mixing bowl,[199] thus the immortal human soul-form must be an imitation of the world soul, or with Plato's words, it is akin (συγγενεῖς, 47c1, d1; cf. 90a6, c8) to the world soul. Moreover, being established in the similar way and possessing two circles,[200] the immortal part is able to recognise and move in the similar way as the world soul and the junior gods' souls.[201] The substantial distinction between them rests on their purity, for the former is declared to be 'second and third in degree of purity'[202] – it is not necessary

> by Plato himself, Dillon (pp. 355–356) tends to solve this seemingly problem by declaring that for Plato the physical world is not real, for it is established from the elemental triangles that are 'immaterial entities', and he cites Aristotle's criticism in *De caelo* to prove this argument. Yet our research in section 1.1.2.2 has already revealed that this Aristotelian criticism is not true, and the elemental triangles are material entities. Therefore, to prove that there exists no body-soul problem it would be better to resort to the vehicle-theory.

[199] For an interpretation of the 'mixing-bowl', see Proclus' conclusion at *In Tim.* III 249, 27–250, 8. His main argument is: the mixing-bowl is separate from the Demiurge, rather it is productive of soul (ψυχογονικός), for the Demiurge uses it only by establishing the souls. In this sense it has determinate responsibility for the souls. Being responsible for the generation of the souls, it belongs to the same rank as the Demiurge, though not superior to him, which implies that it is also a kind of intellective god, and, when the Demiurge is fontal-like, so is the mixing-bowl.

[200] Cf. *Tim.* 44d3–45a2, 69c5–6.

[201] On the difference of soul's essence and activity, see Steel (1978) 70–73; (1997b) 296–297; Finamore & Kutash (2017) 123–129 (especially on the world soul).

[202] Usually, the second and third degree of purity is deemed to be relevant to the rebirth of man in woman and animal (*Tim.* 42a1–2, 42b3–c4), yet one should consider the passage of *Rep.* 456a10, where Plato asserts that man and woman have the same nature, Calcidius (*In Tim.* § 191) also stresses that the distinction rests only on their gender and bodily powers. So (1) it is very possible that in the *Timaeus* Plato intends to speak of the 'virile' and 'effeminate'

for the Demiurge to fashion two same forms or beings, as Plato declares at *Republic* 597c1–d6, thus the world soul and young gods' souls are the souls of one determinate form, while the immoral human souls of another. Because after generation the divine souls continue to stay in the mixing-bowl, whereas the immortal human souls, as soon as they are generated, are immediately and wholly separated from the mixing-bowl and mounted in their own vehicles, therefore the divine souls and the immortal human souls are 'both the same and different species' (καὶ τὰ γένη ταὐτά ἐστι καὶ ἕτερα).[203] (2) As stipulated by the Demiurge, the original dwellings of the immortal human souls are the stars. Given that the human being is born in the earth, there should be a descent starts from the stars to the earth. Meanwhile, being sowed in the stars implies these individual souls' ability to recognise things in the same way as these astral souls,[204] including the capacity of perception. (3) The immortal human souls are mounted in their chariot-vehicles,[205] which enable them to wander in the stars. In annotating this text Proclus argues that the individual souls are firstly established, then distributed to the stars and mounted in the vehicles. After hearing 'the fated laws' (νόμους τε τοὺς εἱμαρμένους, *Tim.* 41e2–3) they are made the citizens of the whole universe.[206] One important point in this process is the generation of the vehicles of these individual souls, and we must explain what they are: in his commentary (*In Tim.* III 266, 24–268, 21; 233, 23–234,5) Proclus has recourse to Iamblichus' explanation, for the latter asserts that the vehicles of the souls are generated from the whole ether (ἀπὸ παντὸς τοῦ αἰθέρος, III 266, 27),[207] so

characters that can exist in both man and woman, as Proclus argues at *In Tim.* III 283, 27–30 and 293, 5–19. (2) The description of the rebirth in woman, as a part of the 'possible account' (κατὰ λόγον τὸν εἰκότα, 90e8), functions in the context as a punishment inflicted on the disobedient people, as affirmed by Timaeus of Locros, see *De nat.*, 224, 13–225, 15, esp. 224, 14–15 (κόλασις [...] ἅ ἐκ τῶν λόγων) and 224, 19 (ψευδέσι λόγοις). While Taylor (1928) 263 wrongly insists that this phrase should be read literally, and the woman should take a chance to reborn as a man.

[203] Proclus, *In Tim.* III 245, 10–19.

[204] For a discussion of the cosmic, daimonic and individual souls, see *Ibid.* III 251, 29–256, 21.

[205] Before this reference in the *Timaeus* the vehicle of the soul emerges already in the myth of the winged charioteer in *Phaedr.* 246a–249d, and Proclus' interpretation of this passage can be found in his *Platonic Theology* IV. The Proclean commentary on this *Phaedrus*-passage is summarised by Van den Berg (2017) 228–231.

[206] See Proclus, *In Tim.* III 266, 1–14. According to Tarrant (2017) 154n423, the point of 'making the souls the citizens of the world' is also mentioned in III 238, 5 and 276, 28. For the fated laws, cf. the myth of Er at *Republic* X 614aff. and *Laws* 903b–905d (on the divine rightness and the fate of soul).

[207] The Platonic ether is viewed as the purest and most luminous form of air (*Tim.* 58d1–2: κατὰ ταὐτὰ δὲ ἀέρος, τὸ μὲν εὐαέστατον ἐπίκλην αἰθὴρ καλούμενος. *Phaed.* 111b1–2: ὁ δὲ ἡμῖν ἀήρ, ἐκείνοις τὸν αἰθέρα. b5–6: ᾗπερ ἀήρ τε ὕδατος ἀφέστηκεν καὶ αἰθὴρ ἀέρος πρὸς καθαρότητα. Cf. *Crat.* 410b6–8). However, it is not only a kind of air, rather it forms the pure heaven in which we find all stars and planets (*Phaed.* 109b6–c1; *Laws* 898e10–899a1). In *Crat.* (408d8–e1: καὶ γῆς καὶ αἰθέρος καὶ ἀέρος καὶ πυρὸς καὶ ὕδατος) ether appears to be one element in addition to the canonical four elements, and this point is apparently asserted in Ps.-Plato's *Epin.* 981c5–6: πῦρ χρὴ φάναι καὶ ὕδωρ εἶναι καὶ τρίτον ἀέρα, τέταρτον δὲ γῆν, πέμπτον δὲ αἰθέρα. Such a concept of 'fifth element' is accepted and developed by Aristotle and the other Platonists. For this notion in Aristotle, see Althoff (2005) 14–15; in Xenocrates,

they are 'simple and immaterial' (ἁπλοῦν καὶ ἄυλον, III 285,13), and have a generative dynamis. Without ether the bodies of the astral gods would be diminished, while being fashioned from ether we can conclude that the vehicles of the individual souls must be moulded in accordance with the lives of the gods.[208] Moreover, the Demiurge himself is the begetter of the vehicles, and he institutes them with the (rest) ingredients for the astral bodies, i.e., the ether, so that they are possibly like the stars.[209] Given that he is the agent who mounts the immortal human souls in their vehicles, if he does not mould the vehicles by himself, whom else should be obliged to? Thus, the Demiurge is responsible for the institution and distribution of the individual souls and their vehicles, and he authorises the souls to govern their own instruments (τὴν ἀρχὴν τῶν οἰκείων ὀργάνων, III 267, 10–11). Proclus argues that what is remarkable here is that the Demiurge creates the vehicles without taking ingredients from the whole beings that are already being moulded, rather from the rest ingredients, which makes the vehicles necessarily independent, and more importantly, everlasting, so that the individual souls can always be the encosmic citizens (III 267, 13–30). To illustrate this point Proclus resorts to the myths of *Phaedo* 113d5–6 and *Phaedrus* 247b1–3, where the souls are described to use their vehicles in Hades and in the heaven (III 268, 1–10). Furthermore, he points out the distinction between the individual souls and the souls of the astral gods: the latter hold the 'single and unchangeable intelligence' (μιᾷ δὲ καὶ ἀτρέπτῳ νοήσει, III 268, 14–15), and their bodies are set into them without being stipulated to be governed by the souls, which implies that the astral souls always govern their bodies, while the individual souls are subject to the possibility of being overpowered by their 'bodies', so the Demiurge mounts them in the vehicles and empowers the souls to control over them.

To sum up, the Demiurge begets the immortal individual souls by moulding the rest ingredients with the mixing-bowl. Distributing these souls to the stars he mounts each of them into the ethereal vehicle, which is produced by himself in order that it can be possibly similar to the divine astral body. Dwelling on the stars, governing and moving their own vehicles, the individual souls are the citizens of the whole universe. Both these souls and their vehicles are not mortal, rather as divine entities formed by the demiurgic dynamis they are essentially everlasting. However, unlike the divine world soul and the astral souls, these immortal human souls are enslaved to the fated laws, which implies that they can lose their divinity, descend from the stars, and enter the other (mortal) bodies.

Proclus, however, goes further by determining and analysing the divine human soul-form's intermediate substance of being both divisible and indivisible:[210] As mentioned above, each soul, including the soul of human beings, is a mean between the indivisible Substance that is always the same and the divisible Substance that is generated in bodies, thus the divine individual souls also share this determinate substance. As said above, the

---

see Fr. 53 (Heinze) = Simplicius, *In Phy.* 1165, 33–39. In the sense that the souls are mounted on the stars and move together with them, Calcidius attributes the stars to the soul-vehicles, see *In Tim.* § 141.

[208] Proclus, *In Tim.* III 266, 24–30. Cf. Iamblichus, *In Tim.* fr. 84, in Dillon (1973) 198–199, 379–380.

[209] *Ibid.* III 234, 1–2: ἄμφω γοῦν ἀπὸ τοῦ δημιουργοῦ γεννᾶται καθ'ὁμοιοτητα τῶν ἄστρων.

[210] *Ibid.* III 268, 21–270, 2.

vehicle of the divine soul-form is engendered along with it, and the mounting of the latter in the vehicle initiates its homey life. According to Proclus, this kind of life bears a divisible substance, whose paradigm the soul has attained in advance, when it establishes its opinion as the paradigm of sensation in the vehicle, and its own 'policy-making dynamis' (τὴν [...] δύναμιν προαιρετικὴν, III 268, 31) as the paradigm of the appetite (ὄρεξις).[211] All these faculties in the individual souls are plainly divisible, and before them is 'the otherness' (ἡ ἑτερότης)[212] of its many divisions of its substance, in accordance with which the soul is both divisible and has something that is 'indivisible and whole' (ἀμέριστον καὶ ὅλον). Regarding the indivisible substance of the individual souls Proclus handles it by resorting to its relation to the intellect, for according to him the indivisible substance of souls pertaining inherently to the intellect, which is the soul's most powerful cognitive dynamis to discriminate and comprehend the indivisible things:[213] not every individual soul possesses an intellect that is set over it, for in this case the individual souls would always stay on the star, subjecting not to the fated laws. Rather every individual soul is joined to a determinate daimon (δαίμων) possessing the daimonic intellect,[214] and by sharing this kind of intellect the individual souls also own the intellect that is set as an indivisible substance. Thus, every individual soul is both indivisible and divisible: it has its own divisible faculties, as mentioned above, which makes it divisible; participating the indivisible element held commonly with the daimon over it, it is indivisible.

After the explanation of the generation of the immortal human soul-form and its heavenly vehicle we should turn to the becoming of the mortal soul, which is entitled 'the unregulated soul' (ἡ ἄλογος ψυχή) by Proclus.[215]

---

[211] Proclus, *In Tim.* III 284, 24–27, where in explaining the descent of the individual souls Proclus proclaims that they "have previously possessed the uppermost pinnacle of this [life] in the pneuma, and received its causes indivisibly in their opinion-forming life; for that is the principle of sensation". (Tr. Tarrant).

[212] I suppose that this 'otherness' is like the Difference (τοῦ ἑτέρου, *Tim.* 35a4. Cf. θατέρου, 35b3) which co-constitutes the world soul, or it originates somehow from the latter.

[213] This clarifies why Proclus argues that the substance of the souls is not composed of the indivisible and divisible Substances themselves, rather something analogous to them (section 1.1.2.3): the intellect is the faculty that can recognise the indivisible things; considering that both intellect and the thought of the indivisible things are in the soul, they are the same.

[214] See p. 39 demon's role in Plato's Cosmogony (Theology). Cf. the description of immortal soul in next page.

[215] The term 'ἄλογος' should not be translated into 'irrational' or 'unreasoning', as many scholars like Opsomer (2006b); Tarrant (2017); Finamore and Kutash (2017) have done, for it is a translation influenced by the Stoics, see Taylor (1928) 263, who argues that this term should be translated as 'without ratio', or more plainly 'unregulated', 'without measure', which is quite reasonable: the unregulated soul is fabricated by the young gods, so it is the divine image of the rational immortal soul and bears a less pure substance. Yes, it has the desires and emotions relating to the nutrition of our body, but speaking of its responsibility for the necessary desires, we cannot define it as 'irrational'. Hence the terms (rational, unregulated, immortal, mortal) that Plato and Proclus utilised to describe the two parts of the individual souls should not be understood as contradictions, rather they manifest their differences in respect of substance, dynamis, and activity.

Considering the current issue, let us firstly read the contexts involving the generation of this soul-form:

> [1] In so far as it is fitting that something in them should share the name of the immortals, being called divine and ruling over those among them who at any time are willing to follow after righteousness and after you – that part, having sown it as seed and made a beginning, I will hand over to you. For the rest, do you, weaving mortal to immortal, make living beings; bring them to birth, feed them, and cause them to grow; and when they fail, receive them back again (*Tim.* 41c5–d3).
>
> [2] After this sowing he [sc. the Demiurge] left it to the newly made gods to mould mortal bodies, to fashion all that part of a human soul that there was still need to add and all that these things entail, and to govern and guide the mortal creature as noble and good as they are able, save in so far as it should be a cause of evil to itself (*Tim.* 42d5–e4, with reversion).
>
> [3] They [sc. the young gods], imitating him [sc. the Demiurge], when they had taken over an immortal principle of soul, went on to fashion for it a mortal body englobing it round about. For a vehicle they gave it the body as a whole, and therein they built on another form of soul, the mortal, having in itself dread and necessary affections (*Tim.* 69c5–d1).

From these three passages we can conclude that the young gods, who are created by the Demiurge himself, are the establisher of the mortal souls: in text [1] the Demiurge tells them that the immortal human souls are 'made equal to' (ἰσάζοιτ' ἄν, *Tim.* 41c2) the young gods,[216] and credited with the nature to 'share the names of the immortals' (ἀθανάτοις ὁμώνυμο νεῖναι πρόσήκει, *Tim.* 41c6),[217] and he sows them as seeds on the stars, where the young gods dwell. But this is only the beginning of the sowing-work, now he hands the creation-task over to the young gods, whose duty is to weave mortal to immortal (ἀθανάτῳ θνητὸν προσυφαίνοντες, 41d1–2), begetting the living beings like human and animal, giving them food, and receiving their souls back after their death. Evidently these are the particular tasks relating mainly to the mortal lives: not only the creation of the mortal souls and bodies, but also the 'weaving' of them to the immortal souls, through which the generation of the mortal living creatures will be accomplished, and their fate of living, death and re-incarnation will begin – this is also what the Demiurge assigns to them in text [2], where they are told to use their dynamis to govern the mortal creatures as noble and good as possible. Remarkably, in the second passage they are commanded to "fashion all that part of a human soul that there was still need to

---

[216] The present optative form ἰσάζοιτ' ἄν indicates that the divine human soul is advancing towards equality, not already achieve it. See Proclus, *In Tim.* III 225, 13–25. Cf. Tarrant (2017) 106n240. This is the reason why Plato repeatedly expresses that the love of wisdom of the soul is akin to the divine and immortal and what always exists, see *Rep.* 611e1–3. Cf. 490b4, 518e2–3, etc.

[217] Calcidius (*In Tim.* §§ 139–140) attributes the names of 'immortal' and 'divine' to rationality (ratio), the names of 'mortal' and 'woven together' to defective things like irascibility (iram), pleasure (voluptas) and desire (libidinis), so (§ 140) it is the mixture of the latter things make the human soul less pure than the world soul.

add and all that these things entail",²¹⁸ which hints at the generation of the mortal soul-form, and what it needs – according to Proclus and the other Neoplatonists – a vehicle, for just like the immortal soul-form has an everlasting vehicle that is formed by the Demiurge, the mortal soul-form should also possess a vehicle so that it can descend into the material body and be unified with it. This point is manifested in text [3], where the young gods, having taken over the immortal soul from the Demiurge, fashion the whole body as the (third) vehicle of and 'built on' (προσῳκοδόμουν, 69c8) the other form of the human soul, i.e., the mortal one. The way the young gods take to mould the mortal soul-form is by imitating the Demiurge their Father, for they are entitled 'the imitators' (οἱ δὲ μιμούμενοι, 69c5). And as imitators they should mould both the mortal souls and their pneuma-vehicles, just as the Demiurge establishes both the immortal souls and their ethereal vehicles.

Moreover, given that they are immortal and divine imitators differentiating themselves from the human imitators – for example, the painter and poet (*Republic* 601d1–602b12) who are culpable for their unregulated imitation – their divine imitation should also participate in the divinity and immortality, in which sense the young gods can "govern and guide the mortal creature to the best of their powers, save in so far as it should be a cause of evil to itself" (42e2–4). The mortal soul's taking part in the immortality can be substantiated by its preservation after departing from the mortal shell-like body, which is revealed in the myths of *Phaedo* 111c–114b and *Republic* 615a–616a.²¹⁹ Here is an overview of the myth of Er in the latter dialogue: after decoupling from the body Er's soul travels with many others to 'a determinate daimonic place' (τόπον τινὰ δαιμόνιον, 614c2), where there are four openings, two of them in the heaven, the others in the earth, and there are judges seating in the middle, before whom all souls will be sentenced. Er's soul, however, is ordered by the judges to be a messenger to human beings by reporting what is taking place there, so his soul is obligated to 'listen to and observe everything in that place' (ἀκούειν τε καὶ θεᾶσθαι πάντα τὰ ἐν τῷ τόπῳ, 614d4). What it sees (ὁρᾶν, 614d4) and hears is as follow: while some souls are being sentenced and going either in the heaven or in the earth through the openings, from other openings some others, after a long journey, coming down or up to that place again. They exchange their experiences during their travel in the heaven or earth. The souls from the heaven telling the souls from the earth about the unconvincing beauty of 'the experiences and the sights (εὐπαθείας [...] καὶ θέας, 615a3) there, while the latter weeping and lamenting, as they recall (ἀναμιμνησκομένας, 615a1) how much and what sort of things

---

²¹⁸ *Tim.* 42d7–e2: ὅσον ἔτι ἦν ψυχῆς ἀνθρωπίνης δέον προσγενέσθαι τοῦτο καὶ πάνθ᾽ ὅσα ἀκόλουθα ἐκείνοις ἀπεργασαμένους ἄρχειν. Fronterotta (2015) 52 asserts that what the young gods add is nothing but the mortal body, thus he denies the independent existence of the mortal soul by regarding the 'thymos-formed' (θυμοειδές) and the appetitive (ἐπιθυμητικόν) part as two mortal functions of the human soul which are the bodily dynameis 'in its interaction with the immortal soul' (p. 55). He acknowledges that this is a view deviating from the normal interpretation (p. 54n22), yet this is a misunderstanding, for the two mortal forms are independent parts of the mortal soul-form, which has its own generation in comparison with the human body.

²¹⁹ See Proclus, *In Tim.* III 235, 10–21; 238, 10–13; etc. In addition, Tarrant (2017) 118n287 also mentions the myth of *Gorg.* 523a–524a.

– including many 'fears' (φόβων, 616a4) – they 'had suffered and seen' (πάθοιεν καὶ ἴδοιεν, 615a1) on their journey. After seven days all these souls leave there and begin with a new journey until they arrive at a place where they can see (καθοπᾶν, 615b5) the spindle of Necessity (Ἀνάγκης ἄτρακτον, 616c5), below which these souls are asked to choose their new lives from the paradigms (τὰ τῶν βίων παραδείγματα, 618a1). Er's soul sees (ἰδεῖν, 619e7, 620a2, a3, a7, c1, c2) many different choices that are made by the souls according to their memory, perception, and their strength in philosophy.[220] After all souls have chosen their new lives, they receive the touch (ἐφαψάμενον, 620e4) of the goddess Clotho and go to the plain of Lethe, where they have to drink (πιεῖν, 621a7) a certain measure of water from the river of Forgetfulness and lodge there for the night, in which they are carried to their new birth. From this myth we can derive that if the mortal souls (and the pneumatic vehicles) perish immediately after their separation from the shell-like body, the various desires and emotions pertaining originally to them would not preserve, and the punishment of the souls would be nonsense, so no doubt that the mortal soul shares the immortality of the immortal soul and the gods, although it exists not eternally.[221]

After determining that the mortal souls and their vehicles are created by the young gods through imitating the Demiurge, and the mortal souls lasts for a longer time than the earthly body due to its substance as divine imitation of the immortal soul, we shall turn to the so-called pneumatic vehicle, which should be a subtle body in which the cognitive activities and appetitive desires of the mortal soul take place. Firstly, it is requisite to re-assert the necessity of such a vehicle, for (1) the establishment of this vehicle denotes the fulfilment of the divine imitation of the young gods: As the immortal soul rides on its luminous vehicle, the mortal soul as an imitation should also drive its own vehicle. Given that the mortal soul survives the death of the earthly body, there bound to be another vehicle for the mortal soul.

(2) Only with this vehicle the descent into the earthly body is possible. At *Tim.* 42c4–d2 Plato speaks of the purification and ascent of the human soul: "it should not prematurely find release from its transformations and labours, but only when, by following the circuit of the Same and alike within him and after vanquishing through reason the troublesome mass (τὸν πολὺν ὄχλον) that had afterwards adhered (προσψύντα) to him of fire, water, air and earth, confusing and unregulated (θορυβώδη καὶ ἄλογον), it has arrived at the form of its first and best condition".[222] By stressing that only with the circuit of Same the human soul can overcome the 'troublesome mass' and recover its best form Plato implies that the things relating not naturally to this circuit, rather to the circle of Difference, should be vanquished and purified,[223] because the latter is entitled 'the generating-circuit' (τὸν γενεσιουργὸν περιάγει κύκλον, Proclus, *In Tim.* III 296, 22), which brings the soul to generation in an individual life. From the best condition, i.e., the universal, divine and immortal life to the contrary individual, mortal and divisible life with the shell-like body, there must be an intermediate life, like in the establishment of the world body between the opposite fire and earth there should

---

[220] *Rep.* 620b3–4 (μεμνημένην), c5 (μνήμη), 619d1 (φιλοσοφίας) and e1 (φιλοσοφοῖ).
[221] For a summary of the mortality to the mortal soul, see Opsomer (2006b) 161–166.
[222] Translation taken from Tarrant (2017), with slight revision.
[223] See Proclus, *In Tim.* III 296, 7–297, 21.

be intermediate elements air and water. Here the intermediate life involves the mortal soul and its vehicle,[224] for through its being mounted in the middle vehicle the immortal soul is made 'a citizen of generation' (γενέσεως πολῖτις, III 297, 3). Therefore even before the immortal soul is embodied into the earthly body, there is already a second vehicle which is established not from ether, rather from the simple elements which are entitled here the 'troublesome mass', because unlike the immortal vehicle they are materials,[225] and this 'simple and enmattered' (ἁπλοῦν καὶ ἔνυλον, III 285, 13–14) vehicle is 'adhered' to the immortal soul for its descending into the generation-heading life, from which it falls further into the shell-like body and dwells on earth, beginning there its mortal, earthly life – as Proclus annotates, this 'troublesome mass' is so 'confusing and unregulated' that the vehicle built from it is 'made from a variety of garments and weighs the soul down'.[226] So for the sake of the descent to the individual life on earth there must be an intermediate life which is impossible without a middle vehicle – while in order to ascend, the human soul must be released from the cycle of incarnation, and to achieve this goal it should overcome the adherence of the second vehicle and this intermediate life with the help of the circuit of the Same.[227]

---

[224] Proclus, *In Tim.* III 298, 2–299, 9.

[225] In *Elements of Theology*, §§ 207–208 Proclus argues that the first vehicle is created by the demiurgic Intellect and hence it is essentially immaterial, indestructible, and impassive. Cf. Finamore and Kutash (2017) 133.

[226] Proclus, *In Tim.* III 298, 1–2: ἐκ παντοδαπῶν δὲ χιτώνων συγκείμενον, βαρύνοντα δὲ τὰς ψυχάς. Tr. Tarrant (2017).

[227] We must bear in mind that what Plato describes in this passage concerns the whole matter of embodiment, hence, in the view of the purgation, all things – expect for the intellect and the circle of Same – seem to subject to the generation of a mortal life, in which sense they should be overcome. However, Plato does not assert that the circuit of Difference, the mortal soul, and even the pneuma-vehicle should be strictly treated as 'confusing and unregulated', rather, such a character is particularly ascribed to the things 'of fire, water, air and earth', namely the material things adhered to the immortal soul after it is moulded. That's why Plato mentions only the mortal bodies (*Tim.* 42d6–7: σώματα πλάττειν θνητά). Hence, it is requisite to stress the role of the circuit of Same in the purification of the human soul, for what makes the purification necessary and what contradicts this process is naturally unregulated. Yet regarding the circle of Difference, the mortal soul, and the second vehicle we should not assert that they are not valuable at all, rather, proceeding from the divine origins, i.e., the Demiurge and the young gods, they also bear determinate substances, through which they hold certain dynamis that enables them to recognise proper objects and move both themselves and the others. Therefore to achieve the purgation of our souls, these faculties should be ordered to perform their competence in an appropriate way, for as a human being, he has the capacity of perception immediately after birth, which reports to him the external sensible qualities and arouses plenty of pleasures and pains, all these affections are even more powerful than the affection of nutrition, so justifying and correcting all kinds of sensation involving the mortal soul constitutes the very beginning of the process of purification. In fact, both Plato and Proclus do not rule this aspect out, for what they emphasise is always that the ascent to immortal life demands the releasing from the unregulated materials which are naturally not immortal: that is, a division of the immortality from mortality, and the intermediate is the mortal soul and its vehicle.

Now let us take an historical overview of the vehicle theory: Indeed there is already a notion of 'inborn' (σύμφυτος)[228] pneuma involving perception[229] in Aristotle, and this explains perhaps why the second vehicle is entitled 'pneumatic' by Proclus.[230] Yet this theory is officially found in the Neoplatonism: it is established by the Neoplatonists like Porphyry and Iamblichus, and maintained and developed by almost all Neoplatonists like Themistius, Syrianus, Hermias, Philoponus, Damascius, Priscian and Simplicius, while Proclus the pupil of Syrianus is viewed as the one who systematises the whole vehicle theory. Except for the Platonists the first person who talks about the soul-vehicle is Galen.[231] Despite this strong tradition in the Platonism some modern scholars argue that the necessity and possibility of the pneumatic vehicle still needs to be granted, for example Siorvanes lists three reasons to justify it: the pneumatic vehicle exists in the fleshy body and participates in the cognition-activities, feelings, and desires, which can be ascribed to the 'common sensorium' in Aristotle (*De an.* 3.1, *On Sleep* 2); although some bodily parts like hair and nails continue to grow after death, our heart and other decisive organs cease to work, so the essence of vitality is located not in the material body, rather the pneuma; the third argument – it appears already in the Proclean *Timaeus*-commentary – concerns the state of the soul after death: the soul must possess a 'body' in the Hades to receive the rewards or punishments.[232]

One interesting question is whether the term 'pneuma' roots in Plato's own works. No wonder that one cannot find a location where this word is applied to describe the soul-vehicle, for it denotes either wind or a kind of wind or breath.[233] Moreover, in the *Timaeus* Plato mentions only the immortal vehicle (41e2: ὡς ἐς ὄχημα) and the third vehicle, i.e., the shell-like body (69c6–7: ὄχημά τε πᾶν τὸ σῶμα; cf. 44e2). However, in determinate cases this term does relate to body and soul, thus also to perception, just like the 'inborn' pneuma in Aristotle: for instance in the *Laws* there is a location where pneuma (in the sense of 'wind') concerns the negative effect on the soul;[234] in *Philebus*

---

[228] This Aristotelian term σύμφυτος is taken by Proclus to describe the vehicle, see for example *El. Theol.* §§ 209–210. Cf. Siorvanes (1996) 131.

[229] For Aristotle this inborn pneuma exists in all living creatures, it has the seat in the heart and functions as a sender of the sense-affections from heart to the brain. Cf. Oser-Grote (2005), 468.

[230] While Tarrant (2017) 190n542 argues that the question 'why the second vehicle is called pneumatic' is unclear.

[231] Cf. Siorvanes (1996) 131–132; Blumenthal (1996) 28–29, 84–85, 98, 112–113, 125–126; (1997) 284. Siorvanes (1996) 131n27 enumerates the studies of vehicle in Neoplatonists, esp. Dodds (²1963), 313–321; Finamore (1985), and Blumenthal (1992). Lautner (2002) 266n34 gives more literature. The newest studies on the vehicle-theory are made by Opsomer (2006b); Kutash (2011) 196–205; Griffin (2012), and Dillon (2013).

[232] Siorvanes (1996) 132.

[233] For the meaning of wind and a determinate sort of wind, see *Crat.* 410b3: πνεῦμα ἐξ αὐτοῦ γίγνεται ῥέοντος. Cf. *Rep.* 394d8, 488d6, 496d7; *Phaedr.* 255c4; *Tim.* 49c2, 77a1; *Laws*, 845d6, 865c1. For 'breathing' see *Tim.* 66e7, 79b2, 84d2, 91c6–7.

[234] *Laws* 747d6: διὰ πνεύματα παντοῖα [...] ταῖς δὲ ψυχαῖς οὐχ ἧττον δυναμένην πάντα τὰ τοιαῦτα ἐμποιεῖν. Cf. 797d11 (the change in the wind and the possible harmful influence on body and soul).

47a6–9, pneuma (as 'breath') is said to be changed because of our bodily pleasure;[235] in the *Phaedo* two times this term is used to describe the separation of our soul from the material body on the occasion of death:[236] according to the context of *Phaedo* 70a4–6, death takes place when the soul leaves the body 'as' (ὥσπερ) a pneuma – a similar formulation is applied in *Tim.* 41e2: 'ὡς ἐς ὄχημα'.

To sum up, in Plato one can already discover that the individual life in the shell-like body (vehicle) relates decisively to the pneuma, for one of its fundamental meanings is 'breath', and considering that the death is clarified as the departing of the soul from the body as a pneuma, we can understand why in Proclus the pneuma is explained as something that weighs the soul down to the earthly body.

Moreover, during the soul's dwelling in the earthly body the pneuma functions as the faculty of perception, as displayed by the case in the *Philebus*, and a change of pneuma can arouse effect on the body as well as on the soul, as revealed in the *Laws* – through this examination we can also conjecture that such a pneuma is composed of four elements, for it can be aroused by the bodily pleasure and affect the body and soul. To achieve Proclus' theory of the second vehicle one still has a long way to go, but according to this account we can find at least a trace of such a theory in Plato.[237]

Going back to the mortal soul, we should not forget that there are two further parts in it: one part is responsible for the feelings like anger, courage, rage, honour, shame, and so on, and is thus entitled 'thymos-formed' (θυμοειδές),[238] the other relates inherently to all kinds of bodily desires and appetites, hence it is named 'appetitive' (ἐπιθυμητικόν).[239] Although the mortal souls are moulded 'as perfect as possible' (ὡς ἄριστον, 71d7), they are established not from the same ingredients of the immortal souls. Moreover, these two parts also own different nature: the superior one of them is assistant of the divine soul-form (*Tim.* 70a5, d6), for it is (merely) able to obey the logos of

---

[235] *Phileb.* 47a6–9: τὸ δ' αὖ τῆς ἡδονῆς πολὺ πλέον ἐγκεχυμένον συντείνει τε καὶ ἐνίοτε πηδᾶν ποιεῖ [...] παντοῖα δὲ πνεύματα ἀπεργαζόμενον. For the motif 'bodily pleasure' in the *Philebus*, see Frede (1997) 277–279.

[236] See *Phaed.* 70a4–6: εὐθὺς ἀπαλλαττομένη τοῦ σώματος καὶ ἐκβαίνουσα, ὥσπερ πνεῦμα ἢ καπνὸς διασκεδασθεῖσα. Cf. 77e2.

[237] Strikingly, at Ps.-Plato's *Axiochus* 370c4–6 the author asserts that in the soul there is divine pneuma (θεῖον πνεῦμα), through which one attains comprehension and cognition: εἰ μή τι θεῖον ὄντως ἐνῆν πνεῦμα τῇ ψυχῇ, δι' οὗ τὴν τῶν τηλικῶνδε περίονοιαν καὶ γνῶσιν ἔσχεν. For this 'divine pneuma', see Männlein-Robert (2012) 55n93.

[238] There is no proper word in the modern western languages to translate the Platonic term θυμοειδές or θυμός, at *Tim.* 70a2 we are told that the θυμός relates to 'a manly spirit and ambitious of victory', and in *Rep.* 439e6f, the well-known Leontius-example reveals that it involves also anger and shame, so I translate the θυμοειδές into 'thymos-formed'. For the studies about this notion in Plato, see for example Büttner (2000) 26–37; (2006) 86–88; Schmitt (2012) 278, 299–302; (2015) 313–316.

[239] Epistemologically, the thymos-formed part possesses according to Proclus remembrance (superior form of phantasia), while the other has perception (inferior form of phantasia). Cf. Lauter (2006) 128–130; Opsomer (2006b) 143–144. For Proclus, the mortal soul and the mortal life has no ability of opinion, the lowest level of rational life, rather only perception and phantasia. For the Proclean doctrine of opinion and phantasia, see Lautner (2002) 257–269.

the highest part by recognising its message through opinion. The inferior appetitive part, however, is called 'the baser part' (τὸ φαῦλον, 71d8), sharing not in logos and reason (λόγου καὶ φρονήσεως, 71d4–5), driving itself (and through which the whole soul) easily to a wrong direction (70b6).[240]

After this investigation we can describe the generation of the human soul with the five Proclean aspects (substantial existence, harmony, form, dynamis, and activity) that are utilised to interpret the establishment of the world soul: (1) The essential existence of the immortal soul-form is similar to that of the world soul, for both this human soul-form and its heavenly vehicle are created by the Demiurge, and after the establishment the immortal soul-form lives a divine life on the heavenly stars. However, in contrast with the world soul or the souls of the astral gods the immortal soul-form is less pure – partially due to its order in the generation of all kinds of souls and the way of its constitution, and according to this distinguished substantial existence it will descend into a fated temporal life in the earthly body.[241] The mortal soul-form and its pneuma-vehicle, being established by the young gods by way of imitating the Demiurge their father, are images of the immortal soul-form and its heavenly vehicle. Because this pneumatic vehicle consists of simple material elements, it enables the intermediate life by weighing the immortal soul down from the divine life. This mortal soul and its vehicle, however, as imitations of the demiurgic work, perish not immediately after the shell-like body is exhausted, for only in this way the rewards and punishments after death are possible. (2) Considering that the immortal soul-form is fashioned in the similar manner as the world soul, it must be divided and re-combined according to the same harmony, as Timaeus declares at 43d5–7: "the intervals of the double and the triple; three of each sort, and the connecting means of the ratios, 3/2 and 4/3 and 9/8". The mortal form of the human soul also shares the harmony of the world soul, albeit merely in a necessary degree, so that it can be held in agreement with the divine soul-form. (3) In the divine soul-form there exist two circles, similarly to the world soul. The difference is that these two circular movements can be easily interrupted by the corporal affections like nourishment and sensation initiated by the mortal soul-form, which hardly bear these two circular movements, for as the imitation of the immortal form though, the mortal part does not have the ability of discursive thinking and intellect, and its pneumatic vehicle is the location where the sensation and remembrance take place – that is to say, the mortal soul-form is essentially distinct from the immortal soul-form, thus its activities can disturb the movements of the immortal soul part. (4) The immortal human soul has the similar twofold-dynamis as the world soul: it participates in intellect, discursive thinking, right opinion and belief,[242] and its self-motion initiates the generation of life, whereas the mortal form bears sense perception and remembrance, which enables it to discern the sensible qualities and move the earthly body.[243] (5) In addition to the

---

[240] Due to this essential difference of the mortal and immortal soul-forms, Timaeus points out two different desires at *Tim.* 88a8–b2: the former desires nourishment, while the latter desires reason (φρονήσις).

[241] *Tim.* 41e6: ὄργανα χρόνων. Cf. Proclus, *El. Theol.* § 192.

[242] Cf. Cornford (1937) 142.

[243] The opinion that all physical bodies are the organs of the soul is asserted by Aristotle at *De an*, 415b18–19.

activities of cognition and motion, the human soul-forms subject to a peculiar activity due to the fated laws, i.e., the descent and ascent, for the pneumatic vehicle and the mortal soul-from initiate the process of descent by weighing the immortal soul down into the earthly body, and after the death of the earthly individual body they enable the reincarnation; while the ascent and purgation of the immortal soul is contained in overcoming their influence and releasing from the cycle of (mortal) generation.

1.2.2.2 The generation of the human body

The whole earthly body is asserted to be the third vehicle of the human soul, being established from a multitude of elements it is 'combined and enmattered' (σύνθετον καὶ ἔνυλον, Proclus, *In Tim*. III 285, 14). On the generation of the human body, it is also appropriate to resort to the five-aspects-model, although Proclus does not utilise this model to clarify this issue:

(1) The substantial existence of the human body (*Tim*. 42e8–43a1). The physical body is sensible and material, and all sensible materials are composed of the four elements in the χώρα. In this respect the young gods borrow a multitude of four elements from the world and fashion the human body by imitating their Father. Being borrowed these four elements must be repaid, i.e., they cannot be always held within the human body, thus this kind of body is mortal. As a perishable body it is the third vehicle of the human soul, and its ensoulment is the inception of the individual life, which is also perishable.

(2) The limited harmony of the body (*Tim*. 43a1–5). The young gods, having borrowed the elements from the world, glue all these elements together into one unity, not with the insoluble bonds, as in the case of the world body, rather by welding them with many rivets which are invisible because of their smallness. This indicates that the harmony of the human body is much less than that of the world body, the bodies of the fixed stars, and planets, and even the other two vehicles of the human soul. Such a tiny harmony (a) can hold the body as the substrate and vehicle of the unified human soul (namely both its immortal and mortal part), but it maintains the body merely in a certain period, (b) cannot always keep the body naturally in harmony with the human soul, for occasionally the bodily affections originating from outside and inside are able to assail and disturb the divine circular motion of the soul and thus bring forth disorder and chaos.

(3) The form and shape of the human body (*Tim*. 44d3–45b2). According to the Platonic Timaeus, the human, seen from outside, possesses a head and a body with four limbs. The head is created as an imitation of the whole universe which has a round shape (44d3–4). To serve the head the gods send it the complete body with four limbs, for the head possesses all movements and with its body it can travel to every region and in every direction. Moreover, considering that the front is more honourable than the back, the most movements bestowed to the head are in this direction; in order that the head can distinguish the front from the back, they set face on its front side and join organs into the face for all providence (προνοίᾳ, 45b1) of the soul.

(4) Analogical to the world body the human body is the vehicle of the human soul, but unlike the world body, the human body is not self-sufficient. It is equipped with limbs and other organs in order to maintain its existence and growth,[244] this is why Plato attributes the nature of 'in-flowing and out-flowing' (ἐπίρρυτον σῶμα καὶ ἀπόρρυτον, 43a6) to it, which, however, is not aroused by the body itself, rather by the incarnation of the mortal soul-form, for as mentioned above, although our hair and nails keep growing after the death, the heart and other organs cease to work.[245] Given that the constitution-ingredients of the human body should be paid back, the earthly body must decay and perish, which implies that its dynamis can be held only in a certain period.

(5) The bodily activity is the actuality of its dynamis, namely, to be servant of the soul and to keep living. Being created as the vehicle of the mortal human soul, the activity of the earthly body is factually the actuality of the commands of the (mortal) soul. For this sake the human body, as said above, possesses sense-organs that are set by the gods. Besides, to hold the living life the body requires nutrition, thus there also exists the activity of nourishment. However, considering that the main activity of the earthly body should be attributed to its servant of the soul, this activity should be restricted to the necessary extent.

1.2.2.3 The combination of the human body and soul

There are three passages involving the implantation of the human soul into the earthly body: firstly in the demiurgic declaration of 'the fated laws' (νόμους τε τοὺς εἱμαρμένους, *Tim.* 41e2–3)[246] Plato describes the generation of sensation, desires, and emotions due to the necessary embodiment of the immortal souls (42a3–b2); then the passage at 43a5–44d2 involves the implantation of the immortal soul (τῆς ἀθανάτου ψυχῆς, 43a5); lastly the context 69c5–72e1 depicts the incarnation of the mortal soul-form, which also mentions the becoming of perception, desires with pleasure and pain, and many kinds of emotions. The embodiment of the soul enables the beginning of the living human life, and the immortal and divine part should take care of the whole body, while the dynamis and activity of the mortal soul-form should be strictly limited in accordance with the fated laws.

---

[244] *Tim.* 43b5–6, 44b2. Cf. 70d7–8.

[245] So when the mortal body is engendered, the second vehicle, or the pneuma, must also be established, for although they do have distinctions – the pneuma-vehicle is simple, whereas the earthly body is complex; the pneuma-life educates and even dominates the bodily mixtures, the life in the complex body is bound with the mixture in the body (Proclus, *In Tim.* III 285, 8–12) – nevertheless, both of them are enmattered, being established from all four elements (*Tim.* 42c6–d1, 42e8–43a1), and belonging to the mortal soul. More decisively, without the mortal soul and the pneuma-vehicle the body would not be maintained.

[246] Cornford (1937) 143n1 mentions *Laws* 904c5–8, where Plato asserts that everything sharing the soul can change itself, and such a change is 'in accordance with the order and law of Fate'. For the discussion about the fated laws, see Calcidius, *In Tim.* §§ 142–190. Cf. Boeft (1970); O'Brien (2020) 211–242. Proclus (*In Tim.* III 275, 5–23) suggests that the fated laws are placed by the Demiurge in the immortal souls, for it is according to these laws they take part in governing the universe, moving themselves, doing things right or wrong in their choice, etc.

(1) The general description of the incarnation is firstly revealed in the words of the Demiurge, who shows the immortal souls the nature of the universe and the laws of Fate:

> Whensoever, therefore, they should of necessity have been implanted in bodies, and of their bodies some part should always be coming in and some part passing out, at first, it was necessary that they all have sensation, the one and same for all, arising from violent affections; secondly, love (ἔρωτα) blended with pleasure and pain, and besides these fear (φόβον) and thymos (θυμὸν) and all feelings that accompany these and all that are of a contrary nature (42a3–b2. Tr. Cornford, slightly revised).

These divine immortal souls, after being moulded and mounted in their vehicles by the Demiurge, circling around (περιόδους, 43a5) in the heaven with their heavenly vehicles, helping the gods managing the whole universe.[247] However, due to 'a necessity' (ἐξ ἀνάγκης, 42a3)[248] they must be implanted in the bodies. The term 'necessity' indicates that this sort of embodiment is essentially distinct from that of the world soul and the astral gods' souls, for this sowing is indeed a type that involves the perishable body and leads to a mortal life, which corresponds immanently to the inferior purity of the individual souls themselves; and this necessity, namely living in a mortal life, is a part of the fated laws, while the world soul and the young gods' souls govern the mortal creatures with these laws.[249] Hence the incarnation results necessarily from the souls themselves that are fated to descend, and is realised by the young gods who join the human body and soul into a unity.[250]

The consequences of this embodiment are: (a) The becoming of the human being as a living creature. The soul and the body are originally two separate entities. The young gods, whose task is to finish the rest creation-work in which their Father engages, implant the soul in the earthly body and weave them into a unity, initiating the generation of the human being as an encosmic citizen on the earth. (b) The generation of sensation, love mixed with pleasure and pain, and the feelings such as fear and anger and their companies and all that are contrary to them.[251] Before the implantation the divine soul circles around in the heaven with its first vehicle, subjecting to no influence of the perishable body (vehicle). And the human body, as an other-moved entity, possesses the potentiality of being affected by the external movements (43c1–4) and then moving the others, yet has no chance to move the soul before the combination. After the implantation, however, the forcible affections (ἐκ βιαίων παθημάτων, 42a5–6) can pass through the bodily organs, 'assail' (προσπίπτοιεν, 43c6) and 'shake' (σείουσαι,

---

[247] Proclus, *In Tim.* III 284, 16–21. Cf. the myth about souls and their wings at *Phaedrus* 246a3–249d3.
[248] Cf. *Tim.* 69d5: ἀναγκαίως. At *Phaed.* 95d1–2 Plato describes this incarnation 'like disease' (ὥσπερ νόσος).
[249] Cf. Proclus, *In Tim.* III 285, 16–21 and Cornford (1937) 146–147.
[250] *Ibid.* 284, 23–27: ἡ τῆς θνητῆς ζωῆς συνάρτησις, ὑφισταμένη παρά τε αὐτῶν τῶν ψυχῶν […] καὶ παρὰ τῶν νέων θεῶν.
[251] *Tim.* 42a3–b2. Cf. 44a5–8. For the generation of the affections of sensation, pleasure and pain, see 64a2–65b4.

43d2)[252] the soul, and the latter will discriminate and comprehend these affections, which results in the generation of sensation, love mixed with pleasure and pain – which indicates the complete life of desire, for love is the most violent affection of this life[253] – and the feelings such as anger and fear.[254]

Remarkably, what involves in this passage is not merely the immortal soul as well as its simple and un-enmattered vehicle, rather the whole unified human soul with its vehicles. This context is a statement made by the Demiurge, who prefers to show the just moulded immortal souls the laws of Fate – their descent to the earthly bodies, re-incarnation, and purification – and place these laws in them, in this view this generation seems to concern primarily the immortal souls. However, in the preceding demiurgic announcement given to the young gods (*Tim.* 41a7–d3) the Demiurge declares to hand the rest generation-work of human beings over to them – they are commanded to 'weave mortal onto immortal' (41d1–2), so before the immortal soul is embodied in the shell-like body, the mortal soul and its simple and enmattered pneuma-vehicle must be already created and be woven to the immortal soul, and the combined and enmattered shell-like body should also be established. That is to say, the immortal soul's implantation in the earthly body requires the supplement of the mortal soul with its corresponding vehicle and the creation of the mixed body, which manifests that at the point of generation what is implanted in the body is not only the immortal soul, rather the unified human soul with its immortal and mortal parts and their vehicles. Therefore, what described here is the general fated embodiment of the soul in the body and the generation of the living human being – the first generation of all human beings and the first generation of all sensation in the individual life, as Plato formulates, 'one and (the same) for all' (μία πᾶσιν, *Tim.* 41e4, 42a5) – therefore, this is the providence of the Demiurge.

Following this divine declaration Plato continues with the rest creation-work of the young gods and the specific realization of the immortal soul's embodiment: in the part of creation the young gods mould the mortal soul and its vehicle(s) by imitating their Father, albeit the ingredients that are used to form them are still less pure, consequently the mortal soul and its pneumatic vehicle are mortal, although they last longer than the earthly body due to their own purity. After the creation of the mortal part the created gods go on to fashion the organic body by borrowing the elements from the whole world and welding them together into one unity with 'a multitude of rivets' (πυκνοῖς γόμφοις, *Tim.* 43a4) which are too small to be visible.

We see that the creation-order of the soul-forms and their vehicles is firstly the immortal soul and the heavenly vehicle, then the mortal soul and the pneumatic vehicle, and lastly the earthly body, while the incarnation is performed in reverse order, i.e., the gods set the mortal part firstly in the body, making it in-flowing and out-flowing, then implant the immortal soul into the complex, enmattered, and mortal body. This real creation-order of the human being is opposite to that of the universe, for the latter proceeds from the intellect and soul to the body. The reason is rooted in the fact that the

---

[252] Cf. *Phileb.* 33d5: σεισμόν.
[253] Proclus, *In Tim.* III 287, 29–31: διὰ δὲ τοῦ ἔρωτος τὴν σύμπασαν ζωὴν τῆς ἐπιθυμίας ἐχαρακτήρισε, διότι σφοδράτατόν ἐστι τοῦτο περὶ αὐτὴν τὸ πάθος.
[254] For a more detailed analysis of the generation of this perception, see section 2.1.

generation of the perishable animals is within time,[255] and according to Proclus, "everything arising over time begins from an incomplete point of generation".[256] Moreover, in the case of the mortal lives 'the many' are generated before 'the one', for the many elements are firstly borrowed and welded together into a whole body, then thanks to the bodily need of food and drink involving sensation and appetites, it has an 'in-flowing' and 'out-flowing' nature, which reveals the embodiment of the mortal soul, at last the gods bound the circuits of the immortal soul into this mortal body (*Tim.* 43a5–6), completing the connection of the immortal soul and body.[257]

This whole process manifests the clear distinction of the three kinds of combination of soul and body: the Demiurge 'mounted' (ἐμβιβάσας, *Tim.* 41e1) the divine soul in the first vehicle, the young gods created and 'wove' (προσυφαίνοντες, 41d2) the mortal soul to the immortal soul, and the second vehicle is 'adhered' to the immortal soul, while they 'bound' (ἐνέδουν, 43a5–6) the circuits of the divine soul into the body. Hence, although the narrative order of the embodiment begins from the immortal soul to the mortal soul – namely at first the implantation of the immortal soul (*Tim.* 43a5–44d2), the becoming of the bodily organ of the immortal soul, i.e., the head (44d2f.), then the incarnation of the mortal soul: the whole mortal soul is set in the body, which results in the generation of the three faculties perception, desire and emotional feeling (69c5–d6), and the embodiment of the thymos-formed part (69e5f.) and appetitive part (70d7f.) – the factual becoming order is reversed, i.e., firstly the establishment of the mortal body, then that of the mortal soul, finally the immortal soul.

(2) The embodiment of the immortal soul (43a5–44d2). In this passage we are told that after the implantation of the divine soul-form into the body, i.e., after the birth of every human being, neither the immortal soul nor the material body can control the other, rather 'with force' (βίᾳ, *Tim.* 43a7) they are moved and move mutually, in this situation the whole life moves in all six directions without order or measure (43a7–b4). Contrasting with the other kinds of creatures such as the universe which rotates in the same place without these six movements, and the planets that have orbital revolution 'forwards' though, without the other five movements, the movements of an infant, seen from outside, possess only these six movements. In this period there are cases in which the circular soul-movements easily undergo the influence of the corporal affections like nourishment and perception, especially the latter, which is said to be the 'very frequent and strong' (πλείστην καὶ μεγίστην, 43c8) motion that can prevent and disrupt the movements of the soul, evoking its two revolutions temporarily inactive (43c7–e8). When the immortal soul-form engages in such a situation, it seems to be unregulated and without intellect.[258] Given that what Plato speaks of here is the immortal soul-form, and the revolutions of the world soul and the souls of fixed stars cannot be so severely dislocated by incarnation, it is reasonable to conclude that both the rotation and the

---

[255] *Tim.* 41e6: ὄργανα χρόνων. Cf. 42d5: ὄργανα χρόνου.
[256] Proclus, *In Tim.* III 322, 5–6: πᾶν δὲ τὸ κατὰ χρόνον γιγνόμενον ἐκ τοῦ ἀτελοῦς ἄρχεται τῆς γενέσεως. (Tr. Tarrant).
[257] For the Proclean discussion about the difference between the presentation of the mortal and immortal soul in the mortal body, and the creation of universe and that of the mortal creatures, see *Ibid.* III 321, 25–322, 17.
[258] *Tim.* 43e3: ἀλόγως. Cf. 44b1: ἄνους.

cognitive dynamis and activity of the human soul – due to its lack of purity on the one side, and the less harmoniously fashioned body on the other side – are destined to be affected and sometimes even interrupted by the perishable bodily movements, once it is implanted in the earthly body.[259] This can be exemplified by the fact that an infant sleeps quickly, when it is regularly shaken. Such a situation changes, when the current of growth and nutriment becomes weaker, and the soul revolutions recover their path and lead the whole life (44b2–8). When this trend of recovery is strengthened with 'a correct nourishment of education' (συνεπιλαμβάνηταί τις ὀρθὴ τροφὴ παιδεύσεως, 44b9 –c1), a person will be thoughtful and escape from the worst disease,[260] but if he fails in this matter, he will be 'imperfect and without understanding' (ἀτελὴς καὶ ἀνόητος, 44c3), and must go back to Hades after his death.

(3) The embodiment of the mortal soul-form includes two steps: (a) the implantation of the thymos-formed part in the breast and (b) that of the appetitive form in the belly. At *Timaeus* 69c5–72e1 Plato describes the implantation of 'the other form' (ἄλλο τε εἶδος, 69c7) of the human soul, i.e., the mortal parts called 'thymos-formed' (θυμοειδές) and 'appetitive form' (ἐπιθυμητικόν), and explains why they should be embodied in the organs that are separated from the head.[261] In accordance with the demiurgic announcement in 42a5–7, the incarnation of the mortal soul parts initiates the generation of perception, pleasure and pain, fear and anger and other kinds of feelings and emotions. Although all these faculties belong to the mortal soul, given that the perception is already handled at 42a5–6, 43c6–7, 44a5–8 and 64a6–c6, and the theme 'pleasure and pain', as 'common affections of the whole body' (64a2–3), is discussed at 64c6–65b4,[262] the emotions like anger and fear, which should be attributed to the thymos-formed part, and the desires like drink and eat, which can be explained with the appetitive part, are now left to be explained in detail.

---

[259] Calcidius (*In Tim.* §§ 206–207) annotates that for an infant the rational soul-form is still not firmly formed due to the irrational mental weakness and the excessive bodily affections, for this argument he resorts to *Laws* 666a3–8, where the kind are not allowed to drink wine until 18 years old. Proclus (*In Tim.* III 334, 28–336, 2.) – in my opinion not contradicting Calcidius, rather makes his argument clearer – stresses that what is disturbed and impeded by the sensation-affections is not the substance of the immortal soul, rather its dynamis and activity. For research of the Proclean position, see Steel (1978) 69–73. A concise historical investigation of the body-soul relation following the Platonic *Timaeus* can be found in Sorabji (2003) 152–162. For a discussion of the incarnation of the immortal soul, see also Carpenter (2008) esp. 44–47.

[260] At *Tim.* 86b1–87b9 Plato talks about the disease of the soul due to the excessive disordered bodily affections and the wrong education. In the aforesaid research of the term 'pneuma' we can find that Plato notices even the influence of climate on body and soul.

[261] The immortal soul is incarnated in the spherical head by the young gods (*Tim.* 44d3–5). Thanks to the immortal soul the head is the most divine bodily part. Although the divine soul is set in the head, its dynamis concerns the whole body, *vice versa*, the affections of the bodily parts can also affect the soul, this clarifies why the bodily affections can 'completely' (παντάπασιν, 43d3) hamper the revolution of the divine soul of an infant.

[262] Cf. Cornford (1937) 282.

Timaeus describes them with an interpretation-model of 'position–form (structure) – dynamis': (a) The incarnation of the thymos-formed part in the breast and the role of heart and lung (69d6–70d6). The gods, in fear of a possible pollution of the divine soul-part, prefer to implant the mortal parts not in the head, rather other proper places in the body. Hence, they establish firstly a neck to separate the head and the thorax, then set the mortal soul in the thorax. Given that naturally there is a better part and a worse part in the mortal soul, they divide the hollow of the thorax also into two rooms, implanting the nobler part which 'is of a manly spirit and ambitious of victory' (70a2) in the near of the head, between the diaphragm and the neck, so that it can hear the logos of the divine soul and help forcibly restraining the wrong desires that are generated from the appetitive part, which always prefer a resistance to the commands of the immortal part. This is realised through the organ of the thymos-formed part, i.e., the heart, for it is knot of the veins and origin of the blood moving round through the whole body, when the divine part discovers that some bodily parts are acting in a wrong way, it will send a message to the thymos-formed part. Receiving this message an anger will be aroused in the heart, and through the bloodstream this anger will be transported to those discordant parts, forcing them to be conscious of the commands and threats, and acknowledge the leadership of the divine soul (70b1–c1).[263] Furthermore, foreseeing (προγιγνώσκοντες, 70c3) that the rise of the anger, in the form of a swelling, is done by means of fire,[264] and results in a suffering from the heat, the gods implant the soft, bloodless and perforated lung around the heart like a buffer, and cut canals of the trachea to reach it, in order that it can breath and drink and in this manner cool off the heart. In virtue of this function the lung helps the thymos-formed part in serving the logos of the immortal soul (70c1–d6).

From this account we can derive that the thymos-formed part, being established and located in the breast by the young gods and behaving itself, for example, in the form of anger, is viewed as an assistant of the divine soul-form. To play such a roll it must be able to recognise the messages that are sent by the divine part, which implies that the thymos-formed part has a capacity of opinion that is based on the sense perception.[265]

(b) The implantation of the part of ἐπιθυμία in the belly and the dynamis of liver and spleen (70d7–72d4). This soul-part is the worse part of the mortal soul being responsible for food, drink, and the other bodily requirements, thus it is embodied between the midriff and the navel. Being 'like an untamed beast' (ὡς θρέμμα ἄγριον, 70e4) this part should be cautiously implanted so that there will be a proper order of all parts of soul. The gods are apparently conscious of this necessity, for locating it in the belly, this part

---

[263] For the opinion that anger is the boiling of blood and heat, see also Aristotle, *De an.* 403a30–b3.
[264] Cf. *Tim.* 68 b2 and 80e4, where Timaeus discusses the relation of fire and the blood-colour.
[265] For the relationship of thymos and opinion, see Büttner (2006) esp. 86–88; Schmitt (2012) 288–332. This argument seems to contradict the Proclean doctrine that the mortal soul-form has no dynamis of opinion, yet we should bear in mind that that after incarnation the mortal soul is unified with the immortal soul, being a part of the unified soul the thymos-formed part has the ability of opinion with perception, while for Proclus, before the embodiment the immortal soul-form has the opinion with logos, and the mortal soul-form bears no dynamis of opinion with perception.

is kept as far as possible from the divine soul-form, which enables the latter to take care of the whole body without being affected by the appetitive soul-part (70d7–71a3). The reason of its being like a wild animal rests on its lack of the cognition ability with which it could understand the logos of the divine part (71a3–4). Moreover, even if it can somehow perceive these logoi, it would take no heed of them (71a4–6). Instead, by day and night it would be fascinated by visible images and shadows (εἰδώλων καὶ φαντασμάτων, 71a6). Foreseeing this determinate nature of the appetitive part, the gods conceive a beneficial usage of it by forming the liver and implanting it in the belly. Being smooth and bright, the liver is like a mirror, for receiving the impressions originating from the intellect it can reflect visible images; possessing bitterness it is able to evokes fear in the appetitive part; having sweetness it enables the part of ἐπιθυμία to exercise divination in dreams, through which it can be attached to (προάπτοιτο, 71e1) the truth (71a3–72b5). In addition, for the sake of the liver the gods create and locate the spleen on its left side, which helps to maintain its brightness and cleanliness (72b6–d4).

To summarise: as divine creators of the mortal soul and body the young gods know the essence of body and soul,[266] thus they can foresee what happens when the implantation takes place. To make the human being possibly perfect and good, they conceive a suitable unification in which the soul-forms and bodily parts can harmoniously co-exist through the leadership of the divine immortal soul-form: the so-called θυμοειδές is incarnated in the breast, and its organ, the heart, can reach every bodily part through the flux of blood. When the divine part discovers disorders coming from outside or from the desires within the body, it informs the thymos, and the latter will boil with anger and spread this anger to every region of the body through the flux of blood, causing them to endure the commands from the divine soul-form. Because the boil of anger and the bloodstream are realised by the fire, the heart need be cooled down, which is done by the lung. The gods set the appetitive part in the belly, so that it is far away from the divine part. Given that it is unable to understand the logos of the immortal soul, they establish the liver for it and authorise the liver to reflect images of the logos, to calm down the ἐπιθυμία through its bitterness, and to enable this part to prophesy by virtue of its sweetness. Moreover, in order that the liver can keep bright and pure, the spleen is added to be its neighbouring organ.

Methodically the embodiment of the mortal soul-forms is described in terms of their positions, structures and dynameis. Remarkably these aspects are not depicted in the view of the modern physiology,[267] which indicates that the Darwinism and other modern natural science play no role here. The reason is, for Plato, to set the soul in body is to realise the divine target: a perfect generation[268] which ensures human beings' possible participation in the intellect. To achieve this purpose the bodily organs must be established to serve the soul: the breast and belly are divided so that the two mortal

---

[266] The creation-work are assigned to the young gods at *Tim.* 41d1–3. Considering that the laws of the Destiny (νόμους τοὺς εἰμαρμένους, 41e2–3) are showed to the immortal souls, the young gods must also know them.

[267] Such an opinion is held in many interpretations, for instance Cornford (1937) 282.

[268] *Tim.* 42e2–4, 71d5–7. In the *Phaed.* 96aff. Plato searches for the reason of generation, which begins with the material cause and ends with the intellect, this investigation coordinates with the description in the *Timaeus*.

parts can be separated from each other. The thymos-formed part is set in the near of the divine part, because naturally it is its assistant, while the appetitive part is implanted far from the immortal part, so that it cannot disturb the logos of the latter; the incarnation of the heart, lung, liver and spleen serves to enable the three parts to form an orderly unity, making the human being as similar as possible to his creators. And in the same manner (κατὰ ταὐτὰ, 72e1) the rest bodily parts are consecutively established.

1.2.3 Conclusion

In this chapter, I have discussed the generation of the human being, who is the main perception subject of the Platonic sense perception theory. The statement of this subject matter begins with a description of the four Platonic sensation subjects, viz. the universe, the fixed stars and planets, the human being, and at last the plants. Possessing the highest perceptual form 'joint-perception' (συναίσθησις), the first two kinds of perception are entitled 'unaffected and common'. The sensation of the human being, being 'common and affected', is deemed to be the second kind. The sensation of the plants is defined as 'divided and affected', for it is merely endorsed to discriminate whether the affection is pleasant or painful (1.2.1).

Being unable to perceive without affection, the human being requires a body to receive the external affections; being entitled 'common' the human perception must have a soul. In this view the account of the human generation in terms of perception subject falls into three parts: (1) the generation of the human soul (1.2.2.1). There are two forms, or two parts, of the human soul: the divine part is created by the Demiurge in the same way of establishing the world soul and the astral souls, thus it is a divine imitation of the latter two kinds of souls; the mortal part is established by the young gods by imitating their Father, hence it is an image of the immortal soul-form. The mortal soul-form has two further parts, i.e., the thymos-formed part and the appetitive part. Strikingly, according to Proclus, Plato attributes three vehicles to the human soul: the first heavenly vehicle is established from the fifth element, the ether, and it is created along with the divine soul-form, which means that it is also immortal and divine; the second pneumatic vehicle and the third shell-like vehicle belong to the mortal soul, which are all moulded by the young gods. Both unregulated vehicles are established from the four elements, but the former is simple, the latter is complex. Hence at *In Tim.* III 285, 12–16 Proclus declares that the soul-vehicles are threefold, and "either simple and not enmattered, or simple and enmattered, or combined and enmattered. And there are three lives, one divine, one lasts longer than the body, and the last perishes together with the body." (2) The becoming of the human body (1.2.2.2). The third vehicle is the mortal human body consisting of the four elements that are borrowed from the universe, and this body is bound with many invisible rivets by the young gods. Being borrowed from the world these elements must be paid back, which implies that the human body cannot be eternal; being unified not through the divine harmony, rather with small invisible rivets, the body is not fashioned into a harmonious form like the world body, which signifies its unsteadiness and discontinuity. Thus, the earthly body is mortal, and the individual life on earth perishes when this shell-like body is dead. (3) The combination of the human body and soul (1.2.2.3). Concerning the embodiment of the three soul-parts there are three passages in the *Timaeus*, i.e., 42a3–b2, 43a5–44b2 and 69c5–75e1. The first text focuses on the incarnation of the human soul in the body, and the whole quotation is part of the announcement of the fated laws made by the Demiurge. In this text we can see that the incarnation brings forth the generation of sensation, desire with pleasure and pain, and the feelings like anger and fear. The actual embodiment is realised by the young gods: they mould firstly the mortal body, determine its in-flowing and out-flowing nature by implanting the mortal soul as well as the pneumatic vehicle in the mortal body, then bound the immortal soul in the body. At this point we are taught that for the infant the dynamis and activity of the immortal soul are impeded due to the affections of nourishment and sensation, and its substance stays untouched. So, when the bodily affections are weaker, the circuits of the immortal soul recover their movements and bring the whole life back to order. For the embodiment of the thymos-formed part of our mortal soul the gods choose the breast to be its dwelling and the heart as its very organ, since on the one side it should be set in the near of the head in order that it can quickly receive the message from the divine part, on the other side the heart is unified with all bodily parts through the bloodstream, so that the aroused anger can be delivered to every part. Considering that the appetitive part should be implanted as distant as possible from the divine part – in case it disturbs the divine revolution – it is set in the belly. Foreseeing exactly the fact that, although this appetitive part can somehow perceive, it is unable to understand the logos of the immortal aspect, the young gods fashion a smooth, bright, and bitter liver to make this part submissive. Clearly, these organs are not described in the biological sense, rather in accordance with their dynameis, or their beneficial usage in moulding the three parts of soul in a harmony order and forming a possibly perfect and good human being, and it is in the same manner that the other corporal parts are established.

2 The generation of the affected and unaffected perception

After expounding the generation of the perceptible object, i.e., the whole universe, and that of the sensation subject, viz. the human being, especially his two soul-forms and three kinds of vehicles, logically and factually it is requisite to explore the generation of the human perception and its cognitive ability. Given the complexity of the subject matter this chapter will concentrate on the issue of generation, while the cognitive dynamis will be clarified in chapter 3.

Before we go into the details of the perception generation, we should firstly throw light on the different types of sense perception, since it is very possible that not every kind of perception has the same origin and comes to be in the same way. Indeed, according to our research in section 1.2, there exist three kinds of human perception, with Proclean terms they are the common and unaffected sensation of the immortal vehicle (soul), the common and affected perception in the pneumatic vehicle (the unregulated soul), and the divided and affected sensation in the ensouled shell-like body.[269] In Aristotle the perception is also tripartite:[270] the first two are the perception 'according to themselves' (καθ' αὐτά), i.e., the 'peculiar' (ἴδιον) sensation concerning the sensible qualities like colours, which are exclusively accessible for one of the five sense-organs, and the 'common' (κοινόν) perception involving the commonly perceptible qualities that are reachable for at least two sense-organs, while the third kind of sensation comes to be 'in an incidental way' (κατὰ συμβεβηκός). Both models originate from Plato,[271] and their seemingly difference can be eliminated by a dichotomy: the 'affected sensation' (παθητικὴ αἴσθησις) and 'unaffected sensation' (ἀπαθὴς αἴσθησις): in the Proclean system both the sensation in the pneumatic vehicle and the shell-like body are affected, so is the Aristotelian peculiar and common perception. The divine sensation of the immortal soul, in the eyes of Proclus, is unaffected, which is equal to the Aristotelian incidental perception – for they both discriminate the substances of the sensibles through the 'opinion with perception', which cannot be affected by the affections originating from outside.

With this unaffected-affected sensation framework the first section of this chapter shall begin with an investigation into the generation of the affected sensation: firstly I will examine the general description of the generation of this kind of sensation in the Platonic dialogues, so that the preconditions of the becoming of this perception-sort can be determined, namely the existence of both body and soul, the generation of the sense-affection, its motion from outside to the sentient body and soul, and the actuality of the soul's perception-ability. Then I shall clarify each of these preconditions in a more precise manner (2.1). Following this interpretation, I will turn to the generation of the

---

[269] Proclus, *In Tim.* III 287, 7–10.
[270] Aristotle, *De an.* 418a8–25.
[271] For a detailed explanation of both models and their Platonic foundation, see section 3.1.1.

unaffected sensation which is generated from the combination of the affected sensation and memory (2.2), and at last there will be a summary of this complete subject matter (2.3).

2.1 The generation of the affected perception

As said above, the first part of this chapter will concentrate on the generation of the affected perception, which involves the mortal soul, the second and third vehicle in the Proclean model, and the first two kinds of perception in the Aristotelian framework, namely the peculiar and common sensation. For the question 'how can an affected perception be generated', or in another view, 'from where the affected sensation can be generated', we can find the answer in a multitude of texts such as *Theaetetus* 156a5–b2, *Philebus* 34a3–5, and *Timaeus* 43c1–7. Determining the necessary preconditions of the becoming of such a perception (including the existence of the sensible things and the sensation subject, whose generation is already discussed in the last chapter; the becoming of certain sense-affection; the movement which delivers the potential sense-data in form of sense-affection from outside, through the sense-organ, and finally to the soul; and the soul's alteration due to the influence of the affection, then its discrimination of this affected sense-affection; and so on) is the main concern of section 2.1.1. Expounding these involved factors, especially (1) the generation of the sense-affections, (2) their motion from outside to the soul, and (3) the soul's cognitive ability in discriminating these affections, is the content of section 2.1.2. Our present research, despite the available accounts in Proclus and Aristotle, especially the *De anima*, will begin with the related Platonic contexts. Yet, when necessary, we will resort to the Aristotelian works, and the ancient commentators like Alexander of Aphrodisias, Themistius, Priscian, and Philoponus.

2.1.1 The preconditions of the generation of the affected sense perception

The possibility of the generation of the perceptual discrimination, no matter which kind, is rooted on the one hand in the availability of the sensibles, which demands for the existence of the sensible things, on the other hand in the existence and participation of a perceiver, a living human being. Thus, the first precondition of the generation of the affected sensation lies in the existence of both sensible objects and sensation subject. All sensible things are composed of form and matter: Through form the substance of the sensibles can be determined, with matter, i.e., the four elements which are proportionally reconstructed in respect of number, motion and dynamis, the qualities of the perceptible things are enmattered and become sensible (see section 1.1.2.2). The perceiver consists of body and soul: His body is also established from the four elements, albeit it is made live and credited with sense-organs; as for the human soul, it holds uniquely two further forms which are divided into three parts: one divine form and two mortal parts (see section 1.2.2.1).

To clarify the necessity of the existence of the sensibles and the sensation subject, we should recall the passages like *Timaeus* 42a3–6 and 69c5–d6, which are already mentioned in section 1.2.2.3:

> [1] they [sc. the immortal souls] should of necessity have been implanted in bodies, and of their bodies some part should always be coming in and some part passing out, there must needs be innate in them, firstly, sensation, the one and same for all, arising from violent affections. (Tr. Cornford, slightly revised).

> [2] For a vehicle they gave it the body as a whole, and therein they built on another form (εἶδος) of soul, the mortal, having in itself dread and necessary affections: first pleasure, the strongest lure of evil; next, pains that take flight from good; temerity (θάρρος) moreover and fear, a pair of unwise counsellors; anger (θυμὸν) hard to entreat, and hope (ἐλπίδα) too easily led astray. These they combined with unregulated (ἀλόγῳ) perception and desire that shrinks from no venture and so of necessity compounded the mortal species (of soul). (Tr. Cornford, slightly revised).

From context [1] we can learn that the (affected) sensation arises 'from the violent sense-affections' (ἐκ βιαίων παθημάτων, 42a5–6), which are even 'more forcible and bigger' (ἔτι μείζω θόρυβον, 43b6) than the influence of the nourishment. The origin of these affections should (partially) be the external sensible qualities and their elemental movements, for if these affections generate from inside, they would be called pain, pleasure, or other kinds of feelings and emotions: In this sense Plato emphasises that the sensation with such a genesis is 'the one and same for all' (μία πᾶσιν, 42a5), which reveals that all sensations (of this kind) come to be, when this condition is satisfied, i.e., the existence of the forcible sense-affections.

However, we should not forget that only for the living human being the affections function as one of the preconditions, for the human perception is generated after the embodiment of the immortal soul and the generation of the living human being.[272] Hence both the existence of the forcible affections and that of the living human being are indispensable conditions for the coming to be of the (affected) sensation – this point is also stressed in context [2]: The ensouled body has the affections that bring forth sensations, which are said to be 'unregulated' and relate inherently to the mortal soul-form, for at 69c8 the affections are declared to exist 'in itself' (ἐν ἑαυτῷ), i.e., in the mortal form (τὸ θνητόν, 69c8) of the human soul; and at the end of this passage Plato explicitly states that the unregulated sensation relates naturally to 'the mortal species' (τὸ θνητὸν γένος, 69d5–6) of the human soul. Strikingly, in this text the affections are clearly proclaimed to be held by the mortal soul, which indicates that what involves here is the generation of the affected sensation.

---

[272] Given that this perception results from the embodiment of the human soul which enables the beginning of human lives, in the late antiquity the sensation is deemed to be the criterion of living creatures and those without lives, see for example Aristotle, *De an.* 427b11–13; Calcidius, *In Tim.* § 193. This argument is also utilised to prove of the role of pneuma, see part (2) in section 1.2.2.1.

To sum up, these two passages concern the generation of the (affected) sensation of the first human being and every new-born, and they elucidate that to engender the affected sensation the existence of the living human being and the sensible qualities is necessary. Moreover, we should bear in mind that although the sense-affections originate from outside, finally they are somehow in the mortal soul-form.

The existence of the sensible qualities and human being alone enables, however, no becoming of the affected perception, for the (external) sensible qualitative forms and the human body (i.e., the sense organs) and soul are still not involved in one single perception generation process, which is not obviously stressed in the two *Timaeus*-passages. To realise such a generation, more determinate and necessary preconditions should be supplemented. Yet which kinds of prerequisites? In order to specify them we must resort to more Platonic accounts on this issue, which are primarily presented in the following passages:

> [3] And there are two kinds (εἴδη) of motion, each of them is infinite in multitude, but according to dynamis (δύναμιν) the one kind is to act (τὸ μὲν ποιεῖν ἔχον), the other is to be affected (τὸ δὲ πάσχειν). From the association and friction of these against each other generates offspring, infinite in multitude, but twins: one that is perceptible thing (αἰσθητόν) and one that is perception, which is falling out together with and is generated with what is perceived (*Theaet.* 156a5–b2).

> [4] When the soul and the body come together in a single affection (ἐν ἑνὶ πάθει) and are moved together, if you name this motion 'perception', you will not speak in a wrong way (*Phil.* 34a3–5).

> [5] A yet greater tumult was caused by the affections of the things that assailed them (τὰ τῶν προσπιπτόντων παθήματα), when someone's body chanced to (περιτυχὸν) collide with (προσ-κρούσειε) another (ἀλλοτρίῳ) fire from outside, or solid concretion of earth and softly gliding waters, or was overtaken by the blast of air-borne winds, and the movements caused by all these things passed through the body to the soul and assailed it (προσπίπτοιεν). For this reason, these whole things (συνάπασαι) were later called by the name they still bear – 'perception' (*Tim.* 43b6–c7. Tr. Cornford, slightly revised).

Even at first sight one can grasp that: in text [3] the generation of the affected perception accompanies with that of the perceptible quality, for when we perceive, there must be things that can be perceived for us, i.e., the sensible quality. Yet both the generation of the affected sensation and the sensibles are said to be caused by the 'association and friction' (ὁμιλίας τε καὶ τρίψεως, 156a8) of two kinds of (physical) motion, one 'to act' and the other 'to be affected on', whose origin and substance are not explicitly declared in this passage.[273] What is stressed here is the infinite multitude of both kinds of movements and the results of their association, i.e., the generation of the affected perception and sensible qualities.[274]

---

[273] For the further references of these two kinds of motion, see *Theaet.* 159c14–d1, 182a5–b7.
[274] *Ibid.* 156a6: πλήθει μὲν ἄπειρον ἑκάτερον. 156b1: πλήθει μὲν ἄπειρα.

From the passage [4] we can derive that the becoming of (affected) perception requires the simultaneous engagement of both body and soul in the single affection (ἑνὶ πάθει),[275] which reveals that the affected sense-affection must be engendered prior to this engagement – considering that in text [3] the perception generates from the association of two kinds of motion, the affection should be caused by this very association. The fact that both the sensory body and perceptual soul – which corresponds to text [1] and [2] – take part in the process of perceiving by being 'moved together' (κοινῇ καὶ κινεῖθαι, *Phileb.* 34a4) in the single affection leaves us an impression that during the affection's generation, the body and soul are passive, so that they should be attributed to the side of 'being affected'. Yet this is not true, for the soul is always spontaneous (see section 2.1.2.3).

Text [5] declares explicitly that: the affection is a violent motion caused by the encounter of the bodily elemental movements and the elemental movements from the sensibles; this affection must pass 'through the body', which implies that it moves firstly from the encounter-point to the human body, or precisely the bodily sense-organ, then enter and pass through it; such an affection is violent, for it is claimed to be able to 'assail' the soul of the perceiver, which corresponds to the description in text [1].

In summary, to generate a determinate affected perception the following conditions must be satisfied: (1) the existence of the living human being and external sensible qualities; (2) the emergence of an affected affection due to the encounter of the (homogeneous) elemental movements from the sensibles and the sense-organs; (3) the movement of this sense-affection from outside to the corresponding sense-organ, and through this organ to the soul; (4) the soul's being moved by such this affection, then through its cognitive dynamis it discriminates and comprehends such an affection. These common conditions for the becoming of the affected sensation are confirmed not only by Plato, but also by Aristotle.[276]

2.1.2 Detailed analysis of the preconditions of the affected perception's generation

Now we should observe each of these prerequisites in detail: Given that both the generation of the sensible qualities as well as that of the sensation subject are already expounded in chapter 1, what left to be clarified are the rest three: (1) Speaking of the emergence of the affected sense-affections we must explain what kind of motion the 'acting' and 'being acted upon' belong to, and how can their 'association and friction' be realised – in fact a clue about this issue is already given in text [5], but we are not sure whether this is the general account for all affected affections (2.1.2.1). (2) Regarding the 'movement' of the generated affection from the place where the encounter happens to the perceiving body and through the latter to the soul, a clarification of such a possibility is required. For if this transport is a kind of motion, it appears to be a quite complex one: what involves is not only locomotion, but also alteration of the state of sense-organs (2.1.2.2). (3) As for the soul in the course of perceiving, both text [4] and [5]

---

[275] Cf. *Theaet.* 186b11–c2; *Tim.* 45d2–3.
[276] See *Phy.* 244b11; *GA* 524b25–29; *De an.* 410a25–26, 416b33–35; *De sensu.* 436b6–8; *De somn.* 454a9.

seem to leave it a passive role to play: in text [4] it must 'be moved' in the 'singe affection', while in the latter quotation it is claimed to be assailed by the affection. So, whether it is passive in the generation-process is another issue that shall be treated (2.1.2.3).

2.1.2.1 The motion of acting and being affected and the generation of sense-affection

The investigation into the genesis of the affected sense-affections consists of two parts: (1) primarily I shall explore the substance and origin of these two kinds of motion, i.e., to act and to be acted upon, for it is still unclear in which sense they come to be as two correlated movements whose 'association and friction' is declared to generate the affection, and through which the perception and perceptible things also come to be. Furthermore, there will be an examination about whether this two-fold division is valid for all kinds of motion. After determining their substance and origin, I will (2) turn to explain the becoming of the sense-affections by introducing two new texts in which the medium and the sun (daylight) are also regarded as the necessary preconditions of the affection-generation.

(1) To clarify the substance and origin of the two interrelated movements we should re-examine the quoted texts. In text [3] Plato's Socrates provides a primary description of the perception-theory pertaining to Heraclitus, Protagoras, and their followers. Thus, Socrates begins with an explanation of the generation of the affected sense-affection and perception: supposing that 'all is motion' (τὸ πᾶν κίνησις ἦν) and there is nothing beyond it (*Theaet.* 156a5), the movements are divided into two kinds, viz. the one that is to act and the other that is to be affected upon. This division is made in accordance with their dynameis, which means that under all kinds of motion there are some that can initiate the movement(s) of the others, while the others are to be affected on. Being generated from the very interaction of acting and being affected upon, the infinite 'offspring' (ἔκγονα, 156a8) also fall into two sorts: the affected perception like sight, hearing, smelling, pleasures, pains, desires, and fears, etc.; and the objects that are to be perceived, i.e., the sensible qualities for instance colours, sounds, and tastes (156b3–c2).

However, what Plato expresses here is not his own doctrine,[277] rather it is merely a reconstruction of the Heraclitean and Proragorean perception-theory, which hints at a necessary distinction of the Platonic thought from that of the other two philosophers. There are three main assertions in this passage: (a) the premise that all moves, (b) the division of all movements into two kinds (to act and to be affected on), (c) the association of them engenders all perception and things that can be perceived. Now one can proclaim that none of these claims are originally Platonic, for (a) in general sense Plato would not declare that all things are moving, for we all know that the Rest is one of the five biggest species that are enumerated in the *Sophist*, especially at 254c–255e, which is certainly not neglected in the *Theaetetus*, for he declares later that: "it will be no more

---

[277] See *Theaet.* 156a4 (ἥδε αὐτῶν); 156c6–7 (βούλεται γὰρ δὴ λέγειν). Cf. Irwin (1977) 1–13; Bostock (1988) 153; Polansky (1992) 76–77; Dorter (1994) 77; Becker (2007) 268; Kahn (2013) 54–55.

correct to say that all moves than to say that all rests" (181e6–7). Moreover, the Platonic Socrates is obviously not satisfied with this premise, that is why he re-considers and criticises this all-motion-theory at 181b8–183c4. (b) Nor would Plato assert that generally all kinds of motion can be separated into two kinds 'to act' and 'to be affected on': although this separation appears at first sight to be reasonable, for it is a division that seems to meet simultaneously 'genus and part',[278] nevertheless it is not a suitable one with regard to all kinds of motion, since on the one side this dichotomy cannot explain the generation of every motion, especially the first bodily motion: Reading the term 'to act' literally, it exercises its dynamis not on itself, rather on the other motion, i.e., 'to be acted on', which manifests that this act-acted on model leaves the genesis of the first acting-motion unexplained; on the other side, the bodily movements have two-fold dynamis, i.e., to act and to be affected upon, as Socrates stresses both at *Theaet.* 157a4–7 and *Laws* 894b8–c4, which makes it difficult to split all movements with the act-acted on model, for the motion of 'acting' in one case can be the very motion of 'being acted on' in another case. Thus, this dichotomy does not coincide with the 'genus and part' of all kinds of motion.[279] Obviously what Socrates literally asserts in text [3] is that the two kinds of motion are separated by virtue of their 'dynamis' (*Theaet.* 156a6), so this dichotomy is not conceived according to 'genus and part', but rather 'dynamis and activity (ἐνέργεια or ἐντελέχεια)'.[280] (c) The third point should also not be treated as Plato's own doctrine: what alleged here is that both sense perception and sensible things are generated in the association and rubbing of these two kinds of motion, and as added a bit later (159c14–d5), what acts is the sensibles, what is to be affected upon is perception. Moreover, what has the dynamis to act has 'a certain quality' (ποιόν τι), but not to be 'a quality' (ποιότητα), and what to be affected upon becomes perceptive (αἰσθητικόν), not a perception (182a4–9). Yet the phrases 'τόδε αὐτῶν' (182a4) and 'φάναι αὐτούς' (182a5–6) indicates that all these statements belong to the Heraclitean and Proragorean perception-theory. According to Plato, the generation and existence of the sensibles depends not on the association of acting and being affected upon. Rather, as they are composed of certain form and matter, in the view of the accessory cause, or the matter, they proceed from the gathering of the proportional elemental bodies possessing determinate quantitative and qualitative features, in the respect of form they are finally determined by the Demiurge who set forms and numbers in the Chora, as discussed in section 1.1.2.2. That the perceptible things are generated only when they are perceived

---

[278] *Polit.* 262e7: γένος ἅμα καὶ μέρος. Socrates asserts that this is the criterion of a legitimate dichotomy.

[279] In Plato there does exist such kinds of dichotomy in accordance with genus, e.g., in the *Laws* (see 1.1.2.3) the division of self-motion (soul) and other-motion (bodily motion) can explain the principle and generation of all movements, and perhaps also alteration (ἀλλοίωσις) and locomotion in *Theaet.* 181c–d and *Parm.* 138b–c.

[280] For the studies of this Aristotelian dynamis-activity model, see Menn (1994) esp. 81–83; Cleary (1998) 19–64; Makin (2012) 400–421. However, Plato's influence on this model is disparaged by the scholars, for example, in arguing that Aristotle makes the dynamis a way of being Menn (p. 71) has apparently ignored Plato's statements in *Rep.* 477c1 (δυνάμεις εἶναι γένος τι τῶν ὄντων), *Charm.* 169a2–3 (τῶν ὄντων τὴν αὐτοῦ δύναμιν αὐτὸ πρὸς ἑαυτὸ πέφυκεν ἔχειν), and *Charm.* 168c8–d2, which reveal that dynamis as being is already a doctrine in Plato.

is an idea that belongs to some earlier Nature-Philosophers, as Aristotle announces in the *De anima*.[281] Now it is obvious that what Socrates expresses in text [3] is not the Platonic thought, this clarifies why a bit later Plato evaluates this account with the words "loose use of names and words and fail to examine them with precision".[282]

Bearing this in mind one cannot refrain from querying the value of this text in explaining the emergence of sense-affection. But this kind of worry is factually excessive: Yes, Plato does not express his own ideas in this text and some later passages like 159c14–d5, for as mentioned above, these contexts are primarily a summary of the Heraclitean and Proragorean perception-theory, but this implies not that what he says in these passages is completely on the opposite side of his own doctrine. Because, despite the differences from Plato's doctrine, the three main points of this passage do capture some regular aspects that are also shared by the Platonic perception-theory, for instance (a) they indicate that the affection is generated in manner of the 'association and friction' of two movements, and this very affection results finally in the becoming of sensation – in text [4] and [5] we can also discover this point. (b) Plato agrees that both the perception, sensible things, and the movements causing them to engage in the perception-process are 'infinite in multitude',[283] for they relate to the physical world, which always moves and changes. (c) Although the dichotomy 'to act' and 'to be affected on' is not legitimate in splitting all sorts of motion, in terms of the becoming of the affected perception it does bear certain validity, for after all it corresponds to the dynamis-activity framework: under the homogeneous elemental movements proceeding from the sensibles and the corresponding sense-organs one has the dynamis to move, the other can be acted on, and the actuality of their dynameis results in the generation of the affected sense-affection and through which sensation. In this view Plato, conceding the lack of precision of this primary account and claims that such defect is "in many cases not ignoble" though,[284] stresses that occasionally it is even 'necessary' (ἀναγκαῖον, *Theaet.* 184c4). Therefore, the text [3] remains to be a significant source in clarifying the generation of sense-affection and sensation. Following this explanation it is clear that what act and being acted upon are not the sensible objects and perception, rather the elemental movement originating from certain enmattered sensible qualities and the homogeneous elemental motion of the sense-organs, for both of them have the dynamis to stretch out into the neighbouring area and move the homogeneous movement, albeit the latter is more decisive and active, since it possesses the dynamis to decide how far we can perceive and to discriminate the commensurate elemental movements from outside.

---

[281] 426a20–22: ἀλλ᾽ οἱ πρότερον φυσιολόγοι τοῦτο οὐ καλῶς ἔλεγον, οὐθὲν οἰόμενοι οὔτε λευκὸν οὔτε μέλαν εἶναι ἄνευ ὄψεως, οὐδὲ χυμὸν ἄνευ γεύσεως. Cf. Tuominen (2009) 161.

[282] *Theaet.* 184c1–2: τὸ δὲ εὐχερὲς τῶν ὀνομάτων τε καὶ ῥημάτων καὶ μὴ δι᾽ ἀκριβείας ἐξεταζόμενον.

[283] Similarly at *Laws* 895a1 Socrates declares that what is initiated by the soul are the physical movements of 'thousands upon tens of thousands of things: καὶ οὕτω δὴ χίλια ἐπὶ μυρίοις γίγνηται τὰ κινηθέντα.

[284] *Theaet.* 184c2: τὰ μὲν πολλὰ οὐκ ἀγεννές.

Text [4] explicitly reveals that what engages in the course of perceiving are both body and soul, for the perception takes place only when both of them are affected and moved together, which indicates that if one of them engages not in the single affection, the sensation would not come to be, and such a case is termed 'non-perception' (ἀναισθησία), as Plato announces a bit later.[285] That both soul and body should be moved in the single affection is also stressed in text [5], where Plato announces additionally that the order of body and soul in the process of being affected upon: the bodily organ is moved at first, through which the affection reaches the soul and moves it too.[286]

Now obviously, sense-affection is a motion produced by the encounter of two movements, namely acting and being affected on, and after being generated it moves through the bodily organ to the final perception subject, i.e., the human soul. Without sense-affections there would be no affected perception, but when the affections are too weak to move the soul, they lead naturally to non-perception. This is perhaps why in Text [5] Plato asserts that the affected affection should assail the soul, and the reason of the announcement in text [1] that the normal sense-affections should be 'violent' (ἐκ βιαίων παθημάτων, *Tim.* 42a5–6).[287]

(2) The generation of the sense-affections. Having determined that the two movements acting and being affected upon are divided according to the dynamis-activity model, we should ask in which manner their association takes place, for this is the very way of the generation of the sense-affections. To answer this question, we should resort (again) to context [5] and another two crucial passages.

In text [5] Plato proposes a description of the generation of the sense-affection: when the human body 'chanced to collide with another fire' or the other kinds of elements, there engenders a motion, which is the affected sense-affection. From this description we can conclude that (a) the affection is engendered by the unification of one elemental motion generating from the external sensible qualities and the other elemental movement originating from the human body. Thus, it is demonstrated again that the becoming of affection results not from the perceptible object possessing certain kinds of qualities, rather from the encounter of the elemental movements of such qualities and that of the bodily organs. The reason of such an encounter is the aforesaid principle 'like to like':[288] both the qualities and sense-organs are composed of the

---

[285] *Phileb.* 33e14–34e1: ἀντὶ μὲν τοῦ λεληθέναι τὴν ψυχήν, ὅταν ἀπαθὴς αὕτη γίγνηται τῶν σεισμῶν τῶν τοῦ σώματος, ἣν νῦν λήθην καλεῖς ἀναισθησίαν ἐπονόμασον. Cf. *Tim.* 64a5f., 75e.

[286] Cf. *Tim.* 45d1–3: εἰς ἅπαν τὸ σῶμα μέχρι τῆς ψυχῆς, *Theaet.* 185d3: διὰ τίνος ποτὲ τῶν τοῦ σώματος τῇ ψυχῇ αἰσθανόμεθα.

[287] Cf. *Tim.* 64c9: βίαιον (in case of pleasure and pain); e3: βία (sight-affection); 66c7: τῶν βιαίων παθημάτων (taste); 66e6: βίᾳ (smell); 68a1: βία (colour); and very oft in 63b1–64a1 (touch-affections).

[288] The principle 'like to like' is the criterion used by Theophrastus to divide the pre-Aristotelian perception-doctrines into two sides, those who agree with this principle are Parmenides, Empedocles and Plato, those on the opposite side are Anaxagoras and Heraclitus. See Theophrastus, *De sensibus*, 1. Cf. Baltussen (2000) 16–17, 148–151. For further references of this principle, see text [6], and *Tim.* 67b6–c1 (in interpreting the generation of sounds-affections).

proportional formed triangles and elements which keep moving in regular ways, the elements have the dynamis, to be moved and to move the others (*Tim.* 46e1–2), hence when two homogeneous elemental movements meet each other, they will be joined into one unity, through which the affected sense-affection comes to be. (b) The term 'chanced' (περιτυχὸν), being applied to describe the association of the bodily and external elemental motion, appears to define the becoming of affection as something accidental, if this is true, it would be right to declare that the generation of perception as well as the fulfilment of its cognitive power is nothing but coincidence, thus we must examine this point carefully: at first sight this announcement seems even to be reasonable, for actually we do not perceive all time, and this context (it concerns the embodiment of the immortal soul into the shell-like body, thus what is described is the mental state of the infant: the dynamis and activity of his immortal soul is disturbed, while his mortal soul and its perception-dynamis is strong. In this sense the term 'chanced' precisely describes the frequency of the generation of sense-affection) also involves no discussion of this kind of perception that is engendered because of our desire to perceive. Yet such a speculation should not be exaggerated: Although Plato implies that the encounter is by chance, this term should be read loosely, for both the sensibles and the sense-organs are established from the four elements, so when they are the homogeneous elements, and the other preconditions like the proper distance and the existence of suitable medium are also fulfilled, their encounter will be ensured. Moreover, as argued above (section 1.1.2.3), the soul initiates all physical movements, which means that essentially the chance plays no role in both mental and corporeal motion. Thus, when Plato ascribes the association to chance, he does not mean it in general sense, rather for a single association: when and where it takes place, could be accidental.

That the encounter of the elemental movements of the sensible quality and the sense-organ enables the generation of sense-affection is not merely presented in text [5], rather it is a general theory that appears in many other passages, for example:

> [6] All these things are moving, as we are saying; and there is quickness and slowness in their motion. Now what is slow holds its motion in the same place (ἐν τῷ αὐτῷ), and in relation to the things (movements) that approach it; in this way it generates the offspring, which are quicker, for they move, and the motion of them is by nature in space. So when something commensurate with an eye has come into the neighbourhood of an eye, together the eye and it generate both whiteness and its cognate perception – two things that would never have come to be if either of the two had approached anything else. Sight then moves between them from the eyes, whiteness from the co-producer of the colour, and now the eye is full of sight; now it sees, having become, certainly not sight, rather a seeing eye, and what has co-generated the colour has been filled full of whiteness, having become for its part not whiteness but white, whether a white piece of wood or a white stone or whatever thing happened to have become coloured with this sort of colour. (*Theaet.* 156c6–157a3. Tr. Rowe, with revision).

[7] The eyes that they fabricated to bring us light is first under the organs. [...] Such fire as has the property, not of burning, but of yielding a gentle light, they contrived should become the proper body of each day. For the pure fire within us is akin (ἀδελφόν) to this, and they caused (ἐποίησαν) it to flow through the eyes, making the whole fabric of the eye-ball, and especially the central part (the pupil), smooth and close in texture so as to let nothing pass that is of coarser stuff, but only fire of this description (τὸ τοιοῦτον) to filter through pure by itself. Accordingly, whenever there is daylight round about, the visual current (τὸ τῆς ὄψεως ῥεῦμα) issues forth, like to like (ὅμοιον πρὸς ὅμοιον), and coalesces with it and is formed into a single homogeneous body (ἓν σῶμα οἰκεωθὲν συνέστη) in a direct line with the eyes, in whatever quarter the stream issuing from within strikes upon any object it encounters outside. So the whole, because of its homogeneity (δι' ὁμοιότητα), is similarly affected and passes on the movements of anything it comes in contact with or that comes into contact with it, throughout the whole body, to the soul, and thus causes the sensation we call seeing (*Tim.* 45b2–d3. Tr. Cornford).

Apparently, the encounter-doctrine is reaffirmed in text [6] and [7]: in the former quotation Socrates begins with a re-assertation of the underlying Heraclitean theory, i.e., that all moves (156c6–7), and divides all movements with another dichotomy: the faster and the slower. Although the slower movements moving 'in the same place', they are not isolated from the other movements, rather related to the things that coming towards them from 'outside'. These approaching movements from outside must also be the slow ones, since all movements are either slow or fast, but the quick movements, on this very occasion, are still not come to be;[289] and the preposition πρός ('in relation to') expresses the accessibility of the meeting of two such slow movements – the precondition is, both movements should have the homogeneous elements, for example fire, as text [5] explicitly shows. Now through this very coalescence of the two slow movements the quick motion is engendered and moves fast forwards in the space, which is said to be its very nature (πέφυκεν, *Theaet.* 156d3). Although the term 'affection' appears not in this citation, the example of sight and whiteness reveals the process of sense affection-generation: when the slow motion of the eye meets with another slow motion that is 'commensurate' (συμμέτρων, 156d3–4) to it and within range, they can join in engendering the quick movements: the motion of whiteness and the sight, which moving between the eye and the 'co-producer' (πρὸς τοῦ συναποτίκτοντος, 156e2) of the colour.

[289] For further discussion of slow and quick movements in this context, see Bostock (1988) 62–64; Burnyeat (1990) 16–19; Hardy (2001) 65–68; Becker (2007) 268–271; Tschemplik (2008) 80–81; Kahn (2013) 91–93. For further literature, see Bostock (1988) 62n12. Kahn (2013) 52–60 offers an elaborate comparison of Plato's treatment of the flux-theory in *Theaetetus* and *Cratylus*. Both McDowell (1973) 139 and Grönroos (2001) 27n9 argue that there are many difficulties in connecting *Timaeus* and *Theaetetus* together, while Burnyeat asserts that the understanding of text [6] is twofold: the *Timaeus*-physical perspective and the *Theaetetus*-metaphysical one, and he prefers the second. But as my interpretation shows, one should take both dialogues into account, for in both of them we find important descriptions about the generation of the sense-affection, and they can be used together to offer a comprehensive understanding of this issue. The difference rests only on their distinct aspects.

Therefore, the eye becomes a seeing eye, while the sensible thing becomes something white.[290]

Text [7] announces that a sight-affection will be generated on condition that (a) there are three kinds of fire which are akin to each other – one more kind in comparison to text [6][291] – i.e., the daylight that cannot burn, but has the property of 'yielding a gentle light' (τὸ δὲ παρέχειν φῶς ἥμερον, 45b5), or as Plato says later, it is 'that effluence from flame which does not burn but gives light to eyes' (58c5–7); then 'the pure fire in us', i.e., the visual current; and the colour as "a flaming (φλόγα) that flows off from bodies of every kind and has its parts (μόρια) so commensurate (σύμμετρα) with the visual ray as to yield sensation" (67c5–8), although this kind of fire is not obviously expressed in this text, the text [6] has told us that the colour within range is necessary for the generation of affection and sensation. Furthermore, according to the principle 'like to like' (ὅμοιον πρὸς ὅμοιον), to generate a sight-affection the linear 'homogeneous body' (σῶμα οἰκεωθὲν συνέστη, 45c5) of the daylight and visual current should encounter another motion of the homogeneous element, namely a kind of fire 'from outside' (ὃ τῶν ἔξω, Tim. 45c7), while text [5] clearly proclaims that to arouse an affection the bodily movements should associate with "another fire from outside, or solid concretion of earth and softly gliding waters, or was overtaken by the blast of air-borne winds" (43c1–4). (b) These three fire-streams should meet with each other, come together into a single direct line, and be affected in the same way (ὁμοιοπαθὲς, 45c8) because of their homogeneity. (c) In the coalescence of the daylight with the visual current they are combined in the neighbouring air (τῷ πλησίον ἀέρι, 45d6),[292] which manifests the necessity of air for the becoming of affected sense-affection.

The transparent air functions here as the 'medium',[293] as already mentioned in text [6] (Theat. 156d6: τότε δὴ μεταξύ). For between the perceptibles and the sense-organs there is a certain distance, which is not empty but filled with elemental bodies like air and water, if the three homogeneous movements can join together in the neighbouring realm, this intermediate space must possess something that underlies this kind of motion, e.g., air. To specify the total kinds of medium we can examine Timaeus 61d6–68d2, where the generation of sense-affections are described: in text [7] we are already taught that the becoming of sight-affection happens in the neighbouring air. With reference to sound the air also functions as medium, for the sound is asserted to be generated as the

---

[290] Hence it is unreasonable for Bostock (1988) 63 and Sedley (2004) 42 to declare that the slow movements are the alterations of subject and object. Bostock has wrongly ascribed this doctrine to Plato by asserting: "the Timaeus never suggests that a white stone is giving off that stream of particles which our theory calls a whiteness *only* when it is being perceived, but our theory very clearly does make this claim" (p. 64).

[291] For this three-fold cause of sight, see Calcidius, In Tim. § 245. For a detailed analysis of the sight-mechanism, see Grönroos (2001) 31–35 and Remes (2014) 15–18. In p. 34 Grönroos points out that together with daylight the condition of sight to perceive is 'optimal', for with daylight the vision current can be made firm enough.

[292] Cf. Aristotle, De an. 418b4–9, where Aristotle adds water to the list of sight-medium. To demonstrate the necessity of the transparent air, Aristotle argues that when we put something colored direct on our eyes, it will not be seen (419a11–12. Cf. 26–28, 423b20–22).

[293] Cf. Ibid. 423b1–7, where Aristotle stresses that we perceive everything through the medium.

stroke caused by the air (τὴν [...] ὑπ' ἀέρος [...] πληγὴν διαδιδομένην, 67b2–4).²⁹⁴ Regarding odours Plato mentions both air and water, for the odours are defined to be finer than water but grosser than air, which can be easily demonstrated "when a man forcibly inhales the air through something that obstructs the passage of the breath: then no odour filters through with it; nothing comes but the air robbed of all scent" (66e6–67a1. Tr. Cornford).²⁹⁵ For taste and touch the flesh (includeing the tongue) functions as medium.²⁹⁶ According to this account air and water, which are composed of the simple elemental bodies and exist between the sensibles and the perceiver,²⁹⁷ are the media for the affections of colour, sound and odour, while the medium (flesh) for the tangible perception is in the body. That is to say, for the former three kinds of perception the affections move 'through the media' (ὑπὸ τοῦ μεταξύ), whereas for touch and taste the affections move with the medium (ἅμα τῷ μεταξύ).²⁹⁸

However, if what Timaeus says in Text [7] is true, the daylight would be the main reason of the generation of colour-affection,²⁹⁹ because it enables the meeting of the visual current and the elemental movement of the sensibles. Actually, this is also Plato's doctrine at *Republic* 506b–509b, where he argues that the sunlight is the third species (γένος τρίτον, 507e1) in addition to sight and colour, without which the sight can see nothing, and the colour would be invisible. In this sense Plato praises the sunlight: "the sense of sight and the dynamis of being seen are yoked together with a yoke that, by the measure of a form (ἰδέᾳ) by no means insignificant, is more honourable than the yokes uniting other teams, if light is not without honour" (*Rep.* 507e7–508a2. Tr. Bloom, slightly revised).

Given that the sight and the visible qualities do require the daylight to realise their dynamis, it seems necessary to add this factor to the list of causes of affection-generation. But before this requirement is affirmed, we should examine whether the generation of the other kinds of affections also demand for daylight or a third species. However, such an examination turns out that: (a) Plato proclaims in the *Republic* that for sound, hearing and many others there is no need for a third species (507c12–d3); in the related *Timaeus*-text (61d6–68d2) the daylight is also not regarded as a necessary factor for the generation of sense-affections, nor is another factor mentioned:³⁰⁰ under the affections that concern only an peculiar part of the body the first mentioned are those peculiar to the tongue,³⁰¹ which are declared to occur through combination and separation (διὰ συγκρίσεών τέ τινων καὶ διακρίσεων γίγνεσθαι, 65c4–5), in which there

---

[294] Cf. Aristotle, *De an.* 419b18, 420a11–12, where both water and air are media.
[295] Cf. *Ibid.* 421b9, again the media are air and water.
[296] *Tim.* 61c8, 62b7–8 (for touch), 75a5–6 (taste). Aristotle, *De an.* 423a15–16, b4–26. Cf. Althoff (1992) 123; Kullmann (2007) 434.
[297] Aristotle, *De an.* 422a9: τοῦ μεταξὺ ἀλλοτρίου ὄντος σώματος.
[298] *Ibid.* 423b14–15. For the reason of their being media, see *Tim.* 31b5–32c4 (air and water as bonds of fire and earth), 55d8–56a6 (their orderly physical features) and 58d1–8 (the sort of air and water and their properties).
[299] See *Rep.* 508b9–10: ἆρ' οὖν οὐ καὶ ὁ ἥλιος ὄψις μὲν οὐκ ἔστιν, αἴτιος δ' ὢν αὐτῆς ὁρᾶται ὑπ' αὐτῆς ταύτης. Cf. 509b2–4; Aristotle, *De an.* 418b2–3.
[300] *Tim.* 65b7–8: τά τε πάτη καὶ τὰς αἰτίας αὖ τῶν δρώντων.
[301] At *Tim.* 75a5–6 the tongue is proclaimed to be formed for the sake of sensation: εἰ μή πού τινα αὐτὴν καθ' αὑτὴν αἰσθήσεων ἕνεκα σάρκα οὕτω συνέστησεν, οἷον τὸ τῆς γλώττης εἶδος.

exists no role for a third species to play (65 c1–66c7); in the case of smell (66d1–67a7) both the pleasant and unpleasant odours are proclaimed to generate from substances 'in process of being liquefied or decomposed or dissolved or evaporated" (66d7–8, Tr. Cornford), namely they come to be during water's changing into air or when air becomes water, in which process we also cannot find a third species; the account of the becoming of sound-affection seems to be distinct from that of taste and smell, for sound is defined as a stroke which is imposed on the brain and the blood by the air through the ears and transmitted further to the soul (67b2–4),[302] but still, a third species involves not in this description. Having explored the generation of sound-affection and hearing-affection Timaeus turns to colour-affection (67c4–68d2), which we have already investigated. One wonders why Timaeus does not mention the sense of touch, yet the truth is, the tactile affections are not peculiar affections[303] that involve solely one certain bodily part, rather they are affections that relate to the whole body.[304] Such affections are expounded in the previous text which focuses on the common affections of tactile qualities, pleasure and pain (61c4–65b4). According to this passage these affections for hotness, coldness, hardness, softness, heaviness, lightness, roughness and smoothness are not concerned with a third form, rather their generation is also the result of the elemental movements and their associations, the same as in the case of taste, smell and sound. With reference to pleasure and pain we should firstly ask whether they are perception, given that in terms of perception Plato speaks of action and being acted on, the perceiver and the perceptibles and body and soul, and these are also necessary conditions for the generation of pleasure and pain (64a2–65b4), which should also be attributed to sensation, or a specific species of sensation.[305] Indeed, the context [1] is

---

[302] For an analysis of this hearing-mechanism, see Grönroos (2001) 36–37; Schmitt (2012) 304–307.

[303] *Tim*. 65b7: τὰ δ' ἐν ἰδίοις μέρεσιν ἡμῶν. Cf. 65c2: ἴδια ὄντα παθήματα.

[304] *Ibid*. 64a2–3: τῶν κοινῶν περὶ ὅλον τὸ σῶμα παθημάτων. Cf. 65b5: τὰ μὲν δὴ κοινὰ τοῦ σώματος παντὸς παθήματα. That the Platonic definition of tactile affections is for Theophrastus unreasonable, is based probably on the difference between the Platonic scheme of whole-bodily-organ or single-bodily-organ and the Peripatetic scheme of five sense organs which are all peculiar sensation. Cf. Baltussen (2000) 106, 112.

[305] Pleasure and pain are attributed to perception at *Tim*. 69d1–2 and *Theaet*. 156b5. Plotinus has clearly distinguished the role of the corporeal affections from that of the soul in the generation of perception, such a 'bodily affection/ soul cognition' framework can cover the generation of all kinds of feelings, emotions and the normal sense perception. See *Enn*. 4.4.22.27–23.48. Cf. Blumenthal (1996) 123, 207n10. Solmsen (1968) 613, 615 calls them 'sensation *sui generis*'. To demonstrate the essence of pleasure and pain Solmsen (p. 615) throws light on the terminology in this *Timaeus*-context: "αἴσθησις is a perception of which we become conscious, and αἰσθητόν is what we perceive. ἡδονή and λύπη are not strictly speaking αἰσθήσεις but potential concomitants of αἰσθήσεις; they are παθήματα – a word of even wider range than αἰσθήσεις. αἰσθήσεις as such are not felt but only comprehended. And yet Plato uses the word ἀναίσθητον as the contrary of ἡδύ and λυπηρόν and says that we – or parts of our system – become αἰσθητικά of pleasure". However, he proclaims later that in the senses of touch, taste and smell it is difficult to separate the feelings (pleasure and pain) from perception, which is not right, for although in the case of smell the pleasure and pain are used to help distinguishing the odours, which does makes it difficult to distinguish feelings from perception, the sens-

about the generation of pain and pleasure (42a6–7), which are regarded as the second result of the violent affections, and the text [2] points evidently out that pain and pleasure are 'combined with unregulated perception' (69d4–5), thus no doubt the pain and pleasure have the same origin as the sensation. Be perception as they are, we also cannot find the so-called third species in the account of their generation.

Based on the examination of the becoming of all kinds of affections we can conclude that except for the sight-affections the reason of the becoming of affected sense-affections seems to be related only to the encounter of the elemental movements. If this is true, should we then clarify the generation of all kinds of affections with such a model that is divided into two categories, i.e., sight-affection and non-sight-affections? Obviously, this is not necessary: (a) literally one can say that all affections result from the association of homogenous elemental movements, because the distinction between these two kinds lies mainly on the degree of the requirement of a third species to realise such an association. (b) After all, the ground of the generation of all affections is the same: all sensible qualities and sense-organs are enmattered, which means that they are composed of the elemental triangles that possess proportional multitudes, movements, and dynameis. Therefore, although in comparing with the other sensations (46e8–47c3) the sight deserves a higher position due to the participation of the sunlight,[306] all affections should be regarded as the results of the elemental association. In this view there is no necessity to separate the generation of the sight-affection from the other kinds of affections.

However, the argument that despite the sight-affection the generation of the sense-affections need no sunlight is false: we should not forget the role of Chora in the generation of the sensible world, namely it is the accessory cause. Analogically in the generation of sense-affections the elemental movements should also be attributed to the accessory reason: the proportion of the tringles and elements is initiated by the implantation of the world soul, which is established by the Demiurge. Having a divine soul, the sun is also a god which should be viewed as one of the young gods, whose duty is to help the Demiurge to govern the heaven and the mortal creatures in the sublunary realm. Therefore, regarding the role of sun in the generation of the affections we should bear in mind that (a) it is the reason of the generation, growth, and nourishment of all sensible things on earth, which is apparently stated at *Republic* 509b2–4; (b) the sun also plays an indispensable role in the process of the generation of the proportional affected

---

es of touch and taste, however, can certainly perceive without feeling pleasure or pain, and as Aristotle stresses (*De an.* 421a19–20), the touch-sense is the most precise human perception.

[306] Cf. *Phaedr.* 250d3–4; Olympiodororus, *In Phaed.* 1, 22, 2–3: διὸ καὶ ὄψεως ἐμνημόνευσεν, πρώτη γὰρ αὕτη ἐνέργεια τῶν αἰσθήσεων. Hearing is another divine sense, see *Tim.* 47c5–e2; Aristotle, *Eudemus* (or: *On the Soul*), frag. 47, 48. Cf. Cornford (1937) 152n1. There are two kinds of classifications of the senses in Plato, both have their own criterion and thus rightness: one in respect of the sense-affections, or the degree of their relaying on the body: firstly touch, then pleasure and pain, following with taste and smell, afterwards smell, at last sight (*Tim.* 61c–68d); the other order, according to the perfection of the perception, is opposite to the first arrangement – the sight and hearing are now primary sensation, as Timaeus shows at 47a–e. The latter arrangement is also revealed in Philoponus' commentary (*In de an.* 352, 23–29): firstly sight, then hearing, in the middle smell, and at last touch and taste. Cf. Tuominen (2009) 175.

affections. This can be clarified by the state of the media, which cannot function well without the proportional sunlight, for example with little sunlight the air and water could be too cold to freeze, in which case the odours cannot move though them anymore, and the sounds would also be impeded, likewise when it is too cold or too hot, our flesh would be not less sensitive for the motion of the affections. The reason why Timaeus does not mention the sunlight in 61c–68d is apparently that in this passage he describes the generation of sense-affections exclusively in the perspective of the accessory cause, i.e., the matter. Thus Themistius (*In de an.* 59, 9 and 33–35) proclaims that light is a determinate entelechy (ἐντελέχεια) and perfection (τελειότης) of what is transparent. In this view every kind of affection-generation should be attributed to the dynamis of the proportional elements, the sun, the world soul and finally the divine Demiurge. Hence speaking of the generation of sense-affections the sun – in the sense of a divine soul – should also be attributed to the cause, while the elemental motion is the accessory cause, thus being not mentioned in the description of the affection-generation though, the sun is one of the indispensable factors.

From to this account we can also derive that it is unreasonable to regard the sensible quality as 'active' and the perceiver as 'passive' in the generation-process of the affected sense-affection.[307] For (a) such a framework of 'acting-being affected upon', as mentioned above, belongs obviously not to Plato: in the texts [3] and [6], he does not attributes the motion of acting to the elemental movements of the sensibles, and the motion of being affected upon to that of the sense-organs, and in text [6] he declares explicitly that both the eyes and the sensibles hold the slow movements,[308] later at 182a4–9 he stresses clearly that this kind of perception-theory belongs to the Heracleiteanism (τόδε αὐτῶν, 182a4; 'φάναι αὐτούς', 182a5–6). (b) Even using this framework, it is still not difficult to find that what acting and being affected upon here are not the sensible qualities and the sense-organs, rather their elemental movements – and in the most cases the elemental motion of the sense-organs is more active than that of the sensibles. (b1) The elemental movements of the sense-organs determines whether that of the sensibles are suitable for co-producing the sense-affections: speaking of the generation of sight-affection in text [7] Plato points out that the vision current of our eyes goes out and "strikes upon any object it encounters outside" (*Tim.* 45c6–7), which manifests that the elemental movements of the sense-organs are active in capturing the homogeneous movements from the sensibles. Moreover, a coalescence takes place 'by

---

[307] Unfortunately, they are normal terms that used in interpreting Plato, see for example Cornford (1935), 46n3; Sayre (1983) 209; Bostock (1988) 62; Burnyeat (1990) 16; Polansky (1992) 97; Grönroos (2001) 23–25 (following Frede (1987b) 5); Tschemplik (2008) 80–81; Kahn (2013) 86–87, 90–91. For the argument about the passivity and activity in the view of the Aristotelian perception-theory, see Bernard (1988) 221–233; Schmitt (2012) 303–309. Here I will endeavour to prove this point within Plato's works. The discussion of passivity-activity continues in section 2.1.2.3.

[308] There are always slow changes in the sensibles and sense-organs, see Cornford (1935) 49–50. Nakhnikian (1955) 132 declares six movements in the course of perceiving: (1) πάσχον (sense-organ), (2) ποιοῦν (sensibles), (3) προσβαλλόμεινον, (4) προσβάλλον, (5) ποιότης (sensed quality) and (6) αἴσθησις. Yet we should keep in mind that this declaration is also based on the Heraclitean and Proragorean perception-theory.

chance' (περιτυχὸν, 43c2), as presented in text [5], however, such a chance is decided not only by the fact whether the qualities of sensible things have homogeneous elemental components as the sense-organ or not, but also by their proportion, because some of them are too stark to damage the sense organs,[309] while some others are too weak to be discriminated by the elemental movements of the sense-organs (*Tim.* 64b7–c6) – thus in text [6] the term 'συμμέτρων' (*Theaet.* 156d3–4)[310] is applied to describe an appropriate colour-flaming. Therefore, the elemental movements of the sensibles are decided by that of the sense-organs. Then we should consider the following facts: as material bodies the elements of the sense-organs keep moving and stretching even out over the neighbouring area, and these elemental movements pertaining to the generation of affected sense-affection can be controlled by us, for instance when the eyelids are closed, the generation of a sight-affection will be consequently impeded (*Tim.* 45e1–3), which manifests that our sense-organs are not passive in engendering the sense-affections. Moreover, in many cases of the becoming of touch-affection our touch-organ (flesh) is driven by the soul to touch the external object, thus the perceiver stands on the 'positive' side to reach to the sensible object, while the tactile-qualities like hardness and softness can hardly be called 'active', for these qualities are lack of the elemental mobility to stretch out and act on our sense-organ (flesh). Thus, although in text [6] Plato calls the sensible body the 'co-producer' (συναποτίκτοντος, 156e2) of the colour, its elemental motion would not be entitled 'active'. (b2) Moreover, even if in some cases we can ascribe the 'activeness' to the elemental motion of the sensibles, it is more restricted due to the following reasons: firstly, we can only see, smell and hear in a determinate distance,[311] which signifies that the sensibles locating beyond this certain distance would not be perceived, that is to say, the 'activeness' of the elemental movements of the sensibles depends in certain degree on whether it is in the available perceptible distance, which is decided by the dynamis of the elemental movements of our sense-organ again. Secondly, if we are sick, the sense organs will be changed, and the sensible qualities can be perceived differently as what they originally are, in this respect the 'activeness' of the elemental movements of the sensibles is not altered, but the elemental movements of the sense-organs are changed and thus the sensation could also be different. For example, Plato claims at *Theaet*etus 159c4–e5 that although the wine is always sweet, it is only sweet for the healthy Socrates, while for the sick Socrates it is bitter, this explicitly reveals that at least in the cognitive sense the sense organs (and the soul) do have priority than the sensibles, for in this case whether the taste of the wine is sweet or bitter is decided by the state of our tongue.[312] In this view, when one supposes

---

[309] In the Allegory of Cave, the eyes hurt when we see towards the fire and the sun, and going back to the cave our eyes cannot see because of the darkness there, see *Rep.* 515c8–d1, 515e1–516a2, 516e4–517a1, 518a1–4. Cf. Aristotle, *De an.* 424a29, 426a30–b3, 429a31–33, *insomn.* 459b20–22. Cf. Krapinger (2011) 217n572.

[310] Cf. *Tim.* 65d6: πέρα μὲν τοῦ μετρίου, 66d3: συμμετρία, 67c7: σύμμετρα. But in the case of colour this commensuration is unequal to the same bigness of the fire-particles (τὰ μόιρα), see *Tim.* 67d2–6.

[311] Aristotle, *De an.* 423b2–3. Cf. 434b26–27.

[312] The truth is, in both situations our organs function rightly, because for the sick organ the wine does taste bitter. The healthy and sickness of the organs are in relate to their cognitive states,

that the sense-organs as well as the perceiver should be called 'passive', it is a serious misunderstanding of the Platonic perception-doctrine. Therefore, if we look back to text [3], in which Plato proclaims that the movements 'to act' and 'to be affected on' are divided according to the dynamis, the dynamis of the sense-organs should not be understood as passive,[313] for on the most occasions what is more decisive and active are the elemental movements of the sense-organs. The 'activeness' of the sensibles rests on the very fact that the generation of sense-affection is impossible without its participation as co-producer.

2.1.2.2 The motion of the affection from body to soul

In explaining the generation of the sense-affections we have determined that the sensible qualities enmattered in the external sensible things and the sense-organs must have the homogeneous elements, which enables then an encounter in the outside and the becoming of the sense affection, when all necessary conditions like the certain distance, daylight (especially in the case of sight-affection) and medium are fulfilled. Now we should concentrate on the advance of the generated affection from the outside encounter-point to the inside soul. Obviously, there are two phases in such a progress: (1) from the meeting-point of the elemental movements in the surrounding area back to the sense-organ, and (2) from the bodily organ to the human soul.

(1) Substantially, the movement of the affection from the external realm to the sense-organ should not be regarded as a simple physical or physiological process,[314] rather it is a qualitative motion from dynamis to activity. In text [6] Plato credits the quicker movements with the nature of locomotion, for he says: "the motion of them is by nature in space" (φέρεται γὰρ καὶ ἐν φορᾷ αὐτῶν ἡ κίνησις πέφυκεν, *Theaet.* 156d2–3). However, given that what is proclaimed in this text is still the Heraclitean and Proragorean perception-theory, whether this motion is essentially a locomotion or not, requires further examination: the locomotion is a motion-type that proceeds from one place to another and is usually performed by a physical body, so considering that at *Theaet.* 181c–d and *Parm.* 138b–c Plato divides the movements into alteration (ἀλλοίωσις) and locomotion, it seems reasonable to treat the affection-movement as a spatial motion. Yet in the view of the origin (ἀρχή) and completion (τέλος) such a movement differentiates itself from the normal locomotion: originating from the meeting-place of the elemental movements, the affection is indeed a motion which takes

---

thus, to be 'cognitively active' (τὸ ἐπιστημονικῶς ἐνεργῆσαι) the organs should also be altered when the perceiver is drunk or sick or asleep, see Priscian, *In de an.* 122, 10–11. Traditionally the author of this Neoplatonic commentary is attributed to Simplicius, but it should be Priscian of Lydia, for the concerned discussion, see Steel (1997a) 105–140.

[313] Cornford (1935) 234 asserts that 'dynamis includes passive capacity, receptivity, susceptibility', and gives further analysis about the term 'dynamis' (pp. 234–238). Strikingly, he neglects the positive action of the elements proceeding from the perceiver.

[314] Unfortunately, that this affection-motion is physical and physiological, seems to be a general opinion held by scholars like Taylor (1928) 430–431 and Cornford (1937) 269 (in case of tastes).

the elemental movements as its substrate:[315] in the affection-movement there are at least two parts, i.e., the material elemental motion, and the potentially discriminated sensible quality existing in this elemental motion. Given that all sensible qualities proceed from the proportional properties of the elemental bodies (polyhedrons), as mentioned in section 1.1.2.2, the transport of these perceptible qualities can be accomplished by the homogeneous elemental movements, which means that the locomotion of the elemental movements functions as the substrate of the sense-affection. Now it is evident that the essence of the affection-motion rests not on the elemental locomotion, rather on the potential sensible qualities included in this locomotion.

This affection movement, however, can alter the state of the sense-organ, for in the sense-organ there exists originally no affection, but now there is an affection, and this affection moves even further to the soul. In this view, this affection-motion is essentially a kind of alteration (ἀλλοίωσις),[316] resorting to the dynamis-activity model it can be viewed as a qualitative movement from dynamis to activity.[317]

Theoretically, there are two possibilities to clarify the sense-organ's alteration, for the affection can either enter directly into the organ and change it, or be prevented from going into it, instead some other things take place successively, for instance the organ is affected to generate a similar succession-affection. Although in both ways there emerges an alteration in the organ, they are obviously distinct from each other: if the affection does penetrate the organ, there should be media like air and water in it, for only in this way the affection can enter into it; in the other case there is no need of a medium, rather one should explain how the organs can produce something like succession-affection to continue the affection-process.

Indeed, the *Timaeus*-text shows explicitly that the first suggestion is more reasonable, for there are air and water in all organs: speaking of the odours we are told that if we inhale the air through something that obstructs the passages of nose, no odours can be perceived (66e6–67a1), which indicates that by smelling the odours must enter the nose, in which there are air and water. As said above, sound is generally defined as "the stroke

---

[315] In the sense of substrate, the announcement that locomotion is the nature of affection can be maintained, but it is by virtue of a necessity, not because of its substance, for in terms of perception the material aspect is the auxiliary cause. That is why after the description of the physical process of seeing, Plato (*Tim.* 46c7–d1) attributes all these things to the 'accessory cause' (συναίτια), with which the god can accomplish the form (ἰδέαν, 46c8) as good as possible.

[316] Aristotle, *De an.* 417b12–15, 418a2–3. For the doctrine that perception is a certain alteration (ἀλλοίωσίς τις), see for example *De an.* 416b34–35. In annotating *De caelo* 270a25–35 Simplicius summarises the underlying syllogism used by Aristotle to demonstrate that a circle is without alteration: "what alters changes with respect to quality; what changes with respect to quality changes in affection" (*In de caelo* 111, 6–7, trans. Mueller), thus "things which alter change in affection" (*In de caelo*, 111, 14). This syllogism manifests the general theorem that instead of locomotion the affection is related to alteration. Themistius (*In de an.* 54, 7–8) argues forcibly that "all altered things are altered through determinate affection and movement". For a further analysis of affection as a species of quality, see Aristotle, *Cat.* 9a28–10a9.

[317] Aristotle, *De an.* 417a14–18. For the motion as a process from dynamis to activity, see *Phy.* 201b31–33, 257b8–9; *Metaphy.* 1066a20–22.

inflicted by air on the brain and blood through the ears and passed on to the soul" (67b2–4). As a stroke on brain and blood through the ears, it must penetrate the ears. For the colour-affection the fire-particle, assailing the eyesight and separating from it after having reached the eyes, "forcibly thrusts apart and dissolves the very passages in the eyeball, it causes the discharge of a mass of fire and water".[318] Being surrounded with a multitude of water, the in-going flame is finally quenched in the moisture (68a3–4). Such a penetration is already indicated in text [7], where we are taught that after being formed in a single line, the sight-affection moves "throughout the whole body, to the soul, and thus causes the sensation we call seeing" (45d2–3). So, evidently the colour-affection can forcibly enter the eyes, in which there are air and water. As for touch and taste, their medium is flesh, which is composed of water, fire, and earth (74c6–d2), so the affections can freely enter in and move with the flesh. The argument that all organs consists of water and air is also declared by Aristotle at *De anima* 425a3–9: "sense-organs are made from two of these simples only, air and water (for the pupil of the eye is of water, the organ of hearing of air, and the organ of smell of one or other of these), while fire either belongs to none of them [the organs] or is common to all (for nothing is capable of perceiving without warmth), and earth either belongs to none of them or is a constituent specially and above all of that of touch. So, there would remain no sense-organ apart from those of water and air" (Tr. Gendlin).[319]

According to this exposition we can summarise that the affected sense-affections do forcibly penetrate the organs, for in the organs there also exist media like air, water, and flesh, through (with) which the affections can move into them. And as affections enter the organs, the latter, with the Aristotelian terms, are 'sensibly affected' (τὸ αἰσθητικῶς παθεῖν) and altered to be 'same' (ὅμοιος) to the sensible qualities.[320] This alteration, however, implies that the dynamis of the sense-organs is realised: firstly to stretch their elemental movements out, discriminate the homogeneous and commensurate elemental movements of the sensibles and join with them in giving birth to the affections; then to receive the engendered affections by letting them enter into and pass through themselves.

In this regard we should continue to explore the substance of this very alteration that happens in the organs. Clearly such a change is not a normal qualitative change, rather it looks like a kind of generation. As mentioned in the preceding section, at *Theaet.* 181c–d and *Parmenides* 138b8f. Plato classifies the alteration as a kind of motion contrary to the locomotion, for it is a motion that takes place "in itself" (ἐν τῷ αὐτῷ).[321] Usually

---

[318] *Tim.* 67e7–68a1: προσπίπτουσαν καὶ διακρίνουσαν τὴν ὄψιν μέχρι τῶν ὀμμάτων, αὐτάς τε τῶν ὀφθαλμῶν τὰς διεξόδους βίᾳ διωθοῦσαν καὶ τήκουσαν, πῦρ μὲν ἁθρόον καὶ ὕδωρ. Tr. Cornford. In the eyes the fire is in the centre, surrounded by the water, see 45b8–c1. Cf. Taylor (1928) 482.

[319] Cf. Aristotle, *De an.* 417a4–5 (ἐνόντος πυρὸς καὶ γῆς καὶ τῶν ἄλλων στοιχείων) and Priscian, *In de an.* 118, 6–21; 122, 11–15. Priscian announces that the medium is 'known' (γινώσκεται) through water and air, see his *Metaphrasis in Theophrastum* 19, 14–19.

[320] Aristotle, *De an.* 417a14–21, 418a3–6. Cf. 416a26–b9 (in case of nourishment). Alexander of Aphrodisias uses the term 'assimilate' to describe the similarity of the sense-organ and the sensibles, see *Alexandri De anima liber* 33, 18: ἐξομοιωθῇ; 35, 1: ἐξομοιούσης.

[321] *Theaet.* 181c7, c9–d1; *Parm.* 138c5.

such an alteration denotes a conversion to the contrary quality, for example from white to black, from soft to hard (*Theaet.* 181d1–2), but meanwhile, the substance and substrate remain unchanged.[322] However, the change in the sense-organs is distinguished from this kind of alteration, since: (a) there is no destruction in respect of qualities, rather what happens is that the organs receive the affections, allowing them to enter in and pass through, in which way the organs become cognitively similar as the affections. Therefore, what altered is these organs' state, for after being affected the affections are now in themselves, their dynamis as sense-organs is now realised, and they become thus sensibly affected, which is a joint of activity and being affected upon.[323] With other words, the effect on the bodily organ happens not in respect of their 'disposition' (ἕξις) – an alteration of a specific quality like the hardness of the organs. Hence, Aristotle emphasizes that what happens in the organs is either not an alteration or one of 'a different species' (ἕτερον γένος),[324] for it arouses a change from dynamis to activity, which is factually "a transformation to procession or form, or a change in accordance with the natural condition".[325] (b) Given that what happens in the organs is actually the change from the non-existence to the existence of these sense-affections, i.e., the sense-organs change 'from a blankness to a form' (ἀπὸ στερήσεως εἰς εἶδος), this alteration can also be viewed as a kind of 'generation',[326] and this is essentially distinct from the normal alteration relating to the contrary qualities.

To sum up, essentially the affection-movement is not a locomotion – which functions as the substrate – rather a motion from dynamis to activity, a motion that enters directly into the sense-organ due to the existence of media, and changes the latter in the sense of realising its dynamis, making the organ same to itself through its generation in it. Being sensibly affected though, the sense-organ has no capacity to recognise this affection, which implies that the affection must move further to the soul.

(2) The affection-movements from sense-organs to soul. As the affections penetrate the organs, their dynameis are perfected. However, this perfection enables not the discrimination of the sense-affections, rather they should move further to the soul, for

---

[322] Philoponus, *In de an.* 301, 15–16: ὅπερ μένον κατὰ τὴν οὐσίαν καὶ τὸ ὑποκείμενον τὸ αὐτὸ κατὰ παθητικὴν ποιότητα μεταβολὴν ἴσχει.

[323] Cf. Priscian, *In de an.* 125, 34–35: τὸ τοιοῦτον ὁμοῦ πάθημα καὶ ἐνέργημα ὑπό τε τῶν αἰσθητῶν.

[324] *De an.* 417b6–7. Cf. *Phy.* 244b10–11 (ἀλλοιοῦνται γάρ πως καὶ αἱ αἰσθήσεις) and Alexander, *Alexandri De anima liber*, 39, 2 (διά τινος ἀλλοιώσις). Although what Aristotle speaks here is the perception, not sense-organ, given that what he means is a change from dynamis to activity, it is suitable to resort to this proclaim. For a detailed explanation about the similar termini like 'πάσχειν τι' and 'κίνησίς τις', see Caston (2012) 138n344(3). Remarkably, Aristotle denies later that the perfection of the activity is a movement, for the movement is 'an activity of the imperfect thing' (431a6–7: τοῦ ἀτελοῦς ἐνέργεια), while the activity is 'of what has already been perfected' (431a7: τοῦ τετελεσμένου).

[325] Priscian, *In de an.* 123, 25–26: τὸ ἐπὶ ἕξιν ἢ εἶδος ἢ τὸ κατὰ φύσιν κατάστημα μεταβάλλον. In this sense the sense-organs are somehow like the χώρα, which takes the forms of things and moved by them, yet it changes not its own disposition. See *Tim.* 50c–51a.

[326] Philoponus, *In de an.* 300, 13–14; 301, 10–11. Perhaps this can clarify why in Priscian's commentary (122, 21) on *De anima* 417b3–4 the original text 'τὸ δὲ σωτηρία' is paraphrased as 'τὸ δὲ γένεσις καὶ σωτηρία'.

being sensibly affected and altered to be same to the (forms of) affections though, the sense-organs are not self-sufficient to perceive them.[327] The reason lies in the fact that the sensation-discrimination requires the soul, precisely speaking, in the cognitive sense only the soul holds the competence to perceive, as already revealed in texts [4], [5] and [7]. The soul perceives by way of discrimination (κρίσις), which aims at the forms of the affections, and this dynamis to discriminate is instantly exercised. 'Instantly' because the (mortal) soul can discriminate and comprehend the affected sense-affections as soon as they are in the pneumatic vehicle. Comparing with the perfection of the soul's cognitive dynamis to discriminate the affection, the perception of the dynamis of the sense-organ is naturally not 'a pure activity' (καθαρὸν ἐνέργημα), rather a process that is divisible, corporeal and extends over time (σωματοειδὲς ὑπάρχον καὶ χρόνῳ παρατεινόμενον).[328] In another perspective, the lack of the cognitive dynamis of the sense-organs is already manifested by the completion (τέλος) of their generation, i.e., to serve the soul: we are taught in the *Timaeus* that after the embodiment of the immortal human soul Plato turns to the description of the generation of the human body and soul in accordance with the 'reasons and providence' (αἰτίας καὶ προνοίας, *Tim.* 44c7) of the gods. At the outset of this account the gods implant the immortal soul-form in the spherical head, bestow it the whole body as its vehicle (44d3–e3), set the face on the front side of the head, and "fasten in it organs for all providence of the soul" (ὄργανα ἐνέδησαν τούτῳ πάσῃ τῇ τῆς ψυχῆς προνοίᾳ, 45a7–b1).[329] So apparently the whole body, including all sense-organs, is immanently obedient to the soul, for it is established 'for all providence of the soul'. Being corporeal and divisible, the sense-organs belong to the 'accessory cause' (συναίτια) that possesses the ability to co-produce, receive and transmit the affections, albeit without the cognitive capacity (*Tim.* 46c7–e6). Hence the affection must move from the sense-organ to the soul.

The reason of the soul's dynamis to perceive, i.e., to discriminate and comprehend the sense-affections, rests essentially on the very fact that it is the cause and principle of all physical movements and changes. In the same *Timaeus*-passage (46c7–e6) we are told that while all material things are accessory cause, the soul is the cause. Furthermore, in the first chapter we have determined that the world soul initiates the motion of the whole world body (1.1.1.3), for the implantation of the world soul enables all proportional movements of the elements (1.1.2.2), and in *Laws* (896a5–b9) Plato declares that the soul, as the self-motion, is cause and principle of all kinds of proportional corporeal

---

[327] At *Gorg.* 465c9–e1 Plato proclaims that if the body discriminates by itself (αὐτὸ τὸ σῶμα ἔκρινε) without the soul, all things would be together and there would be no distinction between the contrary things.

[328] Priscian, *In de an.* 125, 36–126, 3.

[329] For the function of the body as ὄργανον, see *Phaedo* 65d7–8, 83a4–6; *Theat.* 184d4–5; *Tim.* 51c2–3, d8–e1. For the discussion about the relation of soul and body in Aristotle and the ancient commentators, see *De an.* 412a27–b6, 415b18–19; Alexander, In *de an.* 16, 1–14; Proclus, *In Tim.* II, 117–119; Priscian, *In de an.* 167, 19–34 (the sense-organs is actuated and characterized as living organs by the soul); Philoponus, *In de an.* 217, 13f. Cf. Perkams (2008) 94–96, 197–198; Arnzen (2013) 29 and 29n115. Themistius attributes the first principle and cause of the living body to the soul in three senses: "from where the motion itself comes, for sake of what, and as form" (*In de an.* 50, 26–29: καὶ γὰρ ὅθεν ἡ κίνησις αὐτή, καὶ οὗ ἕνεκα, καὶ ὡς εἶδος).

movements including locomotion and alteration.[330] Therefore, the soul is the cause of all movements of the perceptible things,[331] more precisely, the beginning, middle and end of the sensible qualities as well as the affections are finally generated from the (world) soul.[332] Given that the human soul is akin to the world soul, the affection-motion from outside to the soul seems to be a reversion to its cause and principle, and as its cause the soul can recognise it instantly. Now we can sum up: considering that the human soul is implanted in the body and the affection has already altered the organs, its advance, or reversion to the soul, is possible and necessary, when the affection is stark enough.

In respect of matter (or the accessory cause) we can also explain the affection's assailing the soul: the mortal human soul-form possesses the pneumatic vehicle, so the affected sense-affection, according to the principle 'like to like', can enter in this vehicle, for the latter is established from all four elements, and it is declared to be 'simple and enmattered', which enables it to function as the Chora in the generation of the sensible universe, i.e., all kinds of sense-affections can enter in this vehicle without changing it. Therefore, entering in the sense-organs the affected affections move further to the pneumatic vehicle, where they assail the soul, so that the soul can touch and discriminate them.

2.1.2.3 The perfection of the soul's perception-ability: discrimination and comprehension

As the texts [4], [5] and [7] explicitly indicated, when the affected sense-affection arrives at the soul and forcibly moves it, the soul will exercise its percipient dynamis on this affection, which engenders a sense perception and brings the course of perceiving to end. On the role of the soul in recognising the sense-affection we should firstly determine which soul-form is responsible for this affection in general sense, then clarify whether the soul is passive in this process, finally affirm the soul's perception-ability, i.e., to discriminate (κρίνειν).

(1) The affected sense-affection is usually perceived by the mortal soul-form. In section 1.2.1 we have already determined that the human perception is a kind that is 'common and affected', and this affected sensation is engendered once the human soul is implanted into the human body. The order of this incarnation begins with the embodiment of the mortal soul (and its pneumatic vehicle) in the established shell-like

---

[330] For the announcement that the soul initiates alteration, see also Aristotle, *De an.* 415b23–24; Themistius, *In de an.* 50, 29–35. Philoponus clarifies this point with an explicit syllogism: "The soul is cause of perception in animals; all what perceives is altered; hence the soul is cause of alteration" (*In de an.* 275, 1–2: ἡ ψυχὴ τοῖς ζῴοις αἰσθήσεώς ἐστιν αἴτιον, πᾶν δὲ τὸ αἰσθανόμενον ἀλλοιοῦται, ἡ ψυχὴ ἄρα ἀλλοιώσεως αἰτία).

[331] Philoponus, *In de an.* 272, 21: τῶν γὰρ αἰσθητῶν αἰτία ἡ ψυχή. Cf. 275, 1.

[332] Indeed, the whole matter of perception can be viewed as a tripartite circle: firstly, from the (world) soul to the generation of all corporeal things, i.e., all sensible objects and their qualities, then from the association of the homogeneous and commensurate elemental movements of the perceptibles and the sense-organs to the generation of affected sense-affection, finally from this affection to the (human) soul.

body and ends with that of the immortal soul. Such a sequence implies that it is reasonable to ascribe the affected perception to the mortal soul, for after its embodiment there engenders various kinds of human perception. To demonstrate this argument one can resort to Plato's own words in text [2]: "for a vehicle they gave it the body as a whole, and therein they built on another form of soul, the mortal, having in itself dread and necessary affections".[333] Evidently what Plato indicates here is that the (affected) affections are in the mortal soul itself, which is declared to be 'dread and necessary'. Another proof lies in the description of the disturbance of the sense-affections upon the immortal soul-form's dynamis and activity at *Tim.* 43e–44b, because from this passage we can conclude that if these affections are naturally in the immortal soul-form, Plato would not declare that its circuits could be severely impeded by such affections: the texts [4], [5] and [7] reveal that the involved soul-form is merely 'assailed', which is distinct from the immortal soul-form's being disturbed. Moreover, both the pneumatic and shell-like vehicle are made of the four elements, although the former is simple, the latter is complex; the immortal vehicle, however, is established from the fifth element, i.e., the ether. Thus, according to the principle 'like knows like', the affections aroused by the four kinds of elemental associations should naturally be recognised by the mortal soul which has material vehicles moulded similarly by these four elements.

(2) In the course of perceiving the soul is not passive, but spontaneous and active. As argued above, the affected sense-affections are in the mortal soul itself, so when the mortal soul recognises these affections, it should not be passive. Yet how can we explain the passages in which the soul is announced to be moved or even assailed by the affections, e.g., in texts [4] and [5]? Well first of all we should re-stress that (a) the terms 'active' and 'passive' should not be utilised to describe the matter of perceiving, for the elemental movements of the sense-organs are naturally 'active' in giving birth to the sense-affection, and such an organ-activity is essentially initiated by the mortal soul, for only after the incarnation of the mortal soul into the earthly body (the third vehicle) the latter has the in-flowing and out-flowing nature and the other activities, as mentioned in section 1.2.2.3. More decisively, the soul is the reason of all affections and actions, so how can it be passive in recognising those affections originating from nowhere else but itself?[334]

(b) If one insists to call it 'passive', this passivity should be understood as a signal that is instantaneously given by this affection, a signal that the soul can decide now whether it exercises its perception-ability on the affection or not. The soul's 'being moved' is different from a physical movement like locomotion, nor can it be attributed to the qualitative motion from whiteness to darkness, rather it manifests that a proper affection is already transformed to the soul, and the soul can act and recognise it by using its inborn perception-dynamis. Therefore 'being moved' denotes nothing but the very fact that the soul is about to actuate its sensation-dynamis. Yet whether this dynamis will be perfected or not is not decided by this instantaneous 'being moved', for even though the soul is 'moved', it can still stay unactuated or concentrate on other

---

[333] *Tim.* 69c6–d1: ὄχημά τε πᾶν τὸ σῶμα ἔδοσαν ἄλλο τε εἶδος ἐν αὐτῷ ψυχῆς προσῳκοδόμουν τὸ θνητόν, δεινὰ καὶ ἀναγκαῖα ἐν ἑαυτῷ παθήματα ἔχον. Tr. Cornford.

[334] At *Laws* 894c5–6 Plato announces that the soul causes all actions and affections: ἐναρμόττουσαν πᾶσιν μὲν ποιήμασι, πᾶσιν δὲ παθήμασι. Cf. 903b7–c1.

things: At *Symposium* 220c–d we are taught that Socrates stands outside and thinks for a whole day without any food or drink, and he feels no heat of the summer. Apparently, he could feel hungry, thirsty and the heat, but his soul drives him in another direction – he is thinking, hence he does not perceive these bodily affections, no matter from outside or inside. Therefore, 'being moved' by the affections does not endorse the announcement of the 'passivity' of soul, since the soul can still decide whether to actuate or not,[335] and if one insists on its 'passivity', it must be confined in the very instantaneous effect engendered by the affection.[336]

(3) The soul's sensation-dynamis is actuated,[337] so that it can discriminate the affected sense-affections from the other kinds of affections and determine the underlying sensible qualities, for such a dynamis of discrimination and comprehension is inborn.[338] This sense-discrimination is revealed in many passages, for example, in the *Republic* Plato proclaims that for the cognition of some sensible qualities the discrimination through perception appears to be sufficient (523b1–2: ὡς ἱκανῶς ὑπὸ τῆς αἰσθήσεως κρινόμενα), but when the soul is confronted with the contrary perception (523c1: ἐναντίαν αἴσθησιν), it will be compelled to ask another soul-ability, i.e., the understanding (νόησις) for help (523a10–b4). This manifests that the ability that enables the soul to

---

[335] Here we have a seemingly difficulty: both the mortal soul-form and the unified soul are said to perceive, so we must determine which is talked about in the specific contexts: Considering the current subject, i.e., the affected sensation, we should stress the impassivity of the mortal soul-form. By the way, it is easier to explain the impassivity of the 'unified soul' than that of the 'mortal soul', for in the view of the unified soul Plato, for example in the *Theaetetus*, declares that the affection 'extends through the body to the soul' (ὅσα διὰ τοῦ σώματος παθήματα ἐπὶ τὴν ψυχὴν τείνει, 186c1–2), where he has no intention to stress that the soul should be moved. And he formulates just a few lines ago that in the case of sense perception the soul investigates 'through the dynamis of the body' (185e6–7: τὰ μὲν αὐτὴ δι' αὑτῆς ἡ ψυχὴ ἐπισκοπεῖν, τὰ δὲ διὰ τῶν τοῦ σώματος δυνάμεων), which mentions no passivity of the soul at all. More strikingly, in the *Timaeus* and *Republic* Plato even tends to stress that the affection (of the mortal soul-form) 'reports' to the unified soul the sensible qualities, see *Tim.* 64b3–6 (ἐξαγγείλῃ, 64b6); *Rep.* 524a1–3 (παραγγέλλει, 524a2), etc.

[336] The impassivity of the soul in the perception-process is a theme that is intensively handled in Aristotle and the Neoplatonism. For the discussion on this subject, see Sorabji (1991) 228f.; Blumenthal (1996) 123–125; Tuominen (2009) 181–184; Perkams (2008) 48, 197–199.

[337] For discussions about this kind of alteration in the perception-soul, see Aristotle, *De an.* 417b2–19; Themistius, *In de an.* 55, 29–56, 17; Priscian, *In de an.* 122, 21–124, 26; Philoponus, *In de an.* 302, 4–307, 19.

[338] *Theaet.* 186b11–c1; *Phaed.* 75b8–9. Cf. *Laws* 653a5–6 (the first childish perception is pleasure and pain); Aristotle, *De an.* 417b16–17. However, the discrimination-dynamis is not restricted to the perception, instead it is also used in many other cases, e.g., the truth (*Theaet.* 150b3), what is recognized (*Polit.* 259e6), the music (*Laws* 658e6–7), the life (*Laws* 734c3), the trial (*Laws* 877b4), etc. In the *Gorgias* we are told that the body cannot discriminate according to itself (*Gorg.* 465d2–3), which also indicates that the soul must be the faculty to discriminate. And Plato also announces that the soul discriminates badly, because it is hidden behind the sense-organs and the whole body (*Gorg.* 523b8–d4). I suppose the reason of the plenty use of this term rests substantially on the oneness and unity of the human soul: it is the same human soul to discriminate the sense-affection and the truth, for the soul is both unified and multi-faced. For this theme, see section 3.1.1.

perceive is entitled 'discrimination', which is a capacity aiming at all determinate sensibles like colours and sounds: to expound why the cognition of the contrary perception requires the understanding, Plato tells us that in perceiving one single finger the most people can grasp its colour (523d3: whiteness and darkness), and shape (523d3–4: thickness and thinness, 523e3: bigness and smallness) with sight (ἡ ὄψις, 523d5), and its shape (523e5–6: thickness and thinness) and tangibility (523e6: hardness and softness, 524a8–9: lightness and heaviness) with touch (ἡ ἁφή, 523e6).[339] At *Theaetetus* 201b7–c2 we are taught that a person knows the fact only by seeing (ἰδόντι μόνον ἔστιν εἰδέναι), while the judge can correctly 'discriminate' by hearing (ἐξ ἀκοῆς κρίνοντες), for through hearing he attains a precise opinion (ἀληθῆ δόξαν λαβόντες), although it is not knowledge, nevertheless, it is adequate for a right discrimination.[340] In another example, Plato argues that the guests can 'discriminate' the pleasure of the food before eating them in the way of smelling (and perhaps also seeing), albeit his discrimination is not better than that of a cook (*Theaet.* 178d8–e4).[341] Moreover, in the case of general sensation Plato writes that the most people tend to make distinction according to pleasure.[342]

We must bear in mind that in strict sense the affected sensation denotes the discrimination of the affection in the soul exclusively, while in broad sense it concerns the sensibles and the whole process of affection-generation: (a) The perfection of the dynamis of sense-discrimination needs neither the external stimulus, i.e., the affections proceeding from the coalescence of the elemental movements of the sensible qualities and the sense-organs, nor the sense-organs, whose dynamis is to discriminate the proper elemental movements of the sensibles, co-producing and transmitting the affections,[343] for this discrimination belongs exclusively to the soul. In this sense the Neoplatonist Damascius stresses that the affected sense perception is not the process of the affections' passing through the body to the soul, rather it is a discrimination stimulated by this process,[344] and Plato asserts that the soul perceives not 'with', rather 'through' (διά) the sense-organs (*Theaet.* 184c1–9). (b) As what the soul discriminates is the internal sense-affection, we can say that, primarily, the perception is internal, subjective, and active, but given that this internal affection originates from the external world, the perception, secondly, can be regarded as external and objective.[345] This is also why Aristotle announces that in this discrimination-activity the sensibles and the perception are the

---

[339] For the general references of touch-sense, see *Phaed.* 75a5; *Theaet.* 184e4–5, 186b2–4; *Tim.* 62b7–8; etc.

[340] For seeing and hearing with reference to discrimination, see *Rep.* 578b1–2 (seeing); *Laws* 658c4–11 (hearing and seeing), 925a2–5 (seeing). For general description of seeing and hearing, see *Rep.* 507b10–c10 (seeing and hearing); *Theaet.* 184d8–9 (seeing); *Soph.* 236b4–6 (seeing), etc.

[341] For a general description of smelling, see firstly *Tim.* 66d1–67a7.

[342] *Phileb.* 67b3. Cf. 33a3–5 (the discrimination of the pleasure), 65b5–6 (distinction in view of the pleasure and intellect).

[343] At *Tim.* 64e3–4 Timaeus declares that the sight cannot produce the violent affection by its own combination and separation: βία γὰρ τὸ πάμπαν οὐκ ἔνι τῇ διακρίσει τε αὐτῆς καὶ συγκρίσει. Cf. Taylor (1928) 462; Cornford (1937) 268n1.

[344] Damascius, *Lectures on the Philebus* 157, 8–12.

[345] Schmitt (2012), esp. 303.

same.³⁴⁶ And generally we can say that although the sensibles and the sensation are different in their being, essentially they belong to the same species.³⁴⁷ Furthermore, speaking of the external sensible qualities, it is reasonable to emphasise that although they are not essentially active in the process of affection-generation, without the existence of such sensible qualities as well as their substrata, i.e., the external objects (albeit those external objects are not discriminated by the perception-dynamis), an affected perception is impossible. Given the important role of the enmattered sensible qualities, one can also claim that perception is a kind of cognition aiming at the external things which can act on our sense-organs.³⁴⁸ Therefore, with the affected perception ability the soul discriminates the sensible qualities through the sense-organs: colours through eyes, sounds through ears, smells through nose, tastes through tongue, tactile qualities through our flesh, whereas the (common) perceptible qualities such as motion, rest, shape, size, number, and one can be discriminated through all sense-organs.

Another important point is that the sensible feelings like pleasure and pain also relate inherently to the sense-discrimination of the mortal soul, for texts [1] and [2] signify that in Plato sense perception, feeling, and desire are generated from the bodily affections, as soon as the mortal soul is incarnated in the third vehicle, the earthly body. Thus, in the case of the affected sensation we see that discrimination, feeling, and desiring are not substantially distinguished from each other, for they belong to the same species, as supposed by the most modern philosophers.³⁴⁹

2.2 The generation of the unaffected sensation

As declared at the outset of this chapter, there are affected and unaffected sensation in the Platonic corpus, and this dichotomy exists also in Aristotle and Proclus. The unaffected perception, in view of the Proclean three-vehicle-model, belongs to the immortal soul-form, whose circuit of Difference distinguishes not only the sensibles qualities like colours and sounds, but also their substances – just like the world soul. In the Aristotelian three-kinds-model, the unaffected perception relates essentially to the incidental perception, which concerns a substance that is incidentally perceptible due to its occasionally characterized qualities such as colours or tastes, for example, 'white is son of Diares' (*De an.* 418a21). Here 'son of Diares' is a substance, yet it is not the object of the affected sense perception, rather due to its incidental whiteness it is sensible. Both the Proclean immortal perception and the Aristotelian incidental sensation involve the substance of the sensible objects, which is doubtlessly unaffected and exists thus beyond the competence of the affected sensation, so it is suitable to call it the unaffected sensation.

---

[346] See Aristotle, *De an.* 425b26–28. Cf. Bernard (1988) 140–146; Schmitt (2019) 170–171.
[347] *Theaet.* 156b7–8: τὸ δ' αὖ αἰσθητὸν γένος τούτων ἑκάσταις ὁμόγονον. 156c2: καὶ ταῖς ἄλλαις αἰσθήσεσι τὰ ἄλλα αἰσθητὰ συγγενῆ γιγνόμενα. Cf. 182b5 and 184d4–5.
[348] This point is discussed by Aristotle (*De an.* 417a2–9) and the ancient commentators (e.g., Alexander, Themistius, Priscian, and Philoponus). For a summary of this discussion, see Bernard (1988) 50–52.
[349] Like Descartes and Kant. Cf. for example Büttner (2006) 79.

As one kind of sensation the unaffected sensation denotes inherently 'the opinion with sensation' (δόξα μετ' αἰσθήσεως), namely the opinion that is generated on the ground of the (affected) sensation.[350] Here we are confronted with the difference of the Aristotelian unaffected perception and the Proclean one: in Aristotle we can assert that this unaffected sensation is the opinion with sensation, for in the mentioned example the son of Diares is incidentally white, such a perception can be right or wrong, while Proclus' unaffected sensation is an opinion about the sensible objects with logos, thus it is always true, for it is the cognitive dynamis of the immortal circuit of Difference.[351] This distinction, however, lies in the criterion of these two models: for Aristotle his three-kind-model is grounded on the different external sensible objects, while Proclus fabricates his framework in accordance with the distinct human soul-forms and their vehicles in the view of their generation. Namely for the immortal soul-form alone its opinion is always right, but when it is unified with the mortal soul-form, the opinion with perception of the unified soul can be wrong, for the immortal soul-form can be impeded by the affected sensation.[352]

Turning to the generation of the unaffected sensation, or the 'opinion with perception', we should assert that it requires the combination of the affected sensation and the proper memory-image. At *Phaedo* 96b4–6 we are told that both opinion and memory originate from the perception,[353] while in the *Philebus* the Platonic Socrates asserts further that the opinion generates from the affected sensation and memory, and to illustrate this announcement he gives an example (38b6–d10): when a person sees an object that exists beside the rock under a tree from a distance, he cannot see it clearly, yet 'wants to discriminate' (βούλεσθαι κρίνειν, 38c7) what he sees (ταῦθ' ἅπερ ὁρᾷ, 38c7–8), so he asks himself what this object is (τί ποτ' ἄρ' ἔστι, 38c13), and answers himself by declaring, if he rightly distinguishes (ἐπιτυχῶς εἰπών, 38d6–7), that 'it is a man' (ὡς ἔστιν ἄνθρωπος, 38d6), whereas on occasion of a mistake, he would opine it as a work (ὡς ἔστι [...] ἔργον, 38d9–10) made by some shepherds and call it 'a statue' (ἄγαλμα,

---

[350] For the text locations of the opinion with perception, see *Charm.* 159a2–3 (αἴσθησίν τινα παρέχειν, ἐξ ἧς δόξα ἄν τίς σοι περὶ αὐτῆς εἴη); *Theaet.* 161d2–3 (εἰ γὰρ δὴ ἑκάστῳ ἀληθὲς ἔσται ὃ ἂν δι' αἰσθήσεως δοξάζῃ); 179c3–4 (ἐξ ὧν αἱ αἰσθήσεις καὶ αἱ κατὰ ταύτας δόξαι γίγνονται); 201b8–c1 (ταῦτα τότε ἐξ ἀκοῆς κρίνοντες, ἀληθῆ δόξα λαβόντες); *Tim.* 28a2–3 (τὸ δ' αὖ δόξῃ μετ' αἰσθήσεως ἀλόγου δοξαστόν); 28c1 (δόξῃ περιληπτὰ μετ' αἰσθήσεως); 52a8 (δόξῃ μετ' αἰσθήσεως περιληπτόν); etc. For the locations about the opinion with logos, see for example *Theaet.* 201c9–d1: ἔφη δὲ τὴν μὲν μετὰ λόγου ἀληθῆ δόξαν ἐπιστήμην εἶναι.

[351] As mentioned in section 1.2.2.1, the immortal soul-form is moulded as an imitation of the world soul, for it is established from the same ingredients and in the similar way. Although it is less pure as the latter, as divine imitation of the world soul it also possesses two circles, which have the dynamis to recognise and to move. Given this fact, it is reasonable to assert that our circuit of Difference has the same cognitive dynamis as that of the world soul, i.e., to opine the substances of the sensibles.

[352] For a detailed analysis of the Aristotelian and Proclean framework of perception and their rightness in the view of Plato's perception-theory, see the following section 3.1.

[353] *Phaed.* 96b4–6: ἢ τούτων μὲν οὐδέν, ὁ δ' ἐγκέφαλός ἐστιν ὁ τὰς αἰσθήσεις παρέχων τοῦ ἀκούειν καὶ ὁρᾶν καὶ ὀσφραίνεσθαι, ἐκ τούτων δὲ γίγνοιτο μνήμη καὶ δόξα.

38d10).³⁵⁴ This example corresponds explicitly to the Aristotelian incidental perception, for the shape of this sensible object can be perceived (a round head with a long body and four limbs), its location (beside the rock under a tree, form a distance) is mentioned to determine this specific appearance, and the discrimination of this appearance (τοιαῦτ' ἄττα κατιδὼν φαντασθέντα, 38d2) leads to the judgement of its substance: a man or a statue of the shepherds. The whole generation-process of the unaffected sensation can be concluded as follows: (a) at the outset the person perceives something in the sense of appearance. The affected sense perception functions as precondition of the generation of opinion, for to opine something we should primarily perceive it, as revealed in this example, and the memory also relies on the sensation-dynamis. Yet not all kinds of affected perception lead directly to the becoming of opinion, for on the one hand if what one perceives is just colour or shape, he could discriminate it with the affected perception-dynamis alone, on the other hand, he must (b) desire to distinguish the substance of the appearance. For unlike the affected perception, whose affection could be engendered 'by chance' (περιτυχὸν, *Tim.* 43c2), as described in text [5], the generation of an opinion depends mostly on the soul itself, thus it should firstly have the desire to discriminate the essence of the appearance. (c) Now the person asks himself what it is, with this inquiring his soul turns to the next phase, i.e., it combines with the discriminated sensation with its memory about such an appearance. This step is crucial for the generation of the opinion, Socrates depicts this in detail at *Philebus* 39a1–7: considering that he has viewed the soul as a book (38e13–14), he argues now that when the memory coincides with (affected) sensation, the '(soul-)procedures' (τὰ παθήματα, 39a2)³⁵⁵ take part in this discrimination by writing words in the soul. (d) At last, the soul acquires the response to this what-is-question, depending on whether this procedure writes rightly or not, the opinion that he attains can be correct or deceptive. Given that the generation-process of the unaffected sensation is in the soul itself (proceeds from perceiving the sensibles and the desire to distinguish its substance, continues with the soul-procedures: the remembrance of the similar images, then comparison and combination of the fresh perception with the memory-image, and ends with soul's self-assertion, this opinion is deemed to be the logos that is carried on by the soul itself.³⁵⁶

Speaking of the logos of the human soul one recalls probably the logos of the world soul, the paradigm of the human soul. In this sense we can clarify why the human soul has this cognitive ability, namely the opinion with affected sensation: at *Timaeus* 37b3–c1 Plato talks about the logos of the world soul in differentiating the sensible objects,³⁵⁷ he proclaims that when the logos 'comes to be related to something sensible' (περὶ τὸ αἰσθητὸν γίγνηται) and moves the circuit of Difference that proceeds in a correct way,

---

[354] For the interpretation of this example, see Davidson (1990) 353–356; Frede (1997) 247–248; Büttner (2000) 80–81.

[355] For the translation of τὰ παθήματα as 'soul-procedures', see Büttner (2000) 80n229. We should bear in mind that here the meaning of this term is distinct from that of the affected sense-affection, which is also named πάθημα, for the latter signifies the external bodily affections, while the πάθημα in the *Philebus* is the ability of the soul itself.

[356] For this assertation of soul, see also *Theaet.* 189e6–190a6; *Soph.* 263e3–264b3. Cf. Davidson (1990) 354n21; Frede (1997) 247n42; Büttner (2000) 80n231; Grönroos (2001) 83–84.

[357] See section 1.1.1.1 and 1.1.2.3 about the world soul. Cf. Proclus, *In Tim.* II 309, 2–312, 5.

the latter reports the sensible thing to the whole soul, then the reliable and true opinion and belief come to be. That is to say, such a logos involving the sensible things moves the circle of Difference to discriminate it and reports it to the whole soul, during which process neither the circuit of Difference nor the world soul distinguishes through the sense-organs, for the world soul envelops the whole universe and needs no sense-organs to perceive. This kind of divine discrimination discerns not only the sensible qualities, but also their substances, hence Proclus attributes it to 'the unaffected and common perception' (ἡ ἀπαθὴς αἴσθησις καὶ κοινή, In Tim. III 287, 7–8). Given that the immortal human soul is formed with the same ingredients of the world soul and in the similar manner, it must possess similar structures and cognitive abilities including the circuit of the Difference, whose cognitive dynamis is to opine the sensible things without being affected by them.

Here, one interesting point that is worthy to mention is, the world soul as well as the human soul discern the substance of the sensibles in the way of (spatial) touching (ἐφάπτηται, Tim. 37a7).[358] Given that the world soul encompasses the whole world body and moves it through its two circles, it is not difficult to understand that the world soul recognises the whole world by touching all objects in it, so in the case of the generation of right opinion about the sensible things we can assert that the world soul discriminates the substance of the sensibles in the manner of touching it by itself – in this sense the term ἐφάπτομαι indeed means 'touch and grasp'. Strikingly, this scene is also appropriate to the human immortal soul: at Phaedo 79c1–d7 the Platonic Socrates proclaims that when the soul touches and grasps the objects that always change in way of the affected perception, it hesitates about itself, and is confused, as if drunk, while when it observes by itself, it 'touches and grasps' (ἐφαπτομένη, 79c9, d6) the things that always exist, immortal, and unchanged, which is the substance of the sensible things. From this passage we can also derive that both the affected and unaffected perception are important for us, for each of them has its specific dynamis and the corresponding objects. Both kinds of perception are the cognitive dynamis of the unified soul, thus for the discrimination of colours, sounds, enmattered shapes, sizes, movements, rests, numbers, and oneness, our soul touches and grasps them through the affected perception, while regarding the substance of the sensibles it discriminates by itself. Since the human soul possesses two forms and three parts, as explored in section 1.2.2.1, and all cognitive abilities are exercised in the soul, Plato stresses at Laws 961d–e that the salvation of every person lies on the combination of the intellect and the noblest sensation into a unity,[359] that is to say, the two forms and three parts of the soul should move with each

---

[358] For the text locations where ἐφάπτομαι is used to connect the soul and its (immaterial) object, see Lys. 220c2–4; Crat. 393b1–4; 404d1–3; Phaed. 65b9; Rep. 484b6; 490b4; 534c5–6; 620e4; Phaedr. 253a2; 265b7; Theaet. 190c5–8; 208d7–9; Tim. 71d6–e3; 90c1; Crit. 116e1–2; Laws 968b5–6. Cf. Aristotle, De an. 429a10–20, 430a10–20. Text locations are partially taken from Fronterotta (2015) 47n16, for the spatial touch of the world soul see his analysis in pp. 46–48.

[359] Laws 961d9–11: συλλήβδην δὲ νοῦς μετὰ τῶν καλλίστων αἰσθήσεων κραθείς, υενόμενός τε εἰς ἕν, σωτηρία ἑκάστων δικαιότατ' ἂν εἴη καλουμένη. Cf. 961e3–4 (τὰς αἰσθήσεις τῷ κυβερνητικῷ νῷ συγκερασάμενοι); 964d6–7 (ἢ τίνα τρόπον τῇ τῶν ἐμφρόνων κεφαλῇ τε καὶ αἰσθήσεσιν ὁμοιωθήσεται ἡμῖν ἡ πόλις); 969b6–7 (κεφαλῆς νοῦ τε κοινωνίας εἰκόνα τινά πως

other in a commensurate way,[360] so that they can touch each other and their objects in an ordered way.

2.3 Conclusion

In this section I have dilated on the generation of sense perception. The main resources invoked to expound this issue are taken from Plato's dialogues, whereas the sensation-doctrines of Aristotle and Proclus are occasionally adduced for the sake of a better detailed interpretation, in addition the commentaries of Alexander, Themistius, Priscian, and Philoponus on the Aristotelian *De anima* are also cited to strengthen the arguments. Considering the complexity of this subject-matter I have raised a dichotomy of all kinds of perception, namely the affected perception and the unaffected sensation, which can cover both the Aristotelian and Proclean three-fold-separation of perception. For the interpretation of the affected sensation's generation, I have firstly proposed a brief answer, then offered a closer exposition. Regarding the generation of the unaffected affection, I have clarified its generation by resorting to the Philebus-passage and its kinship with the opinion of the world soul.

After examining the related passages in the *Theaetetus*, *Philebus* and *Timaeus*, I have argued that to clarify the generation of the affected perception four preconditions should be fulfilled, i.e., the existence of the sensibles and the living human being; the becoming of the affection in the neighbouring area of the perceiver; the affection-movement from outside to the sense-organ and soul; the soul's being moved in order to exercise its perception-dynamis (2.1.1). Given that the first precondition is already discussed in the first chapter, the other three are left to be clarified. Such a clarification falls naturally into three parts (2.1.2): firstly (2.1.2.1) I have expounded the two related factors in engendering the sense-affections, i.e., to act and to be affected upon. In the Heraclitean and Proragorean perception-theory the former signifies the dynamis of the sensibles, or precisely the ability of the certain qualities that are enmattered in the external objects, whereas the latter denotes the capacity of the bodily organ and the human soul. For Plato, however, to act and to be affected upon are factually the elemental movements originating from the sensibles and the sense-organs. The encounter of these two elemental movements takes place in the neighbouring area, according to the principle 'like to like', this coalescence is not essentially 'by chance', rather these elemental movements must be homogeneous. So, one can assert that the elemental movements of the sense-organs stretch out in the neighbourhood, then discriminate and conjoin with the commensurate elemental movements proceeding from the sensibles, and their combination gives birth to the sense-affection, which, after its generation, moves back to the sense-organs and soul. Remarkably in the generation of the sight-affection (1) there must exist media through or with which the elemental movements can move. After

συμμείξαντες); *Phaedr.* 249b8–c1 (δεῖ γὰρ ἄνθρωπον συνιέναι κατ' εἶδος λεγόμενον, ἐκ πολλῶν ἰὸν αἰσθήσεων εἰς ἓν λογισμῷ συναιρούμενον) and *Polit.* 272c2–4 (καὶ πυνθανόμενοι παρὰ πάσης φύσεως εἴ τινά τις ἰδίαν δύναμιν ἔχουσα ᾔσθετό τι διάφορον τῶν ἄλλων εἰς συναγυρμὸν φρονήσεως).

[360] *Tim.* 90a1–2: διὸ φυλακτέον ὅπως ἂν ἔχωσιν τὰς κινήσεις πρὸς ἄλληλα συμμέτρους.

a research of the concerned texts the following media are determined: in the case of sight, smelling and hearing the media are water and air – the two bonds that are utilised to conjoin the fire and earth in establishing the world body, while by tasting and touching the medium is flesh, which consists of water, air and earth; (2) there is a third species, namely the daylight of the sun, which enables the conjunction of the visual ray and the fire particles originating from the sensibles. The existence of the sun enables the generation and growth of all sensible things on earth, and the participation of the daylight in the generation of the sight-affection endorses the priority of the sight under all five kinds of the peculiar perception.

Being already generated the affected sense-affection stays not in the place where it comes to be, rather it moves quickly back to the sense-organ, penetrating it and moving further to the soul (2.1.2.2). The reason of the possibility of its moving into the organs rests on the fact that in the sense-organs there also exist media, through (with) which the affection can freely pass: this also clarifies the accessibility of the further moving from sense-organ to the soul. When the organ is affected, it is altered, not in the sense that its quality is destructed and replaced by the contrary one, rather it is a kind of generation, or in the view of the dynamis-activity model, it is a perfection of its dynamis, which is bestowed on the human being by the gods and is already there after his birth. By virtue of this dynamis the sense-organs can send out the elemental movements which can discriminate the homogeneous elemental movements of the sensibles within a certain distance, conjoining with these elemental movements in producing sense-affections, receiving these affections 'actively', and at last transmitting them to our perceiving soul. Such a dynamis is realised by becoming like the quality or form carried by the affection – for such an affection is now in the organ. Being sensibly affected though, the sense-organs cannot discriminate the affections by themselves, for although being established from the material elements and possessing the dynamis to be altered by the affection, they lack the dynamis to recognise the qualitative forms held by those affections, which is exclusively the sovereignty of the soul. Given this fact the affections must move further to the soul.

The manner in which the soul is moved is termed 'assail', for the affection should be stark enough to affect it, and the soul's being moved, or precisely, such an alteration – again in the sense of perfection of the dynamis – signifies the possibility of the actuality of its perceptive ability which is named 'discrimination'. According to the principle 'like to like' only the soul can discern the forms of the sensible affections, while the sense-organs, being composed of elements and formed by the soul, are only able to co-produce the affected sense-affection and transport it to the soul. Furthermore, as in the case of the generation of the affected sense-affections, in differentiating these affections it is not suitable to describe the soul with the term 'passive', for the advance of the affection at soul is a signal that the soul can recognise the affection immediately, but whether it responses to this signal and acts to distinguish the affection depends on itself, as demonstrated by the example of *Symposium* 220c–d. In the activity of the sense-discrimination we can assert sense perception is both subjective and objective, both internal and external, for on this occasion there exists equality between the sensibles and the perception in the soul (2.1.2.3).

The exposition of the unaffected sensation's generation begins with a determination that such a perception aims at the substance of the sensibles, which indicates that it involves another cognitive ability, i.e., the opinion with perception (2.2). This kind of perception, being distinct from the opinion with logos, originates from t the soul-procedure which combines the fresh affected sensation with the proper memory-image and makes the self-discourse. The reason of the human soul's being able to opine is clarified by resorting to the logos of the world soul, for being similarly moulded, the immortal soul-form also has the circle of Difference which enables the generation of opinion. Moreover, as the word soul touches and grasps the sensible things by itself, our unified soul can also touch and grasp the sensibles through itself, although in the case of differentiating the affected sensation it does this through the bodily organs.

3 The kinds of perception and their cognitive abilities

After the clarification of the generation of the affected and unaffected perception, we should turn to the kinds of perception and their cognitive dynameis, for although we have divided perception into two kinds (affected und unaffected sensation), there exist more types under this dichotomy. Moreover, although we have affirmed that the affected sensation can discriminate the sensible qualities, and the unaffected sensation grasps even their substances, still, there is no conclusion about the range and truth of what the perception discerns, which relates immanently to the sensation-types.

Indeed, we have already discussed about the Proclean and Aristotelian three-fold division of perception, and in section 2.1.2.3 the perceptual discrimination of our soul is also introduced. Now we should continue to explore the harmony of these two models in the view of the Platonic soul-theory. After this research it is suitable to determine the Platonic perception-kinds in a more comprehensive view (3.1). Having specified these sensation-types we shall concentrate on their corresponding cognition-categories and the truth of their discrimination (3.2).

3.1 The kinds of sense perception in Plato

With reference to the sorts of perception we can firstly recall the description of the soul-discrimination in section 2.1.2.3, where I have stressed that for this kind of discrimination there are five peculiar senses, through their sense-organs they can discriminate certain kinds of sensible qualities respectively. But in addition to these qualities there exist other sense-categories that can be commonly discriminated by more than one sense, for instance in *Republic* (523a10–525a8) we are taught that both sight and touch-sense can recognise the enmattered shapes like thickness and thinness (523d3–4, e5–6). In this view there are at least two kinds of perception clearly distinguished from each other, i.e., the peculiar sensation which discriminates determinate objects through one peculiar sense-organ, and the common sensation whose objects are recognised by at least two sense-organs. However, this is a classification in the view of the Aristotelian perception-doctrine, which divides the perception intellectively into three kinds. Except for this tripartite model there is another three-fold framework suggested by Proclus, which is already mentioned at the outset of last chapter, but in order to address ourselves to the subject matter at that time, i.e., the generation of the perception, I have resorted to a dichotomy of the affected-unaffected-perception to harmonise both the Proclean and Aristotelian division of perception-types – therefore there is still no detailed observation of these two models. Moreover, although for the exploration of the generation of perception this bipartite framework is satisfying, there is also disadvantage: it is too vague to exhibit all perception-kinds in Plato's philosophy. According to this account, we should re-consider the Aristotelian and Proclean frameworks in detail, and try to demonstrate that both models are reasonable, and can be harmonised according to

Plato's perception-theory (3.1.1). After the demonstration of the possibility of this harmonisation I will endeavour to investigate the Platonic perception-types in a more comprehensive view (3.1.2).

3.1.1 The Proclean and Aristotelian models and their origins in Plato

The aim of this section rests on the argument that both the Proclean and Aristotelian perception-theory are based on Plato's description of sensation, and on this ground, they can be harmonised in the Platonic perception-theory.

(1) Proclus' perception-doctrine originates evidently from Plato, for what he conceives, the three kinds of soul-vehicles and both the affected and unaffected human perception, exists in his very commentary on Plato's *Timaeus* (see section 1.2). In his *Republic*-commentary, *Elementatio Theologica* and *Theologia Platonica* this theory is remained. Let us firstly concentrate on the most significant points of his interpretation of the three vehicles and the corresponding kinds of human sensation: (a) the generation of the divine, immortal soul is accompanied with the establishment of its heavenly vehicle, which is fashioned with the fifth element, i.e., the ether, which is also used to mould the heaven. Thus, this ethereal vehicle is characterised as 'simple and immaterial' (ἁπλοῦν καὶ ἄυλον, Proclus, *In Tim.* III 285, 13). The creator of the immortal soul-form as well as its vehicle is the Demiurge, hence this human soul-form is 'made equal to' (ἰσάζοιτ' ἄν, *Tim.* 41c2) the young gods and holds the nature to 'share the names of the immortals' (ἀθανάτοις ὁμώνυμο νεῖναι πρόσήκει, *Tim.* 41c6). Due to this divine origin the immortal soul-form, like the world soul, also possesses the dynamis of unaffected sensation, which is defined as 'common and unaffected' and is the ability of the circuit of Difference. This divine circuit of Difference, however, is entitled 'the generating-circuit' (τὸν γενεσιουργὸν περιάγει κύκλον, Proclus, *In Tim.* III 296, 22), for it brings the soul to generation in an individual life due to its contact with the mortal soul-form as well as its vehicles. (b) Taken over the creation-work of the mortal human souls from their Father the young gods mould this mortal form by imitating the Demiurge. Moreover, they are commanded to 'weave mortal to immortal' (*Tim.* 41d1–2), begetting the living human beings, and using their dynameis to guide the mortal creature living a life as noble and good as possible. No doubt that the mortal soul and its pneumatic vehicle are merely imitations of the immortal ones, yet as divine imitations they share the eternity in certain degree, so that they can survive the death and continue to exist together with the immortal soul for a period. The 'simple and enmattered' (ἁπλοῦν καὶ ἔνυλον, Proclus, *In Tim.* III 285, 13–14) pneumatic vehicle of this mortal soul is composed of the four elements, which are entitled 'the troublesome mass' (τὸν πολὺν ὄχλον, *Tim.* 42c6), since unlike the immortal ether all four kinds of elements are used to mould this kind of vehicle, which is 'adhered' (προσψύντα, 42c7) to the immortal soul and weighs it down from its heavenly life. (c) The third, shell-like vehicle is the earthly body of the living human beings, which is also established by the young gods and consists of the four elements, yet it is more complex than the pneuma-vehicle, hence Proclus defines it as 'complex and enmattered' (σύνθετον καὶ ἔνυλον, *In Tim.* III 285, 14). Given that these elements are borrowed from the universe, they must be paid back (*Tim.* 42e6–43a1), which implies that this vehicle is perishable. The earthly body

possesses the sense-organs which are credited with the dynamis to discern the homogeneous elemental movements proceeding from the sensibles, to co-produce the affected sense-affections in the neighbouring area, to receive and transport them to the pneumatic vehicle and the mortal soul, one of whose cognitive capacities is included in the discrimination of these affections.

Moreover, in his *Republic*-commentary Proclus emphasises the substantial differences of the three soul-parts of the one unified soul.[361] In accordance with the *Timaeus* (esp. 69c7–72d4) Plato argues at *Republic* 435b1–441c3 that every human soul possesses three 'forms' (εἴδη/ γένη) or 'parts' (μέρη),[362] i.e., λογιστικόν, θυμοειδές and ἐπιθυμητικόν, each of them holds its own nature and distinguishes itself from the other two forms (parts). Most of the Neoplatonists prior to Proclus agree that the soul has different dynameis, yet as it possesses only one substance,[363] the three parts of soul should not be regarded as three distinguished substances, rather they are the three-fold faculties of one single substance. Despite this strong tradition Proclus holds that for Plato the three parts of one single soul, being analogical to the three cardinal virtues wisdom, courage and prudence, are distinct from each other in their substances.[364] Apparently Proclus intends not to argue against the unity of the individual soul, rather by resorting to the soul's substantial diversity he tries to explain the virtues discussed in the *Republic*, which "can only be explained either as the respective perfections of different entities within the soul or as describing the correct relationship of these different entities among themselves",[365] thus, insisting on the substantial diversity enables Proclus to explain the virtues through the perfection of their corresponding soul-part.

Yet he ceases not at this point, rather goes further to observe the soul, especially its perceptual part, which is distinguished from the soul part λογιστικόν, for the latter is rational, while the sensation is unregulated (ἄλογον).[366] Given that the other two soul parts, θυμοειδές and ἐπιθυμητικόν, are both desiderative (ὀρεκτικά, *In Remp.* I 232, 19) and are distinct from the rational part, they are also unregulated, which implies that their

---

[361] For the diversity of the substance of soul in Proclus, see Perkams (2006) 167–185.

[362] Plato uses the terms εἴδη, γένη, and μέρη in the *Republic*, while in the *Timaeus* only εἶδος (69c7) and γένος (69d6, e5) to delineate the individual soul. Cf. Taylor (1928) 498. The reason, I suppose, is located mainly in the difference of the contexts: in the former dialogue there is a polis-soul likeness, thus, it is reasonable to argue that a polis consists of three parts (μέρη), each of them has a multitude of people composed of body and soul, and to apply the term μέρη further in describing the constitution of the single human soul; while the *Timaeus* concentrates on the human soul's generation, procession, and reversion, therefore, Plato emphasizes not the tripartite constitution of the human soul, rather the distinction of the immortal and mortal soul-form (41d2–3, 42e7–8). Indeed, such a difference is also revealed in the *Republic*, yet not in book IV, rather quite later in book X 611a10–612a6.

[363] For the Neoplatonic doctrine of soul's unity and diversity from Plotinus to Proclus, see Perkams (2006) 168–171. Perkams also mentions the influence of Aristotle (*De an.* 432b4–7) on the Neoplatonists.

[364] Proclus, *In Remp.* I 207, 9–11: ἐν μιᾷ ψυχῇ κατὰ τὸ ἀνάλογον ἀρετὰς καταδήσηται, τὰ μέρη τῆς ψυχῆς ἐπέδειξεν τὰ τρία κατ' οὐσίαν ἀλλήλων διαφέροντα, λόγον θυμὸν ἐπιθυμίαν. Cf. 224, 18–19: διαφέρει οὖν τὰ τρία ἀλλήλων κατ' οὐσίαν.

[365] Perkams (2006) 173.

[366] Proclus, *In Remp.* I 232, 15f.

cognitive abilities contain or correspond to the perception-ability.[367] The difference rests merely on the degree of their dependence on perception: the appetitive part discriminates mainly the momentary sensation, while the corresponding cognition of the thymos-formed part is essentially not restricted by time.

Moreover, in the sense that the unregulated parts θυμοειδές and ἐπιθυμητικόν relate immanently to the perceptible things proportionally ordered and perishable, thus are essentially perishable, while the rational soul part involves inherently the intelligible objects which are coherent and everlasting, hence also more divine, the rational soul can be regarded as the 'form' of the unregulated soul, if the soul can be described as a hylomorphic unity.[368] This relationship between the rational and unregulated soul is equal to that of the immortal and mortal soul, which is described in the Proclean *Timaeus*-commentary, *Elementatio Theologica* and *Theologia Platonica*.[369] The main doctrine of the latter two works is: the mortal soul, as shade or shadow of the immortal soul,[370] possesses the cognitive abilities of perception, memory, and phantasia.[371] For phantasia there are two forms, one concerns the external objects and is ascribed to the perception-dynamis, the other acts in the pneumatic vehicle and functions 'figuratively' (μορφωτικῶς) and 'dimensionally' (διαστατικῶς), which relates to memory.[372] These dynameis of the mortal soul, going back again to the *Republic*-commentary, are asserted as 'images' (εἰκόνες) of the corresponding abilities of the immortal soul: phantasia is image of discursive thinking (διάνοια), while perception is image of opinion[373] – such a relationship is also applied between the pneumatic and earthly vehicles, for in his *Timaeus*-commentary III 237, 24–31, speaking of the immortal souls, Proclus argues that: "their single impassive sensation in that [immortal part] produces a single and passive sensation in the pneumatic vehicle, while this produces many passive senses in the shell-like body; and the single appetitive power in that [immortal part] produces the greater number of appetitive powers in the pneuma, all with some independence from the shell-like body and able to be trained, whereas these [powers] produce the final enmattered ones in this [earthly] body".[374]

---

[367] Proclus, *In Remp.* I 232, 22–23: μετὰ αἰσθήσεων γὰρ αἱ ὀρέξεις. For the distinction of the three parts and their relation, see 211, 7f. Cf. Opsomer (2006b) 140–141.

[368] Proclus, *In Remp.* I 234, 17–30. Cf. Perkams (2006) 176–177. Perkams (p. 177) points out that such a view of hylomorphic scheme appears already in Plotinus, *Enn.* II 4, 3, 4–10; IV 3, 1, 8–14.

[369] For the relationship of the immortal and mortal soul in the *Timaeus*-commentary, see section 1.2; for research of the unregulated soul in the *Elem. Theol.* and *Theol. Plat.*, see Opsomer (2006b) 136–166.

[370] Proclus, *Elem.* § 64 (62, 11–12): οὔτε πᾶσα ψυχῆς ἔλλαμψις ψυχή, ἀλλ' ἔστι καὶ τὰ εἴδωλα τῶν ψυχῶν.

[371] At *Theol. Plat.* III 23, 27–24, 1; 24, 10–11 Proclus attributes the cognitive abilities perception, memory, and phantasia to the mortal soul. Cf. Opsomer (2006b) 139.

[372] Proclus, *In Tim.* I 225, 18–19; 320, 10; 352, 18; II 166, 7; *In Remp.* I 111, 21ff.; 235, 18–19. Cf. Büttner (2000) 88–92; Lautner (2002) 264; Opsomer (2006b) 142–143.

[373] Proclus, *In Remp.* I 235, 11–15. Cf. Opsomer (2006b) 143.

[374] Tr. Tarrant. Cf. Proclus, *In Tim.* III 285, 27–287, 10 in annotating *Timaeus* 42a5–6.

After this exposition we should turn to the point that the Proclean soul-doctrine, on which his theory of perception is based, is directly derived from Plato's corpus, especially the *Timaeus* and *Republic*, for as argued above, it is in his commentaries of Plato's works we find his soul-theory. Considering the results arrived, the single problem left is to clarify the rightness of Proclus' terminology. In determining the substantial diversity of the unified soul Proclus uses the term 'οὐσία', which appears not in Plato's own description of the three-fold soul-constitution. Yet when one considers this term in the view of the Aristotelian terminology, he can find that Proclus fabricates his soul-theory with Aristotle's words. In this sense although the most Neoplatonists, due to the influence of the seeming Aristotelian criticism (*De an.* 432a22–b7) of the Platonic tripartition of soul, hold the idea that the soul is a unity with three different faculties, Proclus annotates the three soul parts, in a broad sense, with the Aristotelian terminology.[375]

(2) Regarding the tripartite perception of Aristotle, it is reasonable to announce that the decisive factors of this doctrine are also rooted in the Platonic sensation-theory. The Aristotelian three-fold model (peculiar perception, common perception, and incidental perception) – both the notions and terms – are frequently proclaimed to be conceived originally by Aristotle,[376] yet the fact is, although the terms 'incidental perception' and 'common sensation' are not utilised by Plato himself, and the term 'incidental' originates really from Aristotle, the notions of these three kinds of perception exist already in Plato's dialogues:

(a) The peculiar and common perception in Plato. To expound the Platonic concept of the peculiar and common sensation we need to observe his application of the terms ἴδιον and κοινόν in his statement about sense perception, because in this way we will easily find that the Aristotelian peculiar perception exists equally in Plato, both the concept and the term; in case of the Aristotelian common sensation this observation will rule out the possibility of the terminological existence in Plato, for the term κοινόν is apparently used in another level, however, it leaves room for another clarification, i.e., Plato does have the concept of the common sensation, albeit he does not formulate it with the same term.

The antithesis 'ἴδιον–κοινόν' is so familiar to Plato[377] that in his description of perception he utilises both words in a more complex and systematic manner than Aristotle: for Plato these two terms relate to (a1) the related bodily part of the affected sense-affections. At *Tim.* 61c4–68d8 in accordance with the (affected) affections Plato divides the perception explicitly into two kinds: the affections involving the whole body[378] are touch, pleasure, and pain (61c4–65b4), while those relate only to a peculiar

---

[375] Perkams (2006) 172 views the Proclean 'οὐσία' as an Aristotelian terminology, yet he offers no proof, which, however, can be found at *Metaph.* 1017b10–26, 1028b8–13; *Cat.* 3a29–32; etc. Cf. Priscian, *In de an.* 288, 3–4; Steel (2013) 92n320.

[376] For example, Beare (1906) 260, 275; Solmsen (1968) 620n1 (with further literature); Herzberg (2010) 137 and Perkams (²2013) 266.

[377] For the application of these two terms in Plato, see *Hipp. mai.* 281d1–2; *Gorg.* 502e6–7; *Rep.* 333d4, 535b8–9, 543b3–4; *Phileb.* 33d5–6; *Tim.* 71a1–2; *Laws* 644c10, 961b7; etc.

[378] *Tim.* 64a2–3: τῶν κοινῶν περὶ ὅλον τὸ σῶμα παθημάτων. 65b5: τὰ κοινὰ τοῦ σώματος παντός. Cf. Büttner (2000) 66n179.

part of the body[379] are taste, smell, hearing, and sight (65b5–68d8). In this regard the words ἴδιον and κοινόν relate primarily to the bodily parts engaging in the generation of the affected sense-affections, and this kind of perception at issue, no matter its affections involve only one peculiar bodily part or the whole body, corresponds to the peculiar and common perception of Aristotle. (a2) The Aristotelian peculiar perception on the one side, the 'common things' involving exclusively the substantial categories on the other. At *Theaetetus* 184c1–186c5 Plato separates the things perceived by the peculiar senses from the common things that are inaccessible for them. The peculiar sensation is one that equipped with 'a peculiar organ' (ὄργανον ἴδιον, 185d9) and an intrinsic dynamis, which enables its determinate competence that is unavailable for another kind of peculiar perception (184e7–185a2) – no doubt this is the very Aristotelian peculiar perception. However, for the common thing (τὸ κοινόν)[380] that is 'over' two (περὶ ἀμφοτέρων, 185a4, περὶ αὐτῶν, 185b8–9) or more peculiar senses there is no corresponding sense-organs like eyes or ears (185a4–6), rather the soul can discriminate and comprehend it only 'by itself' (αὐτὴ δι' αὑτῆς, 185d9–e1, e6). Given that the motif of this passage is the ultimate refutation of the assertion that perception is knowledge, we should be cautious about both the concepts and terms that are ascribed to perception on the one hand, and the common things on the other. Bearing this in mind it is not difficult to notice that at the beginning of this context Plato views the perception exclusively as the peculiar perception (184c1–185c2), but when he determines that what grasps the common things is the soul itself, he joins all five peculiar perception together by attributing them to the determinate dynamis that is 'according to body' (τὰ δὲ διὰ τῶν τοῦ σώματος δυνάμεων, 185e7) or based on 'all bodily affections' (ὅσα διὰ τοῦ σώματος παθήματα, 186c1–2, 186d2) – with the term 'ὅσα' all kinds of perception that generate from the bodily affections, including both the Aristotelian peculiar and common sensation, are now evidently ascribed to one side, while the common character that is discerned by the soul itself to the other. Therefore, what is 'common' here rests evidently out of the range of the Aristotelian common perception, because, in Plato's own words, it locates 'over' all sensibles,[381] i.e., τὸ κοινόν enables all sensible qualities as well as the sensible things to be perceptible. Moreover, these common things are for instance What-is (τὸ ἔστιν, 185c4–5) and What-is-not (τὸ οὐκ ἔστιν, 185c5), Substance and Non-substance (οὐσίαν [...] καὶ τὸ μὴ εἶναι, 185c8), Likeness (ὁμοιότητα, 185c8; τὸ ὅμοιον, 186a6) and Unlikeness (ἀνομοιότητα, 185c9; τὸ ἀνόμοιον, 186a6), the Sameness (τὸ ταὐτόν, 185c9, 186a6) and Difference (τὸ ἕτερον, 185c9, 186a7), the One (ἕν, 185d1) and the other number (τὸν ἄλλον ἀριθμόν, 185d1), even and odd (ἄρτιόν τε καὶ περιττόν, 185d2), etc.[382] From such an account we can conclude that the five senses at issue are the very peculiar perception of Aristotle, but

---

[379] *Tim.* 65b7 (τὰ δ' ἐν ἰδίοις μέρεσιν ἡμῶν); 67a8 (αἰσθητικὸν ἐν ἡμῖν μέρος).
[380] *Theaet.* 185b8. Cf. 185c3–4, e1.
[381] *Ibid.* 185c3–4: τό τ' ἐπὶ πᾶσι κοινὸν καὶ τὸ ἐπὶ τούτοις. Cf. e1: τὰ κοινά μοι φαίνεται περὶ πάντων.
[382] Moreover, the Beautiful and Ugly, the Good and Bad (186a9), the substance of hardness and softness, and other contrary things (186b2–7).

'the common things' are definitely not the Aristotelian common sensation.[383] In these common characters only some of them, like the One and the other numbers, when they are enmattered and generated, can be entitled the 'common sensation' in Aristotle's view[384] – yet the phrases 'περὶ ἀμφοτέρων' at 185a4 and 'τό τ' ἐπὶ πᾶσι κοινὸν καὶ τὸ ἐπὶ τούτοις' in 185c3–4 rule such a possibility out, since apparently τὸ κοινόν refers solely to the entities that are separated from the bodily domain, which, on the contrary, is the very object of the Aristotelian common perception.[385]

According to these two passages we can announce that the Aristotelian 'peculiar perception' appears also in Plato, conceptually and terminologically, but regarding the 'common sensation' there is no evidence that this kind of sensation exists terminologically in Plato, which, however, does not endorse an assertation of the non-existence of this notion in the Platonic corpus,[386] for it is possible that he formulates this concept without utilising the Aristotelian terminology. Indeed, as already indicated by the quotations in section 2.1.2.3, Plato does know the notion of common perception:[387] at *Theaet.* 201b7–c2 Plato declares that as the other people discriminate a case by seeing, the judge can discriminate by hearing; in *Republic* 523d3–4 and e5–6 we are told that the thickness and thinness of a finger can be both seen and touched. Furthermore, all kinds of the Aristotelian common perception can be found in Plato: 'motion (κίνησις)' and 'rest' (ἠρεμία, *De an.* 418a17–18; στάσις, 425a16) in *Charm.* 168e7, *Rep.* 436c9 –

---

[383] Grönroos (2001) 42 rightly asserts that the Platonic 'common things' is unequal to the Aristotelian 'common sensation', yet fails to differ the Platonic 'common number' – which means the number itself – from the Aristotelian enmattered number that can be perceived by the common sensation.

[384] Herzberg (2010) 117n27 also mentions this point.

[385] In this regard Beare (1906) 262 and Helmig (2012) 226 are wrong by treating the common character as the objects of the Aristotelian common perception. Rightly judged by for example Burnyeat (1990) 56f. and Herzberg (2010) 116–117. For a detailed discussion on this topic, see Bostock (1988) 118–128. Bostock (112–114) misleadingly argues that we can make a perceptual discrimination of something which simultaneously includes the common things like Being and a sound or a colour, e.g., we can see 'the colour is'. But these common things at issue cannot be perceived, even when they are enmattered (for we cannot see "is" in the coloured things), as Plato asserts at *Theaet.* 186b2–9. Sedley (2004) 106n164 also points this falsehood out.

[386] Yet this is what Herzberg (2010) 137 intends to assert, when he argues that Aristotle, against Plato, broadens the perception-spectrum by adding the common sensation to the peculiar perception.

[387] Polansky (1992) 164 suggests that perhaps Plato ignores not the Aristotelian common sensation, rather he prefers to insist that 'every type of perception is unique to some type of sense', so Plato might think that "the so-called common sensibles are not really perceived in the same way by different senses, for example, shape visually perceived is radically different from shape apprehended through touch". Polansky is right in arguing that Plato holds that the way of perceiving the common sensibles is distinguished from that of the peculiar sensation, for as mentioned above, they are distinct in the sense of the different involved organs. However, what Plato mainly concerns here is the restriction of the perceptual truth in comparing with the discrimination of the soul itself, in this sense there is no need to distinguish common perception from peculiar sensation, for it makes no difference in highlighting this comparison.

e6 (the example of the spinning tops which seems simultaneously to move and to stand still), *Laws* 653e3–5, 664e3–8; 'size' (μέγεθος) at *Charm.* 154c2, *Rep.* 523e3, 602c7–8, *Theaet.* 154b2 (μέγα), *Soph.* 251a10; 'one' (ἕν) in *Rep.* 525a2–3;[388] 'number' (ἀριθμός) at *Rep.* 525d7–8 and 'shape' (σχῆμα) at *Men.* 75b9–c1, *Soph.* 251a9.[389] More decisively, in the finger-passage of the *Republic*, in order to point out the contradictions aroused through perceiving the common sensible qualities of the 'mixed' (συγκεχυμένον τι, 524c4; cf. κεχωρισμένα, 524b10–c1, διωρισμένα, c7) sensible objects, Plato intentionally leaves the qualities 'white and dark' out, which can be exclusively perceived by the peculiar perception, i.e., the sight: at 523d2–4 he announces that for a single finger among three there is no difference whether it is seen in the middle or at end, whether it is white or dark, thick or thin, for with sight we can perceive it without contradiction, yet some lines later (523e4–6), speaking of perceiving three fingers at the same time, only the sensible categories 'middle and end', 'thickness and thinness' are left. The omission of the qualities 'white and dark' is made purposely, for evidently even in respect of three fingers there is little room to be wrong in discriminating them. In this view Plato must know the difference of the 'peculiar sensation' and 'common perception', although he does not talk about the notion of 'common sensation' terminologically.

Moreover, speaking of the peculiar and common perception we should also stress that even the Aristotelian term 'according to themselves' (καθ' αὐτά), the criterion of his division of the three perception-types, can also be found in Plato's description of (peculiar) perception, although it is not regarded as the criterion of the division of distinct perception-kinds: for example, at *Charmides* 167b5–169a1,[390] the Platonic Socrates inquires his partner Critias whether there is 'one determinate knowledge' (μία τις ἐπιστήμη, 167b9) that is both knowledge of nothing else but itself and of other knowledge-kinds (167b9–c2). As Critias disclaims this possibility, Socrates urges him to think (ἐννόει, 167c5) whether there is a certain sight (ὄψις τις, 167c6) that is not the sight of those things that other sights are of, but is the sight of itself (ἑαυτῆς, 167c7) and of the other sights, and also of the lack of sights, moreover, although it is a sight, is sees no colour, rather there is only itself (αὐτὴν, 167d1) and other sights (167c5–d1). Evidently this is impossible, for there is no sight both of sight itself and of the other sights, nor is this possible for all other perception,[391] and being perceived, the sensibles is determinate, thus the sight is sight of something determinate. Hence Plato declares that the sight, if 'it sees itself' (ὄψεται αὐτὴ ἑαυτήν, 168d7), must possess 'a determinate colour' (χρῶμά τι, 168d7), for it would never see anything without colour (168d6–8), in the same sense the hearing must have certain sound. From this account one can

---

[388] That the enmattered 'one' is object of the common perception, is illustrated by Bernard (1988) 113n2.

[389] Büttner (2000) 74–75 offers a clear interpretation of the relation between colour and shape in Plato, especially in the *Meno*. The locations of colour and shape that are summarised by him are: *Theaet.* 163b8–c1; *Rep.* 373b6, 601a2; *Gorg.* 465b5; *Laws* 669a1. See also *Soph.* 251a9.

[390] For an interpretation of this passage, see Halper (2000) 309–316.

[391] *Tim.* 43c2, see section 2.1.2.1. Halper (2000) 312n4 summarises Aristotle's related opinion in *De an.* 417a2–4, 417b19–24 and 429b31–430a9. Cf. Ficino, *The Philebus Commentary*, § 32, in: Allen (1975) 318.

derive that as a kind of perception the sight relates inherently to colour, and the hearing concerns naturally the sound, and so on. Therefore, for Plato at least the peculiar perception can be called the perception καθ' αὐτήν.

(b) Plato's description of the 'incidental sensation'. For the notion of the 'common sensation' although Plato formulates it not explicitly, literally he does apply the term κοινόν in the matter of perception, this is, however, not the case of the 'incidental perception', for the term 'συμβεβηκός' is an invention of Aristotle.[392] Nevertheless, the concept of 'incidental perception' also appears frequently in the Platonic dialogues, one typical example is offered at *Philebus* 38b6–d10, which is already discussed in section 2.2: when somebody sees an object locating beside the rock under a tree from a distance, he would ask himself what this sensible object is, and answers himself by declaring: "it is a man". Such an example corresponds perfectly to the Aristotelian incidental perception, whose object contains a determinate substance that is incidentally sensible – in the *Philebus* it is 'a man' – and one quality that can be discriminated by the peculiar (or common) sensation – in the *Philebus* for instance the colour and shape. Given that the original purpose of this context is to manifest that the opinion (δόξα) generates from (affected) perception and memory (μνήμη),[393] we can further determine that the Aristotelian incidental perception concerns the cognitive faculty of opinion, which grasps the substance of a determinate sensible object. In this regard one wonders whether the 'common things' mentioned in *Theaetetus* 184c1–186c5 can be understood as the incidental perception, yet the answer is negative: the Platonic 'common characters' denotes (partially) the substances of the sensibles, however, they are primarily observed in the view of themselves, while the Aristotelian incidental perception involves the substance of the sensibles in the 'incidental' manner, not in the manner of the substance itself.

(3) After having demonstrated that both the Proclean and Aristotelian tripartition originate from Plato, we should turn to their harmonisation. At the outset of this endeavour, we should re-examine the seemingly Aristotelian criticism of the Platonic tripartite soul at *De anima* 432a22–b7, for this issue directly concerns the unity and diversity of the human soul and thus relates essentially to the matter of perception. Here is the concerned context:

---

[392] Cessi (1987) 87–94. Cf. Büttner (2000) 79n226. However, this term is potentially utilized by Plato on the sensation-occasions, for he speaks of perceiving 'the incidental results' (τὰ συμβαίνοντα) of the 'speech' (λόγος) at *Gorg.* 479c5, 496e10; *Phaed.* 92b4 and *Phileb.* 35c3–4.

[393] For the explanation of this passage as well as the incidental perception, see Büttner (2000) 79–81. For the Aristotelian incidental perception, see Bernard (1988) 75–81; Herzberg (2010) 137–155; Johansen (2012) 180–185.

A problem arises straightaway, in what way we should speak of parts of the soul and how many there are. For in one way they seem to be infinitely many, and not only those which some authors mention in distinguishing the reasoning (λογιστικόν), the thymos-formed (θυμοειδές), and the appetitive (ἐπιθυμητικόν), or (according to others) the rational and unregulated parts; for in virtue of the differences (διαφοράς) by which they distinguish these parts, others appear as parts too with a greater disparity between them than these, those which we have already discussed, the nutritive, which belongs both to plants and to all animals, and the perceptive, which could not easily be set down as either irrational or rational. There is again the part capable of imagination (φανταστικόν), which is different from all of them in being (εἶναι), although with which of them it is identical or non-identical presents a great problem if we are to posit separate parts of the soul. In addition to these there is the part capable of desire (τὸ ὀρεκτικόν), which is held to be different from all in logos and dynamis. And it would be absurd surely to split this up; for in the part that can reason (λογιστικῷ) there will be rational wish (βούλησις), and in the unregulated part appetite (ἐπιθυμία) and thymos; so if the soul is tripartite there will be desire in each. (Tr. Gendlin, with reversion).

This passage is introduced to determine which part of the soul is responsible for its movement,[394] so Aristotle begins with the general division of the soul in respect of 'how' (πῶς) and 'how many' (πόσα), and mentions the Platonic tripartition, which appears primarily in the *Republic*, *Timaeus* and *Laws*.[395] Aristotle's argument is that in accordance with the differences of such a tripartition there must be more parts in the soul, for example the nutritive part that belongs to plants and all animals; the perceptive part, which is difficult to judge to which soul-form it should be attributed to; the part of imagination distinguishable from all other parts; the desire, existing in both the rational and the unregulated soul, is distinct from all others in respect of logos and dynamis. Aristotle does not elucidate the differences in accordance with which the three Platonic soul-parts are divided, but when he has recourse to 'logos and dynamis'[396] to display the distinction of desire from all others, the 'logos and dynamis' should be regarded as the criterion of the division of soul-parts, according to which the soul possesses not only three parts, rather, as he argues at the outset of this passage: "in one determinate way they seem to be infinitely many" (τρόπον γάρ τινα ἄπειρα φαίνεται, 432a24). However, despite the three Platonic parts Aristotle adds in this context only four another 'parts', which results collectively in seven soul-parts: the threefold Platonic parts reason, thymos, and appetite, and the supplemented parts nourishment, perception, imagination, and desire. This implies that (a) either the soul-parts are infinitely many, but seven parts suffice already for the current subject, or (b) they only 'appear' (φαίνεται) to be many, but indeed only seven. Given that in the aforesaid texts Aristotle has expounded

---

[394] See *De an.* 432a18–22, 432b7–8. Cf. Priscian, *In de an.* 288, 18–22.

[395] For the studies of the tripartite soul in the *Republic*, *Timaeus* and *Laws*, see Büttner (2000) 111–122; (2006) 75–93; for the newest research, see Meinwald (2016) 144–168; Kamtekar (2017) 165–185; Jorgenson (2018) 6–87; Weinstein (2018), 33–42. A collection of essays about this topic can be found in Barney, Brennan and Brittain (2012).

[396] *De an.* 432b3–4: λόγῳ καὶ δυνάμει. Cf. 432a15: κατὰ [...] δυνάμεις; 432a20: λόγῳ.

intellect, discursive thinking (διάνοια), opinion, imagination and three-fold perception,[397] of which some are not mentioned in the current passage, it is evident that (a) should be the better interpretation. Furthermore, unlike the matter that is corporeal, continuous, and divisible, the soul is incorporeal and divisible, and as in the case of the matter the soul-parts are 'infinitely many' due to the different logoi and dynameis:[398] in the view of bipartition the soul is separate (χωριστόν) and non-separate, rational and unregulated, cognitive and motivative, theoretical and desiderative, perfective (τελειοῦντος) and perfected (τελειούμενον), perceptive and non-perceptive.[399] Regarding tripartition we have the Platonic immortal soul-form and two mortal forms, and in accordance with desires that initiate movements the soul is also tripartite, i.e., rational will (βούλησις), thymos and appetite, as manifested in this citation; speaking of the fourfold soul-parts Plato itemizes wisdom, courage, prudence, and justice in the view of virtue; and very possibly we can divide the soul into more parts. However, none of these division can reveal all soul-parts, thus Aristotle lists only seven of them in this passage: after all, for the present theme this is already sufficient. Deriving from this point we can stress that (a) Aristotle does not intend to reject the Platonic tripartition,[400] rather he only insists that despite this tripartition there should be the other parts, and the determination of the part that involves the spatial movement is what he prefers to do after this short discussion. In this view he embraces the three kinds of desires that correspond to the three Platonic soul-parts, and he also agrees with the dichotomy of the rational and unregulated soul (432b5–6), which appears frequently in Plato's works like the *Timaeus*. (b) Given that for Plato the soul can be separated both in bipartition and tripartition, such classifications should not be deemed as the final view of the division of the human soul, rather they suffice the requirement of the subject-matter at issue, i.e., this tripartition is necessary for the practical life.

On this ground we can declare that the Aristotelian soul-theory coincides with Plato's soul-doctrine, for they both agree with soul's bipartition and tripartition. This signifies that the clarification of the harmonisation of the Proclean and Aristotelian perception-theory is based on a detailed interpretation of the Platonic soul-theory, especially its unity, bipartition and tripartition, since the unity and diversity of the Platonic soul corresponds to its unified and differentiated cognitive dynameis, in which we find the perception: (a) the soul's unification can be used to clarify its decisive role in the generation, discrimination and comprehension of the sensation both affected and unaffected, which enables the assertation that the whole course of perception is finally decided by the soul. More decisively, we have determined that the (unified) soul is the

---

[397] In commenting the soul-parts of 'those usually mentioned and those that have been said' (τὰ εἰμθότα λέγεσθαι καὶ τὰ εἰρημένα) at *De an.* 432a21–22 Philoponus (*In de an.* 573, 21–24) supposes that there are eight 'parts' of soul: in Plato there are three, i.e., reason, thymos and appetite, while in Aristotle he has mentioned five parts prior to this passage, namely intellect, discursive thinking, opinion, imagination, and perception both peculiar and common.

[398] For the division of the matter according to dynamis, see Aristotle, *Phy.* 206b14–27. Indeed, the criterion 'logos and dynamis' also signifies the self-motion of the soul, as mentioned in section 1.1.2.3.

[399] Priscian, *In de an.* 289, 1–5.

[400] For the apology of the Platonic tripartition, see Priscian, *In de an.* 289, 9–19.

reason and principle of all physical movements including acting and being affected, locomotion and alteration, separation and connection, etc., namely the complete sensible universe is formed and governed by the soul, thus with regard to perception we can proclaim that all sensibles and their substances are eventually generated from the soul, all sense-organs are actuated and characterized as living organs by the soul, and the whole process of perception can be explained by the dynamis and activity of the soul. The material entity, or the matter does have a role to play in this course, for after all it is also a cause of the generation of the sensibles, yet it is only the accessory cause. This unity of soul is approved both by Proclus and Aristotle, for the latter frequently stresses that the single soul has the dynameis of nutrition, movement, perception, and thinking in the *De anima*,[401] while the former, as commentator of many Platonic dialogues, obviously knows this point. (b) The bipartition of soul denotes the rational and unregulated soul, whose relationship with each other is manifested in many aspects: regarding their substances and generation, the unregulated soul is imitation of the rational one, thus in the unified soul the rational soul is prior to the unregulated soul and should thus govern the whole soul; given that both belong to the unified soul and bear determinate cognitive abilities to discriminate their proper objects, they are akin to each other; in the view that affected sensation is impossible without affections, whereas the unaffected sensation of the rational soul needs no affection from outside, they are different from each other; in discerning the peculiar perceptible qualities such as colours and sounds both kinds of soul can hardly be fallible, yet for the cognition of common and incidental objects the rational soul is also always right, while the latter can err occasionally, in this sense they are both alike and unlike. Speaking of their vehicles, the rational immortal soul is mounted into the ethereal vehicle, where its two circuits discriminate and move in their natural state, whereas the unregulated soul possesses two mortal vehicles according to Proclus,[402] i.e., the simple enmattered pneuma-vehicle and the complex enmattered earthly body. The shell-like body can co-produce the unaffected sense-affections and send them to the pneumatic vehicle, where the mortal soul discriminates these affections; the pneuma-vehicle, however, together with the mortal soul, can preserve and transmit the perceived materials to the immortal vehicle and divine soul, in which sense these two soul-parts are successive. (c) The tripartition signifies one immortal soul-form and two mortal soul-parts, or as revealed in the *Republic*, λογιστικόν, θυμοειδές, and ἐπιθυμητικόν. The mortal soul can be further divided into two parts: the higher form is named thymos-formed, and the lower part is called 'appetitive', thus we have a tripartite soul. Unlike the modern philosophers like Kant, who tends to regard cognition, feeling, and will as three separate parts of the soul, every part of the Platonic soul bears these three aspects: the rational soul-part has the cognitive

---

[401] *De an.* 413b11–414a3, 414a29–415a11. On the harmonisation of Plato and Aristotle in respect of soul's self-motion, see Gertz (2010) 73–87; Menn (2012) 44–67.
[402] Deviating from the most Neoplatonists (like Iamblichus, Damascius and Simplicius), Proclus holds a three-fold vehicle theory to clarify the descent of the immortal soul. Cf. Blumenthal (1992) 174–176.

dynamis of intellect and intelligence, and its will-form is βούλησις, the rational wish;[403] the θυμοειδές-part opines its objects, and thymos is the form of its will; the part of the ἐπιθυμητικόν recognises through perceiving, i.e., sense perception functions as its cognitive-ability, while the appetite is its will-form. All three soul-parts can feel pleasure and pain when they are applying their cognitive capacities, which is revealed for example in *Rep.* 583b1f. Now we can summarise the process from cognition to action: firstly, we discriminate the objects, at the same time we feel pleasure or pain about them, then the corresponding will is aroused, which drive us to act.[404]

I suppose that this exposition enables us to proclaim, at least in the broad sense, that the unified and multi-faced character of the Platonic soul endorses both the Proclean and the Aristotelian perception-theory, especially about the kinds of perception. Conversely, the interpretation of Plato's perception-theory with help of Aristotle and Proclus is reasonable, for their philosophies are both based on Plato.

3.1.2 Comprehensive research of the different kinds of perception in Plato

Having determined that the Platonic perception-doctrine is the very ground of the perception-theories of Aristotle and Proclus, we should turn back to the subject-matter of this section, namely the kinds of perception in Plato's corpus. Let us firstly review the tripartition in Proclus and Aristotle: in the former there are three different kinds of vehicles and hence three corresponding kinds of sensation: in the ethereal vehicle there is common and unaffected sensation, the common and affected perception takes place in the pneumatic vehicle, whereas the earthly body is responsible for the divided and affected sensation. In the view of their generation Proclus asserts that the 'single' (μία) and unaffected sensation of the immortal soul produces the single and affected perception in the pneumatic vehicle, whereas the latter engenders the 'many' (πολλάς) and affected sensation in the shell-like body.[405] For Aristotle the soul is viewed as unified, thus he does not divide the perception in accordance with the different soul-forms, rather his tripartite perception-kinds is rooted in the distinction of the perceptible objects. However, given that both models can be explained with the Platonic soul-theory, the kinds of perception in Plato are presumably more than three, which signifies that a comprehensive investigation into the sorts of sensation should be performed with neither the Proclean framework nor the model of Aristotle.

For a comprehensive research of the kinds of perception, we should re-stress that as human beings we are certain kind of perceiver, which indicates that our perception belongs to a certain species and there are also other species. The discussion of the different species of perception-subjects in section 1.2.1 brings forth four types of

---

[403] Just as in the case of Aristotle: with reference to the concerned soul-parts of virtue he argues at *NE* 1139a20–26 that intellect and rational wish (ἡ δὲ προαίρεσις ὄρεξις βουλευτική, 1139a23) are related respectively to cognition and (the will of) action.
[404] For the difference between the Platonic tripartite soul theory and that of the modern philosophy, especially the Kantian philosophy, see for example Büttner (2000) 22–130; (2006) 75–93; Schmitt (2012) 277–371; (2015) 303–319.
[405] Proclus, *In Tim.* III 237, 24–27.

perception that are ascribed to three classes, the common (κοινή) and affected (παθητική) human perception belongs to the second class, which is distinguished from both the first class – i.e., the unaffected (ἀπαθής) and common perception that is attributed to the whole universe (the first kind), the fixed stars and the planets (the second kind) – and the third class, namely the divided (διῃρημένη) and affected perception of the plants, which can only discriminate pleasure and pain. From this account we can derive that, on the one side, the human perception is neither so divine as the sensation of the living god(s) nor as simple as the kind that discerns only pleasure and pain, rather as living creature the human being has its own form (εἶδος), hence his perception is characterised as 'common and affected'; on the other side, in the view that every sensible quality is discriminated by the unified soul holding all three vehicles, these three classes can be ascribed to the same perception-spectrum, and the human soul can participate the perception abilities of the other two classes – in our souls the divine part is moulded as imitation of the world soul and the souls of young gods, so it can be so perceptive as the astral gods, namely it is able to perceive the essence of the sensibles in the manner of the unaffected and common perception; and our mortal soul, being created by the young gods to be in charge of food and drink (*Tim.* 70d7–8), must also possess the ability of the plants-perception in discerning pleasure and pain. This manifests that only if we take both the unity and diversity of the human soul into account, a complete exploration of the Platonic human perception-kinds is possible. Thus, our research shall be exercised in accordance with the division of the human soul, namely the mortal unregulated soul on one side, and the immortal rational soul on the other, while the unity of the soul should also not be neglected.

(1) The divine, immortal human soul does perceive, albeit it discriminates the sensibles not in the same way as the mortal soul, i.e., not through the sense-organs and bodily affections. The reason rests on the fact that the divine part of our soul is a similar creation of the world soul which has the dynamis of divine perception, i.e., opinion with perception. As the first generated thing of our universe the world soul is announced in the *Timaeus* to possess two circuits, the Same and the Difference, and the latter, controlling the movements of the seven planets and moving itself proportionally (ἐν λόγῳ, 36d6–7), is able to perceive both the sensibles and the 'sensible' substances.[406] Being established from the same ingredients of the world soul as well as the young gods' souls, our immortal soul is declared to be made equal to the young gods (θεοῖς ἰσάζοιτ' ἄν, *Tim.* 41c2), which endorses it to possess two divine circles[407] and thus the dynamis of the 'common and unaffected' sensation – at least during the time in which the divine soul is already generated but still not implanted into the body, or when it is purified and ascends again to the heaven, i.e., during its divine life with the ethereal vehicle on the stars, for in this period the immortal soul stays with the astral gods and helps them governing the heaven, perceiving in the divine way with no restriction of the earthly body.[408]

---

[406] *Tim.* 37b6–9. The sensation of the world soul is always true, for what is generated and further delivered to the circle of Difference as well as the whole soul is said to be the logos, which implies its truth inherently See 37b3–4: λόγος δὲ ὁ κατὰ ταὐτὸν ἀληθὴς γιγνόμενος.
[407] *Ibid.* 43d2–4. Cf. 42c5–6, 44a1–2, b7.
[408] Cf. Taylor (1928) 268. For the motif of immortal soul, see section 1.2.2.1.

What follows now is a puzzle: whether the immortal soul perceives when it is embodied in the shell-like body. Although this question is already solved in section 2.2, where we have determined that the unaffected sensation should also be attributed to sense perception, which signifies that the immortal soul does take part in perception during its individual life. However, considering that this question is addressed here in another respect, i.e., the participation of the different soul-forms in sense perception, we should answer it in another way: the immortal soul-form does perceive, yet whether it engages in perceiving depends on the specific occasion: There do exist many cases in which our immortal soul perceives: (a) Resorting to the cognitive dynamis of the circle of Difference (i.e., opinion), the immortal soul-form discriminates the substance of the sensibles, as the *Philebus*-example (38b6–d10) indicates: the sensible object that locates beside the rock under the tree is determined to be a person. (b) Speaking of the movement of the circle of Same (especially the discursive thinking) of the immortal soul-form there exist also occasions on which it is involved to recognise: When we are confused about what we have perceived through the mortal soul-form, the divine soul-form will be summoned to perceive, or it is directly commanded to discriminate the recognisable objects. To reveal the first point we can resort again to the famous finger-passage of *Republic* 523a10–525a10, where in order to demonstrate the fallibility of the mortal soul's affected perception Plato argues that normally there is no need of summing the understanding (of the immortal soul) to recognise the sensible objects, but when the contrary results emerge via our affected sensation of the mortal soul, we will summon the divine soul-part to solve the problems at issue. The other occasions can be revealed by the following examples, i.e., in perceiving the Being (αἰσθόμενος τοίνυν τὸ ὄν, *Rep.* 538b7); the disarray in the soul;[409] the wisdom (ὅταν αἰσθάνωνται ὅτι ἱκανῶς φρονεῖς, *Lysis* 209d5) and the distinction of the species of the soldier from all other species.[410] Given that the term αἰσθάνομαι in these examples is not metaphorically utilised, we must acknowledge that our immortal soul-form does perform its perception-dynamis during its individual life. Moreover, seeing the heaven or listening to music, our immortal soul-form can also take part in discriminating the objects. This point is affirmed at *Tim.* 46e6–47e2, where sight and hearing are deemed to be two 'gifts' sent by the gods.[411] Their 'highest function for our benefit' (τὸ δὲ μέγιστον αὐτῶν εἰς ὠφελίαν ἔργον, 46e8) is to help us in the study of the nature of the universe, especially the intellective circuits in the heaven and the harmony of the music, since both of them are akin to (συγγενεῖς, 47c1, d1) the revolutions of our own thought. This signifies that in both cases our immortal soul-part can possibly be aroused due to its kinship with the divine movements in the heaven and music that are now 'perceptible' for us, and discern the heavenly motion or the musical harmony – this corresponds to the

---

[409] *Soph.* 228b2–5: ἐν ψυχῇ δόξας ἐπιθυμίαις καὶ θυμὸν ἡδοναῖς καὶ λόγον λύπαις καὶ πάντα ἀλλήλοις ταῦτα τῶν φλαύρως ἐχόντων οὐκ ᾐσθήμεθα διαφερόμενα; – Καὶ σφόδρα γε.
[410] *Tim.* 24b1–3: Καὶ δὴ καὶ τὸ μάχιμον γένος ᾔσθησαί που τῇδε ἀπὸ πάντων τῶν γενῶν κεχωρισμένον.
[411] For sight, see *Tim.* 47b2: δωρηθέν. For hearing, see 47c6: δεδωρῆσθαι.

description of the function of astronomy and music in turning around the direction of our soul in *Republic* 527d1–531c8.[412]

At this point we should emphasise that (a) the immortal soul-form perceives together with, or precisely, through the mortal perception. Living not anymore in the heavenly life, the immortal soul-form, as a part of the unified human soul, lives now in the earthly body. Hence, in perceiving the substance of the sensibles as well as the forms it requires the cognitive materials reported by the affected perception via the mortal soul-form, for indeed, even if it perceives not through the affected perception, it needs the other faculties like phantasia[413] and memory, which originate from nowhere but the mortal perception. In this sense we can assert that in the case of seeing the heaven or hearing the music the reason of the immortal soul's involving in the discrimination rests on the one hand on the kinship of its circuits with that of the heaven or the harmony in the music, on the other hand on the affected perception activated either by chance or by the desire to see or to hear. (b) In addition, for a living human being, even if his immortal soul engages in perceiving the sensibles on those occasions, whether it really discriminates in the right way depends not on this simple engagement, rather on the correct nourishment of education (*Tim.* 44b8–c2).

To summarise: with reference to perception the state of the immortal soul-form should be divided into two phases, i.e., in the heavenly life, and the earthly individual life. For although in both periods it discriminates not only the sensible qualities, but also the enmattered substance, when it wanders in the heaven and helps the gods governing, it discerns all by itself in its heavenly vehicle, while during the earthly life, i.e., being unified with the mortal soul-form and embodied in the shell-like body, it perceives normally through the mortal sensation. Besides, in the earthly life the immortal soul-form engages not in all perception-activities, because we do not need to discriminate the substances of the sensibles on all occasions, for example in discriminating the peculiar sensible qualities like colour and sound. Hence there are determinate occasions left for it to function, e.g., in seeing the heaven and hearing the music, and when the mortal soul fails to discriminate the sensibles.

(2) The sensation-faculty of the living human being is mainly activated by his mortal soul-form. Such a kind of perception is affected, and it encompasses many subordinate types like the Aristotelian peculiar and common sensation, and the Proclean single, affected perception in the pneumatic vehicle as well as the many, affected perception through the shell-like body. Yet to determine all kinds of the affected sensation we should firstly resort to its generation – after all, all kinds of perception are generated. Indeed, the generation of the affected perception is already explored in section 2.1, where we have determined that the mortal perception is generated due to the bodily affections which is produced by the meeting of the elemental movements from the sensibles and the sense-organs. Moreover, in arguing that the Aristotelian three-fold perception-theory is grounded on Plato we have mentioned that in the *Timaeus* 61c4–

---

[412] For a historical summary of the function of sight in philosophy, see Calcidius, *In Tim.* §§ 236–248. For the generation of sounds, see *Tim.* 67a8–c2. Regarding the explanation of their concord and dissonance under the principle 'like knows like', see *Tim.* 80a2–b8.

[413] Cf. Proclus, *In Remp.* II 107, 14–23. Aristotle argues that 'the soul never understands without a phantasma' at *De an.* 431 a 16–17. For a study of this assertation, see Steel (2018) 185–223.

68d8 Plato divides the peculiar senses into two parts in accordance with the sense-organs. On this ground we can conclude that (a) there are two ways leading to the becoming of the affected sensation, one is due to the 'accidental' (περιτυχὸν, *Tim.* 43c2) meeting of the bodily elemental motion and the elemental motion from the external sensibles; the other by virtue of the inner desire,[414] which drives our (mortal) soul to perceive, as manifested by the appetite of Leontius to see the corpses (ἅμα μὲν ἰδεῖν ἐπιθυμοῖ, *Rep.* 439e9).[415] (b) As revealed at *Timaeus* 42a3–b2, 64a2–65b4 and 69c5–d6, the perception, pleasure and pain, and the other feelings and emotions are three kinds of faculties that are generated in the mortal soul, and they are engendered by virtue of the bodily affections, in this view there is perception in strict sense and that in broad sense: the perception in strict sense includes not the feelings and emotions, while in broad sense it does. (c) In respect of the related bodily parts co-producing the affected sense-affections, the strict mortal perception can be divided again into two parts, i.e., the sense of touch as well as pleasure and pain on the one side, whose sense-organ is the whole body, and the senses of sight, hearing, smell, and taste on the other, which take only one determinate bodily part as the sense-organ. Despite these classifications, in the view of generation we should not forget the occasions on which the immortal soul-form perceives, from which we can derive another two dichotomies: (d) no matter the generation of the affected sensation involves the whole body or only a part, it results either in precise discrimination or in contradiction, in the latter case the dynamis of the immortal soul-form would be summoned to discriminate; (e) under the five senses the sight and hearing can benefit our thought, especially when we observing the heaven and hearing the music, whereas the other peculiar senses do not hold such a function.

Therefore, with reference to the affected perception we find at least five classifications and ten subordinate kinds of sensation. All kinds of the affected perception, however, can only perceive the qualities enmattered in the physical things, which means that the substance of the sensibles is unavailable for such a sort of perception. Thus, although both the immortal and mortal soul bear the dynamis to perceive, their perceptual competence are distinct from each other: the mortal perception can neither share the dynamis of the divine perception in the sense of discerning the substance of the sensibles, nor damage it, because: (a) These two kinds of soul-forms are essentially distinctly constructed: the divine one is established by the Demiurge himself, its cognition-abilities right opinion, understanding and intellect are distinct from that of the mortal soul-form created by the young gods. Therefore, although there are occasions on which both soul-forms engage in discrimination, their objects are distinguished from each other. (b) The immortal soul-form cannot be destroyed by something alike or something evil – whether its own or an alien,[416] i.e., although the mortal soul-form may compel it to believe in the fallible opinions and perform against its own nature,[417] as manifested

---

[414] See *Tim.* 69d4–5: αἰσθήσει δὲ ἀλόγῳ καὶ ἐπιχειρητῇ παντὸς ἔρωτι συγκεράμενοι ταῦτα. Cf. 70b6–7.
[415] At *Rep.* 474d2f. Plato enumerates many kinds of desires that can initiate perception: the lovers of seeing things (οἳ φιλοθεάμενες, 475d2); the passionate lover of boys (τὸν φιλόπαιδα, 474d4); the wine-lovers (τῶν ἐρωτικῶν, 475a3); etc.
[416] *Rep.* 610e10–611a2.
[417] Calcidius, *In Tim.* § 207.

by the unjust polis and its citizens in *Republic* Book 8 and 9, this influence relates only to the dynamis and activity, not the essence of the immortal soul-form.

Be distinct as the unaffected (immortal) sensation and the affected (mortal) perception are, they are also related to each other: (a) the mortal soul-form is the imitation of the immortal one, for the young gods mould the mortal soul by imitating their Father. (b) They constitute together the unified human soul, for we are told that the divine soul-form is weighed down from the heavenly life to the individual life on earth, of which we find both immortal and mortal soul-form. (c) On determinate occasions they discriminate the sensibles together. As different parts of the unified human soul there is a natural order for these two soul-forms, i.e., the mortal soul-form should be obedient to the immortal one, for the latter considers for the whole soul. In this sense the intellect of the divine part should be combined with the affected perception, and occasionally they should work together to discriminate and comprehend their objects, for example in observing the heavenly movements, as mentioned above.

Now the Platonic division of perception, in the comprehensive view, can be summed up: firstly, there is a dichotomy of the perception belonging either to the immortal or mortal soul, the former kind of perception is equal to the unaffected perception, for it can grasp the essence of the sensibles, while the latter one is the affected mortal perception, because it cannot perceive without bodily affections. Under the latter species one can find the perception in strict sense, and the sensation in broad sense, which includes perception, pleasure and pain, and the other kinds of feelings and emotions that are also generated due to the bodily affections. Regarding the perception in strict sense, there exists one type whose generation is driven by the desire, while the other sort by chance, although for these two kinds the course of perceiving (from the generation of affection to the soul's discrimination of it) are identical. For all these affected sensation there are occasions on which the sensibles are precisely discriminated, and occasions on which the discrimination leads to contradictions and requires thus the diagnose of the divine soul-form, which processes the dynamis like the right opinion and understanding. All kinds of mortal sensation are generated from the affections involving either the whole body (touch, pleasure and pain) or only a peculiar part of it (sight, hearing, smelling and taste). Moreover, if we divide the mortal perception in the view of its relation to the god(s), or whether it is benefit to our thought, sight and hearing can be separated from the other senses. The unaffected sensation of the immortal soul, as revealed above, engages probably on the occasions of watching the heaven, hearing the music, and when the affected perception-discrimination results in contradictions and the (unified) soul prefers to solve this kind of dilemma. With a diagram we can see all these classifications of perception more clearly:

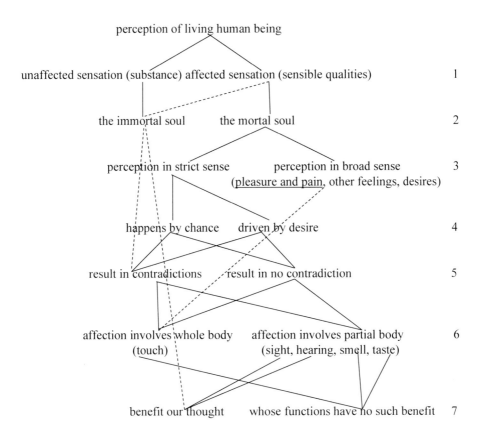

In this diagram there are two points to be clarified, i.e., (a) the crossed lines in level 4 and 5: no matter an affected sensation is generated by chance or driven by our will, the result can be precise and evident, or it contradicts itself, *vice versa*, whether a perception-discrimination contradicts or not, it can be generated either by chance or by desire. In level 5 the reason is the same. (b) The three dotted lines pertaining to the immortal soul reveal the occasions on which it engages in perception (the lines from the 'result in contradictions' in level 5 and the 'benefit our thought' in level 7), and on all those occasions the mortal soul also plays a role (the dotted line from the 'affected sensation' in level 1). Whereas the fourth dotted line between the pleasure and pain (level 3) and 'affection involves whole body' (level 6) signifies that the generation of the affection of pleasure and pain involves the whole body.

This diagram reveals a comprehensive description of the perception-kinds of Plato, and it contains all sorts of sensation in Aristotle and Proclus, for example the Aristotelian peculiar sensation is in level 6, his common sensation can also be attributed to this level, for all common sensation is perceived via the five senses, the incidental sensation can be ascribed to level 1 and 2. The reason rests on the fact that this diagram synthesises the criteria of their models: the distinguished sensible objects, and the view of generation. Moreover, this diagram indicates in certain sense the truth of different sensation-types, which is the theme of the next section.

3.2 The cognitive power of the affected and unaffected perception

Having determined that in Plato the human-perception can be divided into many kinds in accordance with different criteria, and the fundamental criterion rests on the substantial separation of the immortal (rational) and mortal (unregulated) soul-form, which corresponds to the bipartition of the unaffected and affected sensation, it is time to turn to the cognitive ability of the Platonic perception. In general sense this kind of dynamis involves at least three aspects, no matter the engaged soul-form is mortal or immortal: (1) the categories that can be perceived. Normally, the ten Aristotelian categories can be attributed to the perceptible world, through which the physical world can be discriminated and comprehended. In this sense they can be used to determine the cognitive categories of the unaffected and affected sensation: through the unaffected sensation the enmattered Substance of the sensible thing is recognisable, and via the affected sensation we can perceive the rest nine enmattered categories. (2) The truth of the discrimination that varies in accordance with the different kinds of perception. As different kinds of perception hold distinguished degree of truth, the exploration of the sensory dynamis shall fall into two parts, i.e., that of the unaffected sensation and that of the affected sensation, and each includes two steps, namely the determination of the determinate objects, and the clarification of the truth of the sensory discrimination. Considering that the affected sensation encompasses two further sorts, viz. the peculiar sensation and the common perception, the research of the credibility of the affected sensation will begin with the determination of its sensory categories, and continue with the truth of the peculiar sensation, then that of the common sensation, while the explanation of the plausibility of the unaffected sensation goes in the parallel way: firstly its relationship with the first category, the (enmattered) Substance, then its truth in differentiating those 'sensible' substances. (3) The reason of this determinate truth. Logically, after the interpretation of the sensory truth, it is also necessary to clarify such an ability bearing this certain truth.

In this manner the investigation into the affected sensation's corresponding categories, its truth, and the reason of such a cognitive ability constitute the first part of this section (3.2.1), while the determination of the cognitive dynamis of the unaffected perception and the ground of this determinate capacity forms the second part (3.2.2), and at the end there will be a summary of this whole section (3.2.3).

3.2.1 The cognitive ability of the affected sensation

For the affected sensation, according to the description of its generation in section 2.1, we can emphasise that its cognitive dynamis is naturally restricted in many aspects like the distance between the perceiver and the sensibles; the homogeneity and proportion of the elemental movements originating from the sense-organs and the sensibles;[418] the

---

[418] Thus, the perception is entitled 'measuring operation' by Brisson (1997). Cf. Carpenter (2008) 44n17.

kinds of the sensibles at issue; the state of the unified soul; etc. However, despite these limitations the affected sensation still enables the cognition of many determinate objects, i.e., all Aristotelian categories except for the Substance (3.2.1.1.). Speaking of the truth of the affected sensation, we have to concede that although what it perceives, according to nature, is confusing and abstract, through which we cannot discriminate and comprehend the determinate single sensible things, it does have its own rightness, which enables us to begin to recognise the sensible world; besides, it is the foundation of further epistemological dynameis like memory and phantasia, thus the affected sensation can be regarded as the beginning of the empirical cognition (3.2.1.2).

3.2.1.1 The categories of the affected sensation *per se*

In the view of the ancient philosophy the term 'category' primarily denotes the homonymous Aristotelian work, the *Categories*, in which ten categories are stipulated: Substance, Quantity, Quality, Relation (πρός τι), Place, Time, Position (τὸ κεῖσθαι), Possession (τὸ ἔχειν), Acting, and Being Affected.[419] These ten categories, in the sight of the Neoplatonic commentators, despite their various application-possibilities, can be regarded as those of the perceptible things.[420] Given that (1) the Aristotelian perception-theory is grounded on Plato's perception-doctrine, as already illustrated in section 3.1.1, and (2) these ten categories appear also in Plato's corpus,[421] they can be used to clarify the Platonic perception dynamis. Considering the differences of the affected and unaffected perception, their corresponding cognitive categories could also be different, therefore it is requisite to examine the relationship of the sensible categories and both kinds of sensation. Firstly, let us observe the affected sensation and its categories.

---

[419] See *Cat.* 1b25–27.

[420] Porphyry argues that the categories should be treated as an introduction of the physical part of philosophy (καὶ μάλιστα πρὸ τοῦ φυσικοῦ ἂν εἴη μέρους τῆς φιλοσοφίας, *In Cat.* 56, 29–30). Ammonius suggests that the ten categories are for the perceptual things and things in the many (*In Cat.* 33, 25: διαλέγεται περὶ πραγμάτων τῇ τε αἰσθήσει γνωρίμων καὶ τοῖς πολλοῖς. Cf. 41, 9–11: ἐνταῦθα δὲ περὶ τῶν αἰσθητῶν γενῶν καὶ εἰδῶν διαλέγεται, τοῦτ' ἔστι περὶ τῶν ἐν τοῖς πολλοῖς), or the composite substance that undergoes generation and destruction (34, 4–5: περὶ τῆς συνηέτου οὐσίας. Cf. 45, 22: περὶ μόνης τῆς συνθέτου οὐσίας τῆς ἐν γενέσει καὶ φθορᾷ). In the commentary of Simplicius we can find the same declaration, see *In Cat.* 74, 4: περὶ τῶν αἰσθητῶν διαλέγεται. Cf. Gerson (2005) 77n7. For detailed discussions about the theme (σκοπός) of the *Categories* in the Neoplatonic tradition, see Thiel (2004) 11–29 and 67ff.; Tuominen (2009) 204–208.

[421] For example, Substance at *Tim.* 29c2; Quantity at *Soph.* 245d8–10; Quality in *Theaet.* 182a8–10; Relation in *Rep.* 438aff.; Place in *Phaed.* 72a4; Time at *Prot.* 345b2–5; Position in *Phaed.* 80c2; Possession at *Theaet.* 197b9–c5; Acting and Being affected in *Gorg.* 476bff. Cf. Zekl (1998) xx–xxi; Tuominen (2009) 203. Michalewski (2016) 221–222 argues that some of the Middle-Platonists have argued that most or all categories exist already in Plato: in his *On the Generation of the Soul in the Timaeus* 1023E–F Plutarch mentions *Tim.* 37b–c; Alcinous argues in *Handbook of Platonism [Didaskalikos]* 6. 159. 43–44 that Plato summarises the categories in the *Parmenides*; and the *Anonymous Commentary to Theaetetus* (col. 68) holds that in *Theaet.* 152d we can find the categories Substance, Quantity, and Quality.

Indeed, in the view of the Aristotelian perception-theory we can easily certify that the affected sensation does involve all sensible categories expect for the first one, because the qualities perceived by the peculiar sensation corresponds to the categories Quality; while the common sensation objects, i.e., the enmattered motion, rest, oneness, number, shape, and size relate inherently to the rest eight categories: Quantity corresponds to motion, shape, size, and the discrete quantity, i.e., number (*Cat.* 2b23); Relations like 'double, half, bigger' (1b29–2a1) can be clarified with number and size; originally Place and Time belong to the continuous Quantity,[422] therefore the change of Place (ἡ κατὰ τόπον μεταβολή) naturally relates to motion and rest (15b1–16); for the interpretation of Position and Possession one can resort to state (ἕξις), condition (διάθεσις), quality, quantity, etc. (15b17–30), which involve almost all six common perceptual objects; with reference to Acting and Being Affected we have already determined (section 2.1.2.1) that they are two kinds of motion which function as preconditions of the generation of the affected perception. According to this account we can proclaim that all Aristotelian categories except for the Substance relate naturally to the affected perception, through which the universal features of all physical bodies are recognisable.[423]

Yet we should not cease at this point, for such an explanation of the correspondence of the affected sensation and the nine categories is carried out in the view of the Aristotelian perception-theory, which appears not to be plausible enough, that is to say, a determination with Plato's own words would be more persuasive: in the finger-passage of *Republic* (here esp. 523d1–524a4) we are told that through the eyes one can discriminate the whiteness and darkness, bigness and smallness of a single finger, whether it is seen in the middle or at the end. This implies that our sight perceives the Quantity, Quality, Relation and Place of the same finger, which is a sensible entity composed of form and matter and possesses these enmattered categories; for the enmattered Time we are told at *Timaeus* 37c6–39e2 that it has an origin in the generation of the heavenly bodies and their movements, which can also be perceived;[424] for the perceptible category Position we can resort to *Phaedo* 80c2, where the Platonic Socrates argues that our physical body 'rests in the visible world' (ἐν ὁρατῷ κείμενον), thus the physical body, through the determination of its Position, is determined to be sensible – this indicates that for Plato this category Position can be utilised to determine the perceptible things; Possession denotes the states or conditions of the identical subject that relates also to Position,[425] the examples that are given by Aristotle are 'wearing shoes and being armed' (οἷον ὑποδέδεται, ὥπλισται, *Cat.* 2a3), which appear also in Plato's

---

[422] *Cat.* 4b20–25: Τοῦ δὲ ποσοῦ [...] συνεχὲς δὲ γραμμή, ἐπιφάνεια, σῶμα, ἔτι δὲ παρὰ ταῦτα χρόνος καὶ τόπος. Cf. *Tim.* 58b10–c2, where Plato asserts that when something changes its size, it alters its place: μεταβάλλον γὰρ τὸ μέγεθος ἕκαστον καὶ τὴν τόπων μεταβάλλει στάσιν.

[423] For the correspondence of the Substance and the unaffected sensation, see below 3.2.2.1.

[424] Cf. *Tim.* 28a2–4, 28b8–c2. See Mooij (2005) 19–23. For a terminological research of the notion χρόνος in Plato, see George (2014) 166–169.

[425] For the assertation that Position and Possession are the same with respect to subject, yet distinct from each other in the sense of the relation, see Philoponus, *In Cat.* 44,13–45,6.

Charmides 174c5 and *Republic* 551e1,[426] moreover, Plato talks directly about the possession of a cloak in *Theaetetus* 197b9–12; at last, the categories Acting and Being Affected are those with which we are already familiar due to the determination of their necessary pre-existence in the becoming of the affected sense-affections, which is revealed for example at *Theaetetus* 156a5–b2. Given that all six kinds of the Aristotelian common sensible objects are also included in Plato's perception-theory, as mentioned in section 3.1.1, we can proclaim that for Plato the nine categories are also enmattered in the sensible things, which means that through the Platonic affected sensation the sensible world can be described with these nine categories.

On closer inspection, the inherent correspondence of the sensory ability and the enmattered categories can be clarified by one of the substantial features of the sensible world, i.e., its everlasting movement: The objects of the peculiar and common sensation are perceived through motion,[427] because as Aristotle (*De an.* 425a17–20) explains, we perceive "size through motion, and so shape too, for the shape is a determinate size, the rest is perceived through the non-motion (τῷ μὴ κινεῖσθαι, 425a18–19), the number through the negation of continuity, and also by the peculiar objects, for each sense perceives one (ἕν, 425a20)".[428] The motion of the sensibles, furthermore, can be explained by the motion of the matter, which functions as the accessory cause of the generation of all perceptible things. The matter keeps moving, because the basic elements fire, air, water, and earth are always moving. At *Timaeus* 57d7–58a2, following the exposition of the four elements' constitution and generation as well as their transformation into each other, Plato clarifies the reason of the permanent motion of the elements, i.e., their heterogeneity, for on the one hand the four elements are established from four geometrical figures with different shapes, on the other hand, for each kind of these bodies, e.g., the fire-elements, the basic particles that constitute them are also distinct from each other in their magnitude. Because of this heterogeneity when one single element meets another, or when different kinds of elements transform into each other,[429] they either co-produce bigger bodies or are dissolved into smaller ones, and the alteration of their magnitude leads naturally to locomotion. Given that the whole universe is full of elements and there is no empty room left (*Tim.* 58a5–b2), the whole world's beginning to move arouses the increase, decrease, connection, separation, and transformation of the elements, which results in the unceasing movement of all elements and the sensible things (partially) composed of them.[430] The final reason and principle

---

[426] *Charmides* 174c5: ἡ δὲ σκυτικὴ ὑποδεδέσθαι. Cf. *Hipp. mai.* 291a7 (καλῶς δὲ ὑποδεδεμένῳ); *Rep.* 551e1 (τῷ πλήθει ὡπλισμένῳ); *Euthyd.* 299c6; *Tim.* 24b6; *Laws* 833b3.

[427] Aristotle, *De an.* 425a16–17: ταῦτα γὰρ πάντα κινήσει αἰσθανόμεθα.

[428] Cf. *Ibid.* 417b22 (τῶν καθ' ἕκαστον ἡ κατ' ἐνέργειαν αἴσθησις); *An. Post.* 100a16–17 (καὶ γὰρ αἰσθάνεται μὲν τὸ καθ' ἕκαστον). Dexippus stresses that this 'one' is not in accordance with 'one dynamis', rather it implies that each thing is 'one being' (*In Cat.* 30, 14–15: ἓν δὲ ἕκαστον τῶν αἰσθητῶν λέγεται οὐ κατὰ δύναμιν, ἀλλ' ὅτι πάντα εἰς μίαν νεύει οὐσίαν).

[429] For Aristotle's criticism of the transformation-problem between the four elements, see *DC* 306a1–23; for the answers of Proclus and Simplicius, see Simplicius, *In de caelo* 642, 1–648, 10.

[430] So, in the view that 'all things are moving' Plato explains the generation of perception in the *Theaetetus* (section 2.1.2.1), although he can say more about this Heraclitean and Proragorean doctrine, for example, the final reason of the unceasing elemental motion is located in the soul.

of the movement of the sensible world, as revealed in 1.1.1.3 and 1.1.2.3, rests on the soul, whose self-motion enables all other-moved corporeal movements, thus we are told that the world soul initiates and governs all movements of the whole universe. In this view the everlasting motion of the sensibles, resulting eventually from the soul, is the ground of the perception-discrimination of all peculiar and common sensation-objects as well as the nine enmattered categories.

For this interpretation we should bear in mind that (1) both the nine categories and all objects of the peculiar and common sensation (quality, motion, rest, one, number, shape, and size) are enmattered. (a) The nine categories are enmattered, so that we can perceive them, for example the Acting and Being Affected are enmattered in the elemental movements processing from the sensibles and the sense-organs, and evidently, we can perceive the quantity existing in the substratum like finger, which we usually call 'the quantity of the finger', but not the quantity itself, which is essentially not perceptible. (b) The peculiar and common perception-qualities like colours and sounds also exist in the material substrata, e.g., the whiteness is in the matter like wood or stone or any other material surface (*Theaet.* 156e6–7), for only in this way we can discriminate it as whiteness. (c) The reason of their being 'enmattered' can be explained by the substantial character of the affected sensation: its cognitive dynamis is exercised by the mortal soul in the pneumatic and shell-like vehicle, which are established from the four elements, namely they are both enmattered, albeit one of them is simple, the other is complex. This essential feature of the affected sensation determines that the perceptible objects must be enmattered: the sensible qualities are contained in the sense-affections taking the elemental movements as their substrata, and according to the principle 'like to like', only the elemental movements can enter the mortal vehicles and move the mortal soul. Hence, as already discussed in section 2.1.2.1 only through the enmattered affections those sensible qualities can be discriminated.

(2) The objects of the affected perception and the nine discriminated enmattered categories are abstract, universal, and confusing according to nature.[431] That the sensible objects and the nine categories are both enmattered and abstract, is not contradictory, for on the one side they must be enmattered, so that they can be discriminated by the mortal (affected) perception, on the other side, as they are recognised – no matter the sensible things are individual (one finger) or collective (three fingers) – what perceived are the abstract and universal qualities without matter. The reason of the discriminated qualities' being abstract and confusing rests on two factors: (a) the sensible qualities are not restricted in one concrete physical substrate, rather they exist in many if not all corporeal things. For example, as aforesaid, the colour whiteness can be enmattered in wood, stone, or any other material surface (*Theaet.* 156e6–7). Hence, with the discriminated whiteness we cannot determine the concentrate sensible things like a determinate house, for what is white is can also be a box, a car, a cat, and so on. In this sense these perceived qualities – 'qualities' in broad sense, namely all sensible objects of the peculiar and common sensation, or the nine enmattered categories – are confusing, abstract and universal. (b) The physical entities bearing all sensible qualities can be

---

[431] Schmitt (2006a) 153–155; (2012) 309–317. For the further study about the truth of perception and its relationship with other cognitive dynameis in Plato and Aristotle, see Schmitt (2019) 64–74. Cf. 34–42.

altered, which results possibly in their possession of the different or even contrary sensible characters. Plato stresses at *Theaetetus* 182a8–b2 that what possesses the capacity to act comes not to be a quality (ποιότητα, 182a9), rather 'a quality as such' (ποιόν τι, 182a8), namely what is acting becomes for example not the hotness or whiteness, but rather something hot or white.[432] Although what he states here is still the Heraclitean and Proragorean perception-theory – for as discussed in section 2.1.2.1, what is acting should not be attributed to the sensibles – the assertation that what we discriminate through the (affected) sensation becomes for example something white or hot, but not the whiteness or hotness, belongs nevertheless to the Platonic doctrine:[433] as the sensible qualities are perceived, they are enmattered in the physical things, yet essentially those corporeal things cannot hold these qualities forever, for they can change their qualitie. That is to say, the sensible individuals cannot be determined by the affected perception, for what the latter perceives are the sensible qualities that are occasionally enmattered in the perceptible individuals.[434]. On this account Aristotle asserts that the (affected) perception perceives the single things though, what it perceives is something universal.[435]

The sensible physical thing's becoming 'a quality as such' (ποιόν τι) corresponds naturally to the substantial features of the elements: they do not stay still, rather always move and become another element[436] and transform into each other (*Tim.* 49b5–c7, cf. 56d1–57c6), thus each of the elements like fire cannot be entitled 'this' (τοῦτο, 49d2, d6, 49e1, e2) or 'that' (τόδε, 49e1, e2), rather 'like-this' (τὸ τοιοῦτον, 49d6),[437] for it does not have something definite (τινὰ ἔχον βεβαιότητα, 49d8). As the elements cannot be described with the determinate terms or phrases which are suitable for the essentially distinguishable things, it can merely be entitled 'like this' – so is anything else that 'has

---

[432] *Theaetetus*182b1–2: τὸ γὰρ ποιοῦν οὔτε θερμότης οὔτε λευκότης, θερμὸν δὲ καὶ λευκὸν γίγνεται. Cf. 156e5: ἐγένετο οὐ λευκότης αὖ ἀλλὰ λευκόν.

[433] For Plato's accusation against the Presocratic natural philosophy and the Sophists in terms of the perception-theory, see Schmitt (1974) 26–72, 132–240.

[434] In this sense the generation of the affected sense-affection is described with the Aorist-form, for example *Tim.* 43c1 (προσκρούσειε); 45c5 (γενόμενον); *Theaet.* 156d5 (ἐγένετο).

[435] Aristotle, *Phy.* 184a16–b14, where he clearly distinguishes 'what is for us' from 'what is in accordance with nature': what is clear and evident for us, in the sense of our perception, is actually confusing and universal according to nature, hence we must progress from the universal discrimination to the individual, concrete knowledge, for only in this way we can grasp what is according to nature and recognise the sensible thing as something distinct from all others. Cf. *An. Post.* 100a16–b1: καὶ γὰρ αἰσθάνεται μὲν τὸ καθ' ἕκαστον, ἡ δ' αἴσθησις τοῦ καθόλου ἐστιν, οἷον ἀνθρώπου, ἀλλ' οὐ Καλλίου ἀνθρώπου. Although the given example is about the substance, which is the object of the Aristotelian incidental perception and the Platonic unaffected sensation, nevertheless what Aristotle means here is that the objects of sensation are universal and abstract, not concrete. Philoponus (*In Phy.* 14, 3ff.) stresses that what the nature makes are the things particular and concrete, while what for us prior and clearer are things confusing, abstract, and universal. Cf. Schmitt (2012) 312.

[436] *Tim.* 49d5. For the relation of matter and the sensibles' alteration, see Aristotle, *Meta.* 1069b3f.

[437] This translation is taken from Taylor (1928) 316.

a generation',[438] namely all sensible things generating from these elements can only be entitled 'things like this'. Correspondingly, the affected sensible qualities like hotness and whiteness should also be deemed as such and such qualities (ὁποιοῦν τι, 50a2–3). Therefore, Plato asserts that in the sense that all sensible things in the Chora are always generated, attaining their appearance, existing for a period, then vanishing out of it, we can use the words 'this' or 'that' to describe them (49e7–50a2), i.e., these things passing in and out are actually 'imitations of the external beings' (τῶν ὄντων ἀεὶ μιμήματα, 50c4–5).

3.2.1.2 The truth of the affected sensation

Having determined that the nine enmattered categories of the sensible world can be recognised and clarified through the affected sensation, the next question shall be the truth of this kind of perception. As mentioned above, under the affected sensation there are further classifications which bear different degree of truth, for example (1) the peculiar sensation can always precisely perceive its sensible qualities, while the common perception is fallible on certain occasions, and (2) the truth of sensation varies also in accordance with the fact whether it discriminates *per se* or is mixed with other cognitive abilities such as memory and phantasia – this dichotomy appears not in the diagram of the perception-kinds, yet here becomes necessary in the perspective of the sensory truth. On this ground we must concede that it is difficult to certify the credibility of the affected perception as a whole, because it depends on the specific perception-kinds and certain occasions, which indicates that the determination of the truth of affected sensation is possible only in the way of investigating the truth of the two specific kinds of perception respectively. Now considering that the division of the peculiar and common sensation is subordinate to the dichotomy of the perception *per se* and perception with support of other cognitive dynameis, for both the first two kinds belong to the perception *per se*, our research of the perception plausibility shall begin with the peculiar and common sensation.

(1) Under the affected sensation *per se* the peculiar sensation is ensured with truth, while the common perception can be right and wrong. However, no matter precise or fallible, what they perceive, as argued above, is abstract and universal, and relates not to the substances of the sensible things. The peculiar perception, for instance the sight, perceives the enmattered colours which are not accessible for any other peculiar senses, as displayed in *Charmides* 167b5–169a1: there exists no sight that is sight both of itself and of other sights, and sees no colour (167c5–d2), similarly there is no such a hearing or any other (peculiar) sense (157d2–8). Logically, what Plato conceives here seems to be a pattern of contradiction: X is both 'of itself and others' (ἑαυτῆς δὲ καὶ τῶν ἄλλων),[439] and of non-itself. The Platonic Socrates collectively enumerates nine mental

---

[438] *Tim.* 49e6–7: καὶ δὴ καὶ πῦρ τὸ διὰ παντὸς τοιοῦτον, καὶ ἅπαν ὅσονπερ ἂν ἔχῃ γένεσιν.

[439] This phrase and its variants emerge in every example of this passage, see *Charmides* 167c7, d3–4, d6–7, e2, 4, 6–7, 8, 168a2–3, 5–6, c1–2, 3–4, etc. However, as the notion 'dynamis' is introduced, the substantial determination of sight, hearing, motion, and hotness is described with either 'πρὸς ἑαυτὸ' (168d1, e4, 169a3) or 'αὐτὴ ἑαυτήν' (168d4, 7, e7).

faculties that do not conform to this pattern, which can be divided into four groups: perception and the psychic faculties following it, viz. sight, hearing, perception in general sense; appetite, rational will, desire, and fear; opinion; knowledge (167c5–168a6).[440] One solution of this contradiction is to determine whether this involved X has a dynamis by itself, through which it is related to certain things. Namely, to determine its substantial dynamis and the peculiar objects of this dynamis. In the view of categories this solution involves both Substance and Relation, yet this Relation rules the quantitative relation out, for the endeavour of the determination of X's dynamis fails when what involved are things like bigger, double, size and multitude (μεγέθη μὲν γὰρ καὶ πλήθη, 168e5), but succeeds in the cases of qualitative relation like sight, hearing, the motion that moves by itself (κίνησις αὐτὴ ἑαυτὴν κινεῖν, 168e7), hotness (θερμότης, 168e7), and all things of this sort (168b5–169a1). That is to say, the Relation at issue denotes the inherent relationship between the cognitive dynamis which originates from the essence and its proper objects – this is why the Platonic Socrates stresses that anything whose dynamis is relative to itself will also have the substance (τὴν οὐσίαν, 168d2) to which its dynamis is relative. Applying this principle in the peculiar sensation hearing and sight, it is plain that hearing is that of the sound, for the hearing hears the sound by itself; and when the sight exercises its own dynamis, namely when it sees by itself (ὄψεται αὐτὴ ἑαυτήν, 168d7), it must possess a determinate colour, since it cannot see anything without colour (*Charm.* 168d6–8).[441] Socrates proclaims further that just like sight and hearing hold the capacities to see and hear in accordance with their substances, there exists a determinate kind of movement moving (the body) by itself,[442] and

---

[440] I disagree with the separation (three groups of three) that is taken by Schmid (1998) 90, who follows Bruell (1977) 173–176 and Hyland (1981) 114–117 (see Schmid 189n5), because in the sense of generation the desire, appetite, and fear follow perception, as *Tim.* 42a3–b2, 64a4–7, 69c5–d6 and *Theat.* 156b2–7 explicitly illustrate, while the rational will corresponds to the rational cognitive dynamis like intellect. Benardete (2000) 250–251 and Lampert (2010) 204 offer no division of these faculties, while Bloch (1973) 113–115 elaborately explains the relation between perception and these feelings, emotions, and opinion. For the natural difference of perception, opinion, and knowledge as dynameis, see *Rep.* 477a10ff.

[441] For an interpretation of this passage, see Bloch (1973) 112–118; Schmid (1998) 89–96; Lampert (2010) 204–205. Remarkably, Schmid (pp. 95–96) – who follows Tuckey (1951) 46–47 – and Lampert (p. 205) argue that the terms 'ἰδὲ' in 167c2, 'ἐννόει' in 167c5, and 'ὁρᾷς' in 168e2 suggest that the sight of the mind is the very sight that is of itself and of other sights (namely bodily sight) and not of what those other sights are sights of, but Socrates' partner Critias does not see this point. This explanation tends to argue that for Plato there is a metaphorically formulated relation between understanding and mortal perception, for the understanding is treated as the sight of the mind. However, in the *Charmides* speaking of the sight that cannot see colour, yet is sight of itself and of other sights (167b5–d2), Socrates does not hint at a kind of sight in metaphorical sense, i.e., the understanding, rather what he means is merely a kind of sight as sense perception. Besides, we know that for Proclus the mortal sensation in the pneumatic vehicle is the imitation of the divine sensation of the immortal soul, which relates to the circle of Difference, while the understanding involves the circle of Same, thus such a metaphor is unreasonable.

[442] One wonders whether this motion is the self-motion of soul, for the formulation 'κίνησις αὐτὴ ἑαυτὴν κινεῖν' in 168e7 is like the logos of soul at *Laws* 894d3–4 (τὴν αὐτὴν αὑτὴν δυναμένην κινεῖν); 895b5 (τὴν αὐτὴν ἑαυτὴν κινοῦσαν) and 896a1–2 (τὴν δυναμένην αὑτὴν

a certain hotness – with reference to its substantial determinateness – burns (the body) by itself,[443] while size, multitude, and others as such do not possess such a dynamis belonging to themselves.

From this passage we can derive that: (a) dynamis is a determinate species of being which relates to the substance. This point is explicitly manifested when Socrates declares that the dynamis of X relates to its own substance.[444] Moreover, at *Republic* 477c1–4 Plato claims that dynamis is a determinate species (γένος τι) of the beings (τῶν ὄντων), "with which we are able to do what we are able to do, and also anything else is able to do whatever it is able to do",[445] and the examples he offers are the very sight and hearing, for as a perception-form (τὸ εἶδος, 477c4) the sight holds the essential dynamis to discriminate determinate colour and shape.[446] (b) By virtue of this dynamis we can certify the subatance of the peculiar sensation and its corresponding sensible quality. In

---

αὐτὴν κινεῖν κίνησιν). Bloch (1973) 119 argues reasonably that in the second part of this passage (*Charm.* 168dff.) sight and hearing are not treated as concrete mental acts anymore, rather they are observed in the view of their substantial determinateness, which relates to their sensible objects proper, so according to this self-relation the motion under discussion should also be deemed to be one that moves body, for the dynamis of this motion relates essentially to body. In addition to this argument, we can point out that the seemingly similar terms enable not the assertion that what discussed here is the self-motion, for in the case of the qualitative change Plato also uses similar formulation (ἐν τῷ αὐτῷ, *Theaet.* 181c9–d1), he also asserts that all sensible things move themselves (κινεῖσθαι αὐτά, *Theaet.* 181e9), although their motion originates from the soul (*Laws* 894e4–895a3).

[443] One wonders why hotness is viewed as a self-relation faculty like sight and hearing, for hotness seems to be contrary to coldness, as manifested in *Rep.* 438c1–5. However, the point is that here the hotness has a determinate dynamis that relates to its essence, i.e., to burn the body, as argued by Bloch (1937) 119, see also the helpful notes 118n30, 119n34, n35. One decisive proof of this view of self-relation is offered in *Rep.* 335d3–4, where the Platonic Socrates asserts that it is not the function (ἔργον) of hotness to cool things down (ψύχειν), rather the opposite of it, namely the coldness. Such a statement is also suitable for the dynamis of hotness in the *Charmides*, which is intrinsically separated from that of the coldness, for their dynameis and functions are opposite. That the hotness has a certain dynamis to act on other things, is a pre-Socratic doctrine, see Cornford (1937) 180. For a further propose: although sight, hearing, motion and hotness concern the corporeal existence, they should be attributed to different types: sight and hearing are the affected perception possessing the dynamis to perceive the perceptible qualities, while motion and hotness are the state of the sensible things, for their dynameis involve the body. Hence the motion and hotness under discussion, whose dynameis pertaining to body, i.e., proceed from body and relate inherently to body, are the very sensible objects. One text-proof of this suggestion can be found in *Tim.* 61d6–62a5, where Plato explains the generation of hotness, which is considered as a peculiar sensible quality of touch. For the Aristotelian opinion on this issue, see below n447.

[444] *Charm.* 168c8–d2: ὅ τί περ ἂν τὴν ἑαυτοῦ δύναμιν πρὸς ἑαυτὸ ἔχῃ, οὐ καὶ ἐκείνην ἕξει τὴν οὐσίαν, πρὸς ἣν ἡ δύναμις αὐτοῦ ἦν. Cf. 169a2–3: τῶν ὄντων τὴν αὑτοῦ δύναμιν αὐτὸ πρὸς ἑαυτὸ πέφυκεν ἔχειν.

[445] *Rep.* 477c2–3: αἷς δὴ καὶ ἡμεῖς δυνάμεθα ἃ δθνάμεθα καὶ ἄλλο πᾶν ὅ τί περ ἂν δύνηται.

[446] *Ibid.* 477c7: οὔτε τινὰ χρόαν ὁρῶ οὔτε σχῆμα (Plato speaks of the dynamis of knowledge, which is distinguished from that of sight). Cf. *Charm.* 168d7: χρῶμά τι.

both *Charmides* and *Republic*, Plato ascribes certain dynamis to the sense perception by virtue of necessity,[447] which implies that (b1) such a dynamis relates necessarily to sensation, i.e., it is requisite for the (peculiar) senses to have their own dynameis, and what enables this is their own substances. For example, sight and hearing (*Tim.* 46e6–47e2), as mentioned above (section 3.1.2), are the gifts of the gods that enable us to study the nature, especially by observing the celestial movements and hearing the music. To fulfil this providence, they must possess the determinate dynamis relating to their substances on the one hand, and involve the proper objects, i.e., the heavenly colours, shapes, movements, the sounds with rhythm and melody, etc., on the other hand, which turns out to be the dynamis of seeing the colour and hearing the sound. Thus, proceeding from the substance, the dynamis of sight and hearing relates inherently to colours and sounds, and in the same sense the determinate dynamis held by other senses touch, smelling and taste are also specified in Plato's *Timaeus* 61c7–68d8: for touch the tactile qualities like hotness and coldness,[448] for smelling the odours, and for taste the tastes like bitter and sweet. And (b2) these dynameis are necessarily related to the corporeal things, which can be demonstrated in two aspects: firstly, the peculiar sensation perceives through their physical sense-organs – because the dynameis of sight and hearing are realised 'through' (διά) our eyes and ears (*Theaet.* 184b8–c9), 'through sight and hearing' is then synonymous with 'through eyes and ears',[449] that is to say, only through our eyes and ears we can see and hear, for the function (ἔργον) of eyes rests on seeing, that of ears hearing (*Rep.* 352e2–8). In this view the eyes and ears are deemed to be instruments (ὀργάνου, *Theaet.* 185a5),[450] whose dynameis can be ascribed to that of the body (185e7: διὰ τῶν τοῦ σώματος δυνάμεων), although the dynamis of one sense-organ cannot be replaced by another (184e7–185a1): this account corresponds to the statements in the *Charmides*, i.e., the dynamis relates to substance, and thus ensures the truth of the peculiar perception.[451] Secondly what the peculiar sensation-dynamis inherently concerns are things enmattered. For example, the colour must be enmattered, because only in this way it is sensible for our sight, so are the rest peculiar sensible

---

[447] *Charm.* 168d6 (ἀνάγκη); 168d7 (ἀνάγκη); *Rep.* 477b1 (ἀνάγκης). However, the dynamis of knowledge is viewed as natural, see *Charm.* 169a3 (πέφυκεν); *Rep.* 477b12 (πέφυκε).

[448] *Tim.* 61d6–64a1. Cf. Aristotle, *De an.* 422b26–27, where he itemises hot and cold, dry and moist, hard and soft. For Aristotle the qualities hot and cold, dry and moist are fundamental and elemental, for they make the forms and principles of body (*GC* 329b6–17, 330a30–b7; *De an.* 423b27–9. Cf. *Meteor.* 339a13–14; *PA* 648b9–10), while other qualities like hardness and softness, heaviness and lightness, density and rarity are those following them (*PA* 646a16–20; *GC* 330a24–6, 329b32–4). See Caston (2012) 79–80 and n39. Cf. *Tim.* 62c3–4, where Plato clarifies heaviness and lightness in accordance with up and down, which implies that they are not peculiar qualities which can be perceived exclusively by touch-sense. At 63e7–64a1 Plato also implies that the hardness is a common perceptible object. Cf. Büttner (2000) 75.

[449] At *Theaet.* 184b8–185a9 Plato frequently mentions the sense perception of colour and sound: he formulates 'through the eyes', 'through the ears' in 184c6–7, but 'through the sight' and 'through the hearing' at 185a1–2.

[450] For the role of bodily instrument in the process of perceiving, see section 2.1.2.2. That the instrument should be turned together with the whole soul in the education of the philosophers, is stressed in *Rep.* 518c4–d1.

[451] Cf. Aristotle, *De an.* 418a15, 427b11–13, 428b18–19.

objects: sounds, smells, flavour, and tangible qualities. To sum up, all dynameis of the peculiar perception are necessarily related to the bodily things, both in the sense of the involved sense-organs and in respect of their objects like colours and sounds – this reveals that the peculiar sensation is the perception which inherently and necessarily involves the enmattered qualities.

Remarkably, although what we precisely perceive through the peculiar sensation concerns only one of the nine sensation-categories, namely the Quality, its generation, as discussed in section 1.1.1.2, involves nevertheless other categories, especially the Quantity, which is eventually decided by the substance, or the forms of the elemental polyhedrons. For example, the quality of hotness is the consequence of the sharpness of fire,[452] which results from the synthesised reasons such as "the fineness of the edges, the sharpness of the angles, the smallness of the particles and the swiftness of the movement" (*Tim.* 61e1–4), which are substantially perceptible, yet too small to be visible for our human sight – similarly, the polyhedrons of the four elements are also essentially sensible, but not accessible for us because of their restricted magnitude (*Tim.* 56c1–2), hence the determinate quantitative properties of the polyhedrons lead to the generation of the sensible qualities like hotness, and the collection of a multitude of polyhedrons enables us to perceive these qualities through our own sense-organs. That in the level of elements the quantity is prior to the quality, is now revealed,[453] now we should re-stress that this quantity is determined by the shape of the polyhedron bestowed by the Demiurge (*Tim.* 53a8–b7): before the generation of the formed elements, the χώρα is disordered due to its lack of proportion and measure, the Demiurge, whose (rational) will is to create a possibly perfect world (30a1–2), reconstructs the χώρα (pure material) with forms and numbers, for example the four determinate geometrical figures, and establishes the sensible world from the elements composed of these polyhedrons – here we should emphasise that these polyhedrons, possessing the mathematical figures though, are indeed not the pure motionless and indivisible mathematical entities, rather they are merely their imitations which 'suggest the active and demiurgic dynamis of the nature' (δραστικὰς καὶ δημιουργικὰς δυνάμεις τῆς φύσεως αἰνίττεται).[454] Therefore the quantitative character of these polyhedrons are decided by the shapes of these enmattered figures, whereas the substratum, i.e., the matter, is the accessory cause of the generation of these four elemental figures. In this sense we can conclude that the peculiar sensible qualities proceed from the quantitative features of the elemental polyhedrons (with certain forms and numbers), thus, the peculiar sensation enables the discrimination of the (sensible) qualities without fault, albeit is unable to grasp their substances.

The mechanical system of the common sensation is more complex than that of the peculiar sensation, for this kind of perception has no peculiar sense-organ, which

---

[452] Simplicius (*In de caelo* 564, 24–565, 28) annotates that both the Pythagoreans and Democritus tend to explain the generation of hotness and coldness with the enmattered shape from the genus of quantities.

[453] In this sense quantity is closer to the substance. For the studies on this point, see Porphyry, *In Cat.* 100, 10–28; Dexippus, *In Cat.* 65, 15f., Simplicius, *In Cat.* 120, 27–121,12; 206, 8–207, 26. Cf. Strange (1992) 94n227.

[454] Syrianus, *In Meta.* 86, 2. Cf. Opsomer (2012) 168. Timaeus of Locros (*De nat.* 215, 13–17) declares that the four elements consist of matter (as substratum) and form (as logos of shape).

implies that its objects can only be perceived through the five sense-organs and the peculiar sensible objects. For instance, when we perceive size and shape, we can discriminate them through the colour of the peculiar object, namely our soul is primarily affected by the colours, and additionally by the coloured size and shape.[455] In the view that size, shape, and the rest common sensible objects are perceived on the ground of the peculiar sensible objects, the common sensation can also be attributed to the affected perception *per se*.[456] However, the plausibility of this kind of sensation is distinct from that of the peculiar perception: with reference to the peculiar sensation whose dynamis relates substantially to the determinate sensible objects, e.g. the sight to colours, as declared in the *Charmides*-passage, there is little room to be wrong,[457] while the common sensation cannot always rightly discriminate its objects – there exists no sense-organ which belongs exclusively to it, rather its objects are accessible for at least two peculiar senses, and they are additionally and secondly discriminated,[458] namely, the relation of common sensation and its objects is clearly differentiated from the relation of the peculiar sensation and its objects, for the latter relation, as said above, is a self-relation decided by the substance of the peculiar perception, a relation that exists not in the common sensation, for the dynamis of the common sensation relates not essentially to its objects. This clarifies why the attempt of determining the essential dynamis of X fails in the cases of the common sensible objects like 'size and multitude' (μεγέθη μὲν γὰρ καὶ πλήθη, *Charm.* 168e5). Therefore, the common sensation is fallible. For example, in our eyes the fixed stars are motionless in their own places, yet they are moving in the circular way, although they do reside in the same places (*Tim.* 40b4–6); the same things, when seen in water and out of it, appear to be both bent and straight, concave and convex, because on this occasion the sight is misled by the colours (*Rep.* 602c10–d1);[459] the sun appears to us to be merely a foot across (*De an.* 428b3–4), etc.

Although the common sensation is fallible in perceiving its objects, in the view of categories it reports us more about the sensible things and the perceptible world, albeit not include their substances; in another respect, through the common sensation we attain

---

[455] On the clarification that sight perceives size and shape through colours, see *Meno* 75b9–c6; Priscian, *In de an.* 182, 26–29. Cf. Büttner (2000) 74–75; Schmitt (2019) 65.

[456] Thus, the assertation that the common sensation-objects are 'incidentally' (κατὰ συμβεβηκός, *De an.* 425a14–15) perceived by the peculiar senses is not Aristotle's real doctrine. Cf. 425a27–28: τῶν δὲ κοινῶν ἤδε ἔχομεν αἴσθησιν κοινήν, οὐ κατὰ συμβεβηκός. For more clarification on this point, see Themistius, *In de an.* 81, 18–29; Philoponus, *In de an.* 453, 26–457, 25; Priscian, *In de an.* 182, 32–183, 20. For modern studies about this point, see esp. Bernard (1988) 120.

[457] In perceiving the substance and position the peculiar sensation is misleading, see *De an.* 418a16.

[458] At *Meno* 75b9–c1 the shape is regarded as the thing that always follows the colour: ἔστω γὰρ δὴ ἡμῖν τοῦτο σχῆμα, ὃ μόνον τῶν ὄντων τυγχάνει χρώματι ἀεὶ ἑπόμενον. Cf. Büttner (2000) 74.

[459] One wonders how this mistake comes to be, for in differentiating the colours the sight should be always plausible. The reason is that by perceiving shapes and other common sensible objects, our sight discriminates simultaneously at least two kinds of colours, and it must discriminate the positions of these colours, yet in perceiving the positions of the colours the sight can be fallible.

more 'words' or 'names' (τὰ ὀνόματα) relating to the logos (ὁ λόγος), although this relationship is also not essential.[460] As determined above, through the common perception we can perceive the enmattered motion, rest, shape, size, oneness, and number, which correspond to the ten categories of the sensible world except for the Substance, thus, in spite of the fallibility of this kind of sensation, now there are more objects recognisable for us, meanwhile, the actuality of the common sensation brings forth more 'words' like 'seat', 'run', 'one foot across', 'many', 'bent', 'act', and so on. These words, although confusing in the view of the logos and nature (for they are not the discriminated words that relate substantially to the logos, rather they are undiscriminated and cannot be used to constitute the logos of a determinate thing), tell us more about the variety and extension of the logos, for example, for the logos (definition) 'man' we can attribute the words 'round' (head), 'long' (body), 'four' (limbs), 'run', 'seat' to it, which constitutes the beginning of the determination of the definition 'man': on this ground we can announce that the affected sensation *per se* functions as the outset of the empirical cognition of the sensible world.

To summarise: the affected sensation is divided into two types, i.e., the peculiar and common sensation. As for the former, its objects are substantially related to its dynamis, which ensures the credibility of its cognitive discrimination; the latter, however, has another nature, for it holds no peculiar sense-organs, hence, the common sensible objects can only be perceived through the five sense-organs, and this restriction leads to the possible mistakes. What the affected sensation recognises is clear and distinct for us, but not for the sensible things *per se*, because despite the certain degree of the sensory truth, we can only discriminate the things in the sense of 'like this', a discriminated 'this' or 'that' is not achievable.

(2) The truth of the affected sensation with help of further cognition-abilities is grounded on the truth of the affected perception. Regarding the affected sensation *per se* we have determined that its cognitive truth should be occasionally decided, now we should turn to the affected sensation with support of further abilities. Given that the so-called 'further abilities' include memory (μνήμη), opinion, and phantasia,[461] which are based on the affected perception, the exposition of the credibility of this kind of perception should begin with the determination of these two dynameis.

Memory is the (timeless) preservation (σωτηρία) and remembrance of the affected perception in the soul,[462] which functions without the body (ἄνευ τοῦ σώματος).[463] At

---

[460] Cf. Aristotle, *Phy.* 184a26–b14, where he stresses that what we recognise through the perception is something universal, not in the discriminated manner. Through the common sensation we only perceive more universal features of the sensible things, which enables no concrete definition of them. However, we recognise now how many 'words' or 'names' that can be attributed to this 'definition' in the way of perception.

[461] For the sensation mixed with discursive thinking and intellect, see section 3.2.2.2.

[462] *Phileb.* 34a10: σωτηρίαν τοίνυν αἰσθήσεως τὴν μνήμην λέγων ὀρθῶς ἄν τις λέγοι κατά γε τὴν ἐμὴν δόξαν. After this clarification Plato distinguishes memory from recollection (ἀνάμνησις), see 34b2–c2. Proclus declares that "memory is superior to recollection, because memory exists primarily in intellect, which always thinks itself and abides in itself, secondarily also in souls, inasmuch as they pass from one object to another and do not know all things simultaneously and timelessly, and in a third mode it exists also in human souls, in which there are also interruptions by oblivion; memory is superior also because it is similar to

Philebus 34a10–b8 Plato asserts that memory is the preservation of the perception perceived by the soul through the body, namely the preservation of the affected perception. He proclaims further that for the perceived and preserved contents in the soul, when the soul recaptures them by itself, this activity should be entitled 'remember' (μνηνονεύειν). That what we see, hear, and perceive through other ways can be preserved in the soul, is a statement which appears at many locations in Plato's dialogues.[464] The mechanical system of this preservation is expounded in *Theaetetus* 191d–e and 194c–d: in the former passage we are taught that the memory of our souls seems like a waxen block, whose features like size, purity, and quality (hardness or softness) can be individually different. As a gift from the goddess Memory the memory has a significant capacity, i.e., to imprint the perceived image (τὸ εἴδωλον, 191d9) in the wax and remember the imprinted images so long as they remain. In the second context Plato states that when the block of wax in someone's soul is deep, abundant, smooth, and of proper kneading, the perceived impressions printed in such a wax block are so clear and deep that they can stay there for a long time, a person of this kind is the one having good memories and learns quickly, for he would not confuse the imprints (τὰ σημεῖα, 194d4) of his sensation. From these two passages we can derive that the memory, originating from the gods, is a soul-ability that can not only keep what we have perceived, but also remember it, which indicates that such an ability is also one cognitive dynamis distinct from the affected sense-affection,[465] although its strength is individually different. The dynamis of imprinting the perceived images in the soul is clarified here through the simile of wax-tablet, while in section 1.2 we have clarified that the vehicle of the mortal soul includes the pneumatic vehicle and the earthly body, the former is the very place where the affected perception happens,[466] so I suppose that

> eternity, being always directed to the same object, whereas recollection resembles time because of its transitional character; thirdly, because there is memory also where there is no forgetting, but recollection exists only where oblivion occurs; finally, because the more efficacious causes communicate themselves to a greater number, while the weaker ones have a more limited range of communication, and for this reason memory is found in unregulated animals too, while recollection goes no farther than rational souls." (Tr. Westerink, with slight reversion). See Olympiodorus, *In Phaed.* 11. 4. 9–18; Damascius, *In Phaed.* I 256. Cf. Gertz (2011) 117. For the studies of the Platonic recollection, see Lee (2001) esp. 82–185; Kahn (2006) 119–132; Gertz (2011) 109–122; Helmig (2012) 39–86; etc.

[463] *Phileb.* 34b7. Cf. Damascius, *In Phileb.* 158, 1: σώματος χωρίς.
[464] For example, *Theaet.* 163e8–11; 191d4–6; *Epist. II* 314a8–b3.
[465] For the memory as a cognitive ability, see *Laws* 645e1–2: τί δ' αὖ τὰς αἰσθήσεις καὶ μνήμας καὶ δόξας καὶ φρονήσεις. Cf. 723c5–7; 896d1. For the existence of memory in different levels of epistemology, see Damascius, *In Phileb.* 159, 1–5.
[466] Proclus (*In Tim.* III 286, 17–29) distinguishes the divisible and affected sensation from the unaffected and pure sensation in the pneumatic vehicle, which has the same nature as phantasia. With this division the affected sensation is characterised by proceeding to the external world, namely it happens not in the pneuma-vehicle, rather through the shell-like body, while the phantasia is defined to remain in the pneuma-vehicle. In arguing that this vehicle exists further after the departing of the soul from the earthly body, Syrianus and Proclus resort to the Myth of Er, in which the souls choose their new lives according to their

the waxen block in the soul should be understood as the pneuma-vehicle of the unregulated soul-form: this kind of vehicle is composed of the four elements whose constitution is simpler than that of the shell-like body, i.e., it is 'simple and enmattered' (ἁπλοῦν καὶ ἔνυλον), considering that these elements belong originally to those regulated χώρα-elements which are utilised to mould the whole universe and every sensible thing, the sensible qualities existing in the physical things can be discriminated, printed, and preserved in this homogeneous vehicle without being changed or changing themselves, just like the χώρα, which takes the forms of sensible things and remains unchanged (*Tim.* 50c1–3).

The combination of memory and the affected affection gives birth to opinion with affected sensation. According to Plato this kind of opinion denotes the self-discourse of the soul, which answers the question: "what is this determinate sensible thing"? As illustrated at *Phileb.* 38b12–e8, such a dynamis opines the substance of the sensible object, for example, the sensible object that beside the rock under a tree is a man or a statue. In this sense the opinion with affected sensation is entitled the unaffected sensation, which can be both right and wrong (see below 3.2.2.1).

Phantasia is the ability to (re-)shape and (re-)mould the preserved images, which means that it is a cognitive dynamis subjecting not to the bodily sense-affections. Plato's concept of phantasia is complicated, for in the *Theaetetus*, *Sophist*, *Republic*, and *Philebus* it is described with different aspects, and not each of them concerns the cognitive ability grounded on the affected sensation.[467] For our momentary theme we should concentrate on the context of *Philebus* 39b3–c6, where in comparison with the cognitive dynamis opinion, which is typified by a writer in the soul, Plato treats the phantasia as a painter (ζωγράφος) in the soul, who, after the writer gets the opinions (assertions) of the substances of the sensible things, paints the images of what is opined or asserted in the soul, thus we can see these images in ourselves. The term 'πώς' at *Philebus* 39c1 explicitly indicates that the painter holds a determinate dynamis which acts after the affected sensation, while the phrase 'ἐν αὐτῷ ὁρᾷ' manifests that this dynamis depends not on the momentary affected sensation, rather it is factually an ability of drawing the images of all involved sensible qualities which, according to the opinion or the assertion of the soul, relate to the single, concrete thing like 'a man beside the rock under a tree'.[468] Namely, what we can 'see' through the painter in our

---

memories of their preceding lives (*Rep.* 620b4–5, c5), which manifests that the memory also acts in the pneumatic vehicle.

[467] The term φαντασία has several similar forms like φάντασμα, φανταστικός, and the verb-forms are φαίνεται and φαντάζεσθαι, while the words 'appearance', 'appearing' and 'imagination' are normally applied to translate the term φαντασία. For the studies of this concept in the framework of sensation-appearance-opinion of the *Theaetetus* and *Sophist* as well as the criticism of Aristotle, see Grönroos (2001) 101–129. Büttner (2018) 149–173 elaborately demonstrates that the phantasia in the *Philebus* is equivalent to that of Aristotle's *De anima*, he also expounds the role of phantasia in mathematics (esp. geometry), arts (poetry, myth) and ethics. For a study of the notion 'phantasia' in the ancient philosophy with special respect in aesthetics, see Sheppard (2014).

[468] Büttner (2018) 160. For his whole analysis of the *Philebus*-phantasia, see pp. 159–163.

souls are all impressions or images that are perceived,[469] and they are not arbitrarily, rather regularly painted and attributed to something determinate, for instance 'a man' or 'a statue', no matter it really exists or not. Furthermore, being not restricted by the momentary perception, we can also 'see' the images of the past and the future through phantasia, and in doing this we usually have course to our memory.[470] Therefore the phantasia, as a cognitive dynamis, is able to handle its objects figuratively (μορφωτικῶς) and dimensionally (διαστατικῶς),[471] while the affected sensation merely affectively (παθητικῶς).

Through the clarification of what the memory, phantasia are, it is evident that what we discriminate through 'perception with help of other abilities' is either the preserved impressions or the re-shaped images or the opined substance. The truth of memory depends on the credibility of the imprinted images originating directly from the affected sensation, for example when something hot is perceived, it will also be imprinted as something hot, when the memory-dynamis of the soul is in its natural state. What we imagine through phantasia can also be right and wrong, for it can re-shape the perceived images. The affected sensation with opinion is equal to the unaffected perception, whose truth will be explored in next part.

Now we should summarise what we have determined in exploring the cognitive ability of the affected sensation, and ask for the reason of their specific truth: at the outset of this section we have certified that there exists an inherent relationship between the nine sensible categories (Quantity, Quality, Relation, Place, Time, Position, Possession, Acting, Being Affected), and the affected perception including the peculiar and common sensation, for these nine categories can be clarified with the affected sensible objects, i.e., the qualities of the peculiar sensation, the enmattered motion, rest, oneness, number, shape, and size of the common sensation. This correspondence leads to the conclusion that through the competence of the affected sensation alone we can already discriminate and comprehend many determinate objects enmattered in the sensible things, one of whose substantial character is their everlasting motion originating partially from the moving elements. After this clarification I have turned to the examination the truth of the affected sensation, which begins with its two subordinate kinds, i.e., the peculiar and common perception. The credibility of the peculiar sensation is

---

[469] See *Soph.* 264a4–6, where Plato stresses that phantasia results from sense perception: τί δ' ὅταν μὴ καθ' αὑτὴν ἀλλὰ δι' αἰσθήσεως παρῇ τινι, τὸ τοιοῦτον αὖ πάθος ἆρ' οἷόν τε ὀρθῶς εἰπεῖν ἕτερόν τι πλὴν φαντασίαν. Correspondingly, Proclus (*In Tim.* III 286, 20–29) attributes phantasia to the higher form of perception which takes place in the soul.

[470] Such an explanation of phantasia corresponds evidently to that of Aristotle, see *De an.* 427b14–26, where he distinguishes phantasia from perception, opinion, and thinking, and argues that we can imagine as we wish. Strikingly Aristotle (427b21–24) argues that when we imagine something terrible, we would not be affected and have such a feeling, for this happens merely by opining, while Proclus (*In Tim.* I 395, 22–29) holds the opposite doctrine. Cf. Lautner (2002) 265, his clarification for this anti-Aristotelian opinion is that in the Proclean bipartite soul-structure the phantasia is the highest ability of the unregulated soul, whose capacity can influence the lower capacities, thus in imagining the terrible things we are simultaneously emotionally affected.

[471] For the terms 'μορφωτικῶς' and 'διαστατικῶς', see Proclus, *In Tim.* I 255, 18–19; 352, 18; II 166, 7. Cf. Lautner (2002) 264.

rooted in the self-relationship of its dynamis and its peculiar object, which is determined by its substance. For example, sight must have a certain colour (χρώμά τι), i.e., without colour we can see nothing, as revealed in the *Charmides*. In this view when the sight discriminates the colour, it perceives something pertaining to itself, which guarantees the truth of sight. Similarly, the other kinds of peculiar sensation hearing, smell, taste, and touch also possess determinate kinds of qualities, namely sounds, odours, tastes like bitterness and sweetness, and the tactile qualities like hotness and coldness. The truth of the common perception, however, is not ensured, for it does not possess its own sense-organ, hence, its cognitive dynamis can only be performed through the peculiar sense-organs, which results in the possible mistakes. More significantly, what we discriminate through the affected sense perception are the enmattered categories or sensible qualities in broad sense, i.e., they must exist in the substrata, for only in this way they are sensible for us. Yet the discriminated sensible qualities are abstract, confusing, and universal, namely these sensible qualities, for example the whiteness, belongs not exclusively to any single sensible thing, rather it is a general perceptible quality that can be shared by most physical things, and although the concrete corporeal thing comes to be white when it is perceived, it can be altered and becomes for example red. In this sense we can declare that the affected sensation discriminates the enmattered qualities or categories which can potentially be enmattered in almost all physical entities.

This substantial feature of the affected sensation (partially) determines that it fails to determine the substance of the sensible things, which are composed of the sensible materials and invisible forms. The reason rests primarily on the fact that the (affected) perception cannot come to be without the bodily organs and the external sensibles which bring forth the sense-affections, and what the affected perception concerns are all external sensible qualities, whose generation and truth relates inherently to the body and bodily entities. In this sense the affected sensation is entitled 'σωματοειδής'.[472] The other reason relates to the soul: the affected sensation involves the mortal and unregulated soul-form, which is the image (εἴδωλον)[473] or imitation of the immortal and rational soul-form. Due to this very fact the mortal soul is unable to discriminate the enmattered substance, rather, it can only recognise the confusing qualities, quantities, and the rest enmattered categories of the sensible things. This point is explicitly manifested in the *Timaeus*: firstly, Plato's Timaeus declares that the young gods, being afraid that the unregulated soul-form would pollute (μιαίνειν, 69d6) the divine part, implant the mortal parts not in the head, in which the rational soul dwells, rather in different places in the body (*Tim.* 69d6–e1): If the mortal soul-form is homogeneous to the divine soul-form, the gods would not have such a worrying, but now the thymos-formed part is implanted in the breast (69e5–70d6), and the appetitive part in the belly (70d7–72d4). The relative nobler part, the θυμοειδές, being viewed as a soul-form which 'is of a manly spirit and ambitious of victory' (70a2), is set close to the head, so that it can easily hear the logos of the divine soul-form,[474] and helps to restrain the wrong desires that proceed from the relative worse part, i.e., the ἐπιθυμητικόν, which tends to resist

---

[472] *Phaed.* 81c2, b5, 83d2. Cf. *Rep.* 532c7–d11; *Tim.* 31b5; Aristotle, *De an.* 404b23–24.
[473] Proclus, *Theol. Plat.* III 23, 18–25. Cf. Opsomer (2006b) 137.
[474] *Tim.* 70a5: τοῦ λόγου κατήκοον. Cf. 70b (καὶ τὸ βέλτιστον οὕτως ἐν αὐτοῖς πᾶσιν ἡγεμονεῖν ἐῷ); 70d6 (μᾶλλον τῷ λόγῳ μετὰ θυμοῦ δύναιτο ὑπηρετεῖν).

the commands of the rational soul-form (70a7–b1). Given that the activities of the mortal soul-form are heterogeneous to that of the divine soul-form (for they either follow the logos of the divine soul-form, when they are in their best states, or conflict with it, while the divine soul-form always concerns itself about all of them and governs the mortal soul-form[475]), it should also not hold the same cognitive dynamis as the latter: Plato clearly formulates that the mortal soul-form cannot understand the logos, discursive thinking (διάνοια) and intelligence (φρόνησις) of the immortal soul,[476] rather it works through the perception-ability.[477] Therefore, without the dynamis of the rational soul the affected perception in the mortal soul is apparently unregulated (ἀλόγῳ, 69d4), which disables it to discriminate and comprehend the substance of the sensible objects.

If we observe the soul not in the view of its bipartition, rather as a unified entity, we can also clarify the affected sensation's inability to recognise the substance by asserting that the soul's different cognitive abilities enable the determination of different objects: an affected perception reports the sensible qualities to the soul, however, these reported contents involve only the nine categories that are enmattered in the sensible things, not their substances, i.e., the proper objects of the affected sensation embrace not the substance: to discriminate and comprehend the substances of the sensibles the soul should turn to other mental faculty, namely the opinion, and even the discursive thinking. This view is manifested in the finger-passage of the *Republic*, which will be discussed in detail at the end of section 3.2.2.

Despite the fallibility in the case of the common sensation and the inaccessibility of the substance of the sensible objects, the affected sensation, born with us, does enable us to discriminate the nine (enmattered) categories, which is the very beginning of the empirical cognition and the real knowledge,[478] for the perceived objects are things that 'what is for us clear', as Aristotle asserts in *Physics* 184a16–b14: (a) through the peculiar sensation we grasp the perceptible qualities like whiteness and hotness, with the common perception we are able to comprehend more enmattered categories such as Quantity, Relation, Space, Time, Position, Possession, Acting, and Being Affected, hence, the affected perception enables already the cognition of the determinate objects. Although these discriminated sensible qualities are abstract, confusing, universal, and relate not to the (sensible) substances, they can nevertheless be regarded as the basic words that are valuable in describing and defining the natural generated things. (b) Based on the affected sensation the memory and phantasia are generated, which are the precondition of the generation of opinion and discursive thinking, for the becoming of

---

[475] That the rational soul has the right to govern the unregulated soul, see *Tim*. 42b2–3: ὧν εἰ μὲν κρατήσοιεν, δίκῃ βιώσοιντο, κρατηθέντες δὲ ἀδικίᾳ. The relationship of the three parts (forms) of soul is the main concern of the *Republic*, esp. book IV.

[476] See the term 'logos' in *Tim*. 70a5; 7; b4; d6; 71a3; 71d4; διάνοια at 71c4; φρόνησις in 71d5. Cf: 71e2: ἀφροσύνη.

[477] This is revealed in 70b6–8, where the heart is described to function in the way of perception, and at 71a3–7, where the appetitive part is said to possess the sensation dynamis, and 'would most readily fall under the spell of images (εἰδώλων) and phantoms (φαντασμάτων) both by night and by day'. (Tr. Cornford).

[478] That the perception is the beginning of knowledge is originally a doctrine of the Peripatos, yet also accepted by the Platonists, see for example Olympiodorus, *In Phaed.* 4, 8, 7.

opinion requires memory, while the mathematics like geometry is normally studied through phantasia.[479] (c) The affected sensation supplies the materials to the rational cognitive abilities: firstly by observing the discriminated sensible qualities the opinion can recognise their substances, and the discursive thinking grasps the causes of these substances, or the 'common things' that are mentioned in *Theaetetus* 185c4f.; secondly the senses like sight and hearing can benefit our thought because of their kindship of the heavenly motion with the circuits of the soul, and that of the soul-movements with the harmony in the music.

The usefulness of the affected human sensation reveals the rational will of the gods. In *Tim.* 42d7–e4 we are taught that the young gods are commanded to mould the mortal bodies and souls, and to rule and guide the mortal life as noble and good as possible, thus the mortal soul is established 'as perfect as possible' (ὡς ἄριστον, *Tim.* 71d7), and its cognitive abilities, i.e., perception, memory and phantasia, are established by imitating the immortal, divine, and rational soul, which endorses their determinate cognitive capacities including the sensible qualities.[480] Hence, the legitimation of the affected sensation's cognitive dynamis is ensured by its very divine origin.

3.2.2 The cognitive dynamis of the unaffected sensation

Following the examination of the truth of the affected perception we should inquire the cognitive competence of the unaffected sensation, which is equal to the Aristotelian incidental perception and in broad sense the sensation of the divine soul-form in the view of Proclus. Taking the investigation of the cognitive ability of the affected sensation as model, we should firstly clarify whether the unaffected sensation relates inherently to the first Aristotelian category, i.e., the Substance (3.2.2.1), then turn to the range of its epistemological capacity and the truth of its discrimination, last but not least, the reason of such a competence will also be explored (3.2.2.2).

3.2.2.1 The first category 'Substance' and the unaffected sensation *per se*

That the affected sensation can grasp all Aristotelian categories expect for the first one, i.e., the Substance, is demonstrated in section 3.2.1.1 – the reason rests on their natural correspondence: the peculiar sensation endorses the discrimination of the sensible qualities, while the common perception enables the determination of the other eight enmattered categories. Now speaking of the unaffected sensation, it is reasonable to doubt whether it can grasp the first category. As mentioned many times above, the unaffected perception, i.e., the opinion with affected sensation, does have the dynamis to distinguish the substance of the sensibles, for in the *Timaeus* we are told that all

---

[479] Cf. Lautner (2002) 267; Büttner (2018) 164–165. Aristotle (*De an.* 431a16–17) claims that 'the soul never understands without phantasia'. For a Neoplatonic clarification of this assertation, see Steel (2018) 185–223.

[480] In this view Proclus (*In Remp.* I 235, 13–21) proclaims that phantasia is the εἰκών of νόησις, and perception is that of the opinion. Cf. Lautner (2002) 266.

sensibles can be grasped by 'opinion with sensation' (δόξῃ περιληπτὰ μετ' αἰσθήσεως, 28c1), and in *Philebus* 38b6–d10 we are told that the opinion, originating from the combination of memory and the affected perception in the soul, discriminates what the perceived thing is (τί ποτ' ἄρ' ἔστι, 38c13), namely the substances of the sensible things like 'a certain man', 'a determinate statue', etc .

However, this Platonic unaffected sensation-discrimination seems not to be consistent with the first Aristotelian category, since the latter denotes not the substance of the perceived objects like 'man' or 'circle', rather the substance of the single discriminated things like Socrates, or son of Cleon, which corresponds to the very objects of the Aristotelian incidental sensation.[481] That is to say, this Aristotelian category is clearly discriminated from the forms and genera, whereas in the *Philebus*-context we see that what is discerned is 'a man' (ὡς ἔστιν ἄνθρωπος, 38d6), which, at the first sight, should be ascribed to the form of the Aristotelian Substance. If this is true, we should concede that there is an inherent contradiction or divergence between the unaffected sensation and the first Aristotelian category: although it does grasp the substance of the sensibles, such a substance corresponds not strictly to the Aristotelian Substance.

To clarify this seemingly contradiction we should re-examine the related contexts and stress that: (1) there are two kinds of Substance in the *Categories*, i.e., the primary and secondary Substance, and what the incidental perception discriminates is the primary one. At 2a11–19 Aristotle formulates explicitly:

> A substance – that which is called a substance most strictly, primarily, and most of all (κυριώτατά τε καὶ πρώτως καὶ μάλιστα) – is that which is neither said of a substrate (καθ' ὑποκειμένου τινός) nor in a substrate (ἐν ὑποκειμένῳ τινί), e.g., the determinate man (ὁ τὶς ἄνθρωπος) or the determinate horse (ὁ τὶς ἵπος). The forms (εἴδεσιν) in which the things primarily called substances (αἱ πρώτως οὐσίαι) are, are called secondary (δεύτεραι) substances, as also are the genera (γένη) of these forms. For example, the determinate man belongs in a species, man, and animal is a genus of the forms; so these – both man and animal – are called secondary substances. (Tr. Ackrill, with slight reversion).

In this passage Aristotle divides the substance into two types, viz. the primary substance and the secondary one, and gives examples to illustrate this separation: (a) the primary substance denotes for example 'the determinate man' and 'the determinate horse', which is said neither 'of a substrate' nor 'in a substrate'. Such a substance is the composite substance, because both the determinate man and the determinate horse are determinate composition of body (matter) and soul (form). And as a composition, this substance is sensible.[482] (b) The forms and genera are the secondary substance. And the

---

[481] For example, *De an.* 418a21 (son of Diarous), 425a25–26 (son of Cleon).
[482] That the involved substance is the composite substance, is held by Ammonius (*In Cat.* 36, 2: ἀλλὰ περὶ τῆς συνθέτου καὶ σχετικῆς), Philoponus (*In Cat.* 50, 1: ἀλλὰ περὶ τῆς συνθέτου μόνης), and Simplicius (*In Cat.* 80, 18–19: πρώτην οὐσίαν τὴν σύνθετόν φησιν καὶ ἄτομον. Cf. 80, 31–81, 14). For the fact that the composite substance is sensible, see Simplicius, *In Cat.* 81, 8–12; 82, 3–6. Cf. Thiel (2004) 67f. In pp. 58–66 Thiel discriminates the substances in the *Categories* from those in *Meta.* Book VII: in the former work Aristotle speaks of the individual sensible things (whose ontological constitution is not concerned) and the secondary

form encompasses the first substance, the genus embraces the forms. For example, the form 'man' includes the primary substance 'the determinate man', whereas the genus 'animal' includes 'man' – thus for Aristotle 'man' is a secondary substance.

Here 'the determinate man' is entitled the 'primary substance', because (a) on the one side its character of not being 'said of a subject' is peculiar to 'the individual substance' (τῆς ἀτόμου οὐσίας) which is indivisible (ἀδιαίρετος), whereas the secondary substance is predicated (said) of a subject. For the sensible composite substance, in the view that it is the substrate of the substances themselves, is the substance in strict and primary sense, without which the others cannot exist.[483] (b) On the other side, the primary substance like 'the individual man' is 'for us' (πρὸς ἡμᾶς) primary, not 'by nature' (τῇ φύσει): we experience at first the composite and individual substance, then discriminate and comprehend the simple and common one, i.e., forms and genera having their being (τὸ εἶναι) in the individual substance.[484] However, when observed by nature, the forms and genera are primary, for the simples (τὰ ἁπλᾶ), the commons (τὰ καθόλου), the causes (τὰ αἴτια), the non-enmattered (τὰ ἄυλα), and the undivided (τὰ ἀμέριστα) are prior to the contrary entities.[485] Therefore the sort of substance like 'the determinate man' is the primary substance in the view that it is the substance 'according to itself' (καθ' αὑτὴν)[486] and 'for us', since it is the substance that we first encounter in our empirical cognition. Given this account it is reasonable to declare that the Aristotelian incidental perception discriminates the primary substance, which is a sensible composition. The secondary substance, however, can only be comprehended after we have perceived the sensible things and discriminated their primary substance, because this is the normal order of the empirical cognition that begins with perception. For instance, through the beautiful sensible appearance we discriminate Charmides as the determinate person (*Charm*. 154b7–c9), and by pointing out the visible position in a group of people, Theodorus introduces Theaetetus, son of Euphronius, to Socrates (*Theat*. 144b8–c4).

(2) In the *Philebus*-example what is discussed should be treated as the primary substance, not the form. Seeing the object that exists beside the rock under a tree, the perceiver prefers to discriminate the substance of such an object. He asks himself what

---

form and genus, yet in the latter book the distinction of the individual thing and its ontological constitution – namely the (first) matter, form and composition – is the very beginning of the metaphysical explanation, while the 'secondary substance' is not discussed any more. Indeed, in *Meta*. 1069a30–b2 Aristotle claims that there are three kinds of substance, i.e., the sensible-eternal, the sensible-perishable, and the unmoved. The examples given for the sensible-perishable substance are (sublunary) plants and living creatures, and the principles of the sensible substance are form, privation, and matter. Cf. Simplicius, *In Cat*. 76, 17–77, 11; Rapp (2016) 87–117. Considering this assertion and the other proofs like the examples of Socrates and Callias at *Meta*.1070a13, the sensible substance here is equal to the primary substance in the *Categories*.

[483] Simplicius, *In Cat*. 80, 22–27.
[484] *Ibid*. 80, 28–31.
[485] *Ibid*. 82, 17–22. Cf. 84, 12–85, 1; Ammonius, *In Cat*. 36, 2–14; Philoponus, *In Cat*. 50, 6–14.
[486] That the primary substance is characterised by being in virtue of itself, according to Simplicius, is already emphasised by Archytas, see Simplicius, *In Cat*. 76, 9–12; 79, 19; 121, 13–18; etc. The announcement that what is said by itself is substance itself is also agreed by Philoponus, see for example his *In Cat*. 49, 16–22.

such a sensible thing is (τί ποτ' ἄρ' ἔστι, 38c13). Resorting to the opinion ability he discerns this sensible composition as a man, yet strictly speaking not 'a man', rather 'a man standing beside the rock under a tree', i.e., the determinate man. Because this man, due to his determinate location (and perhaps also the certain shape), is discriminated from all other things like a statue. Namely, what the perceiver differentiates is the substance of this sensible object in the determinate position, which results not in a judgement of its form and genus, rather of its primary substance. For this reason, we are endorsed to claim that the unaffected sensation corresponds to the first Aristotelian category.

One can still question that if this kind of sensation brings forth discrimination of the primary substance, why the answer of this discrimination appears to be the form – the phrase 'ὡς ἔστιν ἄνθρωπος' at 38d6 indicates not the determinate man, rather the secondary substance. This interpretation, however, is a misunderstanding of the *Philebus*-passage: what the perceiver discriminates here is not merely a man, rather a man standing beside the rock under a tree, i.e., it is a discrimination which discerns the primary substance of this sensible object, for with such a judgement he distinguishes this sensible object not only from the determinate horse or the determinate statue, but also from the other men who is now for example in Athen, or anywhere else. Hence, although this phrase tells us nothing more than a simple and common substance – the form. Considering the whole context, it should not be treated as the secondary substance, rather it is used to define the sensible object, i.e., 'a man who stands beside the rock under a tree', which denotes the primary substance. In this sense it makes even no difference whether we discriminate this object as a man or a statue (τὸ καυορώμενον ἄγαλμα, 38c10), for both concern the primary substance of the sensible object which is determined by its sensible location.

To supplement our demonstration, we should roughly prove that the primary substance is not merely an Aristotelian notion, in Plato we can also find its trace: at *Republic* 478d5–9 he argues that the opinable things turn out both to be and not to be (ἅμα ὄν τε καὶ μὴ ὄν), while the thinkable thing belongs to 'what purely is' (τοῦ εἰλικρινῶς ὄντος), which means that the opinable things can be viewed as things bearing a determinate kind of substance that is distinguished from the forms.[487] A few pages later, in 585b9f. he compares the form of the sensible things with the form of true opinion, knowledge and intellect, and claims that the latter participates more in the substance (μᾶλλον καθαρᾶς οὐσίας μετέχειν, 585b11), which reveals that in Plato there are at least two kinds of substances, and one of them relates to the sensibles.[488]

---

[487] Gerson (2020) 47. In n32 He gives further text-locations like *Theaet.* 156a5 and *Tim.* 52b3–5.
[488] For the substances of the generated things, see *Polit.* 283d8–9; *Laws* 903c3–5; 966e1–2. Sometimes Plato divides the substance into what really is and what not really is, for example in *Soph.* 262c2 (οὐδὲ οὐσίαν ὄντος οὐδὲ μὴ ὄντος) and *Polit.* 296b10 (πέρι τῆς τοῦ μὴ ὄντος οὐσίας). At *Tim.* 35a1–4 Plato mentions even two kinds of substance, i.e., one indivisible and always the same, the other divisible and comes to be, and credits the soul with an intermediate position. In annotating this lexis Proclus (*In Tim.* 129, 31–130, 1) says "the soul similarly has proceeded to the middle position between what is intelligible simpliciter and the sensibles, and between the beings which only are always and those that are generated simpliciter" (Tr. Baltzly). Thus, the sensible things possess certain kind of substance.

Moreover, at *Laws* 895d1–5 he stresses that we can think about 'everything' (ἕκαστον) in three-fold: substance, logos of the substance, and name (word).[489] Given that this assertation is valid for 'everything', the sensible things must also be suitable for this frame – this can even be illustrated in *Laws* 894a6, where the Platonic Socrates describes the generated things with the phrase 'ὄντως ὄν'. Therefore, it is reasonable to declare that the Platonic unaffected sensation discriminates the composite substance of the sensibles.

In this regard we should explain how we can discriminate the substance of the sensible things. Through the affected sensation we cannot discriminate the primary substance, no matter how many times we have perceived and how long time we have taken to perceive, for although what we determinate through this kind of perception are the abstract, confusing and universal features decided by and originate from the substance, substantially they are not equal to the primary substance itself. Therefore, we must turn to the other kind of sensation, namely the unaffected sensation. Given that the activity of this kind of sensation requires the other cognition-abilities such as memory, as manifested in *Philebus* 39a1–7, the unaffected sensation is equal to the perception with support of the other abilities. The cognitive ability of this perception, which is generated due to the combination of the affected sensation and memory, is entitled 'opinion', or precisely, 'opinion with perception' (δόξα μετ' αἰσθήσεως) – in the *Philebus* the specific location of the sensible object is perceived by the affected sensation, while the discrimination of its substance requires the opinion with perception. The dynamis of such a kind of opinion, i.e., discerning the substance of the sensibles, is manifested, when Plato proclaims that the 'opinion with unregulated perception' (δόξῃ μετ' αἰσθήσεως ἀλόγου, *Tim.* 28a2–3) discriminates the things that come to be and pass away, but never have the real being. Such an announcement credits the realm of generation with not only sensation, but also opinion. For through sensation, precisely speaking, the affected sensation, we can discriminate the nine categories of the physical world, while only through the opinion, which is unaffected, we are able to determine the nature of the sensible things, namely their substances.[490] So the natural physical world, encompassing form and matter, is neither merely sensible nor merely opinable (δοξαστόν), rather both sensible and opinable: sensible through the affected sense perception, opinable according to the unaffected sensation, or the opinion with (affected) sensation.

As human being we are born with the ability of perception (*Tim.* 42a5–6), and the rational soul-form constructed by the Demiurge ensures our souls' capacity of opinion. Plato credits the circle of Difference of the world soul with the capacity of discriminating both the sensible things and their substances (*Tim.* 37b6–c1), given that the human soul, as the divine imitation of the world soul, possesses an immortal, divine form (part) which also has two circles like the world soul, the human soul does bear the ability of distinguishing and recognising the whole realm of generation, i.e., the sensible world, by discriminating all its ten categories through the affected and unaffected sensation.

---

[489] Cf. *Epist. VII* 342a7ff.; *Theaet.* 202b5; etc.
[490] Cf. the detailed clarification of the phrase 'opinion with (unregulated) sensation' at Proclus, *In Tim.* I 248, 7–252, 10.

3.2.2.2 The truth of the unaffected sensation and its reason

Regarding the truth of the unaffected perception, we should first (1) determine whether it has different kinds, and what is the range of its cognitive dynamis. For as in the case of the affected sensation, it is possible that the cognitive truth of the unaffected sensation also varies in accordance with its different types: they could recognise different sorts of objects, and the range of their cognitive abilities could also be distinct from each other. Then (2) concentrate on the truth of this kind of perception, and the reason of such a truth. If the unaffected sensation possesses different kinds and cognitive realms, the precision of their discrimination would also be distinct, in which sense a determination of the credibility of each kind, and an investigation into the reason of this discrimination is necessary.

(1) For the current investigation of the cognitive dynamis of the unaffected sensation, it will be more reasonable, when we divide it into two further kinds, i.e., the unaffected sensation by itself and that with support of further cognitive capacities, for although it can be separated into many different kinds, this dichotomy is the one that corresponds to 'logos and dynamis', the criterion of the division of soul: as the Platonic soul could be deemed to be monadic, bipartite or tripartite, the unaffected sensation could also be separated into different kinds, for example: given that the unaffected sensation is always accompanied with the affected sensation, as exemplified in the *Philebus*-context (with the common sensation we perceive the 'location' of the sensible object, a man), it could be divided in accordance with the different kinds of affected perception, namely the opinion with peculiar sensation, and that with common sensation, or with different sorts of categories depending on the substance; considering that the opinion with sensation discriminates not only the substance of the generated physical things, but also the social things like what is justice and injustice, there are opinions involving the natural world and those pertaining to the practical realm; depending on whether the unaffected sensation takes place with further support like discursive thinking or intellect, the objects of the opinion-discrimination could also be distinct, i.e., there exists the unaffected sensation alone on the one side, and that with help of further cognitive abilities on the other; when the engaged opinable object is a single opinable entity like a single finger, the unaffected sensation reports us nothing contradicts, however, when the opinable object at issue is mixed with other things, such as three fingers, its discrimination leads possibly to contradictions: the same finger could simultaneously be bigger than the second, but smaller than the third – in this case there is opinion for the single determinate entity and that for the mingled things; and so on. Under these different classifications, however, the most decisive dichotomy is that of the unaffected sensation alone, and that with support of further cognitive dynameis, for all other separations either bring forth no essential distinction or originate from this very dichotomy: whether the accompanying perception is peculiar or common, the opinion-discrimination will not be influenced, for what it recognises is the substance, which concerns, yet not decided by other categories; so is the division of the opinion involving the physical things and that of the social matters, since on both occasions the opinion discriminates the substance; for the dichotomy of the unaffected sensation in accordance with the single or mixed object, the

results could be different, for in the former case what we opine tends to be true, or as least the results of the opinion-discrimination can be corrected by itself (for example, in the *Philebus*-example when the perceiver goes closer to the sensible and opinable object, whether it is really a man or a statue would be naturally obvious; and in the case of the sameness of the big and small letters at *Republic* 368d1–7, the sameness will be affirmed or denied, once we standing before them), whereas when the objects are mixed, like the three fingers, the activity of the unaffected sensation could possibly results in contradiction that is unable to be solved by itself: According to Plato, feeling confused in this case, the soul summons the discursive thinking to discriminate the mixed objects. That is to say, the dichotomy in accordance with the single or mixed object coincides with the bipartite division of the opinion alone and that with help of other cognitive abilities. Thus, we should take this separation as the standard one.

Given that the unaffected sensation includes two further kinds, the exploration of its cognitive range should be exercised respectively: (a) the opinion with sensation by itself, or the unaffected sensation *per se*, enables the discrimination of the substance and function of all generated physical things and, in certain degree, the Platonic 'common things' introduced in *Theaetetus* 185c3f. That the unaffected sensation enables the discrimination of the corporeal things that are generated is already proved above, here we must supplement that this discrimination can be understood in two aspects, or two dimensions: it recognises not only the single generated things like 'a man', 'a statue', which is the primary object of opinion, but also the general ones like 'the fathers', 'the philosophers'; and it discerns both the natural things like the wood and stone, and the social affairs like justice. (a1) Our affected sensation is temporally and spatially, for its objects are enmattered in the individual things, and what is discriminates is confusing, abstract, and universal according to nature. Based on the affected sensation the unaffected perception proceeds from the discrimination of the substance of an individual thing, yet it ceases not at this point, rather seeks to derive a universal allegation from this single discrimination. For example, Aristotle (*Phy.* 184b2–5) tells us that an infant tends to call all men 'father', and all women 'mother', for a child does rightly perceive the deep voice, the appearance like certain height or the Adam's apple of a man, and opines that this object with deep voice is 'father', so when he hears a man's deep voice or sees the Adam's apple, he tends to call him 'father'.[491] Apparently perceiving the sensible qualities like the deep voice or other perceptible feature(s) enables the children to opine such an object as father and differentiate him from the mother, yet he opines further: father has a deep voice; this sensible man has a deep voice; so he is father too. Or: a father has a deep voice, all men have deep voice, so all men are father. Hence, the opinion that is made about a single sensible thing tends to stretch out to all homogenous sensible things. (a2) The opinion's dynamis is not confined in the natural world, rather it expands

---

[491] Cf. Schmitt (2012) 314, 318–322. Strikingly, in the *Republic* Plato asserts that all old men should be called 'father', and the guardians cannot distinguish (διαγνώσονται, 461d1) their own fathers, but this is not according to nature, but law (νόμος, 461e3), and the laws about marriages and procreations are factually lies and deceptions (συχνῷ τῷ ψεύδει καὶ τῇ ἀπάτῃ, 459c8), which are made by the rulers (459c8) for the unity of the whole city. So Plato must know the phenomenon that the children call the men 'father', and he does not assert that this is naturally right, but only practically beneficial for the whole city.

further into the realms of arts and humanities. This point can be explicitly revealed by resorting to the first book of the *Republic*, where we are taught that through opinion we can grasp many things' functions generated from their substances, and determine the best one under many similar things, for example at 353a1–8 Plato asserts that although in pruning a vine one can use a dagger or a carving knife, a pruning knife is better than both of them, for with a pruning knife one can remove the determinate new branches locating in many new branches, and cut off the dead boughs from a cluster of many living ones: it has two handles and a certain bigness, through which one can get the determinate branches; it holds short and keen cutting edges, which enables it to prune the branches cleanly and neatly, without hurting the others. Observing the determinate structure of a pruning knife or seeing a farmer using such a knife pruning the new and dead branches, one can naturally discern that a pruning knife functions better than the other kinds of knives. Once we opine this very function of the pruning knife, its form, goodness, and beauty will also be determined: for its form enables its function, when it rightly functions, it is good, with its proportional shape and size it can finish its job in a perfect way, so it must be beautiful.[492]

Moreover, in this book the Platonic Socrates endeavours to determine a suitable answer to the question: what is justice? And the responses that he receives, or what he summarises for his partners' answers, are as follows: speaking the truth and giving back what one has borrowed from the other (331c2–3; d2–3); to give to each what is owed to him (331e3–4; 332a7–8); friends owe something good to their friends and nothing bad (332a9–10); to give to each what is fitting (332c2); doing good things to friends and harming the enemies (332d7–8; 334b8–9); to do good to the friend, if he is really good, and to harm the enemy, provided he is bad (335a8–9); what is advantageous for the stronger, i.e., the ruler (338c3; 339a3–4); to obey the rulers (339b9–10); whatever laws the rulers set down must be done by the ruled (339c10–11); someone else's good, the advantage of the stronger and the ruler, a harm to the obeyed and ruled (343c1–5); the very high-minded innocence (348c12); justice belongs to the things that are in contrast to virtue and wisdom (348 e2–3); a just man tends not to do better than someone like himself, but someone unlike himself (349c11–d2); and so on. During the dialogue with his partners Socrates also gives some of his own opinions about what the justice is, for example it is 'human virtue' (ἀνθρωπεία ἀρετή, 335c4), and he also opines that the just man is a good man (335d10), and justice is something of advantage (339b5–6). One would wonder whether these judgements are made by the opinion with sensation, for the term δόξα appears only three times in the first book, and the first time concerns even not the substance of justice.[493] For this confusion (a2.1) we should remember that opinion concerns the composite substance, and answers the question 'what is (the determinate) X', which is the theme of the first book of the *Republic*: to determine what is justice. Therefore, although the term 'opinion' is not frequently utilised in this passage, what the context concerns is still the opinable issue, i.e., the substance of the justice. (a2.2) The frequently appeared term 'logos' hints at the opinion with perception. In the *Philebus*-passage about the generation of opinion (unaffected sensation), Plato

---

[492] Schmitt (2015), 286–289. For the theme 'the synthetic character of the empiric objects', see his (2011) 23–29.
[493] Namely δόξαζεις at 327c6 and δόξαν in 346a3 and 350e5. Cf. Brandwood (1976) 256.

169

explicitly declares that opinion is logos,[494] precisely speaking, a kind of logos performed in the soul and concerns the substance of the sensible entity, for the perceiver, in order to discriminate "what is the object that stands beside the rock under the tree", asks himself and answers himself; in doing this he is alone and 'thinks' (διανοούμενος, 38e7) the same thing 'by himself' (πρὸς αὑτόν), thus the generation of the opinion, i.e., the psychic process of combining the determinate affected sensation with memory-images, is the same as the becoming of the self-discourse in the way of thinking.[495] According to this account, the frequent application of the term 'logos' in the *Republic*[496] reveals nothing else but the logos of the substance (taken the model of 'substance-logos of substance-name' in *Laws* 895d1–5 into consideration), precisely, the logos about the substance of justice, which turns out to be the object of opinion with perception. As the opinion is now utilised to determine the justice, we are endorsed to declare that its cognitive ability is not restricted in the natural world, rather it distinguishes also the social and political affairs, i.e., its cognitive range covers all things that coming to be in our world.

Now we can go further by stressing that the opinion with (affected) sensation can also recognise the Platonic 'common things' such as What-is (τὸ ἔστιν, *Theaet.* 185c4–5), What-is-not (τὸ οὐκ ἔστιν, 185c5), Substance and Non-substance (οὐσίαν [...] καὶ τὸ μὴ εἶναι, 185c8), Likeness (ὁμοιότητα, 185c8; τὸ ὅμοιον, 186a6), Unlikeness (ἀνομοιότητα, 185c9; τὸ ἀνόμοιον, 186 a6), Sameness (τὸ ταὐτόν, 185c9, 186a6), Difference (τὸ ἕτερον, 185c9, 186a7), One (ἕν, 185d1), the other Number (τὸν ἄλλον ἀριθμόν, 185d1), Even and Odd (ἄρτιόν τε καὶ περιττόν, 185d2), Beautiful and Ugly (186a9), Good and Bad (186a9), though only in certain degree – for what it discriminates are only the images of those things. This is different from the discrimination of the substance of the perceptible things due to the very fact that on the latter occasion what we opine are the primary substance of the sensibles, while the Platonic common things are invisible and everlasting by themselves, i.e., they are the ontological categories and the cause of the primary substances of the sensible things.[497] In fact, the discrimination of these 'common things' is the underlying impulse and the final aim that exists even at the outset of the empirical cognition, i.e., the affected sensation: at *Phaedo* 74b1–76b2 in arguing the existence of the forms and that learning is recollection, Plato asserts that by performing our perception dynamis we 'think over' (ἐνενοήσαμεν, 75a1) that all things in the sensation are striving for 'what equal is' (ὃ ἔστιν ἴσον), and although they strive to be like the equal, they fell short of it (75a1–b1). Despite the theme of this con-

---

[494] *Phileb.* 38e3–4: καὶ λόγος δὴ γέγονεν οὕτως ὃ τότε δόξαν ἐκαλοῦμεν.

[495] For the opinion as the logos of the soul, see also *Theaet.* 189e6–190a6 and *Soph.* 263e3–264b3. Given that in the world soul there exist also logoi of opinion, nous, and knowledge, the self-discourse of soul, or the different kinds of logoi with corresponding cognitive abilities in the soul, should be regarded as a general doctrine of Plato.

[496] λόγος: 334a9, d6, 343a2, 351b6, 352d7; λόγου: 331e1, 336b2, d7, 343a1, 348d9, 352b4, 354b7; λόγῳ: 335a3, 341b2, 6, 8, c6, 342b7, 349a5; λόγον: 331d7, 334d3, 336b4, 337e3, 338d3, 339d1, 340e2, 344d3, 4, 6, 345b7, 348a8, 349a10, 351a1, 353d1, e12; λόγων: 336e3; λόγοις: 340d2, 341a7. Cf. Brandwood (1976) 537–539.

[497] For the newest research of the Platonic and Aristotelian ontology as well as the ontological categories (or the being-categories) in them, see Schmitt (2020) 12–43.

text one can conclude that through the affected sensation our soul notices the distinction between the enmattered equality and the equal itself. Discriminating the latter requires a dymanis beyond the affected sensation though, beginning with the cognition of the sensible objects we can finally arrive at recollection of the equality itself.[498] Or as Plato formulates, for the most people they cannot think the intelligible reality over unless through the perception and sensible things (75a4–6)[499] – for the sensible things are composed of form and matter, i.e., they are both one and many,[500] and for the human beings they are the first things that we encounter in the fields of epistemology. Therefore, although the ability of determining the equal itself belongs not to the affected sensation, through its actuality the soul does think the equal itself over. In this sense the striving for determining the common things functions as the impulse and aim of the affected perception, albeit the latter is still too weak to grasp these things by itself. Now given that the unaffected sensation discriminates the substances of the generated things, it bears correspondingly more competence in recognising those so-called 'common things': at *Theaetetus* 190b2–8 Plato mentions beautiful, ugly, unjust, just, and odd in the context about the fallible opinion, a few pages later, the relations of the numbers five, seven, eleven, and twelve are discussed in the view of opinion (195e8f.); in the Line Analogy of *Republic* (509d6–511e5) we are taught that the opinable things – all living creatures as well as the whole class of the manufactured things – are the imitations (τοῖς τότε μιμηθεῖσιν, 510b4) of the knowable things, especially the things that are comprehensible for the discursive thinking (διάνοια), which implies that through opinion we can grasp the images of those things that are now clearly proclaimed to be the Platonic common things – or at least the things that concern geometry and calculation, like the odd and the even, and other things akin to them (510c1–5).

(b) The unaffected sensation with support of further cognitive dynameis like the discursive thinking and intellect recognises not only the substance, but also its cause and principle. As revealed in the Analogy of Line, what the discursive thinking and intellect discriminate are the knowable entities forming the opinable and sensible things, thus when the unaffected sensation is companied with these abilities, it can discern not only the substances of all generated things, but also their causes. For example in discriminating the man standing beside the rock under a tree we perceive his determinate location (and shape) through the peculiar and common sensation, we determine his being a human by applying our unaffected sensation, while with the discursive thinking we know that the reason of his being a human: he has the divine and mortal soul forms existing in his earthly body, he is able to learn arithmetic, geometry, astronomy, music, and the dialectic, and so on. Namely thorough opinion we grasp the determinate man, while with discursive thinking we can understand the reason of his being a man. Therefore, it is reasonable to declare that all cognitive abilities, i.e., the affected and unaffected sensation, the discursive thinking, and intellect, have their own determinate objects, i.e., what is recognisable is something determinate: the affected sensation recognises the

---

[498] Olympiodorus, *In Phaed.* 4, 8, 8–9: διότι ἐκ τῶν αἰσθητῶν εἰς ἀνάμνησιν ἀφικνούμεθα.
[499] Cf. Damascius, *In Phaed.* I 304, 1–2: Πῶς 'οὐ δυνατὸν ἐννοῆσαι' μὴ διὰ τῶν αἰσθητῶν τὰ νοητά; – Ἡ τάς γε πλείστας τῶν ψυχῶν.
[500] At *Rep.* 525a5 the Platonic Glaucon stresses that: ἅμα γὰρ ταὐτὸν ὡς ἕν τε ὁρῶμεν καὶ ὡς ἄπειρα τὸ πλῆθος.

changeable and divisible sensible qualities; the unaffected perception determines the 'einai' in the determinate form, i.e., the enmattered substance; the discursive thinking discriminates the 'einai' of something itself, or the cause of the substance; and the intellect discerns the 'einai' itself, i.e., the first principle initiates all cognitive abilities and their objects.[501] That these distinct cognitive abilities endorse the discrimination and comprehension of different objects clarifies why Plato stresses that sensation should be joined up with the intellect,[502] and the intention of the education and the laws of the polis is to cultivate and maintain the right order of the different soul-forms in us.[503]

(2) Speaking of the cognitive truth of the two kinds of unaffected affection we should clarify them respectively: (a) the unaffected sensation by itself can be right and false: 'right' in the sense that there is true opinion (τὸ δοξάζειν ἀληθῆ, *Theaet.* 200e5) without knowledge,[504] 'false' means not that an opinion is wrong, rather there exists the possibility leading to the so-called 'mis-opinion' or 'other-opinion' (ἀλλοδοξίαν, 189b12; τὸ [...] ἀλλοδοξεῖν, 189d5; τὸ ἑτεροδοξεῖν, 190e2),[505] for such an opinion occurs when the soul mixes (παραλλάττουσι, 194 d3–4) one substance up with another, as manifested in *Philebus* 38d5–7, where Plato announces that in discerning the object that stands beside the rock under a tree one can probably muddle the substance 'a man' with 'a statue' made by the shepherds. The opinion that 'such an object is a determinate statue' is an 'other-opinion' in comparing with the opinion of its being a certain man. Therefore, a better expression should be that the unaffected sensation *per se* leads occasionally to right and missed opinions. (b) The opinion with companion of other abilities, however, by virtue of its inherent cognitive dynamis, makes no mistakes in discriminating its objects.

As for the reason of the distinct credibility of these two types of the unaffected sensation we should also clarify one after another. (a) That the opinion with the affected sensation enables probably an other-opinion, results mainly from two factors: (a1) In the view of the origin of this cognitive faculty there is a possible mis-combination between the present affected sense perception and the memory-image reserved in the soul. This point is explicitly displayed at *Theaet.* 190e5ff., where to explain the generation of the other-opinion Plato introduces a well-known theory, i.e., the wax tablet, which is already introduced in section 3.2.1.2: the human soul contains a block of wax that is the gift of the goddess Memory, mother of the Muses. What we have perceived (or thought by ourselves) is imprinted in this block, and so long as the image (τὸ εἴδωλον) or the

---

[501] On this point Proclus (*In Tim.* I 352, 15–19) has offered a more systematic summary: "let us rather think that the manner of knowing differs according to the diversity of the knowers. For the very same object is known by god unitarily, by intellect holistically, by reason universally, by imagination figuratively, by sense perception passively. And it is not the case that because the object of knowledge is also one [and the same]". (Tr. Runia & Share).
[502] See *Laws* 961d9: συλλήβδην δὲ νοῦς μετὰ τῶν καλλίστων αἰσθήσεων κραθείς, γενόμενός τε εἰς ἕν. Cf. 961e1–5.
[503] Cf. *Rep.* 441e7f.; *Tim.* 42b2–3; *Laws* 653a5–c4, 747b3–c2; etc.
[504] *Theaet.* 200d6–201c7.
[505] For the discussion that false opinion is actually 'other-opinion', see for example *Theaet.* 189b12–190e4.

imprint (τὸ σημεῖον) remains in the soul, we can remember it (191c8–e1).[506] The 'other-opinion' happens, especially when the soul assigns the fresh affected sensation to a heterogenous image existing already in it,[507] i.e., the generation of this 'another-opinion' is the combination of the present sensation with a seemingly likely memory-image known for the soul. Such a mis-matching, however, originates from the goodness or badness of the memory-faculty which leads to the distinct or indistinct (ἀσαφῆ, 194d14; d15) memory-images – in this sense a good memory is an important philosophical nature for Plato[508] – for although the memory-images are imprinted in the soul with names, when the memory ability is too weak to distinguish one image from the others, the soul tends to attribute the fresh impression to an incorrect image, and misses the 'real beings' or the primary substance of the opinable things.[509] (a2) The fallibility of the unaffected sensation is generated by virtue of the mis-discrimination of the sensory features. Essentially the objects of the opinion, in the view of the Neoplatonic tradition, are the Forms-in-Matter (τὰ ἔνυλα εἴδη), which corresponds to the fourth hypothesis of the *Parmenides* (157b5–159b2): when the One exists, the Forms-in-Matter, or the opinable things share it in a determinate way.[510] The One ensures the possible opinion of the substance of these objects in the sense that it ensures the existence of the forms in them, while the Matter, or the Others (τἆλλα), leads probably to a fallible judgement, because it changes the appearances of the sensibles from time to time and brings forth heterogeneity, making it difficult to discern the sensible features, which leads occasionally to the mis-discrimination of the substance. In another view, the generation of the other-opinion results possibly from the mis-discrimination of the sensibles due to the objective restriction like the physical distance, as revealed in both *Philebus* and *Theaetetus*:[511] because of the distance we are unable to perceive the determinate sensible qualities through the peculiar and common sensation, which results necessarily in a fresh impression that is too unclear to be attributed to the proper memory-image, and further a possible mis-discrimination of the substance of the sensible entity.

(b) The certainty of the opinion with other cognitive abilities is ensured because of the determinate competence of this combination. Firstly, let us recollect the cognitive capacities of the world soul, paradigm of the divine form of the human soul: from the passage of *Timaeus* 37b3–c3 we can derive that there are three kinds of logos pertaining to the world soul: the 'opinative' (δοξαστικός) logos, the 'scientific' (ἐπιστημονικός)

---

[506] Plato points out three cases in which it is impossible for the generation of an 'other-opinion', i.e., when neither object is perceived; if what involved is merely the affected sensation; and if what involved are both knowledge and affected perception. Cf. Cornford (1935) 122.

[507] *Theaet.* 193b9–d2, 194a6–b6, 194d3–4, 195a5–9, c7–d2, etc.

[508] See esp. *Rep.* 586d2, 487a4, 490c10, 503c1, 535c1; *Laws* 747b3–6; etc.

[509] Cf. *Theaet.* 194d6 (ἃ δὴ ὄντα καλεῖται); 195a8–9 (καὶ καλοῦνται αὖ οὗτοι ἐψευσμένοι τε δὴ τῶν ὄντων). Remarkably, at 196d–199c Plato also explores the mistaken opinions which involve no perception.

[510] Proclus, *In Parm.* 1060, 13–15; 1060, 22–1061, 16; 1064, 5–7; etc. Ahbel-Rappe (2010) 26 points out that Damascius (*In Parm.* 434) shares the same idea, which originates from Plutarch. As argued above, Aristotle (*De an.* 417b22; *An. Post.* 100a16–17) also asserts the existence of the One in the sensibles.

[511] See *Phileb.* 38c6 (πόρρωθεν); *Theaet.* 193c1–2 (διὰ μακροῦ καὶ μὴ ἱκανῶς ὁρῶν). Cf. the Letter-Analogy in *Rep.* 368d3–4: πόρρωθεν [...] μὴ πάνυ ὀξὺ βλέπουσιν.

logos, and the 'intellective' (νοερός) logos.[512] All three kinds also exist in our human soul. Regarding our current motif the logos of opinion with perception is the unaffected sensation, while the scientific logos and the intellective logos correspond respectively to the discursive thinking and intellect, the third and fourth section of the famous Line-Analogy. As opinion, knowledge, and intellect of the world soul are three distinct kinds of one single unified logos (*Tim.* 37b3–c3), the unaffected sensation, discursive thinking, and intellect can also be joined into oneness and function collectively. Given that the logoi of the world soul are always discriminated and trustworthy, the parallel discrimination of the logoi in the divine human soul should also be always right.[513]

At last, we should stress that sense perception can be mingled with the other cognitive abilities, is a general Platonic doctrine which is revealed in the perception-theory of the first Platonists, i.e., Speusippus and Xenocrates: in Speusippus, according to the studies of Tarán and Dillon, the classification of substances begins with the One, continues with the principles numbers, magnitude (μέγεθη) and soul, then with the other levels until the sensibles. The sensible entity is 'a kind of monad or point', and the relations of Same, Difference, and Likeness focused in it endorse its difference and essence.[514] Correspondingly, the 'scientific perception' (ἐπιστημονικὴ αἴσθησις) – in our words the unaffected sensation with help of other cognitive abilities, here (here discursive thinking) – participates in the cognitive dynamis of the 'scientific logos' (ἐπιστημονικὸς λόγος) and possesses inherently an unerring dynamis in discriminating the sensibles.[515] The example that Speusippus gives for this kind of perception is the artistic activity of the fingers of the flute-player or harper, which is not primarily performed by virtue of the touch perception of the fingers, rather it involves reasoning, for the cognitive dynamis of perception "shares in the cognitive experience derived from reason for the infallible discrimination of its objects".[516] In Xenocrates we can discover that the sensible things are treated as a kind of substance, and the cognitive dynamis of perception is true: For him there are three kinds of substance,[517] i.e., 'the sensible' (ἡ αἰσθητή), 'the intelligible' (ἡ νοητή), and the composition of them, 'the opinable' (ἡ δοξαστή). What is sensible exists below the heaven, the intelligible things are in the outside of the heaven, whereas the opinable and composite denotes the heaven itself, for it is visible through the perception, but intelligible according to astronomy. In accordance with those three sorts of existence there exists a tripartite discrimination, namely perception (which is true, but not in the same way as the knowledge), knowledge, and opinion (mixed with truth and falsehood).

---

[512] See Proclus, *In Tim.* I 246, 19–20.

[513] The cognitive abilities of the discursive thinking and intellect are originally not our main concern, so our research ends after the clarification of the combination-possibility of the three kinds of logoi. For the explanation of the discursive thinking and intellect in Plato, see for example Cludius (1997) esp. 152–223; Schmitt (1974) 132–232; (2007) 89–112; (2011) 91–155; (2012) 208–276; (2019) 81–127.

[514] Tarán (1981) 48, 57, 60; Dillon (2003) 79.

[515] Tarán (1981) 54, 57, 433–435; Dillon (2003) 78–79.

[516] Tarán (1981) 433–434.

[517] See Sextus Empiricus, *Adv. Math.* 7, 147–149 = fg. 5 Heinze; fg. 83 Isnardi Parente. Cf. Dörrie & Blates (1996) 52–55, 272–274; Dillon (²1996) 30; (2003) 124–125.

Obviously, for Plato and the first Platonists including Aristotle the sensible things possess a kind of substance, and the perception's cognitive dynamis is capable of differentiating and comprehending determinate objects enmattered in the sensible things, because the affected sensation of the mortal soul grasps the changeable and divisible qualities in them, while the unaffected sensation of the immortal soul recognises their substances. Both kinds of perception can be combined with other dynameis which are able to distinguish the invisible objects. This assertation contradicts the notorious Two-World-Theory, which is wrongly ascribed to Plato. For when he discriminates the sensible world from the thinkable world, like in the *Phaedo* and *Republic*, his aim is not to present such a division and to keep this cleft, rather he tends to introduce his Form-Theory: the sensible things are different from the forms, and we cannot clarify their essence and generation with the basic material elements, which, substantially, are also generated, divisible, and changeable. Rather we should turn to the causes which are indivisible and everlasting, in which sense the necessity and rightness of the forms are revealed. Thus, we can assert that there are two worlds in the sense that they hold their own substances and can be properly recognised by distinct cognitive dynameis, but since they are proper objects of the different soul-forms, there is no need to hold this division as an absolute one.

3.2.3 Conclusion: different kinds of sensation and their determinate cognitive dynameis

Now let us summarise the research of the cognitive abilities of the Platonic perception and give an example for this whole explanation, i.e., the finger-passage of the *Republic*. At the outset of this investigation, we have determined that the division of the immortal and mortal human soul-form corresponds to the dichotomy of the unaffected and affected sensation, and further to the division of the first category and the other nine categories of the generated things, or the physical world that is sensible and opinable. Thus, the study of the cognitive dynameis of the Platonic sense perception encompasses two parts: the discrimination of the affected sensation (3.2.1) and that of the unaffected sensation (3.2.2), and each part is performed in the same manner: it begins with the determination of the immanent relationship between the affected or unaffected sensation and their corresponding enmattered categories, continues with the clarification of the cognitive range and its truth of the subordinate kinds of affected or unaffected perception – since each of them includes two further types: the affected or unaffected perception *per se* and that mixed with other cognitive abilities, i.e., for the former the memory and phantasia, and for the latter the discursive thinking and intellect.

That through the affected sensation we can grasp the nine Aristotelian categories, is clarified in section 3.2.1.1. The correspondence between the affected sensation and the enmattered categories is grounded on the fact that these categories Quantity, Quality, Relation, Place, Time, Position, Possession, Acting and Being Affected, in the sense that they are enmattered and thus applied to explain the sensible world, can be clarified with the objects of the affected sensation, i.e., of the peculiar and common sensation. Because the former discriminates the Quality, and the latter grasps the enmattered motion, rest, oneness, number, shape, and size, which cover the rest eight categories. The underlying reason of this agreement is located at one of the essential features of the sensible world, namely it moves all time: the six common sensible objects are all graspable through motion, and the quality itself is a kind of motion. Correspondingly, the nine categories are enmattered, which indicates that they also keep moving and changing. This fact is partially decided by the reconstructed matter co-producing all sensible things – all four elements are moving in certain ways and their motion is unceasing, no matter they are merely elements or fashioned as the specific substrate of the sensible objects. Considering that the Aristotelian sense-theory originates from Plato, and in Plato we find the same categories used in the description of sense perception, we can conclude that the Platonic affected sensation discriminates and comprehends the nine sensible categories.

What follows this clarification is an observation of the cognitive dynamis of this kind of perception (3.2.1.2). Given that the affected sensation can be divided into two kinds, i.e., the affected sensation *per se* and that with further cognitive abilities like memory and phantasia, this research begins with the first kind of the affected sensation which is separated further into two sorts: the peculiar sensation and the common sensation. The former has the ability that relates essentially to the determinate objects, for example the sight perceives colours, and the hearing discriminates sounds, and as this relationship is essential, what the peculiar sensation discriminates and comprehends is naturally true. The *Charmides*-passage 167b5–169a1 is introduced to illustrate this point. On the contrary, the common sensation possesses no peculiar sense-organ, hence it can only perceive through the five sense-organs and the peculiar sensible objects, which leads to a potential fallibility of its discrimination. Be occasionally right or wrong as it may, this kind of sensation brings forth more 'words' to describe and define the sensible world, or it enables the cognition of the sensible things with more categories. The distinguished contents of the peculiar and common sensation, however, are abstract, confusing, and universal, because this is the way that is prior and clearer for us, no for the nature: what we perceive are the changeable and divisible qualities which are enmattered in almost all sensible things, while the determinate substances of the sensibles, or the forms, are inaccessible for this kind of perception. Therefore, the affected sensation *per se* can perceive the nine enmattered categories, through which the sensible world is distinguishable and comprehensible for us for the first time, however, leaving the substances of the sensibles untouched, the recognised contents of the affected sensation are still abstract, universal, and confusing.

The nest theme is the affected sensation with the other cognitive abilities, namely those proceeding from the affected sensation, viz. memory and phantasia, which are faculties realised without the bodily affections: memory is the preservation and remembrance of the affected sensation, for the perceived things can be imprinted in our souls like the impression in a wax-block, and these preserved images can also be remembered when we will – both the preservation and remembrance of these memory-images have nothing to do with the affected sense-affections anymore, which reveals that memory is an ability grounded on, yet goes beyond the affected sensation. Phantasia is described as a painter in the soul, whose ability rests on the (re-)shaping and (re-)moulding of the opined things, namely not the impressions that are perceived, rather the images that are already opined and attributed to a certain substance, thus what it paints are things like 'man' or 'statue'. Given that the cognitive process of memory and phantasia is distinct from that of the affected sensation, this kind of sensation should be ascribed to the affected sensation with help of further dynameis. And because both dynameis are based on the affected sensation, their truth depends also on the latter, namely they can be precise or fallible. However, despite the distinct truth of its different kinds, the affected sense perception should be deemed to be the very beginning of our empirical cognition, for it discriminates certain sensible qualities, offers us the initial recognisable materials, and enables the further discrimination-abilities like memory and phantasia, through which the opinion with affected sensation, discursive thinking, and intellect are possible for us.

The exploration of the epistemological ability of the unaffected sensation is realised in section 3.2.2. Following the research-model in the case of the affected perception, the clarification primarily involves the cognitive category of this kind of perception: the first Aristotelian category, i.e., the Substance, or precisely the primary substance, for this kind of substance such as the determinate man or the determinate horse can be grasped by the opinion with affected sensation, as revealed in the *Philebus*: the sensible thing standing beside the rock under a tree is opined as a man, this 'man' indicates neither the Form nor the Genus, rather the determinate man who stands beside the rock under a tree, namely the Form-in-Matter. From this clarification we can derive that the unaffected sensation, or the opinion with (affected) sensation, holds the capacity to discriminate the substances of all generated things, which is also asserted in *Tim.* 37b6–c1. After this determination we come to the last point of this whole chapter (3.2.2.2), i.e., the investigation of the cognitive range and truth of the opinion with affected sensation, and the reason for such a precision. Given that the unaffected sensation encompasses two subordinate types, namely the unaffected sensation by itself and that with help of higher dynameis like discursive thinking and intellect, the exploration of its cognitive range and truth should be respectively performed. With reference to the former type, we have certified that it can discriminate and comprehend the substances of the generated things including not only the individual and general things, but also the natural and social things, in addition to this cognitive range it also enables the cognition of the objects which belong originally to the discursive thinking and intellect, for the opinable things are images of these objects. The truth of the opinion with affected perception, however, depends on both sides: whether the soul combines the fresh impression with the right memory-image, and whether we can have a right discrimination made by the affected sensation. To explain the first factor Plato introduces the theory of the wax-block in *Theaet.* 191c8: the memory of the soul is like a block of wax, in which the perceived qualities can be imprinted and preserved. After having perceived a sensible object, the soul assigns the present impression to a preserved memory-image and in this way grasps the substance of the sensibles. When the images of the waxen block are not clear and evident enough to be precisely attributed to the fresh impression, there would be wrong judgement. On the other side we are told that if the sensible thing locates too far from us, or when our senses are not so sensitive, we will fail to obtain a discriminated perceptual impression, and to combine it with the correct memory-image.

The unaffected sensation with help of higher cognitive abilities like discursive thinking and intellect discriminates not only all sensible substances, but also the causes, for the discursive thinking knows the numbers and forms themselves, and the intellect recognises the highest principle of all things, i.e., the One. These things (the One, numbers, forms) are the principle and cause of the substances of all sensible things. The

existence of this kind of sensation, for example in Plato's *Laws* 961d9 and 961e1–5, explicitly reputes the so-called Two-World-Theory, and manifests that in Plato different faculties discriminates and comprehends naturally determinate objects: the affected sensation *per se* grasps the abstract and universal sensible qualities or the nine enmattered categories; the opinion with affected perception discriminates the primary substance of the sensibles; the discursive thinking distinguishes the numbers, beauty, ugly, good, bad, and other Platonic 'common things' initiating the generation and substances of the individual things; while the intellect is able to comprehend the eventual principle and cause of all things, i.e., the One. Considering that the sensible things are Forms-in-Matter, and that they participate in both the One and the Others, every kind of cognitive capacities can recognise a determinate aspect of them.

Now let us see an example which manifests the cognitive ability of the Platonic perception: the finger-passage in *Republic* 523a10–525a8. In order to clarify what the nature of arithmetic is, Plato introduces an investigation beginning with the cognitive dynamis of perception, where the competence of both affected and unaffected perception is clearly revealed: firstly he divides (διαιροῦμαι, 523a6) the sensation into two kinds, i.e., the type that leads to a summoning for the understanding (νοήσις), and that not, and explains the criterion for such a division, then offers the finger-example for this division:

> "Here, I show," I said, "if you can make it out, that via the sensation some do not summon the understanding to the activity of investigation because they seem to be adequately discriminated by perception, while others bid it in every way to undertake a consideration because sensation seems to produce nothing healthy."
> [...]
> "The ones that don't summon the understanding," I said, "are all those that don't at the same time go over to the opposite sensation. But the ones that do go over I class among those that summon the understanding, when the sensation doesn't reveal one thing any more than its opposite, regardless of whether the object strikes the senses from near or far off. But you will see my meaning more clearly this way: these, we say, would be three fingers – the smallest, the second, and the middle." (*Rep.* 523a10–c6. Trans. Bloom, with reversion).

Before this passage Plato speaks of the things that lead us to the mathematics, which turns out to be the very sensation. The term ἀγωγά (leadings) at 523a6 indicates (1) the difference of two these cognitive faculties, for what leads to the discursive thinking cannot function as it, taken the perception as example, it has no cognitive ability held by the discursive thinking; (2) the clear relationship of perception as well as the sensibles[518] and the understanding: through the former two we can go over to the latter, i.e., mathematics.[519] Yet not all perception or sensibles have such a function, since some sensible things 'seem to be adequately discriminated by perception' (ὡς ἱκανῶς ὑπὸ τῆς

---

[518] In this passage the perception and the sensibles are treated as the same species, as indicated in *Theaet.* 156b1–c2.

[519] For the different kinds of leadings to understanding, see *Laws* 645a1–b1; *Rep.* 440a10–441e6; etc. Cf. Schöpsdau (1977) 61n52.

αἰσθήσεως κρινόμενα, 523b1-2).[520] Thus the unified soul summons the understanding, only when the sensation brings forth something 'unhealthy' (οὐδὲν ὑγιές, 523b4), i.e., due to the restriction of its cognitive dynamis it could 'at the same time go over to the opposite sensation' (ἐκβαίνει εἰς ἐναντίαν αἴσθησιν ἅμα, 523b9-c1). Here we can see that the reason of the leading function of perception and the sensibles rests *prima facie* on the results of the discrimination of the sensibles: when it arouses contradictions at the same time and 'reports' this to the soul,[521] the understanding will be summoned to participate in the activity of cognition. This decision of turning from perception to understanding is made by our unified soul, which bears all kinds of cognitive abilities, i.e., affected sensation, memory, phantasia, opinion, discursive thinking, and intellect. Therefore, when we cannot grasp the truth through the cognitive ability of the mortal soul-form and this is known by unified soul, it will ask the divine part to utilise its dynamis to solve the problem, in this way the mathematical knowledge must be summoned. To illuminate this argument Plato introduces the well-known finger-example:

> "Surely each of them looks equally like a finger, and in this respect it makes no difference whether it's seen in the middle or on the extremes, whether it's white or black, or whether it's thick or thin, or anything else of the sort. In all these things the soul of the many is not compelled to ask the understanding what a finger is. For the sight at no point indicates to the soul that the finger is at the same time the opposite of a finger."
> "No," he said, "it doesn't"
> "Then," I said, "it isn't likely that anything of the sort would be apt to summon or awaken the activity of understanding."

---

[520] The term "ὡς" implies that whether these objects are really recognised is still a question to ask, because, as mentioned above, the affected sensation grasps no substance of the sensibles.

[521] Storey (2014) 110 summarises the formulations that are utilised to describe the report of sensation to soul: "perception gives 'reports to the soul' (παραγγέλει τῇ ψυχῇ, 524a3); 'declares' or 'indicates' (σημαίνει) things to be a certain way (524a7, 534a10); 'says' (λέγει) something to us (524a8); gives 'interpretations' or 'explanations' (ἑρμηνεῖαι, 524b1); and makes conflicting 'announcements' (εἰσαγγελλομένων, 524b5)". After this summary Storey announces that the language in this passage is 'metaphorical'. Such a judgement results perhaps from the fact that he neglects the contexts in the *Republic*, especially the unity and multiplicity of the soul that is already expounded in book IV: each human soul has three parts or forms, and every form possesses certain dynamis. In the description of the competence and limit of perception, it is viewed as a cognitive faculty of the appetitive soul-part, or generally the mortal part. In addition to this form there exists still a soul-form corresponding to understanding, i.e., the λογιστικόν, or the immortal part. Hence in this passage it is the unified soul on the one side, the specific soul forms, namely the mortal and immortal soul, on the other, and when sensation (of the mortal soul-form) fails to discriminate the objects, our unified soul falls in doubt (ἀπορεῖν, 524a7), and makes decision to summon another soul-form, the part of understanding, to recognise the confusing object. In this view those summarised terms are used to delineate the relation of the unified soul and its mortal part. On this same ground Plato formulates at *Tim.* 64b5-6 that the affection 'reports' (ἐξαγγείλῃ) to soul. For another case of unity and multiplicity in Plato, see the unified and four-fold virtue in *Laws* 963af.

"No, it's not likely."
"Now what about this? Does the sight see their bigness and littleness adequately, and does it make no difference to it whether a finger lies in the middle or on the extremes? And similarly with the touch, for thickness and thinness or softness and hardness? And do the other senses reveal such things without insufficiency? Or doesn't each of them do the following: first, the sense set over the hard is also compelled to be set over the soft; and it reports to the soul that the same thing is sensed by it as both hard and soft?"
"So it does," he said.
"Isn't it necessary," I said, "that in such cases the soul be at a loss as to what this sensation indicates by the hard, if it says that the same thing is also soft, and what the sensation of the light and of the heavy indicates by the light and heavy, if it indicates that the heavy is light and the light heavy?"
"Yes, indeed," I said, "these are strange interpretations received by the soul and require further consideration."
"Therefore," I said, "it's likely that in such cases a soul, summoning calculation and understanding, first tries to determine whether each of the things reported to it is one or two."
"Of course". (*Rep.* 523d1–524b6. Tr. Bloom, with slight revision).

In the aforesaid sections, some elements in this passage like the omission of 'white and black' in the list of the sensible qualities causing contradict perception are already discussed, here we should address ourselves to the following points: (1) at the beginning of this context Plato emphasises that in perceiving a single finger the (unified) soul would not be 'compelled' (ἀναγκάζεται, 523d5) to summon the understanding. The reason is, each of the three fingers can be 'equally' (ὁμοίως, 523d1) perceived by the sensation, and what a specific quality of this single finger is perceived makes no difference,[522] because, so long as such a quality exists in this single finger, our affected and unaffected perception can discriminate it without conflict and reports it to the soul: for the affected sensation this object is white (or black), thick (or thin), soft (or hard), for the unaffected sensation this object with such a colour, shape, size, and so on, is a finger – there could be a mis-discrimination, but a contradiction, for example, this finger is both big and small, comes not to be. That is to say, discriminating the sensible qualities and enmattered substance of one determinate finger does not need to ask the understanding what the whiteness is, or 'what a finger itself is' (τί ποτ' ἐστι δάκτυλος, 523d6). Thus (2) it is the very indeterminacy of the sensible and opinable object and the consequent opposite discrimination leads to the summoning of understanding. With reference to three fingers,[523] the discrimination of their determinate qualities[524] precipitates our soul into aporia (524a6–7). The ground of this aporia rests primarily on the mixed state of the objects at issue, i.e., three fingers. As they are perceived at the same time, the finger in the middle, comparing to the other two fingers, can simultaneously be thick

---

[522] Plato stresses that for 'anything else of the sort' (πᾶν ὅ τι τοιοῦτον, 523d4), namely for all kinds of perceptual qualities.
[523] The pronoun 'αὐτῶν' at 523e3 implies that what involves now are three fingers.
[524] As mentioned above in section 3.1.1, here what involves is the Aristotelian common perception, not the peculiar perception and its object proper like colours. This is the reason why in this quotation Plato rules white and black out.

and thin, soft and hard, heavy and light, and so on. Neither the affected perception nor the opinion holds the ability to overcome these contradictions. For instance, the sight perceives bigness and smallness 'not separated, but mixed up together' (ἀλλ' οὐ κεχωρισμένον, ἀλλὰ συγκεχυμένον τι, 524c3–4). Rather it reports them directly to the unified soul, transmitting this disorder to the latter and causing it to engage in doubt. Now it is requisite for our soul to summon the calculation and understanding to determine whether "each of the things reported to it is one or two" (εἴτε ἓν εἴτε δύο ἐστὶν ἕκαστα τῶν εἰσαγγελλομένων, 524b5), furthermore, the substance of these sensible qualities, like "what the big and the little are" (τί οὖν ποτ' ἐστὶ τὸ μέγα αὖ καὶ τὸ σμικρόν, 524c11).

This complete passage can be clarified in respect of 'the oneness' (τὸ ἕν, 524e1), which determines the possibility of cognition: if it exists in the sensible qualities and the opinable things, as in the case of one single finger, these objects will be determinate, and the discrimination of them shall lead to no contradiction (524d9–e2). However (524e2–525a2), in the case of three fingers the sensible and opinable objects are not determined by the oneness, and the unified soul would be puzzled and compelled to think 'what the oneness itself is' (τί ποτέ ἐστιν αὐτὸ τὸ ἕν). In this case the study of the oneness itself would be among those faculties that can turn the soul around and look at what really is (τοῦ ὄντος, 525a2). Thus, in the view of the oneness we can conclude that if each of the sensibles and opinables share it, there will be no problem in discrimination and comprehension of the sensible and opinable objects: the peculiar sensation perceives the qualities like colours and sounds, the common sensation discriminates the sensible objects like the enmattered motion, shape and size, while the unaffected perception opines the substance of the sensibles. The upshot is, this whole finger-passage reveals on the one side the different kinds of cognitive abilities like perception, opinion, and understanding, and their determinate objects, on the other side it shows us that something determinate is the criterion of the possible cognition, and the oneness is the inner measure of this cognition.

Bibliography

1 Ancient Authors

Ammonius (1895) In aristetelis categorias commentaries, ed. A. Busse, CAG 4.4, Berlin.
Aristotle (1894) Aristotelis Ethica Nicomachea, ed. I. Bywater, Oxford.
——. (1949) Aristotelis Categoriae et Liber de interpretatione, ed. L. Minio-Paluello, Oxford.
——. (1950) Aristotelis Physica, ed. W. D. Ross, Oxford.
——. (1955) Aristotelis Fragmenta Selecta, ed. W. D. Ross, Oxford.
——. (1957) Aristotelis Metaphysica, ed. W. Jaeger, Oxford.
——. (1961) Aristotle De Anima, ed. W. D. Ross, Oxford.
——. (1964) Aristotelis Analytica Priora et Posteriora, ed. W. D. Ross, Oxford.
Asclepius (1888) In aristotelis metaphysicorum libros a–z commentaria, ed. M. Hayduck, CAG 6.2. Berlin.
Calcidius (2016) On Plato's *Timaeus*, ed. and tr. J. Magee, Cambridge, MA.
Dexippus (1888) Dexippi in aristotelis categorias commentarium, ed. A. Busse. CAG 4.2, Berlin.
Elias (1900) In Porphyrii Isagogen et Aristotelis Categorias Commentaria, ed. A. Busse. CAG 18.1, Berlin.
Damascius (1959) Lectures on the *Philebus*, ed. L. G. Westerink, Amsterdam.
——. (1977) The Greek Commentaries on Plato's *Phaedo*, vol. 2, ed. L. G. Westerink, Amsterdam.
Iamblichus (1973) Iamblichi Chalcidensis: In Platons Dialogos Commentariorum Fragmenta, ed. J. M. Dillon, Leiden.
Numenius (1973) Numénius: Fragments, ed. E. Des Places, Paris.
Olympiodorus (1970) Olympiodori in Platonis Gorgiam commentaria, ed. L. G. Westerink, Leipzig.
——. (1976) The Greek Commentaries on Plato's *Phaedo*, vol. 1, ed. L. G. Westerink, Amsterdam.
Orpheus (1922) Orphicorum fragmenta, ed. O. Kern, Berlin.
Philoponus, John. (1897) In aristotelis de anima libros commentaria, ed. M. Hayduck. CAG 15, Berlin.
——. (1899) Ioannes philoponus de aeternitate mundi contra proclum, ed. H. Rabe, Leipzig.
——. (1909) In aristotelis analytica posteriora commentaria, ed. M. Wallies, CAG 13.3. Berlin.
Plato (1900) (1902) Platonis Opera, ed. J. Burnet, 5 vols., Oxford.
——. (1995) Platonis Opera: Tome I, ed. E. Duke, W. Hicken, W. Nicoll, D. Robinson, and J. Strachan, Oxford.
——. (2003) Platonis Rempublicam, ed. S. Slings, Oxford.
Plotinus, Plotini Opera, ed. P.Henry and H.-R. Schwyzer, 3 vols., Oxford 1964–1982.
Plutarch (1927) (2004) Moralia, 16 vols. tr. F. C. Babbitt, Cambridge (MA).
Porphyry (1964) Porphyrii in Platonis Timaeum Commentariorum fragmenta, ed. A. R. Sodano, Naples.

——. (1993) Porphyrii philosophi fragmenta, ed. A. Smith, Stuttgart.
——. (1997) Storia della filosofia, ed. A. Sodano and G. Girgenti, Milan.
Priscian (Ps.-Simplicius) (1882) Simplicii in libros aristotelis de anima commentaria, ed. M. Hayduck, CAG 11, Berlin.
Proclus (1864) Procli Commentarius in Platonis Parmenidem, ed. V. Cousin, Paris.
——. (1899) (1901) Procli Diadochi in Platonis rem publicam commentarii, 2 vols., ed. W. Kroll, Leipzig.
——. (^{2}1963) Proclus: The Elements of Theology, ed. E. R. Dodds, Oxford:
——. (1965) Procli Diadochi in Platonis Timaeum commentaria, 3 vols., ed. E. Diehl, Amsterdam.
Sextus Empiricus (1914–1958) Opera. 3 vols, ed. H. Mutschmann and J. Mau. Vol. 4 Indices, ed.K. Janaceck, 1962, Leipzig.
Simplicius (1882) (1895) Simplicii in aristotelis physicorum libros commentaria, 2 vols., ed. H. Diels, CAG 9 and 10, Berlin.
——. (1894) In aristotelis quattuor libros de caelo commentaria, ed. J. L. Leiberg, CAG 7, Berlin.
——. (1907) In aristotelis categorias commentarium, ed. K. Kalbfleisch, CAG 8, Berlin.
Syrianus (1892) Syriani in metaphysica commentaria, ed. H. Rabe, CAG 6.1, Berlin.
Themistius (1899) In libros aristotelis de anima paraphrasis, ed. R. Heinze. CAG 5.3, Berlin.
Theon of Smyrna (1878) Philosophi Platonici expositio rerum mathematicarum ad legendum Platonem utilium, ed. E. Hiller, Leipzig.
Timaeus of Locros (1972) De natura mundi et animae, ed. W. Marg, Leiden.
Xenocrates (1892) Xenocrates: Darstellung der Lehre und Sammlung der Fragmente, ed. R. Heinze, Leipzig.

2 Modern Authors, Editors and Translators

Adamson, P. (2015) "Neoplatonism: The Last Ten Years", in *The International Journal of the Platonic Tradition* 9 (2015) 205–220.
Ahbel-Rappe, S. (2010) Damascius' Problems and Solutions Concerning First Principles, Oxford.
Allen, M. J. B. (1975) Marsilio Ficino: The *Philebus* Commentary, Berkeley. (Rep. 2000).
Althoff, J. (1992) Warm, kalt, flüssig und fest bei Aristoteles. Die Elementarqualitäten in den zoologischen Schriften, Stuttgart (Hermes Einzelschriften 57).
——. (2005) "aithêr/ Äther", in O. Höffe (ed.) Aristotle-Lexikon, Stuttgart, 14–15.
Annas, J. (1999) Platonic Ethics: Old and New, Ithaca.
——. (2019) "Plato's Ethics", in G. Fine (ed.) The Oxford Handbook of Plato, Oxford, 531–549.
Armstrong, J. (2004) "After the Ascent: Plato on Becoming Like God", in *Oxford Studies in Ancient Philosophy* 26: 171–183.
Arnzen, R. (2013) Proclus on Plato's *Timaeus* 89e3–90c7, in *Arabic Sciences and Philosophy*, 23 (2013), 1–45.
Arthur, O. L. (1936) The Great Chain of Being: A Study of the History of an Idea, Cambridge, MA.
Baltes, M. (1972) Timaios Lokros. Über die Natur des Kosmos und der Seele, Leiden 1972 (Philosophia Antiqua 21).
——. (1996) "Γέγονεν (Platon *Tim.* 28 b 7): ist die Welt real entstanden oder nicht? ", In K. A. Algra, P. van der Horst and D. T. Runia (eds.), Polyhistor: Studies in the History and Histo-

riography of Ancient Philosophy Presented to Jaap Mansfeld on his Sixtieth Birthday, Leiden, 76–96 = M.-L. Lakmann, A. Hüffmeier and M. Vorwerk (1999) Dianoēmata: kleine Schriften zu Platon und zum Platonismus, 303–326.
Baltussen, H. (2000) Theophrastus Against the Presocratics and Plato. Peripapetic Dialectic in the *De sensibus*, Leiden.
Baltzly, D. (1996) Socratic Anti-Empiricism in the *Phaedo,* in *Apeiron* 29: 121–142.
——. (2007) Proclus. Commentary on Plato's *Timaeus*, vol. III, Book 3, Part I: Proclus on the World's Body, Cambridge.
——. (2009a) Proclus. Commentary on Plato's *Timaeus*, vol. IV, Book 3, Part II: Proclus on the World Soul, Cambridge.
——. (2009b), "Gaia Gets to Know Herself: Proclus on the World's Self-Perception", in *Phronesis* 54 (3): 261–285.
Barney, R., Brennan, T. and Brittain, C. (eds.) (2012) Plato and the Divided Self, Cambridge.
Barnouw, J. (2004) Propositional perception. Phantasia, predication and sign in Plato, Aristotle and the Stoics, Lanham (University Press of America).
Beare, J. I. (1906) Greek Theories of Elementary Cognition: From Alcmaeon to Aristotle, Oxford.
Bedu-Addo, J. T. (1991) "Sense-Experience and the argument for recollection in Plato's *Phaedo*", in *Phronesis* 36: 27–60.
Becker, A. (2007) Platon Theätet, Frankfurt.
Bernard, W. (1988) Rezeptivität und Spontaneität der Wahrnehmung bei Aristotle. Versuch einer Bestimmung der spontanen Erkenntnisleistung der Wahrnehmung bei Aristoteles in Abgrenzung gegen die rezeptive Auslegung der Sinnlichkeit bei Descartes und Kant, Baden-Baden.
——. (1998) "'Teleologie' und Naturphilosophie bei Platon", in H. J. Wendel and W. Bernar (eds.) Antike Philosophie und moderne Wissenschaft. Rostocker Hochschulwoche vom 3.–5. September 1996, Rostock, 1–29.
——. (2002) "Die Entvölkerung des Himmels. Der moderne Naturbegriff und die platonische Daimonologie", in H.-J. Horn (ed.) Jakobs Traum. Zur Bedeutung der Zwischenwelt in der Tradition des Platonismus, St. Katharinen, 9–24.
——. (2018) "Das wissenschaftliche Werk Arbogast Schmits. Versuch einer Annäherung", in B. Kappl and S. Meiner (eds.) Gnothi Sauton: Festschrift für Arbogast Schmitt zum 75. Geburtstag, Heidelberg, 9–20.
Benardete, S. (2000) The Argument of the Action: Essays on Greek Poetry and Philosophy, Chicago/ London.
Bloch, G. (1973) Platons *Charmides*. Die Erscheinung des Seins im Gespräch. (Ph. D. dissertation, University of Tübingen).
Blumenthal, H. J. (1982) "Proclus on perception", in *Bulletin of the Institute of Classical Studies* 29: 1–11.
——. (1992) "Soul Vehicles in Simplicius", in G. Gersh and C. Kannengiesser (eds.) Platonism in Late Antiquity, Notre Dame, 173–188. (Rep. in *Soul and Intellect,* Study XVII).
——. (1996) Aristotle and Neoplatonism in Late Antiquity: Interpretations of the *De anima*, London.
——. (1997) "The Psychology of Plotinus and Later Platonism", in Cleary, J. J. (ed.) The Perennial Tradition of Neoplatonism, Leuven, 269–290.
Boeft, J. den (1970) Calcidius on Fate: His Doctrine and Sources, Leiden. (Philsophia Antiqua 18).
Bostock, D. (1988) Plato's *Theaetetus*, Oxford. (Rep. 2005).

Brandwood, L. (1976) A Word Index to Plato, Leeds.
Brisson, L. (1974) Le même et l'autre dans la structure ontologique du Timée de Platon. Un commentaire systématique du Timée de Platon, Paris.
——. (1997) "Plato's Theory of Sense Perception in the *Timaeus*", in *Bosten Area Colloquium in Ancient Philosophy* 13: 147–176.
——. (2003) "How and Why is the Building Blocks of the Universe Change Constantly in Plato's *Timaeus* (52a–61c)?" In C. Natali and S. Maso (eds.) Plato Physicus. Cosmologia e antropologia nel Timeo, Armstedam, 189–205.
——. (2006) "Plato's Natural Philosophy and Metaphysics", in M. L. Gill and P. Pellegrin (eds.) A Companion to Ancient Philosophy, Malden, MA/ Oxford, 212–231.
Brisson, L. and Meyerstein, F. W. (1995) Inventing the Universe. Plato's Timaeus, the Big Bang, and the Problem of Scientific Knowledge, New York (SUNY series in Ancient Greek Philosophy).
Broadie, S. (2012) Nature and Divinity in Plato's *Timaeus*, Cambridge.
Bruell, C. (1977) "Socratic Politics and Self-Knowledge", in *Interpretation* 6: 141–203.
Büttner, S. (2000) Die Literaturtheorie bei Platon und ihre anthropologische Begründung, Tübingen/ Basel.
——. (2006) "The Tripartition of the Soul in Plato's *Republic*", in F.-G. Herrmann (ed.) New Essays on Plato: Language and Thought in Fourth-Century Greek Philosophy, Swansea, 75–93.
——. (2018) Vorstellung (φαντασία) bei Platon, in B. Kappl and S. Meiner (eds.) Gnothi Sauton: Festschrift für Arbogast Schmitt zum 75. Geburtstag, Heidelberg, 149–174.
Burkert, W. (1972) Lore and Science in Ancient Pythagoreanism, Cambridge, Mass. [USA].
Burnyeat, M. (1990) The *Theaetetus* of Plato. With a Translation of Plato's Theaetetus by M. J. Levett, Indianapolis/ Cambridge.
Busche, H. (2005) article 'aisthêsis/ Wahrnehmung', in Höffe, O. (ed.) Aristotle-Lexikon, Stuttgart, 10–14.
Calvo, T. and Brisson, L. (eds.) (1997) Interpreting the *Timaeus-Critias*. Proceedings of the IV Symposium Platonicum: Selected Papers, Sankt Augustin.
Calvo, Z. and Maria, J. (2018) "The Crafting of Mortal Soul in Plato's *Timaeus*", in *Filozofia* 73 (2): 119–132.
Campbell, G. (2000) "Zoogony and Evolution in Plato's *Timaeus*: The Presocratics, Lucretius and Darwin", in M. R. Wright (ed.) Essays on Plato's *Timaeus*, 2000, 145–180.
Carone, G. R. (2005) Plato's Cosmology and Its Ethical Dimensions, Cambridge.
Carpenter, A. D. (2008) "Embodying Intelligence. Animals and Us in Plato's *Timaeus*", in J. Dillon and M.-É. Zovko (eds.) Platonism and Forms of Intelligence, Berlin 2008, 39–57.
Caston, V. (2012) Alexander of Aphrodisias: On the Soul, Part 1. London/ New York.
Cessi, V. (1987) Erkennen und Handeln in der Theorie des Tragischen bei Aristoteles, Frankfurt. (Beiträge zur klassischen Philologie 180)
Chase, M. (2003) Simplicius: On Aristotle's Categories 1–4, Ithaca.
Cherniss, H. (1944) Aristotle's Criticisms of Plato and the Academy, Baltimore. (Rep. 1962).
Chiaradonna, R. and Galluzzo, G. (eds.) (2013) Universals in Ancient Philosophy, Pisa.
Chlup, R. (2012) Proclus: An Introduction, Cambridge.
Claghorn, G. S. (1954) Aristotle's Criticism of Plato's *Timaeus*, The Hague.
Cleary, J. (1998) "'Powers that Be': The Concept of Potency in Plato and Aristotle", in: *Méthexis* 11: 19–64. Rep. in J. Dillon, B. O'Byrne and F. O'Rourke (eds.) (2013) Studies on Plato, Ar-

istotle and Proclus: Collected Essays on Ancient Philosophy of John J. Cleary, Leiden/ Bosten, 251–297.
Cludius, M. (1997) Die Grundlegung der Erkenntnistheorie in Platons Politeia. Ein Kommentar zu Platons Unterscheidung von Meinen und Wissen und zum Liniengleichnis. (Dissertation of University Marburg)
Cornford, F. M. (1935) Plato's Theory of Knowledge: The *Theaetetus* and the *Sophist* of Plato, London.
——. (1937) Plato's Cosmology: The *Timaeus* of Plato, Translated with a Running Commentary, London.
Coulter, J. A. (1976) The Literary Microcosm: Theories of Interpretation of the Later Neoplatonists, Leiden.
Craig, L. (2001) "The strange misperception of Plato's Meno", in Z. Planinc (ed.) Politics, Philosophy, Writing: Plato's Art of Caring for Souls Politics, Columbia/ London, 60–79.
Darchia, I. (2003) "Colour Perception in Plato's *Phaedo* and Democritus' Treatise *About Colours*", in *Phasis. Greek and Roman studies* 5–6: 35–38.
Davidson, D. (1990) Plato's *Philebus*, London/ New York.
Day, J. M. (1995) "The Theory of Perception in Plato's *Theaeteus* 152–183", in *Oxford Studies of Ancient Philosophy* 15: 51–80.
D'Hoine, P. and Martijn, M. (eds.) All from One: A Guide to Proclus, Oxford 2017.
Dillon, J. M. (^{2}1996) The Middle Platonists: A Study of Platonism 80 BC to AD 220, London.
——. (2003) The Heirs of Plato: A Study of the Old Academy (347–274 BC), Oxford.
——. (2013) "Plotinus and the Vehicle of the Soul", in K. Corrigan and T. Rasimus (eds.) Gnosticism, Platonism and the Late Ancient World: Essays in Honour of John. D. Turner, Leiden/ Bosten, 485–496.
——. (2016) "The Reception of Aristotle in Antiochus and Cicero", in A. Falcon (ed.) Brill's Companion to the Reception of Aristotle in Antiquity, Leiden/ Bosten, 183–201. (Brill' Companions to Classical Reception 7)
——. (2020) "How Does the Soul Direct the Body, After All? Traces of a Dispute on Mind-Body Relation in the Old Academy", in D. Frede and B. Reis (eds.) Body and Soul in Ancient Philosophy, Berlin/ New York, 349–356.
Dörrie, H. and Baltes, M. (eds.) (1996) Der Platonismus in der Antike, Bd. 4, Stuttgart.
——. (eds.) (1998) Der Platonismus in der Antike, Bd. 5, Stuttgart.
Dorter, K. (1994) Form and Good in Plato's Eleatic Dialogues: The *Parmenides*, *Theaetetus*, *Sophist*, and *Statesman*, Berkeley/ Los Angelos/ Lodon.
Eisenstadt, M. (2011) "The Affects and Senses in Plato's *Charmides*", in *Hermes* 139: 84–87.
Erler, M. (2007) (eds.) Die Philosophie der Antike Bd. 2/2: Platon, Basel.
Everson, S. (1997) Aristotle on Perception, Oxford.
Finamore, J. F. (1985) Iamblichus and the Theory of the Vehicle of the Soul, Chico.
Finamore, J. F. and Kutash, E. (2017) "Proclus on the *Psychē*: World Soul and the Individual Soul", in P. D'Hoine and M. Martijn (eds.) All from One: A Guide to Proclus, Oxford, 122–138.
Fletcher, E. (2016) "Aisthēsis, Reason and Appetite in the *Timaeus*", in: *Phronesis* 61: 397–434.
Frede, D. (1997) Platon: *Philebos*, Göttingen.
Frede, M. (1987a) "Numenius", in *ANRW* II. 36.2, Berlin/ New York, 1034–1075.
——. (1987b) Essays in Ancient Philosophy, Minneapolis.

Fronterotta, F. (2015) "Plato's Conception of the Self: The Mind-Body Problem and its Ancient Origin in the *Timaeus*", in D. D. Brasi and S. Föllinger (eds.) Anthropologie in Antike und Gegenwart: Biologische und philosophische Entwürfe vom Menschen, Freiburg/ München, 35–57.

Gaiser, K. (^{2}1968) Platons Ungeschriebene Lehre: Studien zur Systematischen und geschichtlichen Begründung der Wissenschaften in der Platonischen Schule, Stuttgart.

Ganson, T. S. (2005) "The Platonic Approach to Sense-Perception", in *History of Philosophy Quarterly* 22: 1–15.

Gendlin, E. T. (2012) Line by Line Commentary on Aristotle's *De Anima*, New York.

George, C. H. (2014) Expressions of Time in Ancient Greek, Cambridge.

Gerson, L. (1990) God and Greek Philosophy: Studies in Early History of Natural Theology, London/ New York.

——. (2005) Aristotle and Other Platonists, Ithaca/ London.

——. (2006) "On the Harmony of Plato and Aristotle", in H. Tarrant and D. Baltzly (eds.) Reading Plato in Antiquity, London, 195–221.

——. (ed.) (2010) The Cambridge History of Philosophy in Late Antiquity, Cambridge.

——. (2020) Platonism and Naturalism: The Possibility of Philosophy, Ithaca/ London.

Gertz, S. (2010) "Do Plato and Aristotle Agree on Self-Motion in Souls?" in J. F. Finamore and R. M. Berchman (eds.) Conversations Platonic and Neoplatonic: Intellect, Soul and Nature, Sankt Augustin, 73–87.

——. (2011) Death and Immortality in Late Neoplatonism Studies on the Ancient Commentaries on Plato's *Phaedo*, Leiden/ Bosten.

Giannopoulou, Z. (2013) Plato's *Theaetetus* as a Second *Apology*, Oxford.

Gloy, K. (2000) "Platons Timaios und die Gegenwart", in A. Neschke-Hentschke (ed.) Le Timée de Platon: contributions à l'histoire de sa réception, Paris, 317–332.

Golitsis, P. (2018) "Simplicius, Syrianus and the Harmony of Ancient Philosophers", in B. Strobel (ed.) Die Kunst der philosophischen Exegese bei den spätantiken Platon- und Aristoteles-Kommentatoren, Berlin, 69–99.

Gregoric, P. (2007) Aristotle on the Common Sense, Oxford.

Gregory, A. (2000) Plato's Philosophy of Science, London.

——. (2007) Ancient Greek Cosmogony, London.

Grifffin, M. (2012) "Proclus on Place as the Luminous Vehicle of the Soul", in *Dionysius*, 30: 161–186.

Grönroos, G. (2001) Plato on Perceptual Cognition, Edsbruck.

Guthrie, W. K. C. (1978) A History of Greek Philosophy, vol. V: The Later Plato and the Academy, Cambridge.

Hackforth, R. (1936) "Plato's Theism", in *Classical Quarterly* 30 (1): 4–9. Rep. in R. E. Allen (ed.) (1965) Studies in Plato's Metaphysics, London, 439–447.

Hadot, I. (2015) Athenian and Alexandrian Neoplatonism and the Harmonization of Aristotle and Plato, tr. by M. Chase, Leiden/ Bosten.

Halper, E. (2000) "Is Knowledge of Knowledge Possible? *Charmides* 167a–169d", in T. M. Robinson and L. Brisson (eds.) Plato: *Euthydemus*, *Lysis*, *Charmides*. Proceedings of the V Symposium Platonicum. Slected Papers, Sankt Augustin, 309–316.

Hardy, J. (2001) Platons Theorie des Wissens im "Theaitet", Göttingen (Hypomnemata 128).

Helmig, C. (2009) "'The Truth can never be Refuted' – Syrianus' View(s) on Aristotle Reconsidered", in A. Longo (ed.) Syrianus et la Métaphysique de l'Antiquité tardive (Actes du colloque international, Université de Genève, 29 sep.–1er oct. 2006), Bibliopolis, 347–380.

——. (2012) Forms and Concepts: Concept Formation in the Platonic Tradition, Berlin.

Herzberg, S. (2010) Wahrnehmung und Wissen bei Aristoteles: Zur epistemologischen Funktion der Wahrnehmung, Berlin.

Hirsch, U. (1997) Sinnesqualitiiten und ihre Namen (zu *Tim.* 61–69)", in T. Calvo and L. Brisson (eds.) Interpreting the *Timaeus-Critias*. Proceedings of the IV Symposium Platonicum: Selected Papers, Sankt Augustin, 317–324.

Hoenig, C. (2018) Plato's *Timaeus* and the Latin Tradition, Cambridge.

Hoffmann, M. (1996) Die Entstehung von Ordnung. Zur Bestimmung von Sein, Erkennen und Handeln in der späteren Philosphie Platons, Stuttgart (Beiträge zur Altertumskunde 81).

Huby, P. and Steel, C. (1997a) Priscian on Theophrastus on the senses, with 'Simplicius' on Aristotle *De anima* 2.5–12, London.

Hyland, D. (1981) The Virtue of Philosophy, Athens.

Ierodiakonou, K. (2005) "Plato's Theory of Colours in the *Timaeus*", in *Rhizai* 2: 219–233.

Irwin, T. (1977) "Plato's Heracleiteanism", in *The Philosophical Quarterly*, 27: 1–13.

Johansen, T. K. (1997) Aristotle on the Sense-Organs, Cambridge.

——. (2004) Plato's Natural Philosophy: A Study of the *Timaeus-Critias*, Cambridge. (rep. 2006).

——. (2008) "The Timaeus on the Principles of Cosmology", in G. Fine (ed.) The Oxford Handbook of Plato: Second Edition, Oxford, 463–483.

——. (2012) The Powers of Aristotle's Soul, Oxford.

Jones, D. E. H. (2017) Why are We Conscious? A Scientist's Take on Consciousness and Extrasensory Perception, Singapore.

Jorgenson, C. (2018) The Embodied Soul in Plato's Later Thought, Cambridge.

Kahn, C. H. (2006) "Plato on Recollection", in H. H. Benson (ed.) A Companion to Plato, 119–132.

——. (2010) "The Place of Cosmology in Plato's Later Dialogues", in R. D. Mohr and B. M. Sattler (eds.) One Book, the Whole Universe: Plato's *Timaeus* Today, Las Vegas/ Zurich/ Athens, 69–77.

——. (2013) Plato and the Post-Socratic Dialogue: The Return to the Philosophy of Nature, Cambridge.

Kamtekar, R. (2017) Plato's Moral Psychology: Intellectualism, the Divided Soul, and the Desire for God, Oxford.

Karamanolis, G. (2006) Plato and Aristotle in Agreement? Platonists on Aristotle from Antiochus to Porphyry, Oxford.

Karfík, F. (2004) Die Beseelung des Kosmos: Untersuchungen zur Kosmologie, Seelenlehre und Theologie in Platons Phaidon und Timaios, Berlin (Beiträge zur Altertumskunde 199).

Keeling, E. (2019) "Pathos in the *Theaetetus*", in L. Pitteloud and E. Keeling (eds.) Psychology and Ontology in Plato, Cham (Switzerland), 55–66.

King, R. A. H. (2016) "Sensation in the *Philebus*: Common to Body and Soul", in J. Jirsa, F. Karfík and Š. Špinka, Plato's *Philebus*: Proceedings of the Ninth Symposium Platonicum Pragense, Praha, 93–103.

Krapinger, G. (2011) Aristoteles: Über die Seele, Griechisch/ Deutsch, Stuttgart.

Kullmann, W. (2007) Aristoteles: Über die Teile der Lebewesen, Berlin (Aristoteles, Werke in deutscher Übersetzung 17/I).

Kutash, E. (2011) The Ten Gifts of the Demiurge: Proclus' Commentary on Plato's *Timaeus*, London/ New York.

Lampert, L. (2010) How Philosophy Became Socratic: A Study of Plato's *Protagoras, Charmides*, and *Republic*, Chicago/ London.

Larsen, P. D. (2017) The Place of Perception in Plato's Tripartite Soul, in *Proceedings of the Boston Area Colloquium in Ancient Philosophy* 32: 69–99.

——. (2018) "Are there Forms of Sensible Qualities in Plato?" In *Journal of the American Philosophical Association* 4 (2): 225–242.

Lautner, P. (2002) "The Distinction between ΦΑΝΤΑΣΙΑ and ΔΟΞΑ in Proclus' *In Timaeus*", in *Classical Quarterly* (52) 1: 257–269.

——. (2005) "The *Timaeus* on Sounds and Hearing, with Some Implications for Plato's General Account of Sense-Perception", in *Rhizai* 2: 235–253.

——. (2006) "Some Clarifications of Proclus' Fourfold Division of Sense-perception in the *Timaeus* Commentary", in M. Perkams and R. M. Piccione (eds.) Proklos: Methode, Seelenlehre, Metaphysik, Leiden, 117–136.

Lee, E. N. (1976) "Reason and Rotation: Circular Movement as the Model of Mind (Nous) in Later Plato", in Werkmeister, W. H. (ed.) Facets of Plato's Philosophy, Van Gorcum, 70–102.

Lee, M. (1999) Thinking and Perception in Plato's *Theaetetus*, in *Apeiron* 32, 1999, 37–54.

Lee, S.-I. (2001) Anamnesis im *Menon* Platons. Überlegungen zu Möglichkeit und Methode eines den Ideen gemäßen Wissenserwerbes, Frankfurt.

Leggett, A. J. (2010) "Plato's *Timaeus*: Some Resonances in Modern Physics and Cosmology", in R. D. Mohr and B. M. Sattler (eds.) (2010) One Book, the Whole Universe: Plato's *Timaeus* Today, Las Vegas/ Yurich/ London, 31–36.

Levine, D. L. (1976) Plato's *Charmides*. (Ph. D. dissertation, Pennsylvania State University).

Lisi, F. L. (2007) "Individual Soul, World Soul and the Form of the Good in Plato's *Republic* and *Timaeus*", in *Études Platoniciennes* 4: 105–118.

Long, A. A. (2010) "Cosmic Craftsmanship in Plato and Stoicism", in R. D. Mohr and B. M. Sattler (eds.) One Book, The Whole Universe. Plato's *Timaeus* Today, Las Vegas/ Zurich/ Athens, 37–53.

Lorenz, H. (2012) "The cognition of appetite in Plato's *Timaeus*", in R. Barney, T. Brennan and C. Brittain (eds.) Plato and the Divided Self, Cambridge, 238–258.

Männlein-Robert, I. (ed.) (2012) Ps.-Platon: Über den Tod, Tübingen.

Makin, S. (2012) "Energeia and Dunamis", in C. Shields (ed.) The Oxford Handbook of Aristotle, Oxford, 400–421.

Martijn, M. (2010) Proclus on Nature: Philosophy of Nature and Its Methods in Proclus' Commentary on Plato's *Timaeus*, Leiden/ Bosten.

Mather, G. (2011) Essentials of Sensation and Perception, London/ New York.

May, M. (2007) Sensation and Perception, New York.

McDowell, J. (1973) Plato: *Theaetetus*. Translated with Notes, Oxford.

McCready-Flora, I. (2018) "Affect and Sensation: Plato's Embodied Cognition", in *Phronesis* 63: 117–147.

Meinwald, C. (2016) Plato, London/ New York. (Routledge Philosophers)

Menn, S. (1992) "Aristotle and Plato on God as Nous and as the Good", in *Review of Metaphysics* 45: 543–573.

——. (1994) "The Origins of Aristotle's Concept of Energeia: Energeia and Dynamis", in *Ancient Philosophy* 14: 73–114.

——. (1995) Plato on God as Nous, Carbondale/ Edwardsville [USA]. (Rep. 2002).

——. (2012) "Self-Motion and Reflection: Hermias and Proclus on the Harmony of Plato and Aristotle on the Soul", in James Wilberding and Christopf Horn (edd.) Neoplatonism and the Philosophy of Nature, Oxford, 44–67.

Merki, H. (1952) Ὁμοίωσις θεῷ. Von der platonischen Angleichung an Gott zur Gottähnlichkeit bei Gregor von Nyssa, Freiburg.

Michalewski, A. (2016) "The Reception of Aristotle in Middle Platonism: From Eudorus of Alexandria to Ammonius Saccas", in A. Falcon (ed.) Brill's Companion to the Reception of Aristotle in Antiquity, Leiden/ Bosten, 218–237. (Brill' Companions to Classical Reception 7)

Modrak, D. K. W. (2006) "Plato: A Theory of Perception or a Nod to Sensation?" In H. H. Benson (ed.) A Companion to Plato, Malden, MA/ Oxford, 133–145.

Mohr, R. D. (1985) The Platonic Cosmology, Leiden.

——. (2005) God and Forms in Plato, Las Vegas.

Mohr, R. D. and Sattler, B. M. (eds.) (2010) One Book, the Whole Universe: Plato's *Timaeus* Today, Las Vegas/ Zurich/ London.

Mooij, J. J. A. (2005) Time and Mind: The History of a Philosophical Problem, tr. P. Mason, Leiden/ Bosten. (Brill's Studies in Interllectual History 129)

Morrow, G. R. and Dillon J. (1987) Proclus' Commentary on Plato's Parmenides, Princeton.

Mueller, I. (2005) Simplicius: On Aristotle On the Heavens 2.10–14, London/ New York.

Müller, J. (2017) "Psychologie", in C. Horn, J. Müller and J. Sörder (eds.) Platon-Handbuch: Leben–Werk–Wirkung, Stuttgart, 147–160.

Nakhnikian, G. (1955) "Plato's Theory of Sensation", in: *Review of Metaphysics* 9: 129–148, 306–327.

O'Brien, C. S. (2015) The Demiurge in Ancient Thought: Secondary Gods and Divine Mediators, Cambridge.

——. (2020) "Calcidius on Fate and the World Soul", in C. Helmig (ed.) World Soul-Anima Mundi: On the Origins and Fortunes of a Fundamental Idea, Berlin, 211–242.

Opsomer, J. (2000) "Proclus on Demiurge and Procession in the *Timaeus*", in M. R. Wright (ed.) Reason and Necessity: Essays on Plato's *Timaeus*, London, 113–143.

——. (2006a) "To Find the Maker and Father. Proclus' Exegesis of Plato *Tim.* 28c3–5", in *Études platoniciennes* 2: 261–283.

——. (2006b) "Was sind Irrationale Seelen?" In M. Perkams and R. M. Piccione (eds.) Proklos: Methode, Seelenlehre, Metaphsik, Leiden/ Bosten, 136–166.

——. (2012) "In Defense of Geometric Atomism: Explaining Elemental Properties", in J. Wilberding and C. Horn (eds.) Neoplatonism and Philosophy of Nature, Oxford, 147–173.

Osborne, C. (2003) "Knowledge is Perception: A Defence of *Theaetetus*", in W. Detel, A. Becker and P. Scholz (eds.) Ideal and Culture of Knowledge in Plato: Akten der 4. Tagung der Karl- und-Gertrud-Abel-Stiftung vom 1.–3. September 2000 in Frankfurt, 159–173.

Oser-Grote, C. (2005) "Pneuma", in O. Höffe (ed.) Aristoteles-Lexikon, Stuttgart, 467–468.

Ostenfeld, E. (1997) "The Role and Status of the Forms in the *Timaeus*: Paradigmatism Revised?" In T. Calvo and L. Brisson (eds.) Interpreting the *Timaeus-Critias*. Proceedings of the IV Symposium Platonicum. Selected Papers, Sankt Augustin, 167–177.

Paparazzo, E. (2015) "Does Present-Day Symmetry Underlie the Cosmology of Plato's Timaeus? A Response to D. R. Lloyd", in *Apeiron* 48 (2): 123–148.

Passmore, J. (1970) The Perfectibility of Man, London.
Perkams, M. and Piccione, R. M. (2006) Proklos: Methode, Seelemlehre, Metaphysik, Leiden.
——. (2008) Selbstbewusstsein in der Spätantike: Die neuplatonischen Kommentare zu Aristoteles' *De anima*, Berlin/ New York. (Quellen und Studien zur Philosophie 85)
——. (^{2}2013) "Sinneswahrnehmung (aisthêsis)", in C. Schäfer (ed.) Platon-Lexikon, Darmstadt, 265–268.
Perl, E. D. (1997) "Sense-Perception and Intellect in Plato", in *Revue de philosophie ancienne* 15: 15–34.
Pietsch, C. (ed.) (2008) Der Platonismus in der Antike, Bd. 7.1, Stuttgart.
——. (2014) "Schöpfungsvorstellungen in der griechischen Antike: Zur Diskussion um die Entstehung der Welt", in *Antike Welt* 5: 26–32.
Pitteloud, L. (2014) "Is the Sensible an Illusion? The Revisited Ontology of the *Sophist*", in *Aufklärung: revista de filosofia* 1: 33–57.
Polansky, R. M. (1992) Philosophy and Knowledge: A Commentary on Plato's *Theaetetus*, London/ Toronto.
Pritchard, P. (1990) "The Meaning of Dynamis at *Timaeus* 31c", in *Phronesis* 35: 182–193.
Radke-Ulmann, G. (2002) "Platons Ideenlehre", in F. Gniffke and N. Herold (eds.) Klassische Fragen der Philosophiegeschichte I: Antike bis Renaissance, Münster, 17–64,
——. (2003) Die Theorie der Zahl im Platonismus: Ein systematisches Lehrbuch, Tübingen/ Basel.
——. (2012) Kriteriengeleitete Empirie – Überlegungen zum Zusammenhang von Hören und Begreifen von Musik bei Platon, in: D. Koch, I. Männlein-Robert and N. Weidtmann (eds.) Platon und die Mousike, Tübingen, 195–226.
Rapp, C. (2016) The Principles of Sensible Substance in *Metaphysics* Λ 2–5, in C. Horn (ed.) Aristotle's *Metaphysics* Lambda – New Essays, Berlin, 87–117.
Rashed, M. (2009) On the Authorship of the Treatise on the Harmonization of the Opinions of the Two Sages Attributed to al-Farabi, in *Arabic Sciences and Philosophy* 19 (2009), 43–82.
Remes, P. (2014) "Plato: Interaction Between the External Body and the Perceiver in the *Timaeus*", in J. F. Silva and M. Yrjönsuuri (eds.) Active Perception in the History of Philosophy: From Plato to Modern Philosophy, Dordrecht, 9–30.
Reydams-Schils, G. (1997) "Plato's World Soul: Grasping Sensible Without Sense-Perception", in T. Calvo and L. Brisson (eds.) Interpreting the *Timaeus-Critias*. Proceedings of the IV Symposium Platonicum: Selected Papers, Sankt Augustin, 261–265.
Rheins, J. G. (2010) The Intelligible Creator-God and the Intelligent Soul of the Cosmos in Plato's Theology and Metaphysics, Ann Arbor. (Dissertation of the University of Pennsylvania)
Robinson, T. (^{2}1995) Plato's Psychology, Toronto.
Röd, W. (2000) "Platonische und neuzeitliche Kosmologie", in A. Neschke-Hentschke (ed.) Le Timée de Platon: contributions à l'histoire de sa réception, Paris, 237–253.
Roloff, D. (1970) Gottähnlichkeit und Erhöhung zum seligen Leben. Untersuchungen zur Herkunft der platonischen Angleichung an Gott, Berlin.
Rosen, S. (1999) "The Problem of Sense Perception in Plato's *Philebus*", in J. M. Van Ophuijsen (ed.) Plato and Platonism, Washington, 242–260. (Studies in philosophy and the history of philosophy 33)
Runia, D. T. and Share, M. (2008) Proclus: Commentary on Plato's *Timaeus*, Vol. II, Book 2: Proclus on the Causes of the Cosmos and its Creation, Cambridge.

Sansone, D. (1996) "Socrates' 'Tragic' Definition of Color (Pla. *Men.*76d–e)", in *Classical Philology* 91: 339–345.

Sathian, K. and Ramachamdran, V. S. (eds.) (2020) Multisensory Perception: From Laboratory to Clinic, London.

Sayre, K. M. (1983) Plato's Late Ontology: A Riddle Resolved, Princeton.

Schäfer, L. (2005) Das Paradigma am Himmel: Platon über Natur und Staat, Freiburg/ München.

Schellenberg, S. (2018) The Unity of Perception: Content, Consciousness, Evidence, Oxford.

Schmid, W. T. (1998) Plato's *Charmides* and the Socratic Ideal of Rationality, New York. (SUNY series in Ancient Greek Philosophy)

Schmitt, A. (1974) Die Bedeutung der sophistischen Logik für die mittlere Dialektik Platons. (Dissertation of University Würzburg)

——. (1989) Zur Erkenntnistheorie bei Platon und Descartes, in: *Antike und Abendland* 35: 54–82.

——. (2002) Synästhesie im Urteil aristotelischer Philosophie, in: H. Adler (Hg.) Synästhesie – Historisch und aktuell, Würzburg, 109–148.

——. (2006a) Platonism and Empiricism, tr. Christopher Forlini, in *Graduate Faculty Philosophy Journal* 27: 151–192.

——. (2006b) "Platon und das empirische Denken der Neuzeit", in: *Sitzungsberichte der Wissenschaftlichen Gesellschaft an der Johann Wolfgang Goethe-Universität Frankfurt am Main* 43.3, Stuttgart, 77–109.

——. (2007) "Worin besteht die Sicherheit des Erkennens? Platons Ideenlehre und die Absicherung des Wissens in der Erfahrung", in: B. Reis (ed.) Zwischen PISA und Athen - Antike Philosophie im Schulunterricht, Göttingen 2007, 89–112.

——. (2011) Denken und Sein bei Platon und Descartes. Kritische Anmerkungen zur ‚Überwindung' der antiken Seinsphilosophie durch die moderne Philosophie des Subjekts, Heidelberg (Studien zu Literatur und Erkenntnis 1).

——. (2012) Modernity and Plato: Two Paradigms of Rationality, tr. V. Adluri, New York.

——. (2015) "Gerechtigkeit bei Platon. Zur anthropologischen Grundlegung der Moral in der Platonischen *Politeia*", in: D. D. Brasi and S. Föllinger (eds.) Anthropologie in der Antike und Gegenwart. Biologische und philosophischen Entwürfe vom Menschen, Freiburg/ Munich, 279–328.

——. (2016) Wie aufgeklärt ist die Vernunft der Aufklärung? Eine Kritik aus aristotelischer Sicht, Heidelberg.

——. (2019) Gibt es ein Wissen von Gott? Plädoyer für einen rationalen Gottesbegriff, Heidelberg.

——. (2020) "Klassische griechische Philosophie (I): Platon"; "Klassische griechische Philosophie (II): Aristoteles", in J. Urbich and J. Zimmer (eds.) Handbuch Ontologie, 12–26; 27–43.

Schöpsdau, K. (1977) Platon Werke, Bd. 8, I. Teil: Nomoi, Tomoi 1–6 (Gesetze, Buch I–VI), Darmstadt.

Sedley, D. (1997) "'Becoming Like the God' in the *Timaeus* and Aristotle", in T. Calvo. and L. Brisson (eds.) Symposium Platonicum 4 (congrès), Sankt Augustin, 327–339.

——. (1999) "The Idea of Godlikeness", in G. Fine (ed.) Plato, vol. 2, Oxford, 309–328.

——. (2004) The Midwife of Platonism. Text and Subtext in Plato's *Theaetetus*, Oxford.

——. (2007) Creationism and Its Critics in Antiquity, Berkeley/ Los Angeles/ London.

——. (2017) "Becoming Godlike", in C. Bobonich (ed.) The Cambridge Companion to Ancient Ethics, 319–337.

——. (2019) "Plato's Theology", in G. Fine (ed.) The Oxford Handbook of Plato, Oxford, 627–644.
Sharples, R. W. and Sheppard, A. (eds.) (2003) Ancient Approaches to Plato's *Timaeus*, London (BICS Supplement 78).
Sheppard, A. (2014) The Poetics of Phantasia. Imagination in Ancient Aesthetics, London.
Shottenkirk, D., Curado, M. and Gouveia, S. S. (eds.) (2019) Perception, Cognition and Aesthetics, London/ New York.
Silverman, A. (2010) "Philosopher-Kings and Craftsman-Gods", in R. D. Mohr and B. M. Sattler (eds.) One Book, the Whole Universe. Plato's *Timaeus* Today, Las Vegas/ Zurich/ Athens, 55–67.
Siorvanes, L. (1996) Proclus: Neo-Platonic Philosophy and Science, Edinburgh.
Solmsen, F. (1942) Plato's Theology, Ithaca. (Rep. 1967).
——. (1968) Kleine Schriften, Bd. 1, Hildesheim.
Sorabji, R. (1991) "From Aristotle to Brentano: The Development of the Concept of Intentionality", in *Oxford Studies in Ancient Philosophy*, Supplementary Vol. 1991: 227–259.
——. (2003) "The Mind-Body Relation in the Wake of Plato's *Timaeus*", in G. J. Reydams-Schils, (ed.) Plato's *Timaeus* as Cultural Icon, Notre Dame, 152–162.
Steel, C. (1978). The Changing Self: A Study on the Soul in Later Neoplatonism: Iamblichus, Damascius and Priscianus, Brussels.
——. (1997b) "Breathing Thought: Proclus on the Innate Knowledge of the Soul", in J. J. Cleary (ed.) The Perennial Tradition of Neoplatonism, Leuven, 293–309.
——. (2013) Simplicius. On Aristotle *On the Soul* 3.6–13, London/ New York.
——. (2018) "'The Soul Never Thinks Without a Phantasma': How Platonic Commentators Interpret a Controversial Aristotelian Thesis", in B. Strobel (ed.) Die Kunst der philosophischen Exegese bei den spätantiken Platon- und Aristoteles-Kommentatoren, Berlin, 185–223. (Philosophie der Antike 36)
Storey, D. (2014) "Appearance, Perception, and Non-Rational Belief: *Republic* 602C–603A", in Oxford Studies in Ancient Philosophy 47: 81–118.
Strange, S. K. (1992) Porphyry: On Aristotle Categories, London/ New York.
——. (2000) "The Double Explanation in the *Timaeus*", in G. Fine (ed.) Plato, Oxford, 399–417.
Szaif, J. (^{2}2017) "Epistemologie", in C. Horn, J. Müller and J. Sörder (eds.) Platon-Handbuch: Leben–Werk–Wirkung, Stuttgart, 117–135.
Tarán, L. (1971) "The Creation Myth in Plato's *Timaeus*", in J. Anton and G. Kustas (eds.) Essays in Ancient Greek Philosophy, Albany, 372–407.
——. (1981) Speusippus of Athens: A Critical Study with a Collection of the Related Texts and Commentary, Leiden (Philosophia Antiqua 39).
Tarrant, H. (2008) "Eudorus and the Early Platonist Interpretation of the *Categories*". In Revue Laval théologique et philosophique 64: 583–595.
——. (2011) From the Old Academy to Later Neo-Platonism, Ashgate (Studies in the History of Platonic Thought).
——. (2017) Proclus. Commentary on Plato's *Timaeus*, vol. VI, Book 5: Proclus on the Gods of Generation and the Creation of Humans, Cambridge.
Taylor, A. E. (1928) A Commentary on Plato's *Timaeus*, Oxford.
——. (^{6}1949) Plato. The Man and His Work, London.
Thaler, N. (2016) "Judgment, Logos, and Knowledge in Plato's *Theaetetus*", in *Philosophy Compass* 11: 246–255.

Theiler, W. (²1965) Zur Geschichte der Teleologischen Naturbetrachtung bis auf Aristoteles, Berlin.

Thiel, R. (2004) Aristoteles' Kategorienschrift in ihrer antiken Kommentierung, Tübingen (Philosophische Untersuchungen 11)

Tschemplik, A. (2008) Knowledge and Self-Knowledge in Plato's *Theaetetus*, Lanham.

Tuckey, T. G. (1951) Plato's *Charmides*, Cambridge. (Rep. Amsterdam 1968).

Tuominen, M. (2009) The Ancient Commentators on Plato and Aristotle, Stocksfield.

Tuozzo, T. M. (2018) "Sense Perception and Explanation in the *Phaedo*", in G. Cornelli, T. Robinson and F. Bravo (eds.) Plato's *Phaedo*: Selected Papers from the Eleventh Symposium Platonicum, Baden-Baden, 11: 310–318.

Van den Berg, R. (2003) "'Becoming like God' according to Proclus' interpretations of the *Timaeus*, the Eleusinian Mysteries, and the *Chaldaean Oracles*", in *Bulletin of the Institute of Classical Studies. Supplement* 78: 189–202.

——. (2017) "Theurgy in the Context of Proclus' Philosophy", in P. D'Hoine and M. Martijn (eds.) All from One: A Guide to Proclus, Oxford, 223–239.

Van Riel, G. (2013) Plato's Gods, London/ New York.

——. (2017) "How Can the Perceptible World be Perceptible? Proclus on the Causes of Perceptibility", in Roskam, G. and Verheyden, J. (eds.) Light on Creation: Ancient Commentators in Dialogue and Debate on the Origin of the World, Tübingen, 49–59.

Vlastos, G. (1964) "Creation in the Timaeus: Is it a Fiction?" In R. E. Allen (ed.) (1965) Studies in Plato's Metaphysics, London, 401–419 = Vlastos, G. (1970) Studies in Greek Philosophy, II: Socrates, Plato and their Tradition, Princeton, 264–284.

Weinstein, J. I. (2018) Plato's Threefold City and Soul, Cambridge.

Westerink, L. G. (1962) Anonymous Prolegomena to Platonic Philosophy, Amsterdam.

Wilson, N. G. (1994) Photius: The Bibliotheca, London/ New York.

Wolfe, J. R. (2010) Aretē and Physics: The Lessen of Plato's *Timaeus*, Ann Arbor.

Wolfsdorf, D. (2014) "Timaeus' Explanation of Sense-Perceptual Pleasure", in *Journal of Hellenic Studies* 134: 120–135.

Wright, M. R. (ed.) (2000) Reason and Necessity: Essays on Plato's *Timaeus*, London.

Zekl, H. G. (1998) Aristoteles, Organon Bd.2: Kategorien/ Hermeneutik, Hamburg.

Zhmud, L. (2013) "Pythagorean Number Doctrine in the Academy", in G. Cornelli, R. Mckirahan and C. Macris (eds.) On Pythagoreanism, Berlin, 323–344.